MW01633464

pages 223 Shiva-REE
andy-OVER

DRINKing cup 195
STORE CREDIT-249
BOOK-257-259-260-261-263
289 Shuy

APPENDIX i BOOKS

ON BEYOND LEATHERBARK:

The Cass Saga

BY ROY B. CLARKSON

mpc

McClain Printing Company
Parsons, West Virginia

**PARSONS, WEST VIRGINIA
1990**

Frontispiece. Rugged, resolute, independent; an unknown Cheat Mountain Logger typifies the thousands of men and women whose sweat, and sometimes blood, made Cass.

International Standard Book Number 0-9624709-0-2
Library of Congress Control Number 89-91476
Printed in the United States of America
Copyright © 1990 by Roy B. Clarkson
Westover, West Virginia 26505
All Rights Reserved

First Printing 1990
Second Printing 1994
Third Printing 2002
Fourth Printing 2015

McClain Printing Company
Parsons, WV
www.mcclainprinting.com
2015

This book is dedicated to all those persons who lived, loved, hated or died in and around the town of Cass.

JUNE

You are the moonlight of my nights,
You are the sunlight of my days,
You are the twinkle of my stars,
You are the compass of my ways.

Your touch is like cool water
In the burning heat of day.
Your laughter is a bubbling brook
Washing all my cares away.
And, when into your eyes I look,
Darkest night is turned to day.

You are the beauty of my flowers,
You are the ripples of my streams,
You are the music of my songs,
You are the visions of my dreams.

Junie, I love you.

CONTENTS

PREFACE

As I am writing this Chronicle, the town of Cass, West Virginia, stands mutely awaiting the forces that will continue to shape its destiny. Its location has passed through eons of undisturbed forest; it has seen the silent Indian pass, leaving only moccasin tracks in the moss; a brief pastoral disturbance in the area now occupied by the town was followed in the early part of this century by uproarious years of a booming lumber town. Then, as the original timber became depleted, the town waned. Its once riotous streets became silent. It was saved from the oblivion that overtook many similar lumber towns in West Virginia by the establishment of the Cass Scenic Railroad State Park by the State of West Virginia. Now tourists crowd the sidewalks as they arrive to see the smoke-belching Shays and ride the "rails through history," browse in the Country Store or pause to contemplate the past and the future of this unique community.

It is a rare privilege to write a history of one's hometown. While researching this book, I have come across hundreds of names, incidents and events. Many of the persons I have known, most of the events I have heard of while a youngster at Cass. It is a thrill to find, in the county newspapers, old company records and personal interviews, accounts of events and people who, until then, were vague memories. It is an equal thrill to record these in book form that will preserve them for the future.

Cass was a unique town, made up of many ethnic and social strata, a true "melting pot." It was a violent town through much of its history; at the same time it was a loving town. Those of us fortunate enough to have lived there have had our lives greatly enriched by the many cherished friends, neighbors, and relatives who shared our experiences.

It is the purpose of this narrative to give an understanding of the town of Cass through significant facts and to include only material that can be verified. Extensive references are made to the sources of information not known personally by the author. Despite exhaustive efforts, mistakes and omissions are the omnipresent companions of a work such as this. The writer takes full responsibility for such shortcomings. Additional information and corrections will be welcome by him.

The Author
142 Jackson Street
Westover, WV 26505

ACKNOWLEDGMENTS

I acknowledge the profound assistance of my wife, June. Though she didn't live to see it completed she made this book possible through her encouragement, inspiration and love.

I want to recognize the special help of two other persons: Kyle J. "Catty" Neighbors and Philip Bagdon.

"Catty" Neighbors' untiring efforts to collect and preserve historical records and pictures of Cass resulted in the preservation of over forty boxes of early letters and records of the West Virginia Pulp and Paper Company. The records are now a part of the West Virginia & Regional History Collection at West Virginia University, Morgantown, West Virginia. Over three hundred pictures collected by "Catty" were placed at my use by his wife, Ina, and their daughter, Mary Snyder. The original source of many of these pictures is not known and they are referenced here as from the Kyle J. Neighbors Collection.

Philip Bagdon was interested in the history of Cass from boyhood when his father brought him to ride the Cass train. For several years, Phil collected information on Cass through personal interviews and by studying records and pictures. He unselfishly turned over to me fourteen notebooks, a number of photographs, and several boxes of material.

Other persons who were of special assistance were Ivan and Ernestine Clarkson, Ben and Lola Jackson and Russell and Pearl Clarkson.

The following persons helped by giving me letters, photographs or unpublished manuscripts: Terry Arbogast, Eugene Burner, Marlene Chittum, Harry Clark, Ivan Clarkson, Anna Plyler Ervine, George A. Fizer, Connell A. Gillespie, Margaret Hannah Gluck, Reed W. Griffith, Charles Gum, Gordon Hamrick, Emory L. Kemp II, Monta McLaughlin Mace, H. E. Matics, William P. McNeel, Stella Blackhurst, Truman Miller, Jesse Pennington, Betty Wooddell Ralson, William Sampson, Raymond F. Schuck, Beatrice Blackhurst Sheets, Roy C. Siple, Dorothy Tacy, Mary Margaret Tacy Sharp, Lucy Weber, and E. C. Wyatt. Sources of photographs and photographers, when known, are acknowledged in the captions.

The following persons gave invaluable assistance during interviews by either Philip Bagdon or the author: Artie Barkley, Allen J. "Farmer" Blackhurst, Jennings Bradford, Paul Bradley,

Warren "Doodle" Brown, Eugene Burner, Edward "Puzo" Cassell, Odey Cassell, Bedford "Buck" Chestnut, Charlie Chromer, Ivan O. Clarkson, Ernestine Clarkson, Mertie V. Clarkson, Paul Dolkos, Pat Ellisy, "Rocky" Fisher, Preston "Springy" Galford, Eunice Gibson, Connell Gillespie, Forrest Griffin, Reed W. Griffin, Russell Hamrick, Willis Hertig, Ed Howell, Ben Jackson, Lola Clarkson Jackson, Harold Lee, Maggie Meeks, Kyle "Catty" Neighbors, T. M. Pharr, Frank Puffenbarger, Georgia Dougherty Robinson, S. S. "Si" Sharp, Woodrow Sharp, William Simmons, Roy C. Siple, Belva Sheets, Charlie Sheets, Carl Summerfield, Ether Tyson, Maggie Myers Tyson, Johnny Varner, Sam Waugh, Fred Weber, Valley Clarkson Wilkes, "Bud" Wolfe, Laban Wolfe, Stanley Wooddell, and E. C. Wyatt.

The author is grateful to Doris W. Larson and Michelle L. Mullenax who edited the book, to Gerald Futej who read the chapters on "Woods Operations" and "The Town of Spruce," to Dr. George Deike who read the chapter on "The Lumber Railroad," and to Margaret Hannah Gluck who read the chapter on "The Town of Cass." Their comments were very helpful. Assistance of the staff of the West Virginia and Regional History Collection at West Virginia University is acknowledged.

I am especially indebted to my children George Roy, Karen Sue, and Kimeran Ann, and my other relatives and friends who helped give me the will to complete the book.

The efforts of William A. Lunk in producing the painting for the dust jacket, of my daughter, Kimeran Ann, who spent many hours of valuable time preparing the line drawings, and of Paul Liston who prepared the map are appreciated.

The assistance of Jean Shellito in typing early copies of the manuscript and of Joyce Costain and Donna Pancoast in typing the final copies is acknowledged.

I
GENESIS OF A WILDERNESS

A Wilderness Develops

The affairs of modern men are often determined by events occurring in the far distant past. This is nowhere more evident than in the region around Cass, West Virginia, where events of thousands of years have sculpted the destinies of the inhabitants. The forests now covering much of the land are the results of ancient forces that shaped and reshaped the surface features of the earth. All parts of the earth have been profoundly affected by the alternate rising and subsiding of its restless crust, the shifting of continental masses, and the constant erosion of exposed surfaces. The landscape in what is now Eastern North America has undergone many such changes. Ages ago parts of the region subsided to form a shallow inland sea in which an abundance of marine animals lived and died, depositing shell material that was transformed into thick layers of limestone. Periods of uplift and erosion alternating with subsidence and deposition continued eon after eon. About 300 million years ago, lush swamplands, dominated by giant horsetails, clubmosses, ferns, and seed ferns, covered parts of the countryside. Over millions of years, these "botanical dinosaurs" built up thick layers of organic matter: in its turn, the organic material was covered by hundreds of feet of sediment that eroded from neighboring highlands. Eventually the plant remains turned to coal.

The modern landscape had its genesis some 225-270 million years ago when the Appalachian Orogeny resulted in the uplift of rocks, some of which were over a billion years old, into a rugged mountain chain. The Appalachians have been subjected to constant erosion since that time and have remained exposed, one of the oldest mountain ranges in the world, providing habitats where land plants and animals evolved.[1] The years since the uplift of the Appalachians have seen the shifting about of continents, vast climatic changes, and a gradual evolution of seed plants and mammals into the dominant life forms.

In the Cretaceous Period, about 200 million years ago, events began which resulted in a progressive cooling of the northern continents. In many areas tropical floras were replaced by forms more tolerant of cooler climate. This trend continued and, by about two million years ago, the flora and fauna of the northern hemisphere contained many modern forms.

The last two million years have been characterized by a series of profound cyclic temperature changes. Much of this time, known as the Pleistocene Epoch, was characterized by the alternate forming and melting of great glaciers. A number of glacial periods alternated with warmer interglacial times. Each had a tremendous effect on the plant and animal life of the region. The Southern Appalachians, including present West Virginia, were spared the ravages of glacial ice, but as glaciers formed in the north and moved southward, the climate here was modified and the vegetation gradually became more boreal. During warming periods, the reverse occurred.

The last great ice sheet began to melt about 18,000 years ago, and the boreal forest which extended far into the south slowly moved northward and was replaced over much of the southern lands by broad-leaved, flower-bearing, angiosperms. However, on the higher elevations in the Appalachians, the climate remained comparatively severe, and elements of the northern forest, notably red spruce and associated species, were able to survive until modern times. It is this red spruce forest, molded by geologic and climatic factors for thousands of years, that attracted lumbermen to these mountains and set the stage for the exploitation that followed.

The influence of man on this area has been profound. Following the American Revolution, conditions became crowded on the coastal plain east of the Appalachians; people began seeking ways to expand westward. As passes through the mountains were discovered, explorers and settlers poured through them to the rolling hills and rich prairies to the west. The mountains themselves were ill-suited to farming and were bypassed leaving their forested grandeur largely intact until industrial pressures developed after the Civil War. At that time, railroad men, timbermen and others began taking a closer look at these forbidding highlands which lay so close to eastern markets. What they saw was an amazing wealth in timber, coal, and other resources awaiting persons daring enough to risk the capital necessary to harvest this wilderness bounty.

Before we follow their story, let us look at the primeval forest as they saw it. Red spruce was the most important forest type in the higher Allegheny Mountains of West Virginia. It occurred mostly at elevations above 2,500 feet and formed extensive pure stands on the plateaus and mountains above 4,000 feet. Red spruce reached the apex of its development in this area and averaged 30,000 to 50,000 — sometimes reached 75,000 — board feet per acre.

An early writer described this spruce forest as: "At the time of the Civil War, . . . 'there was not a stick amiss' in that region. It was one of the most impenetrable forests in the United States. The soil over most of it was composed of moss and humus often a foot, occasionally two feet thick."[2]

Augustus M. Van Dyke, a member of the Fourteenth Indiana Infantry Regiment during the early part of the Civil War, was stationed at Cheat Summit Fort (Fort Milroy) on Cheat Mountain in Randolph County, in the heart of the West Virginia red spruce country. He described the forest poetically: "Here was the forest primeval, its murmuring pines [red spruce] and its hemlocks, deep, dark, almost impenetrable, as inhospitable as the caverns that concealed themselves under the moss that shrouded its bowlders [sic], where the rain it raineth everyday, and it snows in August. . . . To one who loves the wildly picturesque in nature . . . this region could not fail to awe, to please, to fascinate. The great bowlders [sic] lie scattered in inextricable confusion, as if they had fallen from the hands of giants in battle against each other, and over them there creeps the straggling, trailing tendrils of what is vulgarly called the 'sheep laurel' [mountain laurel]."[3]

Below four thousand feet in elevation, red spruce was usually mixed with northern hardwoods, which grew best in a zone from about three to four thousand feet. The dominant tree associated with red spruce was often yellow birch. In addition to yellow birch, the northern hardwoods included many valuable trees such as sugar maple, beech, black cherry, red oak and chestnut. Hemlock also occurred with Northern hardwoods, particularly in moist spots.

At elevations below about three thousand feet, the northern hardwoods were mixed with and replaced by a mixed hardwood forest. This forest reached its best development on moist, north-facing slopes and in rich coves. The mixed hardwood forest had great diversity and contained over one hundred tree species. White oak and chestnut were the most valuable timber trees in this association. Tuliptree (yellow-poplar), basswood, cucumber tree, beech, red maple, red oak, shagbark hickory, black cherry, black walnut, and sugar maple were other common and valuable species.

Along the Greenbrier River and its tributaries were extensive stands of large white pine. These forests were of excellent quality and were often pure stands, sometimes measuring as much as sixty-five thousand board feet to the acre.[4]

This magnificent wilderness, shaped by ages of climatic and geologic forces, undisturbed except by natural events during its thousands of years of development, sat waiting, until, at the appointed time, man appeared.

WILDERNESS DEFILED — THE BEGINNING

The upper Greenbrier wilderness provided deer, elk, bison, bear, wild turkey, and lesser game animals to the Indians for hundreds of years. In the vicinity of present-day Cass, small, temporary, Indian settlements were located on the bluff overlooking the mouth of Deer Creek, below Cass, and near where North Fork enters Deer Creek southwest of the present town of Green Bank. Their presence there, in earlier times, is witnessed by the many stone points and flint chips found at these locations. Little is known of the tribe or nature of these early inhabitants, for, by the time white men arrived in the vicinity, these small Indian towns were abandoned, and the area, like most of West Virginia, was considered a common hunting ground by Shawnee, Delaware, Miami, and Mingo tribesmen. The Greenbrier River, the most prominent stream in the area, was well-known to the Indians. It was called the *We-o-to-we* by the Miami Indians and the *O-ne-pa-ke* by the Delaware.[5]

We will probably never know the names of the first intrepid white men who slacked their thirst with the waters of the upper Greenbrier River. Perhaps they were French trappers who sought the mink, otter, beaver and other prime furbearing animals in the primeval forest. Or they could have been English explorers from across the mountains to the east. Whether they descended into the upper Greenbrier from the high Shaver's Fork country to the north and west or found their way up the Greenbrier from the south also is not known. According to Thwaites, the Greenbrier River was named by John Lewis in 1751. Lewis, then seventy-three years old, was assisting his son, Andrew, with a survey of a land grant and became so entangled in the thickets of greenbriers growing along the stream that he named it the Greenbrier River.[6] However, Myers[7] gives evidence that the name Greenbrier antedated Lewis' time and was originally applied to the stream by the French. Early French influence remains in a local geographic name, Ronceverte, a town on the Greenbrier River. The name Ronceverte is literally translated into English *Ronce* = brier, *verte* = green or Greenbrier.[8]

The first settlement by white men west of the Allegheny Mountains was along the Greenbrier River. In 1749, Jacob Marlin and Stephen Sewell crossed the mountains from Virginia and settled near the mouth of Knapp Creek where the town of Marlinton is now located. Their stay was temporary, fraught with argument, and ended when Sewell was killed by Indians and Marlin returned to Virginia.[9]

Other settlers, many of Scotch-Irish descent, soon entered the region and, by 1770, there were numerous homesteads throughout the Greenbrier Valley. These early farmers were subjected to danger from marauding Indians and rough forts were built where settlers could gather in time of danger. One such fort was located on land owned by Jacob Warwick on Deer Creek near the mouth of North Fork some four miles east of Cass.[10] There was never a large-scale attack on this fort, but according to tradition, an Indian shot an arrow into it from a mound-like knoll located where Route 92 now crosses North Fork.[11]

Indian raiding parties passed through the vicinity of Cass on their way to attack white settlers further south along the Greenbrier. On such a raid, one of the best-known residents of the valley, Moses Moore, was captured along the Greenbrier River near the present location of Cass. The Indians took him southwest a couple of miles and halted at a beautiful spring at the head of a run. Leaving Moses securely tied, they departed to return shortly with a good supply of lead. This caused later residents to believe there was a lead mine nearby.[12] The probable explanation is that the raiding party had cached the lead on their way eastward, to avoid carrying it, and had picked it up on the return trip. The creek on which their camp was made has since been known as Moses Spring Run. Moses escaped from the Indians and made his way back home.[13]

Around 1770, early settlers in the Green Bank area were impressed with a bald spot that reflected the morning sun near the top of a knob on Back Allegheny Mountain a few miles westward. Little did they dream that this knob, which they designated "Bald Knob," would someday be the terminis of a scenic railway carrying thousands of persons to the second highest point of a state yet to be formed in a nation not yet born.

Sometime after the Revolution, when the danger of Indian attack had abated, an intrepid farmer carved a road across Little Mountain west of Green Bank and began clearing a farm in the narrow valley of the Greenbrier. An abundance of a shrub, leatherwood (*Dirca palustris* L.), grew along a small stream tumbling eastward into the Greenbrier from the vicinity of Bald Knob. Appropriately, the stream was named Leatherbark, a name applied also to the small community that later developed south of the stream mouth.

In time, three farms would occupy the valley between the hill known as Chestnut Ridge on the west (Company Pasture) and the ridge east of the river (Burner's Hill). Still later in time, a large sawmill would be built near the mouth of Leatherbark Creek, and the boisterous logging town of Cass would come riotously into existence, only to wane after sixty years before it would gradually develop into the focus of one of West Virginia's most popular and unique state parks, the Cass Scenic Railroad State Park.

~ II
RIVER DRIVES ON THE GREENBRIER

The Greenbrier River had a great influence on developments in the Cass area. This stream heads in the northern part of Pocahontas County and flows in a south-westerly direction for over 160 miles to join the New River in Summers County.[1] The upper Greenbrier, during much of the year, is a low-level stream filled with rock bars and riffles. However, during flood season in the spring and irregularly at other seasons of the year, it becomes a swollen torrent suitable for transporting logs. Use of the lower part of the river for this purpose dates back at least to 1825. From 1849 until the Civil War, logs were floated on the Greenbrier (usually in rafts) to small mills at Riverside (near Marlinton).[2]

During and after the Civil War, explorations were made of the wild countryside west and north of the present location of Cass. As the immense timber stands became known, speculators and financiers became interested in the area. Because of the general north-south orientation of the Alleghenies and the ruggedness of the topography, development came slowly. To understand these developments, it is necessary to summarize the activities of several corporations and to discuss them separately, for they were independent factors that worked together to culminate in one of the largest lumbering ventures in the Eastern United States.

The westward movement that bypassed the rough Alleghenies is aptly described in this paragraph written in 1899:

> Speculation following the Civil War took Eastern capital to the West. Immigration was large, and naturally sought the unsettled lands which the Government offered at a nominal price to those who would occupy them. Trans-continental railroads, with branches in all directions, were projected and built, and the gold and silver of the Western Mountains beckoned men on. Iron furnaces were fed from the ore of Lake Superior; Pennsylvania, Ohio and Illinois provided the fuel to keep them going. Michigan and Wisconsin largely supplied the lumber markets. Texas and adjoining states kept busy the looms in the woolen mills. All avenues of industrial wealth led to the West. They passed by and through the State of West Virginia, and those who traveled these roads little knew, and took little note of the wealth of opportunity through which they were passing, waiting to be gathered. The tide of Western development, having reached its flood, began to ebb, and, when the light of inquiry was turned upon the fields of investment at home, they found treasures neglected. The Alleghenies were as rich in coal and lumber as the Rockies were in the precious metals. The heart of the wealth of the Alleghenies is in West Virginia, and its throbbing has just begun with the awakening of its industrial life.[3]

A prime necessity for harvesting this wealth of timber, coal, and other natural resources was the building of railroads. The main purpose of early east-west trunk lines through West Virginia was to transport the products of the Middle West to Eastern markets. The Baltimore & Ohio was the first railroad to cross the Alleghenies. It entered the state at Harpers Ferry and proceeded to Grafton where its main line led to Wheeling and on to Chicago. Several branch lines were built. The branch that most affected the Cass area was from Grafton via the Tygart Valley to Belington in Barbour County. The completion of this branch helped stimulate development of the timber resources in the area.[4]

Farther south, another railroad, the Chesapeake & Ohio, was built between Richmond, Virginia, and Huntington, West Virginia. It entered West Virginia a short distance east of White Sulphur Springs. Work began on the Chesapeake and Ohio in 1868 and it was completed to Ronceverte in Greenbrier County in

1872.[5] There was much local opposition to the railroad because it "carried whiskey, killed chickens and cows, scared the horses, and threw the teamsters out of work."[6] This railroad was to prove of greatest importance to developments at Cass.

Some years prior to this, in 1867, Col. Cecil Clay, along with James Waugh, made an examination of the white pine stands on the Greenbrier River in Greenbrier and Pocahontas Counties.[7] In July, 1870, the Greenbrier Lumber Company was formed at Ronceverte by Colonel Clay, Grayson M. Prevost, Charles M. Prevost, Joseph A. Clay, and R. Livingston Kestor. Colonel Clay proceeded to purchase white pine timber and land on Sitlington Creek, Deer Creek, Peters Mountain, and on the Greenbrier River in Pocahontas County in 1871 and 1873. In 1873, he transferred his timber holdings in Pocahontas County to the Greenbrier Lumber Company.[8]

A system of booms and dams was constructed on the Greenbrier River near Ronceverte, and two sawmills known as the "Little Mill" and "Big Mill" were constructed. The "Big Mill" had six boilers with an engine of 250 horsepower. It contained one muley saw, one circular saw, and one gang saw of thirty-six blades (one inch apart). The sawing capacity was 120,000 feet per day.[9]

The St. Lawrence Boom & Manufacturing Company was chartered in February, 1871, by the above men. The land and timber holdings of the Greenbrier Lumber Company, comprising 2,185 acres on Sitlington Creek, Deer Creek, Peters Mountain, and the Greenbrier River, were transferred to this company in 1874 and the sawmill and booms at Ronceverte were transferred in 1882. The St. Lawrence Boom & Manufacturing Company was the major lumber operator in the Greenbrier Valley for many years. It eventually owned land and timber holdings of over 50,000 acres in Pocahontas County and extensive holdings in Greenbrier County.[10]

Cecil Clay, later president of the St. Lawrence Boom & Manufacturing Company, described the extensive white pine stands in the Greenbrier Valley as follows:

> The ordinary run of cuts this winter (1875) is from four to seven 16 feet cuts per tree, averaging five cuts to the 1,000 feet. There are several hundred million feet of good White Pine lumber in this district. The White Pine growing, as it does here, at an

altitude of 2,000 to 2,500 feet. . . . Where the White Pine grows, it takes the ground to itself, but little other timber is found in it. It grows in several localities throughout the valley [Greenbrier]. On Deer and Lithington's [Sitlington's] Creeks are 100,000,000; on Knapp's [sic] Creek and branches another 100,000,000 feet: and Spice, Laurel, and Davy's Runs, with Anthony's Creek, and some outlying patches, would yield a third 100,000,000. . . . It is generally a sound, red-knot timber, with remarkably thin sapwood. This often does not average over half an inch in a lot of 1,000 logs. As much as 40,000 feet can sometimes be cut on an acre.[11]

The most practical way to harvest this timber was to float it down the Greenbrier to their boom and mill near Ronceverte. Log drives on the Greenbrier to Ronceverte had been in progress at least since 1876 when six thousand white pine logs were put into the boom there.[12]

Expertise in cutting and driving the huge white pine reserve on the Greenbrier was obtained in 1882 from New Brunswick via Pennsylvania in the form of Capt. Abner E. Smith. His first job was logging a hollow at the lower end of the George Siple place on Deer Creek east of Leatherbark (present Cass). After two years on Deer Creek, he moved in 1884 to the Geiger Tract facing on the Greenbrier above Leatherbark.

A partnership with James Whiting was formed and, under the name Smith and Whiting, they handled most of the Greenbrier white pine for many years. Smith and Whiting employed skilled lumbermen from as far away as Nova Scotia.

In 1885, Captain Smith moved his operations to the McCutcheon Tract, now part of Seneca State Forest. To move the logs to the bank of Sitlington Creek, he decided to build a railroad. He purchased a seven-ton, saddle-tank, steam locomotive from the H. K. Porter Company and hauled it from Staunton, Virginia, by wagon. He named the locomotive "Little Jim," after his young son. A railroad was constructed up Thomas Creek where "Little Jim" was used to haul logs until the spring of 1890, when it was moved to Cummings Creek. In 1902, the engine was sold to the Marlinton Lumber Company, August, West Virginia, and later to the Kidd, Kirby, and Lilly Lumber Company on Trump Run.[13]

In preparation for a log drive, the timber was cut into logs, peeled and skidded by teams of horses or moved in log slides to landings along the stream. This work continued throughout the year and, when spring arrived, millions of board feet of prime white pine logs were ready to float downstream.

The drive itself was an exciting event. In early spring, after the main ice floe was past, the peeled logs were rolled into the river and the drive began. Houseboats called "arks" were let loose to follow the main body of logs. Men and horses traveled both banks to keep the logs rolled into the stream and moving. When the logs finally reached their destination, they were caught above the millsite in large booms, which consisted of log piers spaced across the stream and filled with stone. Between the piers heavy chains stopped the logs. They were stored there until needed, then were let downstream to the mill.

Arks were constructed upstream for the men and horses accompanying the drive. An ark consisted of a raft seventy to one hundred feet long and about eighteen feet wide. A low log house almost as long as the raft and about sixteen feet wide was erected on each raft. The arks served as bunkhouses, kitchen, and mess hall for the men. A separate raft known as a horse-flat was built for the horses.

The log drives were the high points of the year for farm families living along the stream. They provided not only the excitement of seeing the river choked with logs and talking with the men as they went along but also a chance to sell fresh eggs and meat to the loggers for a bit of cash.

Most log drives on the Greenbrier originated on Deer Creek or points further south. However, in 1890, and probably in 1891, John Driscol drove logs from the vicinity of Durbin. Other drives from the upper Greenbrier were made in 1895 and 1896. In 1899, the West Virginia Pulp & Paper Company acquired timber rights on the upper Greenbrier. Colonel Dan O'Connel and upwards of a hundred men were at work on the R. B. Kerr lands near Durbin, cutting timber for the pulp mill then planned to be built at Covington, Virginia.[14] In 1899, 1900, and 1901, spruce logs were driven down the river to the St. Lawrence Boom & Manufacturing Company's booms at Ronceverte for shipment to the new paper mill at Covington.[15] The 1899 drive is described in the *Pocahontas Times:*

> Sunday the log drive hove in sight. Six arks, or house rafts, each in charge of a Greenbrier pilot, furnished the twenty horses and 107 men living quarters. The arks were made out of spruce hewed

timber for the bottoms, and spruce boards for the sides and tops. They are destined to become postal cards in the near future. Each bore the name of a war-ship penciled in large letters. The 'Iowa' captain, John Buckley; the 'Olympia' captain, Wm. Siple; the 'Merrimac' captain, J. Stretch; the 'Oregon' captain [not given]; 'Mary Trisa' (Maria Teresa) captain, John Rorke; and 'Brooklyn,' Captains Willis Burner and Colbert Duncan.

There was something over six million feet of logs ranging in diameter from 4 in. to 2 ft. After a lot of hard work the logs were driven out of the west branch of the Greenbrier, several days being spent on four miles. The stream was narrow and swift and the logs were jamming continually. Since the main river was reached the drive has been making wonderful speed. Four days brought the drive to Marlinton.

Sunday at sundown the town was apprised of its coming by the hoarse-throated dinner bell on the 'Olympia,' and turned out to see the flotilla come over the Marlin Ford and anchor in the pool below.

Colonel Dan O'Connel was in command. He is extremely fortunate in making such a magnificent beginning on his drive, as the tides on this river in the summer-time are not to be counted on with any certainty. Monday morning they had reached Buckeye by 11 o'clock and were still making fine headway. It will take not more than one small flood to put the logs in the boom at Ronceverte.

The men are still cutting at the forks of the river.[16]

The 1900 drive was described as the most successful log drive ever made on the Greenbrier River. The distance (118 miles[17]) from Traveler's Repose, Pocahontas County, to Bird's Mill, Greenbrier County was covered in eleven days without loss of a man or horse.[18]

The last log drive on the upper Greenbrier was headed by Capt. William Irvine who, in March, 1902, contracted with the West Virginia Spruce Lumber Company to cut six million feet of spruce near Traveler's Repose and drive it to Cass.[19] Log drives continued on the lower Greenbrier until 1908.[20]

The St. Lawrence Boom & Manufacturing Company prospered. During the period 1884-1910, it sawed 433 million board feet, mostly of white pine from the Greenbrier Valley,[21] including the extensive stands in the Deer Creek and upper Greenbrier valleys in the Cass area.

In 1901, the officers and directors of the St. Lawrence Boom & Manufacturing Company were as follows:

Thos. J. Shyrock, President
F.A. Hauck, Secretary and Treasurer
J. W. Harris, Attorney
Directors:

C. C. Homer	W. R. Mahaffey
Thomas J. Shyrock	F. A. Hauck
Porter Kimports	F. T. Homer
Saml. Christ.	J. W. Harris.[22]

EARLY LOGGING AT CHEAT BRIDGE

The first events leading to exploitation of the Cheat Mountain red spruce occurred before the Civil War. As a part of the general road building activity in western Virginia in the late eighteenth and early nineteenth centuries, a road, known as the Staunton-Parkersburg Turnpike, was built in 1847. This highway followed the present general route of U.S. Route 250 through Pocahontas and Randolph Counties and crossed Cheat Mountain and Shavers Fork of Cheat River[1] at what is known today as Cheat Bridge. It was built by Irish workmen who were former laborers on the Baltimore & Ohio Railroad.[2]

At the onset of the Civil War, Union leaders soon saw the need to drive out organized Confederate forces from that part of Virginia lying west of the Allegheny Mountains. This strategy served two important functions: to protect the Baltimore & Ohio Railroad and to encourage the formation of the new state of West Virginia then being planned.[3]

General George McClelland, Union commander stationed at Cincinnati, sent troops across the Ohio and forced the withdrawal of Confederates from Philippi in the first land battle of the Civil War. The Confederates set up strong positions on Rich Mountain for the purpose of controlling turnpikes leading to the

Baltimore & Ohio Railroad. On July 10, 1861, the Confederates were defeated in the battle of Rich Mountain and were forced to retreat eastward.

After the battle of Rich Mountain, McClelland moved his troops successively to Beverly, Huttonsville and Cheat Mountain. He reconnoitered Cheat Mountain Summit in force on July 14, 1861, and on July 16, six companies of the Fourteenth Indiana Infantry Regiment began fortifying Cheat Summit.

Colonel Nathan Kimball, regimental commander, seized the turnpike bridge over Cheat River and threw out a line of pickets along the banks of the river, above and below the bridge. In addition, a strong picket guard was detached in an area of deadwood three miles to the front of the camp. Fortifications were built here that became known as Fort Milroy. They were occupied by Union troops during the fall and winter of 1861-62. On September 12, 1861, these troops repulsed an attack by Confederate forces led by Col. Albert Rust, under the direct command of Gen. Robert E. Lee.[4]

Union forces brought with them a small steam-powered circular sawmill, the first steam sawmill to operate in the red spruce forest in West Virginia.[5] It was but a slight portent of things to come.

The first red spruce timber removed along Cheat River on a commercial scale was cut by W. S. Dewing & Sons of Ashton, Michigan. This company built a large circular sawmill at Point Marion, Pennsylvania, at the confluence of the Cheat and Monongahela Rivers. They purchased extensive acreage of red spruce timber in the vicinity of Winchester (Cheat Bridge), Randolph County, and, as early as 1884, Dewing began blasting the larger rocks from the channel of Cheat River in preparation for driving logs from these lands.[6] Dewing continued purchasing lands in the area, from A. H. and Ella Winchester, as late as 1886 and 1887.[7] In 1890, Dewing & Sons adopted the following trademark to be used in lumber dealings in Randolph County: Ⓓ.[8]

Between 1888 and 1896, Col. Arthur H. Winchester was in charge of cutting Dewing's timber on Cheat River and driving it to Point Marion. He built a large house at Winchester and on June 28, 1888, began establishing a camp.[9]

In addition to Winchester, other key men involved in the building and operation of this camp were Jack Steele, foreman;

Jack Orr, John Flood and Jim Hawthorne, all from Michigan, and Pocahontas County natives Charles P. Carr, George Wilmouth, Tom Houchins, Loring Kerr, and Jesse L. Warwick. The first cooks were James L. and Anderson Sheets. They were followed by Ed Pomeroy and his wife. Garnett House and two of the Greathouse boys were their helpers. Blacksmiths on the job were Benjamin Arbogast, Charles Cassell, and Bill Forbes. Later foremen were Bill Townsend and Frank Campion.

The following list is of other men on this job. From Pocahontas County were: James Carpenter, Pete Arbogast, Lee Trayner, Ellis Hughes, William Sheets, Brown Trayner, Randolph Galford, Porter Rayburn, Cal Rayburn, Bill Bright, Martin Sutton, Phil Rader, John K. Hinkle, Andy Oliver, John Arbogast, Gem Arbogast, Osborn Tracy, Mack Kerr, Joe Kerr, Doc Sheets, Jack Sheets, Jess McLaughlin, Adam Moore, Otis Warwick, Jim Galford, Henry Galford, Kane Crowley, Frank Crowley, Warwick Gum, Kenny Elliott, Norman Wilfong, Peter Kramer, William Gum, Ben Taylor, Rob Bloom, and Loring Nottingham. From Randolph County were Scott Gladwell, Bruce Pritt, Jack Break, Lee Heron, Lee Channell, Wilson Sponangle, Levi Sponangle, Tuck Woolwine, Charles Stalnaker, Pud Triplett, Saul Gladwell, Hayden Break, John Tacy, Charles Thomas, Joel Teter, Lee Wilmer, Ad Mouse, French Quick, Renick Ianer, Henry Conley, Pierre Pritt, Pete Break, George Heron, Isburn Daniels, Hamon Sponangle, Cale Mullenix, John Woolwine, George Stalnaker, Wade Triplett and Bruce Kittle. From Webster County were Bernard B. Hamrick, Clay Holley, Lee Hamrick, and Ad Coger. And from Harrison County, Tom Martin, Emery Martin and Joe Creasy.[10]

Dewing & Sons operated a narrow gauge railroad between Cheat Bridge and Lambert Run to near the top of the mountain, a distance of about three miles. The engine was hauled in by wagon.[11] It was a three-foot gauge Shay (CN31) built April 7, 1882. This small engine had cylinders six inches in diameter with a stroke of six inches and 21-inch drivers.[12] Bruce Kiddle was the engineer.[13]

Dewing also built a splash dam on Cheat River about a half mile above the present iron bridge at Cheat Bridge.[14]

A rather complicated lawsuit clouded the last years of operation by Dewing & Sons at Cheat Bridge. They, through their agent, entered into a contract with Elihu Hutton, by which Hutton was to buy up West Virginia lands for the lumber company.

Hutton was to receive his pay in the difference between what he had to give for the lands and the fixed price he was to receive for them (arranged between Hutton and Dewing).

The arrangement continued in force for a number of years and the transactions ran into the hundreds of thousands of dollars. When, at last, settlement time came, there was a dispute as to the extent of the agreement.

Dewing & Sons brought suit against Hutton and others who had gotten mixed up in the matter in a collateral way. The accounts were submitted to a commissioner, who studied them and reported that Hutton owed Dewing & Sons some $57,000. The Circuit Court of Randolph County gave judgment against Hutton for that amount. Hutton took an appeal and the case was turned over to another commissioner, who reported that Dewing & Sons owed Hutton for that amount, with interest from January 20, 1898. From that judgment, Dewing & Sons appealed to the State Supreme Court. A hearing was held in late December, 1900. The State Supreme Court gave judgment affirming the decision of the Circuit Court that Hutton must pay $57,000 to Dewing.[15]

The Dewing Company's final involvement in the area came about when a deed was recorded in the Courthouse at Marlinton, Pocahontas County, on February 7, 1899, for 67,619 acres of Cheat River land from James W. and Fanny Dewing of Kalamazoo, Michigan, to J. G. Luke of Brooklyn, New York, for $585,000. Notes given for payment were signed by J. G. Luke and endorsed by West Virginia Pulp and Paper Company. The deed also conveyed one sawmill and one planing mill at Point Marion, Pennsylvania, all horses, wagons, and logging materials at Huttonsville, and a logging engine, trucks, and steel rail at or near Cheat Bridge.[16]

The locomotive, steel rails, spikes, etc. were sold by Samuel Slaymaker on behalf of the West Virginia Pulp and Paper Company sometime prior to July 6, 1900. The purchaser was not mentioned.[17] The engine was partially dismantled and removed by wagon.[18]

IV
RAILROADS INTO THE MOUNTAINS

The early lumbering activities described resulted in the river driving of millions of board feet of white pine from the lower slopes and bottomland of the Greenbrier River drainage, some red spruce from the upper Greenbrier and a small amount of red spruce along Cheat River, but they had no effect on the upper slopes and ridges and little effect on the extensive red spruce forests west and north of the Greenbrier drainage.

However, plans were being made on all sides to build railroad feeder lines into this vast timber reserve. One of these was a bold plan developed by Henry Gassaway Davis and his son-in-law, Stephen B. Elkins. During the Civil War, Davis held contracts to furnish the United States Government with horses and mules and to furnish the Baltimore & Ohio Railroad with timber for crossties and bridges.[1] During his extensive travels through the Alleghenies, Davis was impressed by the enormous expanses of timber and the coal reserves he saw there. He bought several thousand acres of timberland at the summit of the Alleghenies and organized the Potomac & Piedmont Coal & Railroad Company to provide transportation to this land. The railroad was to run from Bloomington, Garrett County, Maryland, along the North Branch of the Potomac River to Big Run at Elk Garden, West Virginia.

Continued exploration into West Virginia led Davis to develop a plan to further open up this rich wilderness. With the assistance of Elkins, another rail line was planned. On February 23, 1881, the legislature of West Virginia granted a liberal charter to this line, the West Virginia Central & Pittsburg Railway Company. Track laying commenced immediately and on November 2, 1881, a section from the junction of the Baltimore & Ohio Railroad at Piedmont to the Elk Garden coalfields was opened. On November 1, 1884, tracks were completed to Davis in Tucker County, in the heart of the red spruce country. The town of Davis developed rapidly and was soon the center of a vast timber and pulpwood complex.[2]

Meanwhile, Johnson N. Camden, another capitalist, was promoting railroad building into the area from the south. Camden proposed connecting the West Virginia Central & Pittsburg Railroad and the Chesapeake & Ohio Railroad through an extension from Weston to Covington. He planned a junction with the Chesapeake & Ohio Railroad either by way of Williams River or Cherry River. This plan was modified to connect with a proposed extension of the Hot Springs branch of the Chesapeake & Ohio at Marlinton.[3]

On the basis of this plan in 1880, Col. John T. McGraw, of Grafton, purchased the farms known as Marlin's Bottom along the Greenbrier River in Pocahontas County and planned a town. The site was laid off in lots in 1891 and advertised as a place where a town, to be known as Marlinton, would be built.[4] McGraw projected no less than five railroads into the town of Marlinton; however, the panic of 1893 put an end to those grandiose plans. He retained an interest in development of the area and had a survey made of a tentative rail route from Marlinton to Ronceverte along the Greenbrier River.

The Chesapeake & Ohio Railroad had been interested for several years in extending a branch from the vicinity of Ronceverte, Greenbrier County, into Pocahontas County. On November 16, 1897, a subsidiary, the Greenbrier Railway Company, was founded for this purpose.[5] After surveying several possible routes, a line to be known as the Greenbrier Division was approved by the Greenbrier Railway Board of Directors on April 21, 1899. This line would follow the Greenbrier River the entire distance from Whitcomb, on the main line two and one-half miles north of Ronceverte, to Durbin. Work began immediately and progressed with amazing speed. It is estimated that by September, 1899, over fifteen hundred men were at work on the line, including Blacks, Germans, Italians and various other ethnic groups, many of whom had just emigrated from Europe and could not speak English; they were identified by number tags.[6]

By the end of September, track was being laid at the rate of a mile per day and on October 26, 1900, the official "first train" reached Marlinton. Regular passenger service began to that town on December 17, 1900.[7]

Track laying continued northward at a rapid pace and on December 22, 1900, Cass, the site of the new mill of the West Virginia Pulp and Paper Company, was reached.[8]

Work on the Chesapeake & Ohio between Cass and Durbin proceeded at a slower pace and was not completed until early 1902. Further small extensions were made until it reached Winterburn in 1905. The total distance from Whitcomb to Winterburn was 100.9 miles.[9]

According to McNeel, the cost of building the Greenbrier Division was $2,018,390.32. There was also a toll in human life with nine fatal accidents reported associated with the construction of this line.[10]

Completion of a wye at Cass on February 20, 1901,[11] and a water tank there in early March[12] were steps toward initiation of passenger service, and on June 1, 1901, passenger service to Cass began with one train per day leaving Ronceverte at 7:45 a.m. and reaching Cass at 11:15 a.m. The return trip began at 1:45 p.m. and reached Ronceverte at 5:35 p.m. Passenger service was extended to Durbin on May 26, 1902, and to Winterburn on November 15, 1905. This train ran daily except Sunday.[13]

On August 2, 1903, a second train was scheduled to run seven days a week. Trains Nos. 141 and 143 were southbound, No. 142 and 144 northbound. During the fiscal year ending June 30, 1903, 4,033 passengers boarded the train at Cass. This number increased to 13,190 in fiscal year 1905-06.[14]

Freight traffic on the newly established C&O line was extensive. By 1902, forty-four sawmills, including ten large band sawmills, several large circular mills and numerous small circular sawmills were built near the tracks between Caldwell and Winterburn. Thirty-one of these sawmills were in Pocahontas County.

They had a daily capacity of 293,000 board feet. The largest of these was the Cass mill of the West Virginia Spruce Lumber Company—60,000 feet per day. The smallest was owned by C. C. Wanless and cut 3,000 feet per day.[15]

Tanneries were built at Frank and Marlinton. The numerous farms in the Greenbrier Valley provided additional traffic. Highways were poorly developed, and trucks and buses were non-existent at the time. All transportation of incoming machinery, fuel, mail, supplies, and people and of outgoing products was by way of the railroad.[16]

While the Chesapeake & Ohio Railroad was planning the Greenbrier Division, another railroad that was to affect the Cass area was being planned. As early as 1882, H. G. Davis proposed to extend the West Virginia Central & Pittsburg Railroad from Davis in Tucker County through Randolph, Pocahontas, and Greenbrier Counties to White Sulphur Springs to connect with the Chesapeake & Ohio. In company with Senators Bayard and Camden, Secretary Window, Major Shaw, Baker and Stephen B. Elkins on July 19-26, 1881, he inspected a possible route to White Sulphur Springs and wrote in his journal "The Country from Traveler's Repose [Bartow] to White Sulphur Springs is a remarkably good country to make a railroad through."[17] This plan was never pursued. However, once the Chesapeake & Ohio was committed to building the Greenbrier Branch, Davis made plans to connect with that line at Durbin. The Coal & Iron Railroad Company, a subsidiary of the West Virginia Central & Pittsburg, was chartered in December, 1899, and authorized to build a railroad from Elkins to Greenbrier County. This track was completed to Durbin August 1, 1903, where it made the much-needed connection with the Chesapeake & Ohio that was already in operation there by that time.[18] On November 1, 1905, the Coal & Iron Railroad Company was purchased by the Western Maryland Railway and became known as the Durbin Branch.[19]

V
FORMATION OF THE
WEST VIRGINIA PULP
AND PAPER COMPANY[1]

A summary of events in and around the present location of Cass has been presented to build an understanding of the physical, biological, and cultural factors that have played such important roles in the formation of the town. It is also desirable to present a background of the company that brought the town into existence.

Events that ultimately led to the founding of the town of Cass and the building of a large sawmill there began in Scotland over 150 years ago. They concern a young man named John Luke, who in 1826, completed his apprenticeship as a papermaker and was awarded his certificate of proficiency. He started his own paper mill at Crook-of-Devon, Scotland, and operated it until his death.

In 1829, a son, William Luke, who was to be the founder of the company that built Cass, was born. In the tradition of the day, he started working with his father at the age of twelve and by the time he reached the age of majority, he was an experienced master papermaker.

However, young William was faced with a dilemma. The Fourdrinier papermaking machine had been developed and had started the paper industry on the road from a tedious hand process to a large, highly mechanized part of the industrial revolution. The basic raw material was rags, and, as the supply dwindled and prices soared, many paper mills could not obtain them. William Luke could see that papermaking in Scotland was limited by the scarcity of raw materials as well as by high taxes and a limited labor supply. He became convinced that his future was in a country with large reserves of raw materials and a ready supply of labor. Like many of his countrymen, he said good-bye to his native Scotland and sailed for the United States. That was in 1852 and William Luke was twenty-three years old.

Young men with a professional background of papermaking were in much demand in the growing cities of the United States, and William worked as a special consultant for many small paper companies for ten years. These years were valuable ones for him, as they gave him an opportunity to experiment with new ideas and techniques. The American paper industry utilized straw to supplement rags as a raw material; however, many people, including William Luke, became convinced that pulp from wood fibers was the answer to the ever growing paper manufacturers' needs. A process for producing pulp from wood had been developed in the early 1850s. This process involved grinding soft woods, such as spruce, basswood, or buckeye, against revolving wheels and then mixing the resulting fibers with pulp made from rags.

In 1862, William Luke took a position with the Jessup & Moore Company of Wilmington, Delaware. He soon gained a reputation as one of the world's most knowledgeable papermakers.[2]

The traditions of hard work and excellent products were carried forward by William Luke's oldest son, John Guthrie Luke, who started to work for his father in 1872, at the age of fifteen. After several years of experience, he became associated with the Morrison, Bare & Cass Company paper mill at Tyrone, Pennsylvania. He was manager of this mill from 1875 to 1883. Even though the mill was destroyed by fire in 1882, John G. Luke's work helped put the company on a paying basis, and so impressed Joseph K. Cass, one of the mill's owners, that it later led to the merger of Morrison & Cass with the West Virginia Pulp and Paper Company.

William Luke's other sons, William A. and David Lincoln and later the younger sons, Adam K., James L., and Thomas, also followed their father's footsteps. The Lukes gradually developed the idea of combining their experience into a family-owned company. They soon realized that, in order to do this, a greater knowledge of the chemical properties of wood was needed. Consequently, David L. was sent to college. Five years later he graduated from the University of Pennsylvania with degrees in chemistry and chemical engineering. His training was to culminate in a leadership role in their future company.

The Lukes believed they could design a successful method for making wood pulp using the "sulphite" process, a process several other companies had tried without commercial success. John G. and David Luke worked for the Richmond Paper Company in Providence, Rhode Island, where they and William A. developed their ideas and made plans for a mill of their own. Early in 1886, with their father's advice and financial help, they met at Harper's Ferry, West Virginia, and began plans for a new company that would build a paper mill in the mountains between West Virginia and Maryland close to the immense growth of red spruce in West Virginia. An island, known as Davis Island, in the Potomac River in Allegheny County, Maryland, opposite Piedmont, West Virginia, was purchased from Colonel Henry Davis and Thomas B. Davis. The deed, for forty-one acres, was recorded November 6, 1888. A name was decided upon, and, on October 18, 1888, a charter and certificate of incorporation was granted to the Piedmont Pulp & Paper Company of Allegheny County, Maryland. (This is the original company that eventually led to the present WESTVACO Corporation.) The stockholders were William Luke, John F. Quigley, David L. Luke, John G. Luke, James W. Patten, Daniel W. Strippey and G. T. Reynolds. At the first stockholders meeting at Harper's Ferry on October 27, 1888, William Luke was elected president and David L. Luke, secretary.

To assure the future of the Piedmont Mills, the Lukes realized they would have to acquire an adequate supply of good spruce timber. In the late 1880s, John G. Luke had ridden horseback through the central Appalachian highlands scouting for timber. He saw hundreds of thousands of acres of excellent virgin red spruce stands. The bulk of this was in Tucker, Randolph and Pocahontas Counties, West Virginia.[3] His reports stimulated the Lukes in 1899 to purchase the "Dewing Tract," a boundary of 67,619 acres of virgin red spruce located in the high Cheat Mountain country in the northwest portion of Pocahontas County and the southern edge of Randolph County.[4] This land lays in the heart of the best red spruce timber in the world. Average stands were estimated to contain over forty thousand board feet per acre. It, along with the Dewing mill at Point Marion, Pennsylvania, and other items, cost $585,000.

With the Dewing purchase, the company acquired an employee who was to prove invaluable in dealing with the mountain people in purchasing timber and obtaining rights-of-way as well as in cruising and surveying. This man was Harvey C. Cromer, a native of the Cheat Mountain area of Pocahontas County. A self-taught man, Mr. Cromer was an excellent surveyor and knew practically every acre of timber and every boundary line in the Cheat Mountain country. He was described as a man of rugged character, honest to the core, a real woodsman, quiet, but diligent and thorough in his work. Although he was misunderstood by many people and often referred to as the "snake hunter," he was held in high esteem by the Lukes. It was people like Harvey Cromer who formed a loyal, devoted, and capable working force.

David L. and John G. Luke continued their work at the Providence mill for a time but spent nights and weekends planning the new mill. Utilizing the papermaking backgrounds of their father and grandfather, the experience gained working in the industry, and the chemical knowledge acquired by David L., they were ready in January, 1889, to begin the layout and construction of the Piedmont mill. Their intensive planning was evident when they were able to get the pulp mill in operation in less than seven months from the time they "broke ground."

The first mill was small. It employed sixty persons and produced only thirty tons of pulp per day, but it carried the paper industry a long step forward. Here, through industry, imagination, persistence, and thorough planning, the Lukes established the first commercially successful sulfite operation for the conversion of wood to pulp. Red spruce was an ideal wood for the process, producing a beautiful, strong, lightweight pulp.

At the stockholders meeting on January 28, 1890, John G. Luke was elected vice-president and general manager of the Piedmont pulp operation and plans for expansion were made.

On September 8, 1891, a paper mill was added under the name of West Virginia Paper Company. The original subscribed capital of this company was forty-five thousand dollars. Members of the Luke family were the sole stockholders, and William A. Luke, Adam K. Luke, and James L. Luke were brought into the operation. Officers were: William Luke, president; Adam K. Luke, secretary and treasurer; and William A. Luke, general manager. This operation included two 92-inch wide paper machines. It produced its first paper in mid-January, 1892.

The Lukes believed that, if adequate water and coal were available, pulp could most economically be made near the timber source. Consequently, in 1892, fifty thousand acres of virgin spruce timber in Tucker County were purchased, and a third corporation, the West Virginia Pulp Company, was formed on September 9, 1892, with an original stock of thirty thousand dollars. Its purpose was to build and operate a pulp mill at Davis in Tucker County to convert red spruce into pulp by the sulfite process. The original stockholders of the company were members of the Luke family and John H. Danby, Preston Lea, and David Lindsay. Officers were William Luke, president; William A. Luke, vice-president; and Adam K. Luke, secretary and treasurer. The site for the Davis operation was purchased from the Marshall Coal & Lumber Company on August 13, 1892. When first built, this plant employed seventy-five people and produced thirty-five tons of rolled pulp per day.

The town of Davis, named for Henry Gassaway Davis, had been established in 1884 and was now a thriving lumbering, mining and tanning center. A pulp mill was an ideal addition in this vicinity, for it could utilize much of the smaller timber and tops previously left in the woods by the loggers.

The year 1892 marked a Luke tradition. This was the first year the stockholders received a dividend. The company has paid a dividend every year since, even during the depression. A remarkable record!

By 1894, the Lukes were operating three companies, which employed about 275 persons and produced a variety of paper products. It was thought advisable to open a New York office in order to keep up with business affairs and to make business contacts. Following through with this plan in May, 1894, John G. Luke and Adam K. Luke went to New York and opened an office in the Mutual Reserve Building. Colonel Boone, J. F. Harrison, and Judge Harry Moore joined them at the New York office.

Further expansion was made at the Piedmont plant. This, along with company housing, a company store and other improvements comprised the community known as West Piedmont.[5]

The year 1897 brought about corporate reorganization. The three companies under Luke management had grown and prospered to such an extent that it was decided to merge them into one company. On November 10, 1897, the West Virginia Pulp and Paper Company of West Virginia was organized. The stockholders of the three original Luke companies met on December 7, 1897, and authorized the sale of all their properties and assets to the new corporation at the following values:

Piedmont Pulp & Paper Company	$720,000
West Virginia Paper Company	510,000
West Virginia Pulp Company	270,000
	$1,500,000

This represented a 15-fold growth of the original authorized capital of one hundred thousand dollars for the three companies started only ten years before.

On April 26, 1898, the West Virginia Pulp and Paper Company of West Virginia was formally incorporated. The incorporators were William Luke and all six of his sons. The seven Lukes and John H. Danby were elected directors of the new corporation. Officers were William Luke, president; John G. Luke, vice-president and general manager; David L. Luke, treasurer; and Adam K. Luke, secretary.

The year 1898 was crucial to future developments at the present site of Cass, for in that year it was decided that the company should build another pulp and paper operation on the southern side of the vast red spruce forest in the mountains. The Chesapeake & Ohio Railroad was in the process of constructing a branch from near Ronceverte, Greenbrier County, up the Greenbrier River to connect with a proposed branch of the Coal & Iron Railway near Durbin. This branch was expected to reach Marlinton in 1900, the mouth of Leatherbark Creek in 1901 and Durbin in 1902. The Lukes started exploring this route for a possible location for their new paper mill.

A site at Caldwell, Greenbrier County, West Virginia, was

selected, but, since all mill wastes at the time were dumped into the river, the question of pollution arose. The company had recently won a lawsuit brought by citizens of Cumberland, Maryland, over the pollution of the Potomac River by the mills at West Piedmont (Luke).[6] The Greenbrier River was pollution free and flowed through rich farmlands downstream, making pollution particularly offensive. Furthermore, the city of Hinton threatened to bring a suit against the paper company if the mill was built on the Greenbrier River (Hinton's water supply).[7] In order to attract the company to the Caldwell site, "Captain Matthews, representing the interests of the Greenbrier Valley, offered to raise for the company an indemnifying bond of half a million dollars to save them harmless from persons living on the Greenbrier."[8]

At this point, officials at Covington, Virginia, invited the Lukes to build their new mill at that location on the Jackson River. This stream was already polluted by mining and a tannery, so additional pollution was not seriously objected to. The choice to build at Covington proved to be a wise one, especially years later when southern yellow pine became important as a source of paper fiber.

Money was needed badly by the rapidly expanding company for timberland purchase and construction of mills. The former association of John G. Luke with Morrison, Bare and Cass Company of Tyrone, Pennsylvania, was now an advantage. This company, now known as Morrison and Cass Paper Company, was owned by Joseph K. Cass. A merger between the Morrison and Cass Paper Company and the West Virginia Pulp and Paper Company of West Virginia was arranged. This took place during the summer of 1899 and provided the Lukes capital to expand. The result was the West Virginia Pulp and Paper Company of Delaware. The certificate of incorporation of this company was dated July 10, 1899, with an authorized capital stock of $5 million. The first meeting of stockholders was held on July 14, and the following directors were elected: William Luke, Joseph K. Cass, John G. Luke, David L. Luke and John G. Anderson, Mr. Cass's brother-in-law. Officers were: William Luke, president; Joseph K. Cass, vice-president; John G. Luke, treasurer; Adam K. Luke, assistant treasurer; and David L. Luke, secretary.[9]

On July 22, 1899, the directors adopted the following resolutions:

(a)   To purchase the entire capital stock of Morrison and Cass Paper Company at Tyrone, Pennsylvania, 500 shares, par value of $5,000,000 and deliver to the stockholders of Morrison and Cass 10,000 shares of West Virginia Pulp and Paper of Delaware, par value of $1,000,000.

(b)   To purchase 14,990 shares of West Virginia Pulp and Paper of West Virginia, par value of $1,499,000 in exchange for the same number of shares, same par value, same total.

    On September 21, 1899, the directors authorized the purchase of 3,720 additional shares of West Virginia Pulp and Paper of West Virginia, the balance of the entire stock of the latter company, against which there was issued to them 5,000 shares of the Delaware Company.[10]

In 1899, the company experimented with reforestation, a revolutionary idea for the times. Faced with a seemingly inexhaustible primeval forest, most companies saw little use in reforestation. However, the Lukes set out a plantation of fast growing cottonwoods (*Populus deltoides* Marsh) near their Tyrone mill and experimented with planting red spruce at other localities.[11]

VI
EARLY PLANS
FOR CASS

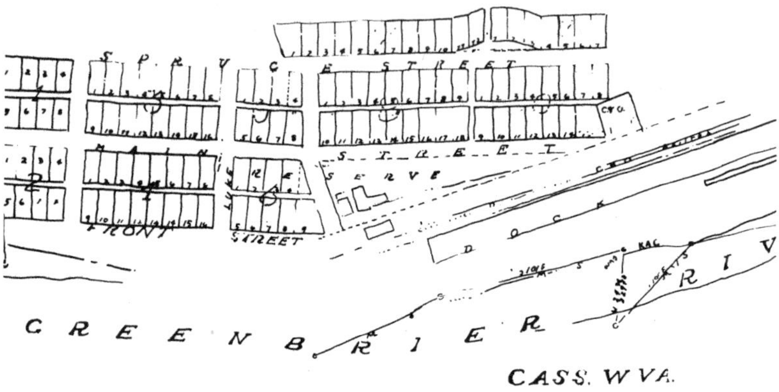

CASS, W VA.

The Lukes' primary interest in the vast red spruce stands on Cheat River was to provide a dependable source of wood for paper pulp. It was quite clear, however, that there was an abundance of large timber that had great value as sawlogs, while the smaller trees and tops could furnish the needed pulpwood. The need for either a ready market for sawlogs or the building of a sawmill to manufacture this timber became evident. The first question was how to harvest the Cheat Mountain timber most advantageously?

The red spruce stands were located on the high plateaus, valleys and ridges mostly west of the crest of Back Alleghany Mountain. This ruled out any attempt to drive these logs down the Greenbrier River in the same manner that the white pine on the Greenbrier was being removed. Since the Chesapeake & Ohio branch from Whitcomb to Durbin was being planned, the most obvious solutions were either to move the logs out by rail or to build a sawmill as close as possible to the supply of timber, manufacture the logs there and ship the lumber out. The Lukes were of the opinion that it was more economical to manufacture as close to the raw material as possible, and a search for a site to establish a sawmill was begun.

In 1898 a tract of 136 acres, at the mouth of Leatherbark Run, was bought from Jacob N. "Newt" and Nancy E. Gum for the sum of $1,000.00 or $7.35 per acre.[1] This land was formerly owned by Charles Z. J. and Ida Curry. The purchase would provide a site for the sawmill and an accompanying town.

The newly formed West Virginia Pulp and Paper Company of Delaware faced the additional problem of the sale of lumber. Their background had been in pulp and paper manufacture. If lumber was to be manufactured in large volume, a good sales organization would be needed. They were fortunate to become associated with Samuel E. Slaymaker, an experienced lumberman who had an established sales organization, S. E. Slaymaker & Company, with offices at 4619 Chester Avenue, Philadelphia.[2] Sam Slaymaker already handled the sales for, and had an interest in, several West Virginia lumber companies including the Whitmer Lumber Company at Bayard, Grant County, and the Condon-Lane Boom & Lumber Company at Horton, Randolph County. Shortly before 1900, he sold his interests in these companies and began cruising the timberlands that were soon bought by the West Virginia Pulp and Paper Company.[3] In 1902, his letterhead read, "S. E. Slaymaker & Company, Wholesale Lumber, Representing West Virginia Spruce Lumber Company, 307 Broadway, New York."[4]

S. E. Slaymaker proved to be an excellent choice, both for his own organizational ability and skill in handling lumber sales and for his advice to the Lukes to hire Emory P. Shaffer as manager of their new pulpwood and lumbering operation. Shaffer had been associated with Slaymaker since 1896 when Shaffer became manager of the Whitmer Lumber Company at Bayard. In March 1900, at the age of twenty-nine, E. P. Shaffer rode the West Virginia Central passenger train to Huttonsville and then took a buggy to Leatherbark to assume his new job with the Lukes. Mr. Shaffer was an excellent choice for manager. He proved to be a woodsman, lumberman, master organizer and superb supervisor. He could do almost any job on a logging operation except saw and file in the mill. He became the driving force of the sawmill and lumbering operations then being planned and became one of the most widely known and highly respected lumbermen in the industry. It would be difficult to overestimate the importance of Emory P. Shaffer to the future of the lumber operations at Cass and, consequently, to Cass itself.

The Lukes' decision to locate a sawmill at the mouth of Leatherbark Run placed it on the C&O Railroad when the northward extension from Whitcomb was completed. A logging railroad could be built from the millsite into the timber on Cheat River. Although the grades were steep, it would be possible to reach the top of the mountain, fifteen hundred feet higher than the millsite, by the use of switchbacks, and to haul the logs out by utilizing geared, steam locomotives.

As plans progressed, it was decided to form a subsidiary company. The subsidiary, named the West Virginia Spruce Lumber Company, was incorporated May 8, 1900, with a capital of $1 million. West Virginia Pulp and Paper of Delaware controlled the stock and advanced the money to this company as it was needed. Incorporators were Joseph K. Cass, John G. Luke, S. E. Slaymaker, David L. Luke and C. F. Moore.[5] William Luke was elected president of the newly formed company, A. K. Luke was secretary and treasurer and Samuel E. Slaymaker was vice-president and general manager. The home office was at 540 Drexel Building, Philadelphia.[6] It was moved to 309 Broadway, New York City, on October 1, 1900.[7]

The purpose of this company was to build a large band sawmill at the mouth of Leatherbark Run. It would manufacture timber from the red spruce stands owned by the company on Cheat Mountain and furnish pulpwood to the paper mill being built at Covington, Virginia. Logs above fifteen inches in diameter would be sawed into lumber; the smaller logs, fifteen inches and under, would be cut into pulpwood bolts and shipped by rail to Covington.

Sam E. Slaymaker and E. P. Shaffer were to handle the layout and construction of the sawmill. Shaffer would manage the entire timbering and sawing operations. All lumber of the sawmill would be sold by S. E. Slaymaker and Company.[8]

Another corporation by the name of West Virginia Boom and Spruce Lumber Company was formed on June 21, 1900. The authorized capital was one hundred thousand dollars. Corporators were J. K. Cass, J. G. Luke, David L. Luke, Adam K. Luke and C. F. Moore.

Its purpose was to conduct "a general lumber business with the right to construct and maintain a boom across the Greenbrier River near the mouth of Leatherbark Creek. It was also to construct and operate a sawmill or mills to be used in the manufacture of lumber or any of its products and to operate such logging railways as was necessary for the operation of the business."[9] This company was never activated.

Meanwhile, construction was being rushed on the pulp and paper mill at Covington. On June 13, 1899, a millsite was purchased. William A. Luke, who had been running the pulp mill at Davis, moved to Covington, and construction of the most modern papermaking operation of the time began. The pulp mill started operating shortly before March 21, 1900,[10] and the paper mill was operating by May 24, 1900.[11]

On August 2, 1900, a formal agreement was signed with the West Virginia Spruce Lumber Company for this subsidiary to supply pulpwood to the West Virginia Pulp and Paper Company at a set price. The company already had crews working on the West Fork of the Greenbrier in northern Pocahontas County attempting to drive logs down the Greenbrier to the booms of the St. Lawrence Boom & Lumber Company at Ronceverte. They had a late start for driving, however, and on July 3, 1900, Shaffer wrote to Slaymaker that there "was a small flood in river and they got the rear of the drive down about 4 miles below this place (Leatherbark)." He also said the "arks are about a mile below here."[12] One week later D. L. Luke wrote to Slaymaker "drive made about 15 miles further down the river—it is hardly to be expected it will get any further this season."[13] This problem remained during the summer of 1900 and in November of that year, J. G. Luke was still writing to ask Slaymaker if it was possible to float the wood on the West Fork (of the Greenbrier) down on the flood.[14]

The inability to get logs down the Greenbrier during the summer of 1900 caused the Covington mill to shut down on November 30 and again on December 27 for lack of wood.[15] Furthermore, the company was forced to use hemlock wood, which produced inferior pulp. Considerable concern was expressed about the possible effects of this on future sales.[16]

Effects were also made to secure pulp wood for the Covington mill from the Beaver Creek area along a part of the C&O that was completed in southern Pocahontas County. Dan O'Connell was in charge of this operation. O'Connell's production was not sufficient to please the Lukes, and between October 16, 1900, and the early part of January, 1901, a number of letters passed between various Lukes and Sam Slaymaker criticizing O'Connell's efforts. Typical of these is one on December 13, 1900, from D. L. Luke to S. E. Slaymaker, "There is little doubt that he [O'Connell] can hustle the work along if he tries, but from the reports we get from Beaver Creek, he is giving the operation there but very little of his personal attention, having been at Beaver Creek since the flood, until this week, but twice."[17] O'Connell's work was delayed by floods in late November, 1900, and by a shortage of cars in some instances. Nevertheless, he did ship twelve loads of pulp to Covington on October 15 and began regular shipments in December.[18] O'Connell's efforts improved after early difficulties in getting his operation going were solved, and by early 1901, he had a crew of 200 men on Beaver Creek. His intention was to cut about six million feet of pulpwood and ship it to Covington via the C&O. His tramway formed a junction with the C&O at the mouth of Beaver Creek. Here a small hamlet, named Dan, developed with a depot, telegraph office, some dwellings and a "pig's ear" (saloon). By January, 1901, O'Connell had shipped over 400 carloads of pulpwood to Covington and was loading at the rate of one hundred thousand feet daily.[19]

VII
THE LOGGING RAILROAD

During the late 1890s, there were numerous plans for building railroads into the luxurious virgin timber stands in the mountains of West Virginia. The Lukes were involved in at least two of these. On November 23, 1899, the notification of plans by the Lukes to build a new railroad was published in the *Pocahontas Times* as follows:

> The Secretary of State has issued a certificate of incorporation to the Greenbrier and Cheat River Railroad Company, which proposed to build a railroad commencing at or near the forks of Greenbrier River in Pocahontas County, and running, by the most practicable route, to a point at or near Rowlesburg, in Preston County. The capital stock of the company is $50,000 divided into shares of $100 each, held by David L. Luke, of Piedmont, West Virginia; C.F. Moore, Covington, Virginia; Jos. K. Cass, Tyrone, Pennsylvania; John G. Luke, of New York; Wm. Luke and Preston Lea of Wilmington, Delaware; and Robert D. Hopkins, of Baltimore. The principal office will be at Dunmore.[1]

This plan was not carried through, however, because of the anticipated need for pulpwood at the West Virginia Pulp and

Paper Company's Covington plant, then under construction. To supply this need it was decided that a railroad into the Cheat Mountain red spruce lands owned by the Lukes was necessary. It soon became clear that a line that would meet with the planned C&O Greenbrier Division at the mouth of Leatherbark Run on the Greenbrier River would be most feasible. It was with great urgency that the Leatherbark operation was planned. On December 30, 1899, the minutes of the West Virginia Pulp and Paper Company show that money was advanced to the West Virginia Spruce Lumber Company to build a logging railroad seven miles in length from the mouth of Leatherbark Run to the top of Back Allegheny Mountain. This railroad, named the Greenbrier and Elk River Railroad, would be built and operated by the lumber company.[2] It would be used to transport logs to the West Virginia Spruce Lumber Company mill to be built at the mouth of Leatherbark Run and to deliver pulpwood to the C&O Railroad at the same place for transport over the C&O to the West Virginia Pulp and Paper Company mill at Covington. This limited beginning would become one of the largest lumber railroads in eastern North America. Decades later this same rail line would provide a glimpse into the history and biota of Cheat Mountain for hundreds of thousands of tourists riding the Cass Scenic Railroad.

The primary purpose of the Leatherbark operation was to supply pulpwood to the Covington plant with production of lumber a secondary consideration. This was emphatically stated by John G. Luke in a letter dated February 17, 1900, as follows: "The pulp lands were bought primarily as a protection for our pulp mills, and while we, of course, want to give the lumber plant every possible advantage, we want to have it clearly understood that the question of pulpwood supply is of the first importance."[3]

In 1900, the small community of Leatherbark became the center of frenzied activity. The Greenbrier Division of the C&O was progressing steadily northward along the Greenbrier River. Sam Slaymaker and E. P. Shaffer, who were in charge of constructing the Greenbrier and Elk River Railroad, were determined that, when it arrived at Leatherbark, they would have the roadbed of the lumber railroad ready for laying rails. The mill being constructed at Covington would soon need pulpwood, and no delay in its delivery would be tolerated.

The route to be taken by the lumber railroad was laid out after weeks of surveying. The rise from the mouth of Leatherbark Run (2,436 feet elevation) to the lowest gap in Back Allegheny Mountain leading into the Cheat River Valley (3,950 feet elevation)[4] was 1,514 feet. It was imperative to make this climb as economically as possible. It was finally decided to go up Leatherbark Run a distance of about two miles and a rise of about 400 feet, head into a cove just above the Arbuckle place and construct a switchback. The tracks would then go around the face of the mountain into another cove where a second switchback over 300 feet higher in elevation than the first would be built. The grade between the two switchbacks was to be 6.7 percent in places. The steepest grade on the track going up the mountain, eleven percent, was above the second switchback.[5] From the second switchback, the track would swing around a promontory and along a short ridge to wind along the face of the mountain to the top at the divide, 3,950 feet in elevation. The total distance to the top would be almost 6.8 miles.[6] This part of the track would later be known as the "Cass Hill."

The organizational abilities of both Shaffer and Slaymaker were severely tested during the latter part of 1900. Work was getting underway in June, and on June 27, Shaffer reported to Slaymaker that "we are getting along first rate locating railroad. Have run line down Leatherbark as far as the mill [Robertson's circular steam mill on Leatherbark] and find that can get pretty good place for road."[7] By June 30, 1900, the right-of-way up Leatherbark had been settled.[8] Shaffer also stated that he had hired a carpenter to put up a camp, and if he could get lumber, the camp would be ready for the men the last week of June, 1900.[9] This was a reference to Camp No. 1 being built for Italian track workers. Camp No. 1 was located near the later site of the coal scales behind the Chesapeake and Ohio Railroad depot at Cass.

Shaffer followed this by a report that, on July 2, he had finished locating the railroad from the Gum place down to the mouth of Leatherbark. He also said, "We can go to work right away hauling lumber for the Italian camp today." In the same letter he says he "will go over to Cheat first chance we get" (in reference to locating grade in that area).[10]

"Italian camp completed . . ." stated a telegram from Shaffer to

Slaymaker on July 6, 1900.[11] By July 12, forty Italians and twelve wagonloads of goods had arrived at the mouth of Leatherbark.[12] These first Italian track crews were brought in by Slaymaker from the lumber job at Horton, Randolph County.[13] Some of them did not stay, for on July 17 Shaffer wrote to Slaymaker that grading on the railroad commenced that morning. He said he had sixteen men and expected forty more.[14]

At about the same time, the C&O engineers received orders to install two sidetracks, each twenty-five hundred feet long on each side of the main track near the depot at Cass. These sidings were to accommodate the new mill.[15]

Obtaining sufficient laborers was a problem at first and on August 2, Shaffer wrote to Slaymaker to "send in 40 or 50 more Italians if you can get them."[16] On August 10, Shaffer wired Slaymaker, "Have 35 Italians at work, 50 more hired."[17] In a letter of the same date he said that "40 more have promised to come next week, then we will have about 100 men."[18] Groups of Hungarians and Austrians were also hired. On August 24, Shaffer wrote, "Have commenced to build a new camp in the head of Whitaker [sic] Run for Hungarians who have just arrived. They will work from there to the top of mountain."[19] Italians, Hungarians and Austrians were kept in separate camps and crews because of the difficulty in communication. The Hungarian camp was not numbered and was known only as Whittaker. Nick Naimo was placed in charge of the first twenty-five Hungarians to arrive at the Whittaker Camp.[20]

Obtaining tools for the rapidly expanding work force was a problem. On July 17, Shaffer wrote to Slaymaker, "How did you make out about the tools? Received 24 (2 dozen) picks and one dozen mattocks and ought to have about 3-4 doz. more mattocks—can do more work with them. The bars, drills, and hammers have not arrived."[21] On July 21, he wrote, "Those people at Huttonsville did not send any striking hammers. Suppose the other tools that you bought are at Huttonsville by this time."[22] On July 25, Shaffer reported that he had something over one hundred shovels, but the mattocks had not yet arrived.[23]

Shaffer was also troubled by a lack of horses. In the July 25, letter he wrote, "The horses from Horton have not arrived yet, but have one team here that came from the camp" (O'Connel's).[24] On another occasion he reports buying the roan horse "Frank" from L. B. Waybright of Crab Bottom, Virginia, and paying $115 for him with check #253.[25]

Despite these drawbacks, progress was being made and on August 30, 1900, Shaffer wrote, "Our road has been graded to the end of the first switchback, and two crews are working beyond." On September 4, he reported that 95 men were working, and on the sixth of September, 101 men were at work.[26]

Since the foreign names were hard to pronounce and even harder to spell, numbers were given foreigners for record keeping and pay purposes. On August 30, 1900, Shaffer sent a record to the Philadelphia office of the checks written to Italian workers for the month of August as follows:

Check No. 254 to Italian No. 2 – $34.79
Check No. 255 to Italian No. 3 – 35.40
Check No. 256 to Italian No. 4 – 35.55
Check No. 257 to Italian No. 5 – 30.90
            [and so on to]
Check No. 295 to Italian No. 43 – 23.29

The checks ranged from a low of $15.64 to a high of $46.50. These workers were paid at the rate of $1.50 per day plus room and board. At the same time, various other workers were making $1.35 to $1.67 per day.[27] There is no evidence that foreign workers were paid less than others or were exploited in any unusual manner other than that they were placed in section gangs engaged in digging grade and laying ties and rails, very strenuous and often times disagreeable work. Also, they lived in small shanties that made up a camp instead of the large bunkhouses later used to house the logging crews.

On September 6, Shaffer asked Slaymaker to look into dynamite fuses and caps at Huttonsville, ordered from Furgeson Construction Company sometime before then. In the same letter he mentioned ordering one and one-half tons of dynamite, fuses, and caps from the Ring Powder Company and thought these should be at Huttonsville.[28]

By September, 1900, a great deal of engineering, clearing right-of-way and grading of the railroad were underway. Yet the Company had invested a total of only $8,965.10, distributed as follows:

Commissary, including hauling	$2,500.00
Paid on contract for sawing and piling	
lumber and peeling bark	900.00
Paid for Right-of-Way	150.00
Paid for House	25.00
Paid for Tools	558.81
Paid for Wagon	67.50
Camp Buildings, about	500.00
Undetailed	4,263.79

This did not include the payroll for the month of August which is estimated at $1,500.00 to $3,000.00.[29]

Preparations for the railroad were also being made by other members of the company. D. L. Luke reported to Slaymaker on September 5, that an order had been given Ingalls, Cincinnati, Ohio, for seven hundred tons of rail at twenty-two dollars per ton. This referred to old "Big Four" rails that had an average weight of 54 pounds per yard.[30] This price probably included bolts and angle bars.[31] Rails were also purchased from Rumbarger at Dobbin and shipped via the West Virginia Central and Pittsburg Railroad Company as follows: July 27, WVC Car No. 506, 47,100 lbs.; July 30, WVC No. 684, 43,000 lbs.; August 6, WVC No. 2028, 66,000 lbs.; August 13, WVC No. 506, 58,100 lbs.; August 17, WVC No. 3013, 62,400 lbs.; August 22, WVC No. 512, 59,700 lbs. and August 27, TH&L No. 6013, 13,400 lbs.[32]

In late summer, labor trouble among the track workers began to hamper their efforts. On September 18, Shaffer wrote that the strike was over, and the men were all back to work except sixteen, including two Italian foremen. They had left for New York.[33]

In an attempt to find the best working combination, there was considerable shifting about of men and on September 25, Shaffer wrote that the Austrian crew was working in Austin Field "above the place we got the tomatoes the day you were up there."[34] Mike Linnan[35] had been put in charge of the crew at Whittaker and would be moved to the upper side of Whittaker. The Italian crew on the lower end of the road had connected with the part Linnan had started on and were working back toward the head of the run.[36]

Shaffer also reported that Mr. Dougan, who was putting in the stonework for the bridge across Leatherbark, had lost a fine horse to colic. He requested a good horse book as the rest of the horses looked like they had distemper.[37]

Shaffer was also lining up crossties and on September 22, he wrote, "That old man Henry that was here wanted to make them, price to be 8 cents per tie."[38] However, on October 30, he wrote that he had made a new contract with A. S. Robertson Brothers (A. S. and J. H. Robertson) to cut ties and that he would put crews enough at skidding to keep Robertson's mill running day and night in order to get ties fast enough. Robertson's contract for ties called for oak at $2.75 per one thousand feet and other kinds of wood at $2.50 per one thousand feet.[39] He thought they might have to get Robertson's other mill to help cut out the ties as "There are so many boards on side cuts that it takes considerable sawing to make ties. . . ."[40]

During this period, Shaffer hired eight mules and wagons to help take out the cuts on the grade and by October 29 he had the first cut above the Austrian camp (Whittaker) out and the one in Dr. Austin's field about half out and three other cuts about half out.[41]

The early 1900s were troubled times in the lumber woods with a great deal of friction between various ethnic groups working side by side and between these newly arrived foreigners and "native" Americans. Shaffer presumably feared trouble between the mixture of Italians, Austrians, Hungarians, and Americans working and living in close proximity to each other for he recommended that thirty-two repeating light rifles and twelve brush guns (shotguns) with cartridges and shells be ordered for use at Leatherbark.[42] These were ordered from Supplee Hardware Company, Philadelphia, at a cost of $17.72 each for Winchester repeating rifles and $19.23 each for Winchester brush guns.[43] On October 22, one box of guns arrived at Leatherbark, and the ammunition arrived on October 29.[44]

On October 4, Shaffer reported that the telegraph line to Cass was completed at last.[45] Until that time, telegrams had to be taken by horseback to Green Bank for transmission.

To prepare the way for extension of the railroad when the top of the mountain was reached, Shaffer had a surveyor named R. H. Boal on Cheat River running line from "The Low Place" to the head of the river. On October 22, he wrote, "Boal is still on Cheat River. He has run a line up the river about two and one-half miles and up Black Run two miles and says there is lots of timber and fairly good country to build road."[46]

On November 22, Boal reported that Allegheny Run would be the best to open up first; the other places were so steep and rough that it would be hard to work them in the winter time.[47]

In the meantime, Linnan's crew was making rapid progress in grading above Whittaker. On October 30, he was 1,200 feet from the top of Cheat and on November 3, he was within 500 feet of the top.[48]

The Lukes believed in looking over their jobs in person when possible. At Cass this policy was established early by D. L. and J. G. Luke. In October, 1900, they planned to go by horseback from Davis in Tucker County to Cass on an inspection trip.[49] At Slaymaker's suggestion, they went instead by train and buggy to the vicinity of Horton in Randolph County, then by horseback to the headwaters of the West Fork of the Greenbrier and down to Cass. After looking over progress being made on the mill and railroad at Cass, they went up the new grade over the mountain and down Cheat River to the Club House.[50] The trip included time for hunting, and, while admitting he was not much of a sportsman, D. L. Luke said that, of course, if a deer should happen to be in the way, he would take a shot at it, although he expected it would go on its way the same as if he hadn't been there.[51]

Although no deer was killed on the trip, a few days later Slaymaker had a buck shot and sent it to J. G. Luke's home in New Jersey.[52] Slaymaker later had wild turkeys sent, and on December 13, Luke thanked Slaymaker for sending the wild turkeys and offered to pay him for them and the deer.[53] The Lukes made periodic trips to Cass that sometimes involved hunting deer, turkey, and pheasants (grouse). Occasionally, friends and business associates came along.[54]

Work on the railroad was delayed in late November, 1900, by heavy rains causing the largest flood "that has been in these streams." It tore out all the tramroad that had been built and the first bridge from the mouth of Leatherbark, which had been completed. It washed the grade considerably for the first mile but did not do much damage above that, except for several slides. Shaffer estimated it would take about a week to get the road back into as good shape as it was before the rain.[55]

This set-back prompted Shaffer to urge Slaymaker to obtain,

from Col. John McGraw, timber which he needed badly to replace the stringers on the tramroad and to supply oak for ties. Shaffer had been cutting on the Galford place on Leatherbark, but this was cutting out very fast. Furthermore, he advised opening up the Collins tract (north of Cass along the C&O right-of-way) as with the arrival of the C&O in January it would put them right in the hardest part of winter to commence operations on Cheat.[56]

Meanwhile other necessary preparations had been made for the new railroad. D. L. Luke wrote to Slaymaker, on December 3, that he was pleased to find all angle bars, bolts, and spikes and all railroad construction materials had already been shipped and were either at Ronceverte or at some point in that locality awaiting completion of the Greenbrier Road for their delivery.[57]

On December 10, the ground was frozen enough that wagons could start hauling ties up the new grade.[58] On December 12, Shaffer reported that Linnan had finished taking out the cut above the Italian Camp and that the Austrian crew would finish all the grading on the lower end that day.[59]

Securing ties in sufficient quantity was a critical problem. On December 13, Shaffer said that 400 ties were being made daily; over 200 by the men in the woods and about 150 by Robertson's mill. He had four teams and wagons distributing the ties along the grade. By December 15, 2,100 ties had been obtained and by December 18, they had made between 8,000 and 9,000 ties.[60]

Another concern was voiced on December 11, 1900, when D. L. Luke wrote to Slaymaker that there seemed to be a great deal of smallpox in West Virginia. On the thirteenth he suggested that all men in camps have vaccinations for smallpox and that all strangers be kept out of the camps.[61] This was done immediately and on December 15, Shaffer said some of the men had sore arms from being vaccinated.[62]

Smallpox continued to be a menace and almost a year later on November 5, 1901, Thomas Luke wrote to Slaymaker expressing concern over cases of smallpox in one of the lumber camps.[63] On November 11, 1901, Shaffer reported that ten men were in the pesthouse and that several others were feeling pretty tough probably as a result of the vaccination.[64]

Some items for the railroad were so critical that personal attention was given to their orders. For example, on December 10,

Harry Moore went to Cincinnati to look after obtaining frogs and switches. He arranged with the Weir Frog Company to get No. 5 frogs which would give the railroad a quick turn out and yet could be operated perfectly safely. He arranged for switches from the same company. He also checked on rail shipments and said seven carloads started out on December 16, and others would follow regularly.[65]

In December, after an order had been placed by the lumber company for coal and oil, C. F. Moore asked Slaymaker why it wouldn't be a good idea to have the Pocahontas Supply Company, a company subsidiary that operated the Company Store, order these items from time to time.[66] This suggestion was followed, and the Pocahontas Supply Company became the main supply agency for the company as well as for the developing town and the surrounding countryside.

Shaffer had been keeping close watch on the progress of the Greenbrier Branch of the C&O and had reported frequently to Slaymaker concerning its advance northward along the Greenbrier. For example, on September 22, 1900, he wrote, "It is pretty lively here now at Leatherbark. Mr. Bowers has moved his crew up to grade the sidings. They have a large force of Negroes, Italians, and Slavs." Shaffer also mentioned that Mr. Hankin, chief engineer of the C&O, was there and told him that the company's commissary building was in the way of the depot building site and that they would soon want the ground.[67] On October 26, Shaffer reported the railroad completed to Marlinton and on November 22, it was about eighteen and one-half miles below Leatherbark.[68]

Delays occurred when "The extensive flood in November did extensive damage to the C&O up Greenbrier. Engineers estimated that it will take seventy-five men one month to repair damages to railroad on the first seven miles below Leatherbark."[69] On December 15, Shaffer reported the C&O completed to about three miles below Leatherbark. Construction was being delayed because a good many of the railroad workers were laid up with sore arms from smallpox vaccinations.[70]

Mr. Frazier, who was in charge of C&O construction, was very cooperative with the lumber company efforts. On December 17, Shaffer reported to Slaymaker that Mr. Frazier offered to loan him tools or handcars to use until theirs arrived. At another time Frazier offered the use of a locomotive on a temporary basis.[71]

The C&O track was laid four or five rods above the camp at Cass on December 21, and reached the mouth of Leatherbark on December 22.[72]

"Railroad (the C&O) will reach Leatherbark tomorrow . . . will commence laying our iron Wednesday." This telegram, sent by Shaffer to Slaymaker at 2:40 p.m. December 21, 1900, announced a momentous and long-awaited event.[73] The Greenbrier Division of the C&O was finally completed to the point where steel and other railroad construction items could be obtained at Cass.

On December 26, Shaffer reported that six cars of rails, plates and bolts, but no spikes, had arrived at Cass.[74] Laying steel up Leatherbark commenced immediately upon arrival of the spikes and angle bars. The first rails were laid by skidding with horses until the locomotive was in operation.

Preparations were already underway for obtaining a locomotive for the lumber company as soon as the tracks were ready. Over a year before, in December, 1899, Slaymaker had inquired of Stearns Manufacturing Company of Erie, Pennsylvania, concerning a 35-ton Heisler locomotive. Blueprints were sent on January 10, 1900; comparisons were made with the Shay engine and a price of $6,675 f.o.b. Erie with $450 extra for Westinghouse air brakes was quoted for the Heisler.[75] However, the Lukes decided to order a Shay engine from Lima Locomotive and Machine Company, Inc., Lima, Ohio.[76]

On December 29, 1900, just one week after the C&O reached Leatherbark, the new Shay locomotive, designated No. 1, arrived. It was Lima Construction No. 630. No. 1 was a 40-2 engine with specifications as follows: 40-2, i.e., 40 tons; two trucks, total wheel base: 28'4"; 11-inch diameter cylinders with 12-inch stroke; 29½-inch drivers; tractive power 15,740 pounds. It was fitted with steam brakes and Westinghouse air brakes; couplers and draft gear provided with three pockets for link and pin type couplers arranged at heights of 24½, 29½, and 34½ inches and Lima Automatic Couplers at 34½ inches above rail; one headlight (18-inch Dayton oil); rear entrance type cab; 4-inch syphon with 16-foot hose and 12-inch diamond stack were other specifications.[77] Shay No. 1 soon became known as "Old Barney" by the trainmen and loggers.[78]

Robert Wilson was the first engineer of No. 1. M. H. Zeigler was the first conductor.[79] The locomotive's first task was to help put a derailed C&O engine back on the track at the newly completed C&O wye just south of Cass.[80] No. 1 soon gained local fame by "pushing 14 loaded cars up a grade that an ordinary locomotive could have hardly crept along."[81]

The new century began at Cass with a flurry of activity. On January 6, 1901, Shaffer reported that sixteen hundred feet of track were laid the day before. On January 8, he wrote that thirty-two hundred feet of track were laid on January 7 and 8, and the switchback was put in on the eighth.[82]

Slaymaker was on the scene for part of this early activity and was sending favorable reports to headquarters. On January 8, D. L. Luke wrote to him that he was "glad to note that your Austrians are making out well laying track and that our engine is a dandy and will unquestionably do your work entirely satisfactorily."[83]

To facilitate hauling materials, a hand truck with a platform about five feet square, 2-inch axles and 16-inch wheels was purchased from Tredegar Iron Works, Richmond, Virginia. It cost thirty-five dollars.[84]

Slaymaker returned to New York on January 9, 1901, and progress was reported almost daily to him by Shaffer. On January 9, they laid 1,800 feet of rail and were about 800 feet above the cut back of Gum's house.[85] On January 15, a telegram to Slaymaker read, "Putting in last switchback today. Will take about 10 days to lay track to top of Mountain."[86] On January 18, Shaffer informed Slaymaker that he "Will lay track across Whitaker [sic] Run tomorrow. Laid 1,800 feet today."[87] Work continued, and on January 27, Shaffer wrote that they had laid over 1,900 feet Saturday and had lost two hours because of not having rails. On January 28, 1,500 feet of steel were laid and two cars of pulpwood were loaded—the first loads of pulpwood from the new operation—even though the weather was getting bad and twenty inches of snow fell on Cheat Mountain.[88] Finally, at noon on January 30, 1901, six months and nineteen days after the first laborers arrived, the top of the mountain was reached and the track on the Cass Hill was completed. Shaffer took a supply of cigars to the top with him to celebrate the event.[89]

Rail for the railroad from Leatherbark to the top of the mountain was obtained from Ingalls in Cincinnati. Tredegar Iron

Works, Richmond, Virginia, furnished the angle bars, spikes and fishplates; track bolts and nuts came from the Lake Erie Iron Company;[90] switches and frogs were obtained from the Weir Frog Company of Cincinnati. Coal for the engine, ordered to arrive one carload per week, was furnished by the C&O Coal & Coke Company of Richmond, Virginia; oil was obtained from the Queen City Supply Company of Cincinnati, Ohio.[91] Dynamite was purchased from the Hercules Powder Company at a cost of twelve and three-fourth cents a pound for No. 2, from Arthur Kirk and Sons Company for twelve cents a pound, from Furgeson Construction Company, and from the Ring Powder Company . A Jim Crow Rail Bender was bought from the Queen City Supply Company for $21.50.[92]

During 1900, equipment to haul logs from the mountain was also being secured. Slaymaker wrote to H. C. Savidge of the J. L. Rumbarger Lumber Company, at Dobbin, Grant County, West Virginia, on January 20, 1900, to ask his advice concerning log trucks. Savidge replied,

> Would say I get my log trucks made the same as the trucks under the standard gauge cars, with springs. I would use also, as you state, a 24″ wheel, the size we are using on our trucks here. When you have the cars built, be sure the brake riggings hang to the truck of the car and not fast to the frame or bed of the car as the Lima Locomotive & Machine Company hang theirs. If you have them fast to the frame of the car, when running on curves, the shoes will draw off of the wheels.
>
> The best wheels that I know of are made by the Loebdell Car Wheel Company, Wilmington, Del., or the Pennsylvania Car and Wheel Company, Pittsburgh. It seems to me as if your price, $250, is high for trucks unless it is caused by the advance in iron. You should buy a wheel that has a good chill on it. If you do not get a wheel that has a good chill on it, it will soon wear out on the steep grades and sharp curves usually found on the logging roads.[93]

He also stated, "The capacity you mention in your letter is O.K., 40,000 pounds. Most of the cars we have here are 40,000 capacity."[94]

The first trucks were obtained from Lima Locomotive Works, Lima, Ohio, and skeleton log cars were constructed at Cass.[95] Early in January, 1901 they were putting some of the log cars together. On the first cars they put two brake stems on each car.[96] On February 28, 1901, twelve new log trucks equipped with air brakes were received from the Russell Wheel and Foundry Company, Detroit, Michigan.[97] Shaffer believed twenty-four log cars would be needed to get logs in as fast as wanted.[98] The company soon settled on 40-foot flatcars with air brakes and hand brakes as the standard to be used to haul logs on the Cass job.[99]

Expenditures for the operation were itemized at Cass and sent to the New York office for payment. Meticulous records were kept and errors, no matter how small, were corrected. For example, in the October 17, 1901, payroll ten cents was deducted from F. P. Paterson and credited to Luther Hiveley. This was questioned by the New York office and a letter explaining it was written.[100]

Logging the Headwaters of Cheat River

Pulpwood started to move from the heights of Cheat Mountain to Covington on January 28, 1901, when the first two cars of spruce logs were loaded on C&O cars Nos. 13237 and 15736.[101]

Work on the rail line into the unbroken red spruce along the headwaters of Cheat River progressed at top speed. On February 2 the track was completed to within one mile of Camp 2.[102] "Camp 2 was built near the old McCutcheon hacking which was hacked about 40 years ago by Robert McCutcheon, father of the late John McCutheon."[103] Camp 2 was built of logs on Shavers Fork near the location of Old Spruce at the divide where the railroad crossed the mountain. It housed loggers and railroaders. A pulpwood yard was nearby.

Cars were soon being loaded with pulpwood as fast as they could be obtained.[104] As many logs as possible were peeled before loading, but, in order to increase the flow of logs to Covington, shipments of unpeeled logs were also made.[105] By the first week in March, pulpwood was being shipped at the rate of eight cars a day;[106] by the end of the month, the log train was making three trips a day to Cass.[107]

Production rapidly increased, and company records for September, 1901, showed a total of 225 cars of pulp shipped during the month. Shipment ranged from 5 to 15 cars daily with an average of 9 cars per day. Each car contained from 10½ to 13 cords of pulpwood, and a total of 2,718½ cords were shipped during the month. Cars were owned by the C&O, and most were numbered from the 11600 and 11700 series, with others bearing numbers 2007, 7042, 45959, 45774 and 45775.[108]

Early shipments of pulpwood were made in open cars with stakes holding the logs. This arrangement led to some difficulties, for the stakes spread at the top, allowing them to rub the sides of the tunnels between Ronceverte and Covington.[109]

Thomas Luke personally inspected the cars coming to Covington and found that the standards that had rubbed were nine-foot three inches from the floor on the car to the top of the standards. The wires on the standards (to prevent spreading) were twelve inches from the top. He recommended that the standards be made six or eight inches shorter to prevent further rubbing and a possible accident.[110]

For a time stakes, used to hold the wood on the cars, were returned to be used again. However, this practice was stopped because less than one-half of the stakes made it back to Cass. The others were taken off along the way to be used for firewood.

Trials were made to determine the best cutting and loading procedures. Shipment of pulpwood in 4-foot, 12-foot and 18-foot lengths were made. Every attempt was made to get forty tons of wood on each car.[111]

Production of pulpwood continued to increase and on January 8, 1902, Shaffer reported plans to load 18 cars every day.[112] A lack of cars and other problems held this back somewhat but shipments outstripped the needs of Covington; on January 24, 1902, Shaffer wrote, "We received a letter from the W.Va. P. & P. Co., written by Mr. Cass from New York, instructing us to confine our shipments (of pulpwood) to 10 cars daily, which causes us to cuss mightily and hope that by return mail we will receive other orders to go ahead again."[113]

Eventually, the pulpwood shipments were dramatically increased and by 1905, forty carloads of pulpwood were shipped from Cass to Covington daily. The record year for pulpwood out of Cass was 1909 when nineteen thousand carloads were sent to Covington, an average of sixty-five carloads per day. By that time, a considerable quantity of pulp from the sawmill was loaded at the pulp shed in Cass.[114]

The new pulp mill at Covington used the calcium sulphite method of pulping wood. It produced fifty tons of pure spruce pulp per day. This pulp produced some of the finest paper available, and soon fibers from red spruce trees grown in the rigorous climate of Cheat Mountain, cut and delivered by the sweat and sometimes blood of rough, largely unlettered men, appeared in books, lithographs, maps and parchment. However, the greatest part of it went into magazines such as *Harper's Weekly, Harper's Bazaar, Collier's Weekly, Judge, Leslie's Weekly, Power,* and *Review of Reviews.* [115]

The early operations on Cheat were directed by Fred Tabor under the close supervision of E. P. Shaffer who made almost daily trips to the mountain. [116]

Not everything went smoothly for the new railroad. In September, 1901, dynamite was found on the tracks. Shaffer suspected a man named Galford, who had been arrested shortly before for selling whiskey. He also suspected Andy and Bob Geiger. [117] A reward of $500 was offered and a detective hired to solve the case; however, no record was found that it was ever solved. [118]

The early performance of Shay No. 1 was outstanding. The track had been well built and very little trouble was experienced. The first accident was during the night of October 16, 1901, when No. 1 jumped the track and broke a bolster while going up the mountain. It took the balance of the night and until the next morning to repair it. [119] Later, on March 12, 1902, the crown cogs were stripped, and No. 1 was disabled until repairs could be made. [120]

Cooperation between the C&O and the lumber company continued, and in October, 1901, the lumber railway was hauling stone off the mountain for use by the C&O as ballast north of Cass. [121]

Not all timber was sold as lumber. For example, Sanville and Lingo, sparmakers of Philadelphia, asked prices on spruce spars fourteen inches at butt, eight inches at the top and fifty-five to sixty-five feet long, and for even larger spars twenty inches at butt, fourteen inches at top and from sixty-five to seventy feet long. [122]

A major concern with timbering is loading the logs onto the railroad cars. At first, log ramps from the landing to the log car were used. Logs being loaded were rolled, via the ramp, onto the car by loggers using peavies and cant hooks. This system was feasible only when the landings were located uphill from the railroad and at the best was slow and inefficient. To assist in loading, a steam loader was purchased. However, on December 2, 1901, Shaffer reported that only three cars were loaded with the loader in one day. [123] At first they had trouble holding the loader in place, but after modi-fying its track somewhat, they were able to load eight cars a day by February 13, 1902.[124]

The lumber railroad was extended past Camp 2 (Old Spruce) toward the head of Cheat River, crossing the river three times in a few hundred yards. By July, 1901, Camp 3 was built in the basin formed by the headwaters about one mile up Cheat River from Camp 2.[125] It was built with lumber hauled in by horses when the railroad was still two and one-half miles from camp. H. R. Warner was the first foreman at this camp and Fred Beard was scaler.[126]

The wood hicks at Camp 3 were justly proud of their cook, Jimmie Kirkpatrick, who was praised almost weekly in the camp news until he was replaced in September, 1903, by Burley Smith.[127]

E. P. Shaffer visited the camps frequently and knew exactly what was being done at each. In June, 1901, Mr. Cass made his first visit to the camps on Cheat.[128]

Practically every job associated with cutting, transporting and processing timber was fraught with danger. Death rode the rails with the brakeman, stalked the teamster on the skid road, lurked behind falling trees, hovered in the mill, and visited the lumber-yard. This fact was known to all involved and at the very onset the company sought to avoid legal entanglements by requiring that persons except employees, entering the mill or riding the train be required to sign a pass that stated distinctly that such persons ac-cepted all risk of accident.[129]

The first fatal accident on the new lumber job was the result of drunkenness. On January 30, 1902, Shaffer reported the inci-dent as follows: "Ran over and killed a man by the name of David McDonald this a.m., about 5:30, on top of the mountain. He was in the office yesterday and drew his time. It is presumed by the crew of the log train that he was lying in a drunken stupor, as he had on his person two pint whiskey bottles with one nearly emptied."[130]

The remains were gathered up, rolled in a blanket and trans-ferred to the front porch of the Company Store at Cass where they "laid prey to the curious public's gaze throughout the day, owing to difficulty in getting a coroner."[131] The coroner finally obtained was J. L. Hudson, justice of the peace; special constable was J. H. Bird; the coroner's jury consisted of Edward Rutledge, Lee Hinkle, Harry Carson, Rev. Harry Blackhurst, C. L. C. Burner and Frank Wilson. The medical examination was conducted by Drs. J. A. and J. D. Arbuckle. A coroner's inquest concluded that McDonald came to his death by his own negligence.[132] According to legend, he was buried at Old Spruce and the grave was marked by a piece of iron pipe driven into the ground as a headstone.[133]

February, 1902, gave the men their first real sample of winter on Cheat. Early in the month between two and three feet of snow fell causing the railroad to drift shut. Linnan's crew was put to work shoveling snow off the tracks daily until the middle of the month.[134]

Spring floods were a menace to the new railroad, and in late February, 1902, Shaffer reported Cheat River to be about four feet over the railroad tracks between Camps 2 and 3 and that a later flood in April, 1902, "tore up foundation part of our new stringer road very badly."[135]

Despite the severe weather that occurred on Cheat Mountain, work continued steadily. In addition to the track in the headwater basin, the railroad was extended downstream from the top of the mountain and Camp 5 was built about one and one-half miles downstream from Camp 2.[136] Camp 5 was built with lumber sawn at Cass that was too poor to send out.[137]

Camp 2 was moved to Camp 5 in March, 1902, leaving three camps in operation on Cheat with about 900 [sic] men working.[138] The workers furnished a ready market for peddlers, and it was reported that Mike Durist, a jewelry salesman, was among the boys and made some good sales.[139]

The rapidly expanding operation needed additional tractive power and a locomotive was leased from the M. P. Bock Lumber Company at Boyer for use on the mountain until a second Shay could be obtained from Lima.[140] On March 3, 1902, Shay No. 2 arrived.[141] This carried Construction No. 694. It was a 50-3 locomotive with the following specifications: 50 tons, three trucks, total wheelbase of 35'7"; cylinders, 12-inch diameter, 12-inch stroke; 32-inch drivers and a tractive power of 27,500 pounds.[142]

During shipment, No. 2 struck some rocks that were lying on

the tracks and broke a cylinder and damaged it otherwise.[143] A bill for $30.44 including eight days labor at $3.00 and $6.44 freight for repair parts was sent to Lima for claims against the C&O.[144]

No. 2 was used mainly on the Cass Hill, making daily trips bringing logs to the mill at Cass and pulpwood for shipment to Covington. However, breakdowns plagued the engine and on April 30, 1902, it was "laid up again" because one of the front tires came entirely off, causing the crew to work nearly the entire night to replace it.[145] On July 18, 1902, it was "only doing about half work owing to the brasses being worn out" and they didn't know how long Bob Hivick, engineer of No. 2, could keep her running.[146] For the next two years, No. 2 was repeatedly in and out of the shop for repairs.

The difficulties encountered with Shay No. 2 caused Slaymaker to look again into buying a Heisler engine. On May 1, 1902, a quote was given at $9,000 for a 50-ton Heisler with an additional $400 for Westinghouse air brakes.[147] The decision was made to stick with Shays, however, and on March 4, 1903, Shay No. 3, Construction No. 754, a 65-3 engine was obtained.[148] Its specifications were sixty-five tons, three trucks; cylinders, 12-inch diameter, 15-inch stroke.[149] Engineers were Fred Linnan and Otts Cromer.[150]

As the tracks were extended into the headwaters of Cheat River and northward (downstream) along the mainstream, additional building materials were needed. The costs of rail, angle joints, etc. were given in a quotation from The Steel Rail Supply Company of 100 Broadway, New York, on March 17, 1902, as follows: one hundred tons of new No. 2, sixty pounds per yard steel rail at $33.40 per gross ton and the requisite angle joints for same at $1.10 per complete joint, all delivered F.O.B. at the Cass mill with the freight prepaid to Cass or deducted from the invoice.[151]

By April, 1902, two or three trainloads of logs and pulpwood were shipped daily (except Sunday) from Camps 3, 4 and 5. Supplies for the camps were loaded into boxcars at the Pocahontas Supply Company siding and brought up the Cass Hill twice a week.

Red spruce was also being cut at this time in the upper Greenbrier drainage. Early in 1902, Captain William Irvine secured a contract from the West Virginia Spruce Lumber Company to cut six million feet of spruce near Traveller's Repose. The timber was floated on the Greenbrier River to Cass.[152]

The new operation had been remarkably free of serious accidents, but inevitably these were to occur. The first violent death on the Cass operations of a workman engaged in his job was in February, 1903, when a brakeman, Zack Dolan, was killed near the first switchback above Cass when the logs slipped on one car and jammed him against those of the adjoining car. His brother, Davis Dolan, was killed at the same switchback in November, 1903, when he was putting on the brakes. A brake chain broke, tossing him under the wheels.[153]

Fire was an ever-present danger in the woods and around a lumber camp. Even though precautions were taken and preventative measures instituted, Camp 5 burned in May, 1903, with the complete loss of all contents and an estimated damage of four thousand dollars. Work was scarcely interrupted, however, and the men were moved to Camp 3 temporarily until Camp 5 was rebuilt.[154] Camp 5 was the only lumber camp to burn throughout the sixty years of operation of the Cass job.

Troubles continued to plague Shay No. 2 until finally, in 1904, it was returned to the factory and a second, larger Shay No. 2 was obtained, a 65-3 locomotive bearing Construction No. 836. It weighed sixty-five tons and had three trucks with a total wheelbase of 38'8¼", cylinders with a 12-inch diameter and 15-inch stroke, 32-inch drivers, and a tractive power of 30,200 pounds. The cab was of closed wood design.[155] It had one 16-inch oil headlight and standard draft, coupler mountings, and brakes. Engineers were Robert and Charlie Hivick.[156]

With nearly one thousand men working in a variety of jobs, each dangerous in its own way, the potential for accidents was great. On October 10, 1904, John Ray, aged about twenty-two years, was killed on Cheat by a log slipping from the tongs of a steam loader and crushing him.[157]

As the railroad was extended down Cheat River and additional camps were opened, an additional locomotive was needed. In November, 1904, Shay No. 4, Construction No. 926, was obtained. It was a 75-3 locomotive with a total wheelbase of 44'6", 13½-inch diameter cylinders with a 15-inch stroke, 36-inch drivers, and tractive power of 35,102 pounds.[158] Engineers were Pat Linnan and Lewis "Pinhead" Collins.[159] No. 4 was the largest engine purchased to that time and was used almost entirely on the Cass Hill. The other three engines became "woods engines" and were used mostly in the operations along Cheat River.[160]

Logging red spruce left in its wake huge piles of limbs and tops that dried and became like kindling wood. The company was very concerned about the ever-present danger of fire especially during the early spring and in the fall. Sparks escaping from the engine stacks or hot cinders from the firebox occasionally fell into dry leaves or treetops, igniting them. The first large forest fire on company lands occurred in 1904 when the slope of Bald Knob, east of Camp 5, burned. To help reduce the chance of fire, the company began cleaning up and burning all the debris along the main line and important spurs for a distance of about one hundred feet on each side of the track. During the fire season, campers were turned back and fishermen and others were watched closely. In addition, a man on a motorcar followed every locomotive to extinguish any live coals that fell along the tracks.[161]

The year 1904 was a red-letter year for the operations on Cheat. During that year, the town of Spruce was established.[162] Here a rossing mill was built to cut and peel pulpwood before it was shipped. A double row of houses, a hotel, and a branch of the Pocahontas Supply Company were constructed to house and supply the employees of the pulpwood mill and their families.

Spruce became the staging center for railroad activity on the Cheat (and later Elk River) operations. A shop and water tank were built there to service the trains.[163] Additional information on the town of Spruce is found in Chapter 9.

"Unlucky Day" ran the heading of a short note in the *Pocahontas Times* for March 16, 1905. It was noted that in one day the following events took place on the Cheat workings of the Spruce Lumber Company: the train crushed the foot of an Italian and it had to be amputated; Shay No. 2 ran into No. 3 on a short curve and the engineer of No. 2 received a wrenched back; a steam loader cut loose and rammed into the wreck. On the same day, a breakdown occurred in the mill at Cass.[164]

In the fall of 1905, the Greenbrier and Elk River Railroad was incorporated as a common carrier. This strategy gave some advantages, such as the right of eminent domain, which company officials felt might be convenient.[165]

For a time, caboose service was offered up the Cass Hill to Spruce for fifty cents. This was abandoned because the train crews had a tendency to stay in the warm caboose instead of being out to put on the brakes.[166]

Death struck again on Cheat in December, 1905, when a lumberjack named R. R. Wilson was hit by a falling tree. The cause was listed as "thick weather."[167] Indeed, the weather often becomes so "thick" on Cheat that it is impossible to see more than a few feet.

In January, 1906, yet another fatality occurred when Fry Byrd, aged fifty years, was killed by the train at Galford's Crossing while he was asleep on the tracks.[168]

By the end of 1905, most of the forest in the basin of the headwaters of Cheat River had been cut. Cutting had progressed down Cheat River to Big Run, about five miles below Spruce. Camps 3, 4 and 5 had been moved to that area. Moving a camp meant moving the men and furnishings only. The buildings, except for small sheds, were abandoned and new buildings were provided at the new site. When a camp was moved, it sometimes retained its number during the first few years, although most camps were numbered serially as they were built.[169]

When a camp was "cut out," the railroad spur, if any, leading into the "cut out" area was removed and the rails were reused in another location. Ties were removed if they were in good condition; otherwise, they were left to rot. Only the main lines from Cass to Spruce and from Spruce down Cheat River and later westward on Elk River were "permanent." A summary of early camps follows:

Camp 1	— Italian camp near the former site of the coal scales at Cass.
Whittaker	— Camp for Italian and Hungarian track workers.
Camp 2	— Near Old Spruce. Camp for loggers and railroad crews; pulp yard.
Camp 3	— About one mile up Cheat River from Old Spruce.
Camp 4	— Above Camp 3 on Cheat River.
Camp 5	— Downstream from Old Spruce near head of Leatherbark Run.
Camp 6	— Black Run
Camp 7	— Black Run
Camp 8	— Twin Bridges
Camp 8½	— Italian Camp on Cheat River main line below Camp 8.
Camp 9	— Big Run

On November 1, 1905, another, larger Shay, No. 5, was added to the company roster. No. 5, Construction No. 1503, was an 80-3 engine with other specifications similar to No. 4.[170] The first engineers were George and Charlie Cromer.[171]

During the next two years, an additional locomotive was added. Engine No. 6 was a Climax, made in 1904 by the Climax Manufacturing Company, Corry, Pennsylvania, Construction No. 534. This was a 40-ton locomotive that was purchased second hand in 1906 or 1907 from the Southern Iron and Equipment Company of Atlanta, Georgia. Bob Hivick went to Atlanta and rode the Climax back. It was taken to the Stony River damsite in Grant County and remained there until about 1913.[172]

In 1908, a second engine No. 6 was purchased, and the first No. 6 (Climax) was renumbered No. 9. No. 6 (second) was a 70-3 Shay Construction No. 1907. It had 12-inch cylinders with a 15-inch stroke and 36-inch drivers.[173] Purchased used from the Lewisburg and Ronceverte Railroad, it was used on the Cheat River Division, the Cass Hill and the Elk River Division until it was sold to Preston County Coal Company, Tunnelton, West Virginia. Engineers were Pat Bradley, Claude Wilcox, and Clyde Galford. [174]

By 1905, the railroad was extended up Black Run north and west of Mace Knob a distance of over four miles. Camps 6 and 7 were built on this line. About two years later, the line was extended northward from Camp 6 west of Mace Knob to the headwaters of Tygarts Valley River where another Camp 2 was built. This line included a five percent grade up which loaded cars had to be pulled. This area was cut over by 1908, and a year later only a single camp was operating on Black Run in the upper Cheat River drainage. By 1910, the headwaters had been logged out.[175]

When a spruce stand was cut, no attention was given to reforesting the area because there was almost always an abundance of young trees already present. With their release to the light, a second growth forest soon materialized.

Only in areas that were burned over was there a problem in achieving good reproduction. In 1909, the Company introduced "scientific forestry methods which should assure them a practically inexhaustable supply of timber in their present holdings."[176] In 1909, twenty-five thousand spruce trees were planted on Cheat. The next year one hundred seventy thousand spruce trees and two thousand yellow poplars were planted. By 1911, only about fifteen hundred acres had burned of the twenty-five thousand acres of company land that had been cut over. These lands were being carefully replanted with young trees taken up in unburned areas.[177]

The rapid natural reforestation in most areas, along with replanting in other areas, led to the common belief that the company's timber supply was self-perpetuating and would allow the mill to run at full capacity indefinitely.

Flooding was unpredictable and often caused extensive damage. In early June, 1908, about seven miles of track on Cheat River were washed out by a cloudburst causing damages of about twenty-five thousand dollars.[178]

OPERATING THE CASS HILL

Locomotives in active use but waiting at Cass or Spruce overnight were under care of the hostler. He worked from 6:00 p.m. to 7:00 a.m. seven days a week. His responsibilities were to coal up the engines, take on water, put oil and sand in the engines, pick clinkers from the firebox and keep the ashes shaken from the firebox and hauled to an ash pile. As time for the next shift approached, he had to get the fire hot and have it ready by 7:00 a.m. when the regular train crew took over.[179]

There was no set time for trains to leave Cass for Spruce. The procedure for preparing the locomotive and assembling the train at the beginning of a shift began when the crew took over from the hostler. The engineer looked after oiling the gears and checking over the working parts. The fireman checked the water and the fire. He might find things satisfactory, or he might throw in a little coal and "blow it up a little."

When ready, they would do any shifting or car spotting that was needed in the lumberyard then pull by the mill and pick up empty flatcars on the upper end of the engine and empty pulpwood racks on the lower end. Thirteen carloads of logs were then set in on the tracks by the pond. The engine with a load of empty cars and perhaps a supply car or coal hopper, was then pulled under the water tower, took on water, and headed up the Cass Hill.[180] The train went as far as the first switchback, dropped the flatcars in the runaround at the switchback, backed up, and hooked on to them with the pulpwood racks. This permitted them to set off the racks at the mill at Spruce and to pick up additional empty flatcars.

Supply cars and coal hoppers were always toward the engine when going up or down Cass Hill to keep them out of the way when shifting in logs or picking up empties.[181] On the way up the mountain, all trains stopped for a 15-minute break on the tailtrack of the second switchback. A clear, cold mountain spring here provided drinking water for the crew.[182]

When Charlie Cromer was engineer on Cass Hill, he became interested in a girl who lived on the mountain. In fact, she lived so close to the railroad, on the hill above Limestone Cut (near the second switchback), that Charlie could visit her while making a run. He would step off the engine at Limestone Cut and his fireman would continue to the spring where the crew took a break. The girl's father didn't like men coming to see his daughter, and after a few visits, the old man pulled out his shotgun and went after Charlie. The crew, hearing the shots, thought Charlie was dead, but he was too fast.[183]

As traffic on the Cass Hill became heavy, a runaround track was installed at the upper switchback. This allowed trains with as many as thirteen cars to meet and pass.[184] This was a common practice at the upper switchback and occasionally at the lower. Meetings were arranged by the conductor of the Cass-bound train, who called from the trainmaster's office at Spruce to the shop office at Cass. He instructed the Cass office man when the train was coming. The shop office man would then tell the crew that was heading up the mountain that they would meet the downward train at a certain switchback.

There was no whistle blown in the 1910s or 1920s at Limestone Cut or Gum's Cut for ''Coming Home.'' The only time they blew a whistle coming down the mountain was at the road crossings and at the switchbacks. When they backed out of the switchback, three toots were blown. Two toots signaled the go-ahead.

Loggers walked from Spruce to Cass when a train was not convenient. They followed the tracks from Spruce to "Gobbler's Knob," the name of the point where the path turned down over a steep hill to the first switchback. From the first switchback they followed the track to Cass.

Loggers, hunters, fishermen, and loads of blackberry pickers often rode the train. They rode on the water tender, in the engine cab, or in empty supply cars on the way down. On the trip up, empty flatcars provided lots of room. In cold weather a fire was often built on a flatcar to provide warmth.[185]

The crew on the Cass Hill was made up of the engineer, fireman, conductor, head brakeman, middle brakeman and rear brakeman. Each brakeman had three cars to manage. Brake wheels were on one end of a car only but occasionally, by chance, two brakes would be together, making life a little easier for that brakeman.

The front brakeman stayed toward Cass all the time, the rear brakeman toward Spruce regardless of how the train was headed.[186] Going up the hill, the brakemen and conductor rode out on the cars, not in the engine. In winter they piled the log chains together and built a fire on them, using for fuel the stake butts that were left in the collars on the cars.

Engines used on Cass Hill from 1912-1914 were No. 8 and No. 11. They were used both night and day, depending on the runs. Usually three trips were made each night from Cass to Spruce. Each round trip lasted about three hours. Trips to Slaty Fork and back required all day. Cass Hill engineers were George "Piney" Williams, Charlie Hivick, Sam Waugh, Cal Bradley, Charlie Craddock, Gil Moore, and Walter Good.[187]

"Piney" Williams was one of the most colorful of the Cass engineers. He came to Cass soon after 1900 and was engineer on the Cass Hill until he had a stroke in the cab of his engine in 1935 or 1936.[188] He always smoked a crook-necked pipe. It was against company rules to smoke due to fire hazard, but "Piney" smoked without restraint. One day he was approached by E. P. Shaffer, who started to "ream" "Piney" out for smoking on the job. "Piney" took the pipe from his mouth, showed its empty bowl to Shaffer and said, "Isn't a man allowed to chew on an old stick of wood?"[189]

For years, R. A. "Bob" Hivick was trainmaster at Cass. He had three assistant trainmasters: Andy Faulkner and later Merle

Ervin at Cass, Andy Faulkner on the Elk River Division, and "Stub" O'Dell on the Cheat River Division.[190]

In 1920, wages were twenty-eight to thirty cents per hour. Conductors received a little more than engineers, firemen a little less. Brakemen received a couple pennies less than the fireman.[191]

During the years before 1942, the engines were run facing Cass. On the Cass Hill, because of the switchbacks, the engines alternated between running forward and in reverse. They entered the first switchback in reverse and emerged forward until the second switchback. The engines entered the second switchback forward and emerged in reverse, in which position the remainder of the ascent was made.[192]

The engineer had the ultimate responsibility for the operation of the train. On his skill rested the efficiency of the entire train as well as the safety of the remainder of the crew. The engineer made all decisions concerning operation, attended to routine oiling and inspection of working parts, and ran the engine.

The fireman had a multitude of chores. His most time-and-energy-consuming task was shoveling coal into the firebox when needed. He stepped on a lever to open the clam-like doors of the firebox when coal was added. In addition to keeping the fire at maximum efficiency, he kept track of the fuel supply, the water level in the tank and boiler, and the steam pressure. Both engineer and fireman watched the tracks for obstructions.

The head brakeman (conductor) was an important member of the train crew. He determined the make-up of the trains and laid out the work for the crew. Where some method of dispatching was employed, he maintained contact with the dispatcher. Once his train was made up and was headed down the hill, the head brakeman tried to balance the braking so that the locomotive must exert a small effort to keep the cars rolling down the hill, yet, the brakes must not cause the wheels to slide.[193]

The brake stick (brake club, "Jim Crow," "hickey") was an essential tool of the brakeman. It was a short iron bar with a hook on the end designed to be inserted through the spokes of a brake wheel and around the stem to provide leverage to tighten up the brake. Manipulation of the brakes was a highly specialized art. They had to be set by hand at the top of the grade, and they often required attention during the descent. If the train was moving slowly, the brakeman could hop off the footboards of one load and catch the next space between the cars as it came by; but if the train was moving too fast, or if he had to make his way forward, he must walk or crawl atop the swaying logs.[194]

The dangers of this job can be visualized if we picture a brakeman in a howling snowstorm, moving from car to car atop the ice-and-snow-covered logs and climbing down at the brake wheel on one end of each car to tighten or loosen the brakes as needed. There was no caboose to go into for shelter and no companion to call to in case of trouble; just a man, his brake stick, the elements, and a mighty behemouth to control. Added danger was caused by the air brakes on the train. Sometimes the air brakes would be released just as the brakeman kicked off the ratchet lock to loosen the brake by hand. If so, the brake stick was whirled around with great force and could knock the brakeman off the car.[195]

When a trainload of logs reached Cass, the C&O switchlocks[196] were opened, and the cars were pulled onto the C&O and placed on the siding beside the pond. In later years, the logs were left at the shop and set in at the pond early the next morning. The siding held thirteen carloads, enough logs for one day's cutting by the mill.

Weather presented special problems and hazards, especially in the winter. Those accustomed to thinking of West Virginia as a southern state find it difficult to envision a bad winter on Cheat Mountain. The coldest part of the state is the high elevations of the Cheat River Basin. Temperatures of $-10°$ to $-15°F$ are frequent and lows of $-34°$ and $-44°$ F have been reported.[197] Freezing temperatures have been recorded during every month of the year.[198]

Severe weather presents hardships, inconveniences, and hazards on Cheat Mountain. Prevailing winds in the area are from the west. They are frequently moisture laden, and as they pass over the mountain, they become cooler, resulting in frequent and extensive ice and snowstorms in winter and violent thunderstorms in warmer months. Snowfall averages nearly 130 inches annually and in some years exceeds 170 inches. Snowfalls in excess of 15 inches are not uncommon.[199] Exceptional snow accumulations made logging extremely difficult or impossible. During the winter of 1907-08, seven feet of snow accumulated on Cheat Mountain. Logging was mostly shut down for two to three weeks. Italians and Hungarians shoveled snow off the tracks. Snow plows, consisting of a blade attached to the end of a log car, were made. Through it all, some 200 men continued peeling pulpwood.[200]

Dr. George Deike of Cass has calculated that snowstorms sufficient to stop logging occurred on Cheat in the years 1902, 1905, 1908, 1913, 1914, 1928 (2), 1944, and 1950, while snowfalls sufficient to greatly hamper work occurred in 1900, 1910, 1922, 1926, 1931, 1936, 1940, 1942, 1947, and 1958.[201]

THE CHEAT RIVER DIVISION

As the upper basin of Cheat River was logged, the railroad was steadily extended downstream (northward) from Spruce. By 1905, it reached as far as Big Run, about five miles north of Spruce; by 1908, another five miles of track were in place.

The extension of the railroad provided a new dimension to company operations. East of Snyder Knob, about ten miles north of Spruce, at an elevation of 4,400 feet, explorations showed a sizable seam of Gilbert coal, positioned to make mining feasible. This seam was 5'8" thick but had a 10-inch sandstone parting.[202] The Gilbert coal was satisfactory for steam production and company officials determined that it would be economical to supply their own coal. Accordingly, a mine known as the Hopkins Mine was opened on May 17, 1908,[203] located between Beaver Creek and Buck Run about one-half mile west of Hopkins in Randolph County.[204] By December 1, 1910, the mine was being worked extensively.[205] The Hopkins Mine was the largest company mine.[206]

In the fiscal year 1914, ending June 30 and including 305 working days, 18,833 tons (2,240 pounds per long ton) were mined. There were seventeen employees inside the mine and four outside. R. A. Hivies was in charge of the operation and D. S. Seaman was mine foreman. All mining was done by hand and the coal was hauled to the entrance by mules and horses.[207]

A second mine opened by the company, the Red Run Mine, was on the west side of Cheat River north of Red Run, one and one-half miles north of Cheat Bridge at an elevation of 3,565 feet. This was in the Sewell Coal and contained a 6-foot total seam; however, much of it was slaty. This mine was driven several hundred feet under the mountain before it was abandoned because of the low quality of the coal.[208]

These mines, along with others opened later, provided coal for the company's locomotives, loaders, and skidders and coal for sale to the residents of Spruce, Cass, and the surrounding community. Reportedly, coal was also shipped by rail to the West Virginia Pulp and Paper Company paper mill at Covington.[209]

In 1909, changes were made in the corporate organization of the company, and on January 31, 1910, all assets of the West Virginia Pulp and Paper Company of West Virginia were transferred to the West Virginia Pulp and Paper Company of Delaware.

The change resulted in the payment of one of the largest fees ever paid to that time, to the Secretary of State of West Virginia for a certificate of authority to do business in that state. The fee paid was $5,289. Acreage owned in West Virginia by the company was stated at 98,500 acres.[210] The number of employees in the Cass and Spruce operations and subsidiaries was about two thousand.[211]

Associated with the above change, on November 1, 1909, the West Virginia Pulp and Paper Company of Delaware absorbed the corporate interests of the West Virginia Spruce Lumber Company. Thereafter, the entire property and operations of the latter were conducted under the name of the West Virginia Pulp and Paper Company.[212]

These changes were purely a centralization of interests and did not affect the extensive lumbering operations. Lumber marketing remained under the personal management of Samuel E. Slaymaker of New York, with the firm of S. E. Slaymaker and Company as the lumber sales agent.[213]

On September 27, 1910, the railroad that would become the most famous logging railroad in the East was formed. The Greenbrier, Cheat and Elk Railroad Company was chartered to commence at or near Bemis, Randolph County, proceeding by the most practical route up the Cheat River Valley into Pocahontas County. It would then proceed to Spring Branch of Elk River and by way of the Elk River Valley to some point at or near Webster Springs in Webster County. The charter authorized the company to construct a branch line from the mouth of Slaty Fork of Elk River up Old Field Fork of Elk to some point on the proposed

Marlinton and Camden Railroad. Another branch was authorized to go up Slaty Fork of Elk River to some point on the Chesapeake and Ohio Greenbrier Division near Clover Lick. A third major branch was authorized from the mouth of Valley Fork of Elk to connect with the Valley River Railroad in Randolph County.[214]

Incorporators and shareholders of the GC&E Railroad were S. E. Slaymaker, Henry L. Condit, John G. Luke, George H. Perkins, and George E. Nelson. Each owned ten shares of stock at one hundred dollars per share. The authorized capital was fifty thousand dollars.[215]

As the railroad was extended down Cheat River, spur lines were built along every sizable tributary. Camps were established, landings constructed, and logs skidded in from the surrounding ridges.[216] When a hollow was cut over, the camp was moved to another location. The rails and sometimes ties were moved and used again. In this manner, Cheat Bridge, fifteen miles from Spruce, was reached in 1910, and grading was done several miles further downstream.[217]

Camp 17, located near Cheat Bridge, was the site of a murder in late May, 1910, when an Austrian by the name of Zoezoo was shot and killed by "Frenchy" Phillips and Ed Campbell. Their intention was robbery, but the arrival of a number of men frustrated their plans.[218]

The year 1910 marked the first time a passenger car was pulled over the lumber railroad on Cheat. The occasion was a visit by the Lukes to Cass and the Cheat Mountain operations. The Lukes had made their first visit in 1901, partly via horseback and then by the log train to the top of the mountain.

By 1910, increasing wealth and corporate status made changes in their style of travel. The later visit was made in a plush, private Pullman car. The party, John G. Luke, David Luke, Thomas Luke, William A. Luke, and Joseph K. Cass left New York on May 29, 1910, and stopped to visit the paper and pulp mills at Covington. They then journeyed, via the C&O, to Cass and were joined by Sam Slaymaker, E. P. Shaffer and their attorney, E. D. Talbott. From Cass, they crossed the mountain to Spruce and the next day proceeded to the various camps down the river. By noon, they were at the Cheat Mountain Sportsman's Association Clubhouse.[219] After resting and inspecting the remainder of their Cheat operations, they returned to Spruce, stayed overnight, and then came back to Cass, where the New York party joined the regular passenger train to Durbin and continued homeward through Elkins.[220]

By 1912, the Elk River Division was well underway, and the Cheat River Division was progressing rapidly down Cheat River. A need for additional rolling stock was met by the purchase of several new locomotives. Shay No. 7, a 42-2 engine, Construction No. 2563, was purchased in 1912. No. 7 had 10-inch cylinders with a 12-inch stroke and 29 1/2-inch drivers.[221] A locomotive was needed in the construction of Stony River Dam, Grant County, however, when No. 7 was purchased, and it was taken directly there for three years before coming to Cass. Charlie Cromer was its engineer.[222]

No. 8, the first "big" Shay at Cass, a 100-3 locomotive, Construction No. 2583, was built in 1912 and came new to Cass. It weighed one hundred tons, had three trucks and 15-inch cylinders with a stroke of 17 inches and 40-inch drivers.[223] No. 8 was equipped at the factory with an acetylene headlamp and a steel cab with a side entrance. This big Shay, run by Sam Waugh, was used mostly on the Cass Hill on the night run.[224]

The company's single Climax engine, originally No. 6, was renumbered No. 9. Thus, the next Shay purchased was numbered 10. It was a 70-3 engine, Construction No. 2765, with 12-inch cylinders, a stroke of 15 inches, and 36-inch drivers.[225] Built for the Canadian Government but not delivered to them, it was sold new to West Virginia Pulp and Paper in 1914. It was used on the Elk River Division, Cheat River Division, and Cass Hill, and also to haul logs on the C&O. Engineers were Grover and Charlie Craddock.[226]

Shay No. 11 was purchased in 1914. It was used mostly on the Cass Hill, making more trips from Cass to Spruce and back than any other Shay. It was almost identical to No. 8 in size and specifications and bore Construction No. 2799.[227] The engineer was George "Piney" Williams.[228]

In 1915, a deal was worked out with the North Fork Lumber Company to trade the original Spruce Lumber Company Shay No. 1 (Old Barney) to the smaller company for a 65-3 Shay built in 1905, Construction No. 1519 with 12-inch diameter cylinders with a 15-inch stroke. This became the Second No. 1 on the Cass operations.[229]

The two big Shays, Nos. 8 and 11, were assigned to the Cass Hill run and the long trips upgrade from Slaty Fork to Spruce on the Elk River Division. The smaller engines, Nos. 1, 4, and 5, were transferred to woods work and the long trips down Cheat River.

Fire was a continuing concern in the woods and in October, 1914, a lookout tower was established on Bald Knob, where a person stayed day and night during the fire season to help detect and pinpoint fires before they were large and out of control.[230]

Death visited the lumber woods periodically during this time.

Nineteen hundred nine started on a tragic note when, on January 1, Elza Morton was killed when logs slipped out of the tongs of a loader at Camp 11 and struck him.[231]

This accident was followed the next week by the death of a Swede—name unknown—at Camp 15. He was killed by a tree falling on him as he drilled a hole in a rock with a hand drill.[232]

On August 2, 1911, Harper Smith, trainmaster of the GC&E slipped and fell between two cars. Both legs were cut off below the knees.[233]

In May, 1912, L. B. Nicely, a brakeman on the log train was killed apparently by falling and hitting his head against the coupler. It was thought he slipped as he put the brake on.[234]

In late March, 1913, Wesley Perkins, hostler at Spruce, was killed. He had run the engine to the sand house to fill the oil cans. In getting out the oil, he pulled a heavy barrel off a platform. It fell, pinning his head between the barrel and a knuckle joint on the running gear of the engine.[235]

On October 30, 1913, an Italian grade worker drowned in Elk River while attempting to cross on a footlog during a flood.[236]

On July 14, 1914, Mike Miaki, an Austrian, was killed by a falling limb.[237]

Death took no holidays on the GC&E. In mid-January, 1916, Ralph Riddle, fireman on one of the locomotives, climbed down from the engine to make a coupling. He went between the engine and the first car as the train was making a sharp curve and was crushed. He was twenty-two years of age and a native of Elizabeth, Wirt County, West Virginia.[238]

A brakeman, Ira Coberly, aged twenty, was seriously injured when he fell from the train between Camp 38 and the main line and had his right leg cut off at the knee.[239]

In August, 1918, David Whitmore, brakeman, crawled under the train to remove a large stone from the track. The other crewmen did not notice him and moved the train, cutting him in two.[240]

Work was suspended on the main line down Cheat River in August, 1914, until logging along the branch lines had a chance to catch up.[241] Several months later, work started again, and the final joining of the GC&E with the Western Maryland Railroad was made at Cheat Junction near Bemis in 1918.[242] To speed up the junction, Charlie Cromer took Shay No. 3 from Cass over the C&O and WM to Cheat Junction in 1917, and construction was started from the north to meet the line being built down Cheat River from the south.[243]

Expansion of the operations during World War I necessitated the purchase of additional log cars. Although undocumented, the most accepted story is that around 1918, 200-plus flatcars were purchased from the United States Navy, apparently the largest group of identical cars ever purchased by a logging railroad.[244]

These 40-foot cars were equipped with "K" brakes and arch bar trucks. They were in continuous use until the job closed in 1960. Early passenger cars of the Cass Scenic Railroad were built on some of these cars.[245]

The completion of the Cheat River Division opened areas for additional coal mines along Cheat River as the railroad reached suitable sites. On the west side of Cheat River, 0.9 mile southwest of Cheat Bridge, the Farm Mine (Clubhouse Mine) was opened at an elevation of 3,780 feet. This mine was in the Sewell Coal, which was 4'8" thick at this point. It was in operation in 1917 but was closed by the fall of 1927.[246]

Whitmeadow Mine, also on the west side of Cheat River, was 0.2 mile south of Whitmeadow Run and 3.5 miles north of Cheat Bridge at an elevation of 3,475 feet. Here the Sewell Coal was 2'5" thick. A considerable entry was driven at this point and some coal mined before it was abandoned because of the thinness of the seam.[247]

Linan No. 1 Mine was opened in 1913 on the east side of Cheat River, 0.4 mile north of Crouch Run and about 5.5 miles north of Cheat Bridge at an elevation of 3,415 feet. The Sewell Coal at this point was 3'5" thick and of good quality.[248]

Nearby on the west side of Cheat River, 0.4 mile north of

Crouch Run and about 4.5 miles north of Cheat Bridge, Linan No. 2 Mine was opened. This contained 4'8" of good Sewell Coal. The entrance to this mine was only eighteen feet above the river and the coal had to be raised slightly to get it into the tipple. Its production ranged from 19,294 tons in 1920 to a high of 23,100 tons in 1924. After 1924, production fell to half this figure.[249]

Linan No. 2 was an excellent site for plant fossils coming from the slate and sandstone above the coal. The mine reportedly contained fossils of reptile footprints, but this could not be confirmed.[250]

Another mine operated on Cheat River by the Company was Big John Mine. Located east of the river, 0.6 mile south of Stalnaker Run and five miles south of Cheat Junction at an elevation of 3,210 feet, this mine contained a seam of Sewell coal 3'6" thick.[251]

The Deer Lick Mine was located on the east side of the Cheat River opposite Fall Run, four miles southwest of Bemis at an elevation of 2,985 feet. It was in the Fire Creek Coal and contained a seam 3'8" thick. This mine was opened in 1923 and closed a year later.[252]

According to Fizer,[253] the most distant mine from Spruce was a second Farm Mine located 1.3 miles west of Bemis in the Campbell Creek coal seam.

The coal mines added to the traffic on the Cheat River Division. Several runarounds were built: a one-fourth mile runaround at Cheat Bridge; another, one-fourth mile or more long, at Camp 30 about fifteen to twenty miles downstream from Cheat Bridge; and another long one at Camp 34 about two miles further north.

The woods engines, No. 3 and sometimes No. 4 or No. 1, were kept at Camp 34. They took empties to and brought loaded cars from the landings in the hollows and assembled loaded trains at Camp 34. Nos. 4 and 5 worked day and night, bringing loaded trains to Spruce and taking empties back to Camp 34. Crews on the woods engines consisted of the engineer, fireman, conductor (who doubled as brakeman), and one brakeman.[254]

Water towers were located on Cheat River at Camp 9, just below the First Fork of Cheat and above the Linan Mines.[255] Further down Cheat River, there were water boxes made from wood.[256]

On December 30, 1920 (December 21, 1920, according to Matics),[257] the GC&E transferred a 40-mile portion of the railroad (from Spruce to Cheat Junction) to the West Virginia Pulp and Paper Company, a non-carrier company. The lumber company possibly was moving to resist opening of common carrier traffic to the coal mines along the Cheat River Division.[258] Locomotives purchased after this date were purchased under the name of WVP&P Company, although they were lettered GC&E for Greenbrier, Cheat and Elk Railroad and were known as GC&E engines.

On March 14, 1922, ownership of the remainder of the tracks from Spruce to Cass and of the machine shop were transferred from the GC&E Railroad to the West Virginia Pulp and Paper Company of Delaware.[259] The name Greenbrier, Cheat and Elk Railroad Company continued to be used until 1936 to designate the line between Bemis and Slaty Fork.

The extent of lumber and coal operations, the long hauls from more distant parts of the job, and the necessity to haul loaded cars of logs upgrade from Elk River made the purchase of additional, larger locomotives imperative. This need was met by the addition of three 150-ton Shays.

The most famous locomotive in use at Cass was No. 12, a 150-3 Shay, Construction No. 3156. It had cylinders 17 inches in diameter, with an 18-inch stroke and 48-inch drivers. It was built to West Virginia Pulp and Paper specifications and arrived at Cass in March, 1921. No. 12 weighed 154 tons and had a tractive power of 59,750 pounds. It had a 9-ton coal capacity and carried six thousand gallons of water. Superheating was installed at the factory. It cost $45,007 to build and was sold for $54,034.[260]

No. 12 was first used on the Cass Hill. Each morning it took a load of logs from Spruce to Cass, picked up empty log cars, and took them through Spruce to Slaty Fork. There, the empties were dropped off, and thirteen loaded log cars were picked up and taken up the three percent grade to Spruce to be ready for the trip to Cass the next morning. The engine made this 44-mile round trip daily, six days a week. Later, No. 12 had the regular run from Slaty Fork to Spruce, making two 28-mile round trips a day.

By 1924, No. 12 was making regular daily round trips on the Cheat River Division to Bemis to pick up logs from Fishing Hawk

Run. The daily run was about eighty-five miles long and required fifteen to seventeen hour days, with occasionally longer days. One train crew did all of this. In a single month, September, 1924, they worked 425 hours. Engineers of No. 12 were "Piney" Williams, Cal Bradley and Walter Good.[261] For further detailed information on Shay No. 12 and its activities see Deike.[262]

No. 12 was so successful that in 1923 the company bought an additional 150-ton Shay, No. 13. GC&E No. 13 was a 150-4 engine, Construction No. 1586, built in 1906. Its cylinders were 17 inches in diameter with an 18-inch stroke and 46-inch drivers.[263] The C&O Railroad sold it to WVP&P for twenty-eight hundred dollars in early 1923. Rebuilt in the Cass Shops and with the addition of superheating, it was used on the GC&E Railroad until 1950 and was scrapped at Cass in 1955. Engineers were Ben Carman and Frank Williams.[264]

By the early 1920s, the logging operation had a massive inventory of equipment operating on approximately eighty miles of main line track and many miles of spur lines.

In operation at that time were:

Shay locomotives: Numbers 1,2,3,4,5,8,10,11,12,13, 14 (after 1923-28) (Shay No. 7 and Climax No (6)9 had been sold prior to 1920).

Cabooses: Four or five shuttling between Spruce, Cheat Junction, and Bergoo, numbered according to the engine it was used with.[265]

Flatcars: Around 200; about 100 were Middletown (wooden bolster in archbar trucks); the remainder were Huntingtons (iron bolster in archbar truck).

Skeleton Log Cars: Purchased by Slaymaker in the early 1900s; built at Cass using Climax bunk trunks.

Dump Cars: 200 series. Wooden hopper cars and A.R.R. standard hoppers, 20.

Boxcars: 20 400 series.

Supply cars: double doors, one on each end, 10.

Boxcars: single center door, 10.

Shovels and related equipment:
No. 1 Bycrus-Erie Steam Shovel
No. 2 Marion Steam Shovel
American Ditcher (modified from a log loader)
American Shovel (larger than American loaders)
Buckeye Shovel (removable from railroad car, didn't work on railroad).

Loaders: Eight loaders; numbers 1-6 were Barnhart, Numbers 8 and 9 were American. (According to Deike Nos. 1 and 2 were American Hoist Model C and No. 9 was a Barnhart that was never assembled but was put in parts inventory.)

Skidders: Five (Nos. 1,2 and 3 were purchased in 1922, No. 4 was bought in 1927, No. 5 in 1928.)

Motor Cars: Five or six. One located at every town: Cheat Bridge, Spruce, Laurel Bank, Bergoo, Cass.

Hand Cars: Two pump hand cars.

Speeders: Several individual "speeders" powered by pedals.

Snowplow: One built with two trucks (possibly a caboose frame) with a plow on each end. The plow on the engine end could be raised and a long stringer placed under it, which hooked to the engine.[266]

Pulp Racks: C&O 10,000 Series. Built especially for WVP&P.

Watertanks: Mainline water towers (tanks) on Elk were located at Bergoo, Rose Run, Big Run, Blue Hole Run, Slaty Fork and Spruce. Some were made of metal, others of wood. Tanks were improvised in the woods and on Shavers Fork by building small dams across the creek at a trestle or merely using a deep hole in the creek. Shays could pump water from any suitable place.[267]

In February, 1923, J. C. Cruikshank bought a Ford car to fit up with railroad wheels to travel back and forth from his home at Cass to the Mountain.[268] The company continued to use regular motorcars for business trips into the woods.

The year 1923 was fraught with accidents.[269] On January 25, Cass Hill claimed the life of another brakeman. Page McCloud, son of Clark McCloud, was braking on the rear end of the train and, while tightening his brake, the brake stick broke and threw him under the car. This occurred above the second switchback. He was about thirty years old and had a wife and four children. He was interred in the Olliver Cemetery near Cass by the Loyal Order of Moose.[270]

In October of the same year, Aeorland Hamrick fell under the log train, lost both legs and died in the Marlinton Hospital.[271]

Braking was, by far, the most dangerous job on the entire operation. On December 18, 1923, yet another young brakeman,

Frank Harris, was killed while making a coupling at the "square turn." He was caught between the engine and a car and squeezed to death. His father, Buck Harris, was conductor on the same train.[272]

The company's greatest extent northward was Cheat Junction, near Bemis, Randolph County. A commissary was built at Bemis to accommodate workers in the Fishing Hawk operations. This commissary burned on June 6, 1924, with a complete loss of the building and contents.[273]

Fatal accidents continued to plague the operations. A freak accident occurred on December 17, 1926, when a number of woodsmen and trainmen were riding a boxcar from Spruce to Cass. The car derailed and rolled over several times, killing Fred Shelton, a brakeman who was riding in the car at the time.[274]

On another occasion, a brakeman named Cutright fell between the cars at the coal bin and was decapitated.[275]

The last engine purchased by the WVP&P Company of Cass was Shay No. 14. This 150-4 Shay was built in 1910, Construction No. 2248. Its cylinders were 17 inches in diameter with an 18-inch stroke, drivers were 46 inches. It was sold new to the C&O Railroad and sold by them to the West Virginia Pulp and Paper Company in October, 1928. According to Deike, No. 14 was purchased at the same time as No. 13. It was rebuilt at Cass and used on the GC&E Railroad until sold to the Western Maryland Railroad in July, 1932.[276] Engineers were "Piney" Williams and Guy Stanley.[277]

The Elk River Division

In 1907 the following advertisement was circulated by E. J. S. Hoch, Allentown, Pennsylvania.

FOR SALE

35,000 acres of virgin forest and coal land, lying on the old Field Fork, Big Spring Fork, Dry Fork, Valley Fork, and the main headwaters of Elk River, above the Whitaker Falls[278] in the Counties of Webster, Randolph and Pocahontas, West Virginia. The timber on this tract is as fine as is to be found anywhere, and is very carefully estimated to cut as follows: Spruce 315 million; Hemlock 175 million; Bass Wood [sic] 49 million; Poplar 42 million; Ash 21 million; Red Oak 21 million; Cherry 14 million;

Cucumber 14 million; White Oak 7 million; Chestnut 7 million; other woods 35 million; being a total of 700 million feet of Saw Timber on the Tract. There are also 80,000 cords of Tan Bark on The Tract, and 350,000 cords of Pulpwood worth $6.00 per cord f.o.b. or $4.00 per cord clear to the operator. An additional 300,000 cords of pulpwood would be available by using small Beech, Birch, Maple, Sycamore, and other woods not included in the above pulpwood estimate. Part of this land is underlaid with clear veins of West Virginia *New River* Coal, running from three to six feet thick, there is also a large body of Cement Rock, Fire Clay, Limestone, Marble, etc., on this tract, the value of which altho' great, is altogether unconsidered in the proposition now. The Titles are good, and will be generally warranted by the grantors, the Acreage is practically correct from actual survey. It lies about six miles from the C&O Ry., and within 10 miles of the B&O Ry. The price is $30.00 per Acre.

The above estimate has been made by two of the most reliable timber experts who pronounce it the best Spruce and other timber tract that is now or ever was in the State, and lies in a solid body easily accessible. There is a good and easy route to and through this land from either the C&O on the east, or the B&O on the west.

Considering the Saw Timber alone, the price is at the rate of only $1.50 per M, exclusive of bark and pulpwood, and either the coal or timber is worth several times the price asked for the whole proposition.

For Address of owners write to

E. J. S. Hoch,
Allentown, PA.[279]

When the above was sent to Slaymaker, he wrote to Hoch informing him that they had had this tract under option for some months.[280]

The large tract referred to was controlled by John A. Innes, Canton, Pennsylvania.[281] It joined land owned by the West Virginia Spruce Lumber Company and they were very interested in purchasing it. Slaymaker had been in contact with Innes for sometime and reported that in November, 1906, he had spent several days looking over the property. He estimated that the tract of thirty thousand acres would cut at least 380,000 cords of pulpwood (up to 16 cords per acre in some places) and 334 million board feet of lumber as follows:

Spruce	100,000,000 board feet
Hemlock	100,000,000 board feet
Ash	40,000,000 board feet
Cherry	10,000,000 board feet
Oak, Maple, Chestnut, etc.	84,000,000 board feet[282]

Another tract of forty-one hundred acres, adjoining this one on the south and west, owned by Senator Henry G. Davis and Stephen B. Elkins of Elkins and others, had very heavy stands of spruce, basswood, and poplar.[283]

The Innes' property was taken over in November, 1907, by William A. Cobb of Elkins as agent.[284] In December, 1907, Slaymaker contacted Innes expressing an interest in the timber and asked for sixty days to investigate the land more thoroughly.[285] This request was agreeable to Innes and on December 14, he forwarded maps, options, deeds, and abstracts of the property to Slaymaker for his examination.[286] On December 10, Slaymaker asked James A. Whiting of Ronceverte to examine the property on Elk, telling him to take Charlie Cromer and a couple more men to help out.[287]

Nineteen hundred eight was one of the worse winters known in this region and Whiting and Cromer ran into extreme weather conditions. By January 3, 1908, they had seen only five thousand acres of the tract. On January 8, Slaymaker requested of Innes an extension of sixty days of their option to examine the property. He said one and one-half feet of heavily encrusted snow was slowing the work.[288] Conditions worsened and on January 10, Whiting reported an additional twenty-six inches of snow and said it took four horses and a sled to pull them out.[289] By February 13, Slaymaker reported drifts on Cheat and Elk of five to ten feet deep.[290]

The option was extended to May 19.[291] Whiting and Cromer completed their survey on April 15, 1908, and reported timber to be very tall, large and of good quality with good percentages of spruce, hemlock, yellow poplar (tuliptree), yellow linn (basswood), ash, cherry and red oak.[292]

Slaymaker, upon receiving Whiting's report, considered the timber had not fulfilled his expectations and made an offer of $15.00 per acre for the tract.[293] By May 23, 1908, the Innes' deal was completed at a price of $15.00 per acre,[294] or $1.00 to $1.50

per thousand stumpage, and Slaymaker wrote to E. E. Clark that "the Innes property is the best deal they have made in West Virginia outside of Cheat Mountain property.

"It is unquestionably the nicest lot of spruce and hemlock that I ever saw and also the lower section of it the best hardwoods. I can show you lots of acres in poplar that will cut 50-60,000 feet and lots of trees that will cut 6-8,000 feet to the tree—the finest ash I ever saw anywhere and also the best hardwood. I feel much elated over this purchase and I am quite sure that the property will be worth double the price we paid for it in a year or two." In the same letter, he mentions buying the Davis tract mentioned above.[295]

At this same time, negotiations were in progress with James Gibson for five thousand acres of timberlands on Elk River. The asking price was $16.50 per acre, but Slaymaker was advised that if the "color of some money" were shown, the land could be obtained for $15.50 per acre.[296]

The Innes and Davis purchases added thirty-five thousand acres to the holdings of the West Virginia Spruce Lumber Company. These lands lay in the Elk watershed, and in order to timber them, an extension of the lumber railroad had to be built.

In anticipation of the opening of the Elk River watershed to timbering and coal mining, a corporation, the Greenbrier and Elk River Railroad, was incorporated on August 9, 1905, to build a railroad from Cass to Fishing Hawk on the Coal and Iron Railroad. Incorporators were C. H. Tiffany, John R. Miller, George H. Perkins, A. J. Cody, and C. F. Moore.[297] C. F. Moore was elected president and headquarters were at 309 Broadway, New York. This corporation was never active and on December 19, 1906, the charter and corporate franchise were surrendered to the State of West Virginia.

After the Innes' and Elkins' properties on Elk River were purchased by the Spruce Lumber Company, another railroad company, the Greenbrier, Elk and Valley Railroad, was incorporated on January 30, 1909. Incorporators were John G. Luke, David L. Luke, Adam K. Luke, S. E. Slaymaker, and George E. Nelson. The small capital authorized, five thousand dollars, indicates that this was intended as a "paper" company only. This corporation also was never active.[298]

An announcement of the plans to extend the lumber railroad

to connect with the B&O at Holly Junction and with the WM at Bemis appeared in the *Pocahontas Times* on September 22, 1910. There were great expectations attached to this event. Not only would it enable the cutting of timber in the Elk River watershed; the coal reserves of Gauley Mountain would also become available. Further speculation was that the largest tannery in the United States would be built at the Forks of Elk, along with a large town.[299] This extension would connect with WM, B&O and C&O Railroads and would provide a maximum of flexibility and convenience for development.

Shortly after this, the real plans of the company surfaced on September 27, 1910, when a third corporation, the Greenbrier, Cheat and Elk Railroad, was incorporated with an authorized capital of fifty thousand dollars.[300] The authorized stock was later increased to $3 million.[301]

John A. Handley, of Greenbrier County, was placed in charge of locating the extension of the railroad from Spruce to the Three Forks of Elk River in September, 1910.[302] The progress of Handley and his surveying crew was rapid, and by April 13, 1911, they were at Webster Springs, having located a route down Elk to that point.[303] The survey was uneventful except that one of the surveyors, Adam Baxter, and his crew killed four bears on the headwaters of Tea Creek.[304]

The plan was to continue the survey to Centralia, Braxton County, where a connection would be made with the Richwood Branch of the B&O. The West Virginia Midland Railroad had been completed in 1902 from the B&O at Palmer, Braxton County, to Webster Springs.[305] However, the Midland was a narrow-gauge system and would not serve the needs of the GC&E unless it was modified.

The route of the Elk River extension ran almost due west from Spruce and crossed the divide into the Tygart Valley River watershed at 4,012 feet elevation, about one mile west of Spruce, a climb of 159 feet. It passed north and west of Mace Knob into the Elk River drainage, crossed the highway at Mt. Airy, and meandered along the southeast flank of Middle Mountain to reach Laurel Bank near where Big Spring Fork and Old Field Fork join to form Elk River.

From Laurel Bank, the route continued on the east side of Elk River to a point about one and one-half miles from the

Pocahontas-Randolph County line, where it crossed to the west side and closely followed Elk River to Bergoo.

Work commenced late in 1910. By December, one hundred Italians were working on the western end of the railroad at Mace.[306] To reduce the grade on each side of the divide, a cut was planned starting nearly one mile west of Spruce. This has since been known as the Big Cut.

The Big Cut was started late in 1910 and completed in 1914.[307] Work was done "principally from the west end as there was a large amount of fill material to be used west of it. To begin with, a track was laid across the hill alongside the location of the planned cut. Logs were moved over this road at first, but only a couple of cars could be brought over at a time, because of the steep grade, and the method was abandoned. Logging continued west of the Big Cut, however, and the logs were stockpiled along the tracks in what was "probably the largest pile of logs ever seen in Pocahontas County and probably the world." This stockpile was estimated to contain one thousand carloads of logs.[308]

To make the Big Cut, a 100-ton Marion steam shovel was purchased. It was mounted on railcar trucks and could be easily moved along as the work progressed. The Big Cut was worked from the top, by laying a switch from the line over the hill into the cut for a loading track and working the cut in lifts of about eight feet deep and twenty-five feet wide, changing the loading track each time the shovel worked through. The material was moved with ten 20-yard (standard length) Northwestern dump cars, ten 30-yard Oliver dump cars, and two locomotives.[309] The drilling was done with steam drills in lifts ahead of the shovel and shot light.[310]

Equipment used by the company on this construction included:

50 carts
30 wheelbarrows
50 horses (this number seems high)
one 80-ton steam shovel
one 100-ton steam shovel (Marion)
4 steam drills
2 locomotives
10 20-yard Northwestern dump cars
10 30-yard Oliver dump cars
5 6-yard dump cars
1 American steam ditcher

80 tons of 3' narrow gauge 20 and 30 pound steel rail for use with
    Oliver cars[311]

The Big Cut was nearly two thousand feet long and almost one hundred feet deep at its deepest place.[312] It represented the largest single engineering feat undertaken by the company and probably by any lumber company in the East. Rock removed was used as fill where the highest trestles were further west on the line.

The Big Cut took its toll of life in late June, 1914, when a young Italian, Suddlezio Mossozie, aged nineteen, was "blown to atoms" by a premature discharge of a blast. He was standing directly on the drill hole when the battery switch was thrown.[313]

The heavy reliance on foreign workers for railroad construction was a disadvantage when World War I started in Europe. By August, 1914, swarms of Italian workers were leaving Cheat Mountain. The down train was filled with Italians and Austrians on their way to New York for boat passage home to bear arms for their homelands.[314]

Work between the Big Cut and Laurel Bank was heavy. It was done with horses, carts and narrow gauge dump cars drawn by horses. Temporary narrow gauge track was laid in many areas to facilitate movement of materials.[315]

By the end of 1912, the line from Spruce to Laurel Bank was finished except for the Big Cut. Grading from Laurel Bank to Bergoo was much easier. A 20-ton rock crusher was installed in October, 1912, at the mouth of Old Field Fork on Elk River to provide stone for ballast on the road.[316] The main line was rock ballasted and laid with 85-pound per yard steel.[317] Laying steel was started on July 1, 1913, under the supervision of A. O. Baxter.[318] By May, 1914, the grade was completed to within twelve miles of Webster Springs, and steel was laid fourteen miles below Slaty Fork.[319] On October 14, 1914, this part of the line was opened for operation.[320] On November 4, the GC&E Railroad applied to the Public Service Commission for passenger service from Cass to Webster Springs.[321]

An astute bit of public relations was practiced as the tracks were extended into the populated sections of Elk. When train movements and other work was done on Sunday, orders were given not to blow whistles in order not to disturb observers of the Sabbath and call attention to the work being done.[322]

The company did not wait until the main line was completed to begin timbering. As early as March, 1912, two gangs of men were set to work pushing a spur up the Old Field Fork of Elk. This was eventually sixteen miles long and reached the timber in the headwaters of this stream, and on beyond Spruce Knob (Pocahontas County) into the headwaters of Williams River on Tea Creek Mountain, Webster County.[323]

A "small uprising" occurred during the building of this spur. One camp of track workers consisted of fifty-six Sardinians and a number of Hungarian teamsters. The Sardinians became dissatisfied with their wage of two dollars per 10-hour day and sent a delegation to Joe Hannah, who was in charge of the track extension, asking that their day be shortened one hour for the same pay. Their request was denied.

The Hungarian teamsters did not join them in this effort and when the Hungarians started out the next morning, they were met by a large crowd of Sardinians with clubs, staves, and revolvers. The teamsters retreated to the stables. Some of the leaders of the hostile gang were fired on the spot. However, they refused to leave; and Sheriff Link Cochran was called. He arrested fifteen of them and took them to Marlinton for a hearing before Judge Smith. The judge fined three of the prisoners and turned the remainder free. The incident blew over.[324]

Slaty Fork, also known as Laurel Bank, served as a staging area for the Elk River Division. There were five houses, a company hotel, a branch of the Pocahontas Supply Company, an engine house and assorted other buildings. Lumber for construction of these buildings was brought in from Cass. The company owned a farm just below the town, between the railroad and the river. A slaughter pen was located on the farm in an area still known as Slaughter Pen Hollow. The engine house was located along the railroad, across from the present planing mill of the Beckwith Lumber Company. The present Western Maryland Boarding House was originally the Pocahontas Supply Company Commissary.[325]

When the tracks reached Bergoo, a spur line was started up Leatherwood Creek and continued up the Left Fork to provide access to timber on Red Oak Knob and the headwaters of Leatherwood on the west slope of Gauley Mountain.

The placement of the railroads along streams in narrow valleys made them especially vulnerable to flashflooding. This was impressed on the company on Leatherwood Creek. When the Leatherwood Creek line was constructed, local residents warned the construction superintendent that the trestles across the creek were too small and too low. He allowed that "they might have had a lot of water back in Brother Noah's day, but these bridges will stand anything this creek has to offer." Not long afterward, on September 14, 1916, a cloudburst occurred which caused the water to rise fifteen feet within a few minutes. Thirteen bridges were removed very efficiently and completely. Damage to the railroad was eight thousand dollars.[326] At Camp 11 on Leatherwood, the barn was built near the stream. A group of Austrians tried to get the horses out, and a 40-year-old man named Frank, and two horses drowned. Frank had saved thirty-five hundred dollars to bring his family to this country.[327]

The greatest extension of the railroad on Leatherwood Creek was built in 1919. From the head of Leatherwood Creek it was fifty-one miles by railroad to the mill at Cass.[328]

In 1922, the railroad was extended up the Right Fork of Leatherwood, and a switching yard was established where the creek forks.[329]

Floods continued to plague the operations. In February, 1923, there was a "nine-foot tide" in Elk River, washing out a number of trestles on Leatherwood Creek and a bridge at Slaty Fork.[330]

By 1923, the lumber company had its greatest extension of railroad lines. According to *Railway Age Magazine*, this amounted to 115 miles of main line and 85 miles of spurs[331] although most people would count only about 81 miles as main line.[332]

For several years, Shay Nos. 5 and 6 hauled logs from Leatherwood Creek. Empties were taken from the main line at Bergoo to switching yards at the Forks of Leatherwood. Two or three trips were made daily, taking empties to either the right or left forks of the stream and bringing loads from the landing to the switchyards. From thirty-five to forty loaded cars were delivered in one day. The loaded cars were then assembled at the Forks and brought into the main line at Bergoo.

One of the big main line engines (Shay 12, 13, or 14) brought empties to Bergoo from Slaty Fork and, after shifting cars at Bergoo, left with thirty to thirty-five loaded cars, heading up the gentle grade to Slaty Fork. Arriving at Slaty Fork in three and one-half to four hours, it either dropped half of the load there or double-headed with one of the other big engines over the hill to Spruce. No. 12 could pull thirteen cars on this grade.[333] These engines returned to Slaty Fork and the Cass Hill engines brought the logs to Cass from Spruce, making several runs a day as needed.[334]

During the early 1920s, the run from Slaty Fork to Spruce was the regular assignment of No. 12. It almost always made two trips daily with thirteen loads each trip or about 156 cars a week, less two cars whose tonnage was taken up by supply cars.

Beginning in August, 1924, Shay No. 12 started making daily round trips from Spruce to Bemis, bringing out only six to ten loads of logs a day, although No. 12 could handle twenty-two cars of logs on this run. The round trip from Spruce to Bemis was about eighty-five miles. It regularly required fifteen to seventeen hours a day, with an occasional 20-hour day and on at least one occasion a 26-hour day,[335] all accomplished with the same train crew.

By the end of 1924, Shays Nos. 12, 13, and 14 were making the runs from Bemis up Cheat River to Spruce and from Slaty Fork up Elk River to Spruce. The Cass Hill between Spruce and Cass was handled by the 100-ton engines Nos. 8 and 11. Each of these engines made three trips a day, six days a week, moving nine cars each trip. The larger engines, No. 13 or 14, supplemented these two when more logs were needed at Cass.[336]

The main line trains used cabooses, where the conductor rode.[337] Denny Flynn was a famous trainman on the Elk River run.

Hours were often long and tiring. A typical day for the train crew was as follows:

> We left Bergoo at 6 a.m. and got back from the Right Hand Fork (of Leatherwood) at 6 p.m. The road engine was broken down in Slaty Fork, so we were called to take loads to Spruce. Before we reached Slaty Fork, a flu started leaking and it got worse going to Spruce. At Spruce we ran light to Cass where it took an hour to plug the flu in the shop—they banked the fire during this repair. We left Cass around 12:30 a.m. and went light down Cheat to

below Hopkins to pick up a loader to replace one that had broken down on Leatherwood. We ran with the loader to Slaty Fork and went to bed at about 3 a.m. We slept one and one-half to two hours until the hostler called us to run to Bergoo with the loader. We went back into Leatherwood that day and got back to Bergoo at 6 p.m. I figured that I worked 27 tons of coal all told during this time.[338]

Considering the steep grades and sharp curves in the logging railroad, the scarcity of runaway accidents are a tribute to the men working the trains and to the shop crews who kept the equipment in good condition. One such accident did occur on the Left Fork of Leatherwood Creek when Shay No. 6, with a heavy load of logs, started running about two miles above the Forks. The engineer, knowing the runaway could not make the sharp turn at Rock Run, jumped. The other crewman had already done so. The engine left the tracks and plunged into the creek and was extensively damaged. Fortunately, none of the crew members were injured.[339] An incline was built down to the creek to enable them to get No. 6 out.

The railroad was maintained by section crews, each with a section foreman. In the Elk-Leatherwood area, one section foreman laid up at the mouth of Rose Run, one laid up at Bergoo, and another one at the Forks of Leatherwood. The section foreman at Rose Run for many years was Charlie Simmons.[340] The section crews were mostly foreign workers who wore brass number tags for identification.[341]

Spurs were built as needed. In June, 1919, large amounts of supplies, including twenty kegs of powder, were shipped to the Propst Run spur then being built near Laurel Run.[342] Such spurs used rails that had been used many times before.[343]

The Elk River Division had its share of tragedy. Olliver Gregory, aged twenty-three, was killed on December 13, 1920, by a falling limb while working on Elk River.[344]

William Gibson, Jr. also found the grim reaper on Elk River. In June, 1922, while working as a brakeman on the log train, he was crushed between two cars while making a coupling.[345]

Otts Simmons, section foreman at Rose Run, was killed at Blue Springs on Elk River when he was going around engine No. 13, lost his footing, and fell under the train.[346]

On February 14, 1927, a logger named Jarvis Newsome died from injuries received when a log fell on him while he hooked tongs on a loader.[347]

As the Elk River Division of the railroad was built, mineable coal in that area became available. The first mine on Elk River, West Virginia Pulp and Paper Company Farm Mine, was located before 1920 on Mill Run two and one-half miles southeast of Ralph. It had a 4'3" seam of Sewell Coal.[348]

Two other mines in this area owned by the lumber company were Baldwin Mines 1 and 2. Baldwin No. 1 (also known as the Bergoo or Bergoo Creek Mine) was located on the ridge above the Bergoo Creek spur two and one-half miles east of the Forest Service Boundary. It was on the Bergoo Creek side of the divide between Bergoo Creek and the Left Fork of Leatherwood Creek. Baldwin No. 2 mine (also known as the Bergoo Creek Mine) was located west of Baldwin No. 1. Both of these mines were opened in the late 1920s and continued until 1939.[349]

It was not always easy to get workers for the mines among the outdoor-loving loggers. On one occasion, E. P. Shaffer asked Jim "Cockeyed" Carpenter to leave his saw filing job and go into the mines. Carpenter replied, "By God, I helped skin this country, but I'll be damned if I'm going to gut it."[350]

The GC&E hauled a large amount of coal from the Elk River Fields for the Western Maryland. At times there were five GC&E Shays engaged in hauling coal, Nos. 8, 11, 12, 13, and 14. According to one report, all five locomotives working the same train could bring as many as fifty-seven cars from Slaty Fork to Spruce. The engines were spaced with Nos. 8 and 11 ahead pulling eighteen cars, No. 12 in the middle with thirteen cars and Nos. 13 and 14 behind pushing twenty-six cars.[351]

The Hosterman Division

The company also operated what was known as the Hosterman Division on the C&O Railroad north of Cass. These operations were involved with removing timber on the ridges west of the Greenbrier River north of Cass. In 1916, a spur from the C&O was built up Trout Run, and shortly thereafter, a second spur was built up Allegheny Run. Each of these spurs extended to near the Back Mountain Road. Within the next two years, a spur up Cup Run (Deever Run) was completed. These spurs were built and owned by the WVP&P and connected with the C&O.[352]

One of the infrequent locomotive wrecks occurred on Deever Run in 1919 or 1920. The cause of the accident, that overturned Shay Number 10, has not been ascertained.[353]

Cutting and loading along the C&O between Cass and Hosterman was also done. A loader and empty cars were spotted on the C&O line to load until it was time for a C&O train. Then the logging train would go to one of the sidings or to Cass until the C&O train passed.[354] Shays No. 2, 3 and 10 were used on the Hosterman Division.

On all their rail lines, locomotives owned by the West Virginia Pulp and Paper Company were rented on an hourly basis to the GC&E Railroad. A rental account for March, 1919, which is typical of the period, shows the following:

Cheat Division Locomotives			
1,2,4,5,&6	1014 Hrs. @ $2.50		$2535.00
Elk Division Locomotives			
6	36 Hrs. @ $2.50		90.00
6 (with shovel)	24 Hrs. @ $2.50		60.00
Hosterman Division Locomotive			
3	68 Hrs. @ $2.50		170.00
	1142 Hrs. @ $2.50		$2855.00[355]

THE PEAK AND DECLINE

The operations centered at Cass were at their peak in the early 1920s. The sawmill at Cass was running two 11-hour shifts a day, six days a week. Several carloads of lumber and thirty or more cars of pulpwood were shipped daily. The pulpwood peeling mill at Spruce ran six 11-hour shifts per week.

To supply the mill with sawlogs and the paper mill at Covington with pulpwood, seven woods engines (Nos. 1,2,3,4,5,6,10) brought logs to the main line on Elk and Cheat Rivers. The three big engines, Nos. 12, 13, and 14, took longer trains up Cheat River to Spruce, up Elk River to Slaty Fork, and twice daily up the steep grade from Slaty Fork to Spruce. The two 100-ton engines, Nos. 8 and 11, brought logs down the Cass Hill from Spruce and took empties and supply cars back up. One engine ran at night and one during the day, each making two or three round trips each shift. From 50 to 65 cars of logs and pulpwood were brought off the mountain to Cass each day, six days a week.[356]

The company had from eight to ten lumber camps operating at this time with eight log loaders, four steam skidders and 200 horse teams skidding. About eighty miles of main line railroad and fifty to sixty miles of branch lines served the lumber operations.

In addition, there were five coal mines in operation, three farms, including the large farm between Cass and Green Bank, the large company store at Cass and three branch stores at Bemis, Laurel Bank, and Spruce.

The limited forests owned by the company, great and magnificent as they were, could not long withstand such an onslaught. The first operation to be curtailed was the pulpwood mill at Spruce. In 1925, this operation was closed and the pulpwood operation was moved to Cass. Spruce became a railroad terminal and most of the families moved to Cass or Slaty Fork.[357]

Non-fatal accidents in the lumber woods, pulp mill and mill were common. In the early years these were not reported in the *Pocahontas Times.* During the 1920s, however, frequent reports appeared such as: Cecil Tabor had his jaw and several ribs broken when his clothing was caught in a setscrew on a line shaft in April, 1922.[358] In February, 1924, Fred Sharp suffered a broken leg while hooking tongs on a loader on Cheat.[359] Frank Ward received a badly crushed leg in the pulp mill at Spruce in February, 1924.[360] Carl L. Kincaid was injured on a log loader in March, 1925.[361] Jacob Dean, brakeman, lost his hand when he fell and the train ran over his arm in May, 1926.[362]

The year 1926 marked the end of the first cutting of the remaining company land on Cheat. Camp 67, on Fishing Hawk Creek, near Bemis, was the last camp on Cheat River in the original cutting. Operations were then shifted to the Elk River lands.

In 1925, the company began disposing of its magnificent fleet of Shays by getting rid of the older locomotives. Sometime after June of that year, No. 4 was sold. Later in 1929-30, No. 2 and No. 3 were retired. They were worn out.[363]

In the late 1920s, No. 10 was sold to the Birmingham Rail and

Locomotive Company, Birmingham, Alabama.[364] Shay No. 11 saw its last service in April, 1931, and was placed on the siding at Cass.[365] No. 8 was also retired at about that time. On June 6, 1932, Shay No. 14 was sold to the Western Maryland Railroad where it became W.M. No. 5 on the Chaffee Branch in Maryland.[366] Shays No. 8 and 11 were sold in 1939 to a Clarksburg scrap dealer.[367] The scrap was taken to Spruce in gondolas with two gondolas of scrap set onto the log train for each engine. No. 12 and No. 13 doubleheaded the loads of scrap up the Cass Hill to Spruce. They were shipped over the Western Maryland from Spruce.[368]

In 1933, Herb Shafer and the shop crew at Cass, with assistance from Lima personnel and using new trucks from Lima, converted No. 12 into a 4-truck, 203-ton Shay by doubling the size of the water tender and adding a set of trucks. Parts ordered from Lima cost $560 and consisted of: one right truck frame ($160), one left truck frame and splice ($170) and two right truck boxes and caps.[369] No. 12 was out of service from March 13 to June 13 for the conversion. The idea behind converting No. 12 to a 4-truck engine was to allow it to go from Cass to Slaty Fork without stopping to take on water.[370]

No. 13 passed its last monthly inspection on February 13, 1942. When the annual boiler inspection was made in March, it was found to require new tubing and was taken out of service on March 20, 1942, and was scrapped about 1955.[371]

No. 12 was put out of service by a collision with a Western Maryland locomotive on Cheat which bent the frame of No. 12. Walter Good was engineer.[372] No. 12 was cut up for scrap in 1955 at Cass.[373]

While locomotives were being retired and sold or scrapped, the company was also getting rid of flatcars. As these were worn-out or becoming rotten, they were brought to Cass and burned on the sidings above the shop. In later years, flatcars were abandoned on spurs in the woods and allowed to rot.[374]

The total main line distance from Cheat Junction to Bergoo was 74.31 miles. This included 41.67 miles in Randolph County, 23.71 miles in Pocahontas County and 8.93 miles in Webster County. The company operated this line until March 3, 1927, when it and several miles of siding and the name Greenbrier,

Cheat & Elk Railroad were purchased by the Western Maryland Railway.[375]

An abstract of this deed includes the following:

1. Railroad from Cheat Junction to Bergoo with one hundred feet of right-of-way.

2. Additional lands and right-of-way for yard terminals at Cheat Junction, Spruce, Laurel Bank and Bergoo and as are needed and required for the purpose of providing for possible changes in the line in order to improve existing grades and curvatures, or to avoid "switchback" operations at Spruce and Cheat Junction. Also, additional parcels of land for improvement of existing curvatures at Cheat Bridge and Switchback Curve, Randolph County and at the Big Cut. The Western Maryland agreed to grant and convey to the GC&E Railroad that portion of the GC&E at Spruce that was replaced by a new loop eliminating the wye.[376]

Although it had been used by the lumber company for years as a main line road, this line was in such bad condition, by Western Maryland standards, that they ran only one engine on it, No. 1006, and made only one run to Spruce a week. GC&E Shays No. 12, 13, and 14 hauled coal and log cars between Laurel Bank and Spruce until the road was upgraded in early 1930 to where ordinary main line locomotives of the Western Maryland could haul coal from the mines in the Elk River Valley.[377] The Dixon Construction Company was in charge of the upgrading, a part of which included building a loop at Spruce to bypass the wye configuration used by the lumber company to route trains between Spruce and Cass. Two steel girder bridges, one for the main line and the other for the long passing siding were put in place. The bridges were originally fabricated in 1905 by the Pennsylvania Steel Company and were brought in secondhand and installed at Spruce around 1930.[378]

From the time of purchase, the Western Maryland retained the title of GC&E as a subsidiary, and a number of Baldwin locomotives owned by the Western Maryland were given temporary GC&E numbers.[379] This practice continued until 1936 when the trackage was merged into the Western Maryland, becoming the Webster Springs Subdivision.

On March 14, 1928, the GC&E trackage not sold to the Western Maryland was transferred to the West Virginia Pulp and Paper Company, including the Cass Hill line from Cass to

Spruce, the Cass Shop and spur lines at Bergoo (Leatherwood Creek), and Laurel Bank (Old Field and Crooked Forks).[380]

The lumber company continued to haul the timber from its Elk River camps and coal from mines on both Elk and Cheat rivers. It had to pay the Western Maryland for each locomotive and car moved on the line. The charge from Cheat Cut to Bemis was three dollars per load, with a fifteen-dollar minimum charge per trip.[381]

An unusual trip was made by one of the log trains in 1928 when the U.S. Fisheries arranged to have a load of trout taken over the mountain for stocking in Cheat and Elk rivers. Ted Fearnow of the United States Forest Service described the trip as follows:

> By prearrangement, the U.S. Fisheries' car met the logging train at Cass. The trip on the old logging railroad to Elk River was most memorable. A full rail carload of trout was moved from the White Sulphur Springs Hatchery to Cass. Fish were carried at that time in aluminum pails stowed out of sight in special compartments on the fish car where they were kept supplied with compressed air and ice. At Cass, the cargo was transferred to waiting flatcars on the old logging road. Then we started the long journey across the mountains with Whitaker Falls on Elk River as the ultimate destination. It was a slow trip with frequent stops to liberate trout in small tributary streams along the way. Each aluminum pail had a substantial chunk of ice placed on top. The cold dripping water kept the temperatures down and also helped to supply oxygen for the trout while enroute. The logging train crew had already brought a load of logs out to Cass earlier in the day. They had already put in a good many hours of work. Then as we proceeded across the various divides, stopping to liberate trout in tributaries of the Greenbrier, Cheat and eventually the Elk River, it was getting pretty late when we headed down Elk toward Cowger's Mill and Whittaker Falls. Suddenly the logging train pulled to a grinding halt on the Upper Elk and one of the trainmen came back and announced "the hog law has got us." I soon learned that what he was saying meant that a federal law, restricting railroad workers to a maximum of 16 hours continuous work, was making it necessary to halt the train. It meant get a new crew or give the old crew a night's sleep before proceeding. With no new crew available, it was in effect the end of the line. At this point I scurried around and managed to locate a handcar which was loaded with trout and 'pumped' downstream to points just above Whitaker Falls where the trout were released. On this trip I had with me District Game

Protector Theodore Moore of Marlinton and his young sons Ted
and Curtis. When the train reached the Upper Elk River, we were
met by Webster County sportsmen including a well-known fisher-
man of that day, Levi Gregory. With Levi's help we managed to
get the last of our trout planted in Elk River.[382]

As an example of the amount of traffic on these lines during
the month of May, 1929, Shays No. 11, 12, and 14 were used to
move 539 cars over the Western Maryland Railroad from Laurel
Bank to Spruce: No. 12 made twenty-seven trips; No. 14, twenty
trips and No. 11 eight trips. Doubleheader trains were used on
twenty-three of twenty-seven working days.[383]

Spruce became a midpoint terminal on the "new" GC&E. An
engine terminal was built and an engine yard maintained. A few
houses, a boardinghouse and a school remained of the old town.
Later, in 1951, these facilities were moved to Laurel Bank.

Spruce also served as an interchange point for occasional light
traffic of the Mower Lumber Company. The connection between
Spruce and the Mower line at Old Spruce was abandoned in
1958.

The original plan to connect with the C&O west of Webster
Springs was realized in 1928 when a narrow gauge railroad from
Webster Springs to Bergoo was built by the West Virginia Midland Railroad, operated by Pardee and Curtain Lumber Company. A third rail was added to make it standard gauge. This line
was purchased by the Western Maryland on May 31, 1929.[384]

As the first cutting of the timber on Cheat was completed,
business in general began to slow down. During the latter part of
1927, the night shift at the Cass mill was discontinued and the
work day was reduced to eight hours.[385] Night trains were
discontinued and a general malaise set in. Twelve head of heavy
woods horses, two farm mules, fifty sets of heavy logging
harness, spreaders, grabs, mauls and other general woods equipment were sold.[386]

The drought in the early 1930s dried the cutover woods into
kindling. Fire became a serious problem. One of the company
skidders was burned in a fire on Gauley Mountain.[387]

During the 1930s, Shays Nos. 1, 5, and 6 were kept in the
woods, hauling coal and timber from Gauley Mountain to Slaty

Fork. Nos. 12 and 13 made the haul from Slaty Fork to Spruce and back. Nos. 8 and 11 brought logs from Spruce to Cass.

Logging continued along Elk River and its tributaries during the middle 1930s. Slaty Fork Creek was opened up in 1933 and other tributaries followed.[388] Accidents decreased as the logging activity slowed down; however, in February, 1938, Frank Zebre drowned during a flood in Elk River.[389]

There was a total of about seventy camps on Elk River during the operations there. Finally, the original timber was cut out. Much of the land was sold in 1936 to the federal government to become part of the Monongahela National Forest. The company's holdings north of Cheat Bridge were also sold, leaving only about forty percent of the original acreage in company ownership. This timber lay between Cheat Bridge and the head-waters of the river.[390]

In June, 1942, the Mower Lumber Company of Charleston, West Virginia, bought the Cass operations and continued cutting second growth on Cheat. They also continued hauling hardwood timber in by truck from various other localities. During the war, they cut pulp for the West Virginia Pulp and Paper Company.

Mower made many changes in the supervisory personnel. Clark Phillips was made woods foreman[391] until he became ill in 1956 and died in April, 1957. He was replaced by Rocky Fisher.[392]

The end of lumbering on Cheat was not yet in sight, however. During the almost forty years since the first cut was made, a good second growth stand had developed in some areas. In other places there was some virgin timber bypassed in the original operations. The crews were brought back to Cheat River and began cutting on Glade Run, six miles north of Cheat Bridge.

Despite all precautions, accidents occasionally occurred and on April 19, 1941, Stuart McNeely, aged twenty-nine, died from head and chest injuries received from an accident on the skidder. He was the son of Mr. and Mrs. Saul McNeely.[393]

The logging railroad claimed another victim on May 9, 1948, when Jimmie Cassell, while walking from Cass to the camp on Cheat, went to sleep along the tracks and was struck in the head by a knuckle joint on an engine.[394]

The work progressed upstream getting closer and closer to Spruce and, by 1942, some skidders were on Beaver Creek and along the river six miles from Spruce. Other skidders were set up along the track on Cass Hill where skidder No. 5 made one of the longest "straight in" hauls of the entire operation: five thousand feet from skidder to tail tree.[395] Gordon Rickett was skidder boss on the Cass Hill skidding.

With the shorter locomotive runs from these cuttings, Shay No. 13 was no longer needed and was retired. Mower bought a used 70-3 Shay, CN. 3189 in 1943 (No. 4) which was repaired by the Cass shop crew and put into service. This engine, built in 1920, was sold new to Birch Valley Lumber Company, Tioga, West Virginia, as No. 5. It was renumbered No. 4 by Mower.[396] No. 4 had 12-inch cylinders with a 15-inch stroke and 36-inch drivers. This Shay cost $17,534 to build, and sold for $20,700 when new.[397]

Ten flatcars, converted to low-sides for shipment of coal, were in use during this time. They were numbered: 34, 53, 54, 94, 99, 146, 157, 160, 171, 183. They were used to supply coal to the four skidders still in use and to supply the coal bins at Cass and Cheat Bridge. Also on the roster were hopper cars used to haul coal to Cass and Cheat Bridge.[398]

Nineteen forty-three was off to a bad start when, on January 1, Herbert S. Galford, aged thirty years, was run over by the log train on Cass Hill and killed. He was brakeman on the train and it was thought he fell between the cars.[399]

Mower brought about several changes in the lumber operations. The old camps were replaced with camps built on flatcars. Each camp train had a kitchen car, a dining car, a lobby car and as many bunk cars as needed, usually five or so.[400] These camps could easily be moved and placed on a siding near to the work being done. Shanties were placed next to the camp for coal, supplies, horse barns if it was a team camp, a filing shed and sometimes a shanty for the camp foreman.

Another innovation by Mower was the use of Caterpillar tractors. In 1943 four of these were put in use on Cheat Mountain. They were used for making railroad grades, landings, skid roads, and campsites. They were also used to skid logs in place of horses as the horses were gradually phased out.[401]

By 1946, cutting had reached the headwaters basin of Cheat River where the virgin forest had been removed forty years before. A railroad was built along the original grade to about one-half mile above Slide Run, and skidders were set up at the best places.[402] The new track was extended up a hollow and along the ridge, and a skidder was set on top of the ridge at an elevation of 4,675 feet, one of the highest skidder sets made.[403] By using steam skidders, virgin timber that had been left high on the ridges in the first cutting as well as the second growth timber was harvested.

The year 1946 saw the end of skidding by horses on the Cass operations. Camp 95, at the head of Cheat River, was the last horse camp on the job.[404] Lanty "Midnight" Cole was foreman of one of the last two team camps. His nickname "Midnight" referred to his practice of turning out to work long before daylight. Forrest "Dick" Griffin was foreman of the other team camp. He had five teams and two Caterpillars. The teams were used to bring logs into a point where the "Cat" could get them.[405]

Around 1945, Cole's camp was closed, and all the teams and men worked in one camp under Griffin. The horses were gradually phased out until by 1946 only one team was left. Their names were "Nip," a bay and "Tuck," a gray, driven by Wade Weese.[406] They were later bought by Brice Cassell, who used them on his farm on Back Mountain.[407]

The company maintained four steam skidders during the second cutting in the headwaters of Cheat. One of these was usually rotated to the shop for repairs, and three were kept in use. Two steam loaders were kept in use on the mountain. During this period, two locomotives made the trip from Cass to Spruce, each bringing up six or seven empties and returning with an equal number of loads of logs.

On June 27, 1946, the Cheat operations claimed another victim when Henry Neil Simmons, aged sixty-four, died from injuries received when struck by a falling limb while cutting timber.[408]

In 1948, the railroad was laid up Slide Run near where the log slide was formerly located. Two switchbacks were required to reach the top of the ridge.[409] This track was extended to the head of Black Run where timbering was completed in the fall of 1949. Blacks were employed for track building and section work. They lived in separate section camps. Their boss was "Old Man" Walker.[410]

The track was then extended over the divide into the Cup Run (Elk River drainage) on the west side of the mountain, where a skidder set using a middle tree or angle tree was placed. Logs were skidded from over a mile away by use of the angle tree and two skidder hauls.

Several camps and skidder sets were made on West Ridge. Some of the workers drove from Cass across the CCC Road to Linwood and walked into the camps and sets. A man-trip consisting of a couple of flatcars, a caboose and the locomotive made the run from Cass on Sunday afternoon to take workers back to camp.[411] This was discontinued in 1953.[412]

By this time, 36 to 40-foot logs were being shipped with one tier on a car instead of two tiers of 16-foot logs. This greatly reduced the time involved in skidding and loading. Many of these logs were a foot or less in diameter at the butt and cut very little lumber.

In the early 1950s, an innovation was introduced when the first chain saw on Cheat Mountain was demonstrated west of Thorny Flat. This item, large and heavy by today's standards, was never popular with the cutting crews, although they were used to some extent during the last years of the job.

The next area to be opened to a second cutting was up the west side of Bald Knob from Old Spruce. This operation began in 1950, and by 1958, it had reached the furthest distance high above Cabin Fork of Cheat, twelve miles north of Old Spruce.[413] During this time, the locomotives, skidders and loaders were being phased out. In 1955, Shays No. 12 and 13 were cut up for scrap. In 1958, No. 5 was pulled behind the mill to provide steam during a period when the mill was down because of snow. While there, a cylinder froze and cracked, putting it out of service.[414] By 1958, there were only two Shays, No. 1 and 4, one skidder, one loader and one camp train in operation.

Finally, in 1959, the last spur was constructed to the top of Bald Knob, where some virgin timber had been bypassed in the original cutting. Skidder No. 2, with Gordon Ricket as skidder boss, was set up near the present Cass Scenic Railroad overlook, and timber was cut from the eastern side of the mountain. Shay No. 4 was used on the Cass Hill to take up eight to ten empties and bring back about the same number of loaded cars. The engine took empties to the skidder set, coupled onto the loaded cars, and dropped the train down to the Cabin Fork Turnoff.

There, the loads were dropped off, and the train moved the empties back to the skidder set.[415] Walter "Pop" Good was engineer and Clyde Galford was fireman on the final logging runs.[416]

After a few months on Bald Knob, the skidder was moved to Old Spruce, where it continued skidding until the operation was closed. On June 29, 1960, Pat Ellisy made the last hook,[417] the tower was dropped by "Doodle" Brown, and an era ended. The last skidder crew was: Woodrow Sharp, foreman; "Doodle" Brown, leverman; Pat Ellisy, bull hooker; Cletus Ellisy, bull hooker; Lester Hevener, on landing; Wilson Shreves, rigging crew.[418]

The last steam loader, No. 7, was used at Bald Knob. Some of the logs skidded at Bald Knob and Old Spruce were left in the woods when the job shutdown until they were later removed by trucks.

At the time of the closing, a grade was under construction north of Old Spruce. It would have been constructed around the mountainside high above Leatherbark's head to log the southern slopes of Bald Knob.[419] This grade was never completed, and the Interstate Lumber Company of Bartow later logged the area by truck.[420]

During the winter of 1979-80 a severe storm felled a large number of spruce trees near Bald Knob. These were trimmed, and Shay No. 5 and an American loader, converted from steam to diesel, were used to load them on flat cars in the manner utilized so many years by the lumber company.[421]

In 1983, a book, *The Cass Collection, Volume 2: The Logging Years (1901-1960)* was written by John P. Killoran. The book contains eighty-five photographs depicting most of the locomotives used at Cass along with many other scenes of the logging activity.[422]

The final events in the private ownership of land on the headwaters of Cheat River were concluded in April, 1988, when U.S. Senator Robert Byrd announced that the U.S. Forest Service had completed the purchase of the Shavers Fork tract of 40,745 acres of land formerly owned by the Mower Lumber Company. This was part of the land originally purchased by the West Virginia Pulp and Paper Company from Dewing and Sons in 1898. The area is now part of the Monongahela National Forest. A reserved timber clause, that will permit lumbering for five years, was included under terms of the sale. Deep mining in the area will be permitted for forty-nine years, however, surface mining will not be permitted.[423]

SUMMARY OF SHAY LOCOMOTIVES USED AT CASS DURING THE LOGGING DAYS, 1900-1960.[424]

No.	Construction Number	Date Built	1 Class	Dimensions Cylinders	Drivers	Tractive Effort	Used at Cass
1	630	12/00	40-2	11x12	29.5	15,740	1900-1915
–	662	12/01	25-2	8x12	26.5	9,560	lease 01
2	694	2/02	50-3	12x12	32	27,500	1902-1904
3	754	3/03	65-3	12x15	32	20,140	to 1930
2 (2nd)	836	3/04	65-3	12x15	32	30,200	1904-1930
4	926	11/04	75-3	13.5x15	36	35,102	1904-1925
5	1530	8/05	80-3	13.5x15	36	35,100	1905-CSRR present
6	1907	5/07	70-3	12x15	36	29,800	1908-1947
7	2563	7/12	42-2	10x12	29.5	16,900	1912-1917
8	2583	11/12	100-3	15x17	40	44,100	1912-1939, ret. 1931
10	2765	5/14	70-3	12x15	36	30,350	1914-1929
11	2799	10/14	100-3	15x17	40	44,100	1921-1955, ret. 1931
12	3156	3/21	150-3	17x18	48	59,740	1921-1955, ret. 1950 – (1942?)
13	1586	3/06	150-4	17x18	46	53,000	1923-1955, ret. 1942
14	2248	4/10	150-4	17x18	46	53,000	1923-1932
1 (2nd)	1519	7/05	65-3	12x15	36	29,800	1915-CSRR-1980
4 (2nd)	3189	5/20	70-3	12x15	36	31,350	1943-CSRR-present

CLIMAX LOCOMOTIVE USED AT CASS DURING THE LOGGING DAYS

No.	Construction Number	Date Built					Used at Cass
6 (9)	534	1904					1906- ?

VIII
WOODS
OPERATIONS

THE LOGGERS

The first logging camp built by the company on Cheat, Camp 2, was built in February, 1901. Camp 2 was located at Old Spruce and housed loggers and railroad workers. Edward Hunter was the first foreman.[2]

"Uncle Waldo"[3] reported in the *Pocahontas Times* on July 4, 1901, that the camp was served iced tea and ice cream on Sunday, June 30, made with ice taken from the top of the mountain within about a mile of camp.[4]

After passing Old Spruce, the logging railroad was extended up Shavers Fork and by the fall of 1901, Camp 3 was built.[5] It was at Camp 3 that the term "Johnny Pulp" was coined to designate the West Virginia Pulp and Paper Company.[6] This designation was to survive throughout the existence of the operation at Cass.

On February 6, 1901, "A Woodsman" from Camp 3 reported:

> We have been having lots of snow, followed by rain and sleet the past week. The forest is covered with snow at this writing.
>
> D.J. Tabor, Foreman for the West Virginia Spruce Lumber Company, has a crew of about 90 men.
>
> James Kirkpatrick is our cook and a better one never followed the woods.
>
> Mike Quinlin is our barn boss. Mike is as comical as a parrot and affords amusement for the whole crew.

Our instrumental music is furnished by the Jews Harp Band. The musicians are Pete Kelley and Jake McLaughlin; professionalist, Alex Butterbaugh with Strickler McLaughlin second best, Martin Boblett, mouth organist and everything moves off smoothly.

John Galford is our shoe cobbler, and is a pleasant gentleman.

The West Virginia Spruce Lumber Company has five teams skidding logs. The teamsters are Jake McLaughlin, Alex Butterbaugh, James King, Patty Louis and Joe Gum. The grab drivers Laurence McLaughlin, John Galford and I.B. Shrader.

Martin Boblett is growing a business whisker.

Bill Cassel is our blacksmith with Wild Bill as assistant.

Charley Poling and Adam Dillman are the road monkeys. They kept the sun darkened for two days, throwing dirt in the air. They are all O.K. and understand the art of road making to perfection.

The Company has an American Log Loader in operation. Four men are employed in its operation, and manipulating the logs.

They are extending the railroad line. There will be a camp located within two miles of here. At least three hundred men will be employed on this line, which will give Pocahontas boys continued employment.

A woodsman by the name of Dave McDonald was run over by the log train one day last week, on Cheat Mountain, and instantly killed. It is rumored that he had been drinking during the day at Cass and had started on his way to [from] Cass. He became so intoxicated that he had fallen to [sic.] sleep on the track. He was run over by the log train and much mutilated.

We have a pigs ear near Cass that should be looked into by the officers of the law. These vile men should be brought to justice and thus save many a soul from shame and ruin.[7]

On June 19 "Comical Jim" filed the following report also from Camp 3:

We have been having magnificent weather to labor in the vast forest of waving spruce.

D.J. Tabor our enterprising and skillful foreman has a large crew of about 95 men.

Bark harvest is now the order of the day. 5 saws running to full capacity of 25,000 feet per day. Each crew consists of seven men: 2 sawyers, 2 spudders, 1 fitter and 2 knot bumpers.

H.E. Roberts and I.B. Shrader are the two champion whirlwind spudders.

George Sharp is scaling during the absence of Ed Hudson.

Hanse Ratlig [sic.], while employed on the steam loader fell off of a loaded car, a distance of 14 feet and got badly hurt, dislocating the ribs on one side. He was conveyed to Cass on the mountain engine and is under the skillful treatment of those eminent physicians, the Drs. Arbuckle.

There is a town started by the West Virginia Spruce Lumber Co. on top of Cheat Mountain near Camp No. 2. Three houses are completed and occupied by employees of the company. A petition is out for a post office at this place. Should this be granted it would be a great convenience to the woodman.

We have a mail boy paid by the month to convey our mail, and should there be a post office established in our midst this would defray the expenses of our mail boy.

Hanse Ratliff was not knocked off the car by John Jerom, as reported by some. The fall was accidental.

Elliot Carpenter was out to see his girl Sunday.

Grant Dixon, formerly of Horton, a woods foreman for the Condon Lane Boom and Lumber Co., was with us a few days ago, prospecting a job. The writer would be pleased for him to locate with us.

James Kirkpatrick, our famous cook, still remains with us, but will be out on a short vacation during the Fourth. He is a magnificent cook, and a pleasant gentleman, liked by all.

Dan Dinkle, the cyclone road-monkey and side show performer, keeps his road in grand style and shows his activity with his foot performance and standing on his head. Dan is all OK, and a genuine 18-karett [sic.] road monkey.

P.S. Dilley, the U.S.A. standard spud fitter, will emigrate to Montana in a few days to prospect for gold and run a gold dust factory.

Will Good left camp a few days ago for his home at Lobelia, to see his girl.

Clarence Spinks, President of the Whistle Pig Trust and General Manager of the Ground Hog Parade has returned to his home at Camp 3.[8]

The railroad was extended further into the headwaters of Cheat River and up Black Run, where Camp 4 was established and in operation by December, 1901.[9] D. J. Tabor was made foreman of Camp 4 and was replaced at Camp 3 by Ward Hudson. Camp 4 was located at the low place where the present Snowshoe Road forks to Old Spruce.[10] It housed a full crew of eighty men. It required seven teams skidding and kept three saws running at full capacity of 20,000 feet/day. Morgan Rader was the saw filer.[11] Camp 4 could also be reached by Slide Run.[12]

Slide Run was named for a log slide that was built along it for almost a mile.[13] Logs were skidded to the slide and decked until winter. During winter, the slide was iced by pulling a barrel of water down it. The barrel was tapped to allow a stream of water to flow out on each side as it was pulled along, thus forming a film of ice on each side of the slide. Sliding was often done at night by the light of coal oil (kerosene) lanterns. In the coldest weather, work could go on day and night—one time sliding continued for three days and nights without rest. The cooks sent five-gallon cans of coffee and huge pots of food out to the workers every six hours or so. A crew of 10 men went along the slide periodically and lifted logs in that had jumped out. This was called "sacking" the slide.[14]

By 1905, Camps 5, 6, and 7 had been established. In March of that year, Camp No. 7 reported that the snow was three feet to five feet deep. John Hardy was camp foreman and Edward Smith was cook. The company had four engines and three loaders at work at that time. The writer also expressed the need for a church on Cheat.[15] The religious welfare of loggers in the woods was not totally neglected, however. Preaching was done on an occasional Sunday by Rev. H. W. McLaughlin, who went to the camps on the log train.[16]

When a new camp was established, it was completely built and ready to move into before the men arrived.[17] Sometimes the smaller buildings were loaded on flatcars and moved to the new location. If they moved from another camp, the only things the men brought along were their personal effects and tools.

Bedbugs were a problem in most camps, and weekly treatment with coal oil helped keep them under control. The men welcomed a move to a new camp for this gave them a short respite from bedbugs and the smell of coal oil.[18]

The logging camps on Cheat were designed to house about one hundred men. They typically consisted of one long, narrow, two-story building that served as the main bunkhouse, kitchen, dining room and lobby. The foreman and clerk slept in a separate small shanty, which also served as an office and as a store. "Brown's Mule" plug or "Twist" chewing tobacco and "Five Brothers" for chewing or smoking, as well as two or three brands of snuff and other personal items, could be purchased there. The loggers could make purchases and have the cost deducted from their wages. The cook and "cookees" also occupied a small shanty, and the blacksmith and saw filer shared another.

Camp 15, in operation on Cheat River by 1910, was a typical camp. The skidding teams required their own camp facilities. The stable at Camp 15 was about thirty by ninety-six feet. It had twenty-four stalls, arranged twelve on a side, with the horses facing the walls where each one had a small open window. Each horse was rationed six quarts of oats morning and night, and hay at night. Bedding straw was used sparingly.[19]

The two-story main bunkhouse at Camp 15 was thirty by sixty feet. The lower floor contained the kitchen, eating tables, and lobby. The second floor was one large, open room devoted to sleeping quarters.

The camps on Cheat Mountain were run on the theory that "nothing is too good for a wood hick." This made the Cass operation popular among the available workers and resulted in the West Virginia Pulp and Paper Company getting and holding high quality men.

The woods foreman was boss of three camps with about one hundred men each. He was responsible only to the general superintendent of the job. E. P. Shaffer personally picked the foreman and kept close tabs on the job by frequent visits to the woods.

Typically, workers in a horse camp included a camp foreman, one cook, one or more cookees, a lobby hog, a blacksmith, a saw filer, a buck swamper, several swampers, several road monkeys, five cutting crews—each consisting of a fitter, two sawyers and three knot bumpers, ten teamsters, a grab driver for every two teams, a grab skipper, a stake maker and an improvement crew.[20] The number of men was adjusted according to the terrain and the size of the area to be cut by that camp.

The crew for one or more steam loaders also stayed in the camp. A loader crew was made up of a loaderman, a tong hooker or hook tender, and a top loader.

If steam skidders were being used, the skidding crew also stayed at the camp. A skidding crew consisted of a foreman, a leverman, a fireman, a bull hooker, three bull chokers, a whistle punk, a rigger, three rigger helpers and two road cutters.

Each man's job was clearly understood and he was expected to be proficient in it. A timekeeper kept time for several camps and travelled from one to another on a "speeder."[21]

A good camp foreman maintained a high level of discipline among the men, fostered good morale and got the maximum work from them. He had to be firm and aloof from the crews, leading to a somewhat lonesome existence for him.

The foreman at Camp 15 was Billy Buckingham, a small man who did things in a quiet way and got excellent results. He knew every detail of the work and frequently pitched in to help with a difficult job. His wage was one hundred dollars a month.

The men were an independent lot and moved about from job to job. They were handled fairly. The men realized that the job was run on the square and that if one of them shirked his duty, he would lose favor with his fellow workers who would make his life miserable.

Next to the foreman, the cook was the most important man in camp. All of the cooks on Cheat were men. If a camp had a good cook, the men were willing to work long hours in the worst of weather and perform their jobs, knowing a bountiful, hot meal waited for them.

The cook's day began at 3:30 a.m. when he arose, got the cookees and lobby hog out of bed, and prepared breakfast to be served at 5:30 a.m. He was responsible for determining daily menus, ordering several days' supplies a week or so in advance, and preparing the meals. He also baked all the bread, pies, and cakes used in the camp. He worked seven days a week.[22]

Cooking was done on a big, double range, which cost $120. It burned coal or wood. Large flat pans were used for bread and cakes. Lard cans, washboilers, and huge coffeepots were used on top of the stove. Deep flat pans were used for meats that had to be roasted or fried.

To the left of the range was a sink where dishes were washed. Water was piped in from a spring and was constantly running. Large tanks at the ends of the stove provided hot water.

Along one wall was a table for baked food. Bread was mixed each day on this and, after baking, was spread out to cool. Underneath were flour and cookie barrels, while above were shelves and cupboards for pies and cakes. At the opposite end from the stove were shelves on which were kept a supply of canned foods and such things as cornstarch, baking powder and flavoring extracts.

A good cook was highly respected by men of the camp. He had absolute control of the kitchen and dining room, including the actions of the men while eating. He also took care of sick or injured men between the biweekly visits of the doctor. For all of this, he was paid eighty dollars a month.[23]

The cookees worked for about one-half of the cooks pay ($1.50 per day). They did a variety of jobs associated with preparing and serving the meals. They peeled potatoes and prepared other vegetables and meats, set the dishes on the table, and placed the hot bowls of food and pitchers of coffee on the table. After the meal, they cleaned up the dishes and dining room.[24]

The main part of the dining room was occupied by three long, oilcloth-covered tables that would seat a total of about ninety men. Wooden benches were attached on both sides of the tables.

The food was good and there was plenty of it—it had to be good or the men would refuse to go to work one morning and demand a new cook. Food was served "family style" in large porcelain dishes. Each man had a tinplate, cup and steel knife, fork, and spoon.

Following are sample lists of food served at the different meals:

Breakfast:
    Steak, fried potatoes, eggs
    Boiled kidney beans, stewed tomatoes
    Bread, biscuits, gingerbread, doughnuts, cakes, cookies
    Coffee
    Oatmeal, stewed prunes
Dinner (midday meal):
    Roast beef with dumplings, boiled and fried potatoes
    Sauerkraut, lima beans, corn, tomatoes
    Bread, rolls, gingerbread, yellow cake, doughnuts, cookies,
        mince pie
    Coffee or tea
    Cornmeal mush, stewed peaches.
Supper:
    Beef, boiled, roasted, or stewed with potatoes, pork

Fried potatoes, boiled navy beans, boiled fresh cabbage,
   tomatoes, baked macaroni
Bread, rolls, gingerbread, cake, cookies, pumpkin pie
Tea or coffee
Cornmeal mush, stewed canned blackberries.
The following were kept on the table:
Salt, pepper, sugar, oleo, evaporated milk, corn syrup, mus-
   tard, catsup, and pepper sauce.

The stunt seemed to be to fall in and get enough to eat in about five minutes. There was little talking at the table except on things related to the eating. Some men took off their hats, while others ate with all their clothes on. A man who came late to meals or who did not wash his hands and comb his hair carefully was distinctly unpopular with the cooking staff. The rest of the men had a deep interest in keeping the cook jollied up, so they soon set the erring one straight.

In one week, a camp used eight-quarters of beef, four sides of pork, four barrels of flour, eight barrels of potatoes, a 100-pound sack of beans, four crates of eggs, and other foods in proportion.

Perishable food was kept in a small, double-walled, sawdust-insulated provision house, located just outside the door of the cookroom. Meat was cut there for cooking. All around were barrels of potatoes, sauerkraut, cabbage, and turnips with bags of coffee, beans, and dried peas. A supply car was brought in from Cass twice a week to replenish the stock.

The lobby was at the end of the main bunkhouse, farthest from the kitchen. It was about twenty by thirty feet. It was heated by a large, low, heating stove that burned coal or wood. On top of the stove was a rack of cans heating water. Along three sides of the lobby were wooden benches and other loose seats were scattered about. At the end was a sink nine or ten feet long where the men washed up in tin wash pans. Cold running water was piped in from a spring, and warm water was obtained from the cans on the stove. Six or eight roller towels hung on each side of the sink.[25]

In one corner of the lobby, steps led up to the bunk room which occupied the entire second floor. This room contained two rows of double-iron beds, most of them double-deckers, forty-three in all at Camp 15.[26]

The bunk room was heated by Burnside stoves that burned wood or coal and provided heat to dry out the woolen socks, pants, and shirts worn by the men in winter weather. The clothes were seldom washed during the winter and set up an unbearable odor to which, fortunately, the men became accustomed.

The men usually slept with their clothes on in the winter, taking off only their shoes. They kept personal possessions under the beds.

Clothing worn by the loggers was comfortable while allowing strenuous activity. In winter, heavy strap socks with low-rubber overshoes were popular, but many men wore heavy-corked Cutter shoes the year round. Heavy woolen Pool shirts with a large checkerboard pattern were popular in the following colors — red and black, green and black, black and blue, white and black. When there was snow on the trees, the shirts were worn on the outside of the trousers. Some men wore felt hats with no protection for the ears, while others used a band, made from a sleeve from a knit undershirt, around their head covering the ears. A hat was worn outside of this. Yankee bell-top caps were used in extremely cold weather. Mule skin mittens with knit wristbands were worn by most men.

Rules of conduct in a camp were unwritten yet well understood by all but the newest greenhorn. Each man had his own coat and hat peg just inside the lobby door, his own place at the table and, of course, his own side of the bed. A new man at camp came into the lobby and sat until he was shown where to eat and sleep.

Discipline was usually good in camp. A troublemaker interfered with getting the work done, and he was sent on his way. The camp foreman was empowered to hire and fire men on the spot at his own discretion, no questions asked, no reasons given.

Lights were out at 9:00 p.m. and everyone was soon asleep. This was accomplished easily, for the men were tired after a long day's work and they knew that the 5:30 a.m. breakfast would soon roll around.

The life of a "wood-hick"[27] was an arduous one, involving long hours of hard work, long periods of time in the woods away from one's family, and physical hardships caused by weather and living conditions. Some men cracked under the strain. In January, 1905, Larry Brindle, aged about thirty-two years, had been to Cass where he lost several months' salary while drinking and carousing. He returned to Camp 3 and became very despondent.

After sitting about for awhile, he asked for the loan of a knife. His camp mates were suspicious of his intentions and refused the request. After the lights were out, he asked for a chew of tobacco and then for a knife to cut it. He was given a knife and immediately cut his throat. A locomotive was summoned by telephone and he was taken to the Pocahontas Hospital at Cass where he died. The woodsmen raised a large subscription for his interment, as was usual with them.[28]

The lobby hog was usually an older man or one who had been crippled by an accident on the job. He was frequently the butt of jokes by the other men. His work day started at 4:00 a.m., when he awakened the teamsters quietly to allow them to take care of their teams before breakfast. His job was mainly housekeeping. He made the fires in the cookstove and heater stoves, kept water hot for the men to wash in, scrubbed the lobby floor, emptied and cleaned spittoons and refilled them with ashes or sawdust, washed the towels, carried in coal, and emptied ashes out of the stoves. He also cleaned and filled the coal-oil lamps, showed new men where to eat and sleep and made the beds. His outside duties included shoveling snow off the camp steps, cleaning out the barns, and putting hay in the mangers.[29] His work week was seven days, and he was paid $1.50 a day.[30]

The blacksmith and saw filer slept in a separate, small shanty. The blacksmith kept the horses shod, made and sharpened grabs, cant hook points,[31] and hooks, and made and repaired chains and other iron tools and equipment. He worked six days a week and received $2.50 per day.[32]

The saw filer worked before a large window in his shanty. He was kept busy six days a week, sharpening the crosscut saws used by the sawyers. He could sharpen about twelve to fifteen saws a day,[33] skilled work for which he was paid two dollars a day.[34] The favorite saw of the men on Cheat Mountain was a 5 1/2 or 6-foot Simmons.

The men chose their own brand of axe. Most were double-bitted and weighed three and one-half to four pounds. Some 5-pound axes were used in de-limbing. Common brands of axes were "Warrens" (made by the Warren Axe and Tool Company), "Kellys," "Plumb" and "Sagers." Each man sharpened his own axe on grindstones in a small building provided for that purpose.

They were justly proud of their ability to put "an edge that would stay" on an axe.

Skid roads were located and blazed out by the buck swamper. When a slope was to be cut, the buck swamper started from the landing and ran a rough road into the timber. A crew of ten to twenty swampers followed, cutting all the trees and shrubs at ground level leaving no stumps standing. The skid road was about a rod wide. Larger stones were removed and, if necessary, ones that could not be removed were drilled with hand drills and dynamited. Roads were located so that skidding was done downhill as much as possible and on gentle slopes. A great deal of care and time was put into road building in order to facilitate the skidding and to reduce hazards for the teams. One skid road was used by two or more teams spaced so as to not interfere with each other. The number of teams used on a skid road depended on the distance to the logs and, consequently, how long it took for a team to make a round trip. A "road monkey" was assigned to each skid road. Working with an axe and a mattock, he removed any stumps or rocks left in the road by the swampers and repaired the road when it was damaged by the skidding. He placed crosspieces of small logs in boggy places to allow the horses to step between them while the logs rode on top. The buck swamper was paid $1.50 a day and the swampers and road monkeys were paid $1.35 to $1.50 per day.[35]

Camp 15 had five cutting crews of six men each. The head faller or fitter cleared any brush that was in the way of the sawyers and notched each tree in the direction it was to fall. Trees were felled to be in the best position for skidding. As many as possible were felled across or alongside the skid road.[36] After a tree was felled, the fitter measured the logs with a stick and marked where each cut would be made.

A crosscut saw was used by the two sawyers. Sawing on the side opposite and slightly above the notch prepared by the fitter, they quickly brought a tree crashing down. A bottle of coal oil was carried by the sawyers. The bottle cork had a groove along the side to allow the oil to come out. When needed, the oil was sprinkled on each side of the saw to clean off the pitch. If the tree began to pinch or if the crew needed help to fell a tree in the right direction, wedges were driven in the saw kerf using a sledge. The sawyers carried two wedges attached to each other by a short chain. When the tree was almost cut through, one of the handles was removed from the saw and the blade pulled out from the other side. Then the wedges were driven in, and the tree was thrown.

The knot bumpers, three in number, trimmed the limbs off the fallen tree and cleared them out of the way of the sawyers and the teamsters. The men moved leisurely from one tree to another but when the actual sawing started, they worked very fast. After the sawyers cut the tree into logs, the knot bumpers nosed the logs by cutting a slanting edge around the small end. A six-man crew could prepare about 225 spruce logs or sixteen thousand board feet in one day.[37] Each cutting crew cut for two teams of horses. Sawyers and fitters were paid $1.50 to $1.60 a day, and the knot bumpers received $1.35 to $1.50.

The trees were cut into 16-foot logs unless there was a special order for longer stock, in which case instructions were passed from the job superintendent to the woods foreman and on to the cutting crews. Logs were cut to a size of six inches in diameter at the small end. The smaller logs, under fifteen inches, were used for pulpwood.

There were twenty horses at Camp 15 in January, 1910. They were all big Percherons, Shires, Belgians and a few Clydesdales, weighing two thousand pounds and better per horse.[38]

The teamster and his team had to be experienced and alert. Logs running on snow or ice had a way of hitting a rock or stump and crashing sideways to catch a man's leg.

"J-grabs" were used on the front log on all hauls, allowing the team to step aside or jay off at the top of a slope when the logs started to slide too fast. The ring from the pulling chain slid off the "J-grab," thus freeing the horses and allowing the logs to move ahead. The team would then be brought to the bottom of the slope and attached again to the "J-grab."

The horses had to be able to make heavy pulls with logs, rocks, and brush underfoot. The sturdiness and nerve of some of the horses were outstanding. Teamsters handled their teams skillfully and injuries to the horses were rare. No new horses had to be taken onto Cheat Mountain in the three years prior to 1910, although forty teams were in use.

During the early years, there was no regular veterinarian available to the company. Persons with experience handled injured and sick horses. A favorite horse liniment for sore muscles was:

Oil of Organam . . . . 2 oz.
Oil of Spike . . . . 2 oz.
Oil of Hemlock . . . . 2 oz.
Oil of Turpentine . . . . 2 oz.
Spirits of Ammonia . . . . 4 oz.
Witch Hazel . . . . 1 pint or
Vinegar . . . . 1 pint [39]

A veterinarian named G. A. Rivercomb, from Ronceverte, was called in extreme cases.[40] By 1906, he was making regular visits to Cass on the first and third Saturday of each month.[41]

The average skid for a team was about one-half mile. The longest skid on Cheat with a team was at Big Run. A trip took half a day. Skidding was done day and night when the moon was light enough. Two sets of teams were used, one worked in the daytime and one at night.[42]

During the spring months of May and June, the entire logging crew would be put to peeling pulpwood. During this time, the horses were turned out in grassy fields on Elk River.[43] For example, in June, 1914, seventy-four head were turned out for sixty days in pasture for a rest.[44] Sufficient logs had been stockpiled to keep the mill running.

The teamster was a skilled man with a real regard for the well-being of his horses. He was up before the other men to feed, curry, and water his team before breakfast. After breakfast, he harnessed the team and drove it up his assigned skid road to the logs. Here, he and the grab-driver prepared a train or trail of logs.

One grab-driver served the two teams assigned to one skid road. He had an axe, a sledge, a cant hook, and a block and tackle. He was kept busy moving the logs to their best position when the teams were making a skid. However, the teams were spaced so that when one team's train had been completed and started off, the second team was soon on the scene.

Grabs were made by the blacksmith or were factory made.[45] They consisted of two 5-inch dogs connected by a short chain with a swivel in the middle. The dogs were driven into the adjoining ends of two logs.

To make up a train of logs, the grab-driver placed a "J-grab" on the front end of the log furthest up the hill. The team was hitched up, and they dragged the log until its back end was even with the front end of the next log. These two were then fastened together by a grab. They were then pulled down to the next log and so on until the train was completed.

The number of logs making up a train depended on the size and species of the logs, the condition of the skid road, and the slope. During winter on a good skid road, one team could bring in fifty to seventy-five spruce logs in one trip; however, thirty logs, including a number of smaller ones for pulpwood, was more usual. On average terrain, a team would handle from five to six thousand feet daily on a haul of one-fourth mile.[46]

Teamsters were a hardy lot and pride in their teams led to constant bragging. Brags were backed by bets concerning which team could move the most logs.

The teamster and his team brought the logs to a landing located near a railroad spur. Here the grabs were removed by the grab skipper, using a hammer also called a grab skipper. The grabs were dragged back when the team was taken for another train of logs.

Teamsters were paid $1.50 a day, including Sundays when they took care of their teams, repaired harnesses, etc. Grab drivers received $1.50 a day six days a week.[47]

Some jobs kept men at or near the camp. The stake maker cut small poles (stakes about eight feet long and four to five inches in diameter) and shaped them to fit the metal pockets on the sides of the log cars.[48] The improvement crew built landings, bridges and corduroy roads in the woods. They also built new camps and had the bunkhouse barns, etc. ready so that when the men were brought in they could go directly to work. The building of many of the camps on Cheat was supervised by a man named Watson.[49]

With some modifications in numbers and conditions, from about one thousand men in the first thirty years to one hundred men in the last years labored in this manner on Cheat Mountain for fifty-nine years. Working, living, and sometimes dying in those isolated, rigorous, and exacting conditions, they cut millions of board feet of lumber and pulpwood. They supplied the growing needs of a rarely seen outside world. To house them, a total of about 180 separate camps were used, with as many as eleven camps operating at one time.[50]

STEAM LOADERS

Cutting the trees and skidding the logs to landings were only the first steps in producing lumber or pulpwood. Loading the logs onto railroad cars for shipment was next. To accommodate loading, landings called rollways, were constructed on the uphill side of the railroad. Logs were skidded to the rollway by horses and were then rolled down the rollway as needed for loading. In the early days, log ramps were placed between the rollway and the car, and the logs were rolled onto the train. The cant hook was an indispensable tool for this task.[51] This was slow work and the height to which the logs could be piled on a car was limited.

Such severe limitations led to the development of the steam loader. A steam loader consisted of a boom arrangement supported by adjustable cables. A cable ran through a sheave at the tip of the boom to the cable drums at the base of the boom. Tongs were fastened to the free end of this cable. The cable drums were powered by a steam engine. The drums and engine were enclosed in a cab. The entire affair was mounted on a round gear and could be swung completely through 360 degrees on the American loader and 180 degrees on the Barnhart loader. The round gear was mounted on double-flanged wheels that ran on wooden rails topped with a strip of iron. The rails were placed on the tops of flatcars, enabling the loader to start at one end of a group of log cars, place logs on a car to form a tier and then move forward to place a second tier in the spot just vacated by the loader. Special spacer rails were used to connect cars to enable the loader to move from car to car. The loader pulled itself from one end of a car to the other or from one car to another by means of a cable and winch arrangement. The brake wheel and stem of a log car could be lowered by releasing a locking pin and laying the brake stem down in a bracket on the end of the car. This took the brake stem and wheel out of the way when the loader was moved from one car to another.[52] Each railroad flatcar was forty feet long and held two tiers of 16-foot logs. Skeleton log cars, used by the company in early years, would hold only one pile of logs. Wooden stakes held by U-shaped pockets on the side of the cars held the logs. Heavy chains were hooked across the car from stake to stake when about one-half of a tier of logs was loaded. Another set of chains was placed on top of each tier when the loading was completed.

Three persons were required to run a loader: the loaderman or engineer, the hook tender or tong hooker, and the top loader. To pick up a log, the loaderman swung the boom toward the log and threw the tongs. The tong hooker quickly placed them near the middle of a log and stepped back. The loaderman tightened the cable, which caused the tongs to bite in. He then raised the log with the cable and swung it around to place it on an adjoining flatcar. The top loader helped guide the log into place on the car as it was lowered and knocked the tongs loose. These dangerous jobs killed several men on Cheat Mountain and Elk River while they loaded logs.

In a day, one crew could normally load ten or more flatcars, with two tiers of logs on each car. The record on Cheat Mountain was twenty-one flatcars loaded by one crew in one day.[53]

Logs were stamped on the end with a brand that identified the camp. They were scaled later with a Doyle Rule as they were taken into the mill. Records of the species and the number of logs cut by each camp were kept available to the superintendent of the operation.

A steam log loader had been documented in use on Cheat as early as December, 1901. The crew had problems holding this loader in place, and Shaffer wrote to Slaymaker on December 5 that "The log loader is alright with the exception of the track and that will never be right until it is on the bottom of the car. There is not any trouble loading logs if can get loader to right place and hold it there."[54] These problems were corrected and by February 13, 1902, they were loading eight cars a day with it.[55]

In June, 1902, John Gerow was placed in charge of the loading at all the camps. Ed Hunter was in charge of the woods work.[56]

The first log loaders to be used on Cheat were purchased from the American Hoist and Derrick Company, St. Paul, Minnesota. Later, Barnhart loaders made by the Goodyear Lumber Company, Buffalo, New York, were added.[57] By 1922, the company owned eight steam loaders, including six American loaders and two Barnhart machines.[58]

Steam Skidders

Skidding with horses worked satisfactorily on much of the company lands along Shavers Fork; however, it was slow on long hauls. Skidding uphill with horses was very difficult, a fact which influenced the placement of the railroad. Feed and care for 200 or more horses and pay for half as many teamsters were expensive. These drawbacks to horse skidding caused the company to begin looking into the use of steam skidders. The first steam skidder, purchased for use at Cass before 1913, consisted of a three-drum steam winch and boiler built on wooden skids. It was placed near a large tree and, cables running through blocks (pulleys) on the tree were used to pull logs to the set.[59] The first skidder set was located on an experimental basis at the first switchback. It proved better than horses for skidding logs uphill, but it was too cumbersome and was used very little after the initial set.[60]

In 1922, the company began using steam skidders in earnest with the purchase of three large high-lead tower skidders. Two additional ones were added in 1927 and 1928.[61] Built by the Lidgerwood Manufacturing Company, 96 Liberty Street, New York, these machines were contained on two railroad cars each.

Skidders Nos. 1, 2, and 3 were bought used on October 12, 1922, from the Turkey Foot Lumber Company in North Carolina at a cost of twenty-five thousand dollars. No. 1 was built in 1916.[62] Its original drum had a capacity of two thousand feet of 1½-inch line. It was reconditioned in the Cass Shop and first used on Elk River in 1926. The first set was to take the timber from Tallow Knob across Cupp Run.[63] After this set was completed, the skidder was returned to the shop and refitted with a larger drum with a capacity of thirty to thirty-five hundred feet.[64]

Skidder No. 2 had a drum with a capacity of three thousand feet of 1½-inch line. It was also used when purchased for use at Cass and was rebuilt before being put into service first at Camp 62 on Cheat Mountain in 1926 and later on the Linwood spur. It originally had a telescoping tower forty-five feet high.[65]

The towers on each of these skidders were later modified to the pole-type tower made of sheet metal rolled and welded. These towers were hinged and could be lowered when the skidder was moved.

Robert Howell, an experienced skidder man from North Carolina, came to Cass in 1922 or 1923 when they were rebuilding the first two skidders. His son, George, and Lottie Howell[66] came with him, and another son, Ed, followed in 1926. They were hired by the company to help recondition and run the newly acquired skidders. The experience brought by them was important in the early success of steam skidding on Cheat and Elk.[67]

Skidder No. 3 was built in 1918. It had a drum capacity of three thousand feet of 1½-inch line. It was built originally with a tilt tower and was ready for use when it arrived. The tower was tilted by means of a large hinge at the bottom. The tower had to be turned, as skidding progressed at a set, in order to keep the hinge behind the tower from the direction of skidding.[68] It was equipped with fall blocks, which were removed later when the skidder was rebuilt making it wound "straight to the gun" as were the other skidders. It was the second skidder actually used by the company, and the first of the three "modern" types. Its first set was at Falls of Cheat in 1926.[69]

Skidders were repaired in the woods whenever possible. If necessary, workers from the shop at Cass went out to make the repairs. The skidders were brought to Cass for the installation of new tubes in the boilers or other extensive repairs. Bringing them to the shop involved dismantling guy wires, lowering the tower onto a railroad car, and removing blocking. A special run by the locomotive was necessary to bring the skidder in. Needless to say, they were kept in the woods until major repairs were a necessity. Since there were no standby skidders, loggers at a set moved to another site until an out of service skidder was repaired.[70]

Skidder No. 4 was purchased from the Babcock Lumber Company at Davis, West Virginia, April 23, 1927, for twenty-five hundred dollars.[71] It was larger than the others and had a spool capacity of four thousand feet of 2-inch line. Its original wooden tower was replaced with a round iron tower. It was first used on Hickory Lick on Elk in 1930.[72]

Skidder No. 5, the last and largest skidder bought by the West Virginia Pulp and Paper Company for use at Cass, was built in 1920.[73] It was purchased from the Babcock Lumber Company, Davis, West Virginia, on August 8, 1928, for six thousand dollars.[74] Its spool capacity was over four thousand feet of 2-inch line, and it was equipped with a Mangus skidder tower that was ninety feet long. It was first used in the Bergoo-Leatherwood Creek Area in 1930.[75]

A skidder was built on a railroad car and was moved to a logging site and placed on a siding. Here it was jacked up and blocked to make it as solid as possible, since there was a lot of vibration while running. The tower was erected and guyed with cables. A "tail tree" was selected and secured with guy wires. The tree was rigged with pulleys for the main cable or highline and for the outhaul cable. The tail tree could be two to four thousand feet away depending on the terrain and on the capacity of the skidder. While the rigging was being done, a skid road for the main cable was cut from the tower to the tail tree. Two road cutters were assigned to each skidder set. Only the largest trees that would interfere with raising the main cable were cut. Light cables were dragged by hand from the skidder to the tail tree. Utilizing power from the skidder, the light cables were used to drag the heavy main cable and outhaul cable to the tail tree. A carriage (buggy, bicycle) with pulleys containing the skidding line was placed on the main cable and attached to the outhaul line, and the cables and buggy were raised high in the air. The buggy was pulled back and forth on the main cable by the outhaul line to form a skid road along which logs could be picked up at any point along the road and brought back to the skidder. The pickup was accomplished by hauling the buggy along the main line to where logs were cut and lowering the skidding line, which contained a bull hook on which several chokers were placed. The chokers were pieces of cable with hooks and eyes spliced on them. They were looped around one or more logs about one-third the distance from one end and then hooked to the bull hook. The logs were then lifted into the air and were brought back to the skidder, lowered to the ground, and released in a jumbled pile near the railroad, where the loader could get to them.

A skid road was used until the logs on each side of it were brought in; then the cables were moved to the right to another tail tree and a new skid road. Moving required only one-half hour or so, for the new skid road was prepared ahead of time.

A skidder set was usually in a valley on a siding by the railroad. Skid roads were made one at a time in succession, forming a complete circle, like spokes of a wheel radiating from the skidder. As new skid roads were made, the box on the tower and bands securing the various pulleys were rotated as needed, or on No. 3 the entire tower was rotated while the skidder remained stationary.

Sometimes a middle tree furnished with proper pulleys was used to bring logs from over a ridge or to go over a hump where the main line was too low. In this situation logs were brought to the middle tree and dumped. After as many logs as possible were piled there, the tail was changed to the middle tree, and the logs were hauled to the skidder. On occasion, two skidders were used in this situation, with one skidding to the middle tree and the other skidding from the middle tree to the railroad.[76]

A skidder set lasted one to six months, depending on the terrain, the size of the tract, and the amount of timber.[77]

Coal for the skidder was brought in on a railroad car called a "lowside." This car was placed on a siding next to the skidder, and a plank was placed to bridge the gap. Wheelbarrows were used to haul coal to the skidder.[78] One "lowside" held several tons of coal and would last a skidder two to three weeks.[79]

Wooden water boxes were built at the Cass shop, hauled to the skidder and supplied by whatever natural water supply was available. In later years, after some locomotives were scrapped, their water tenders were used instead of the wooden boxes.[80]

Occasionally on Elk, skid roads crossed over the highway. In these cases, permission to cross the highway had to be obtained from the County Court.[81]

A skidding crew was made up of fourteen men: a foreman; two road cutters who cleared skid roads; a 4-man rigging crew, who took care of moving the rigging to new skid roads; a leverman, who ran the skidder; a fireman, a 4-man choker crew (one bull hooker and three bull chokers), and one bellboy or whistle punk.[82]

The choker crew was often one-half to three-fourths of a mile away from the skidder and out of sight of the leverman. Signals were sent to the leverman by the bellboy, who operated a battery-powered bell. The leverman responded with the proper number of toots on the skidder whistle.[83] In this manner, he knew when to lower cables, when to tighten them, when to bring in the buggy, etc. The following set of 32 signals were used:[84]

    o = short ring or toot
    – = long ring or toot

Clear track or road	o o – –
Fire	– – – – – (or
	o o o o)
Easy in	– o
Stop	o
Pickup	o o
Pickup easy	– o o
Go ahead	o –
Slack off	– o –
Knock out on slack line	o – o
Knock out on rehaul	o o o o o o
Knock out on skidder line	o – o –
Straighten out lines	o o o o
Raise cable	– –
Drop cable	– – o
Knockout on winch line	– o – o
Go ahead on winch line	o o o o o
Go ahead on winch line easy	– o o o o o
Line over cable	– o o o o
Go ahead let skidding line lay	– o o –
Go ahead let slack line lay	– o – o o
Tie bull hooks on landing	– o o
Winch line – one short for each	– o
Back up	o o o
Back up easy	– o o o
Put up chockers	o –
Take off chockers	– – o o
Pick up on slack line	o – – –
Pull on slack on landing – one o for each 10′	– o –
Crew (Come in)	– – – –
Riggers (Come in)	– – – o
Foreman	– – –
Finish	o o o –

The most dangerous occurrance on steam skidders was the breaking of one of the various cables. For example, on one occasion, at Cheat Falls, the big cable broke about one-half mile from the skidder and rolled back along the skid road, killing Stuart McKneeley on the landing.[85] In another accident on April 28, 1941, Earl Barlow, aged twenty-eight years, died from head, chest, and other injuries in an accident on a steam skidder on Cheat Mountain.[86] On another occasion on Big Run, Craig Peterson had a hand cut off when the ½-inch line broke while being spooled in during a skid road changing operation.[87]

The company was very careful to prevent fire in their holdings.

However, in 1934, fire got out of control on Fishinghawk and burned Skidder No. 4. It was completely rebuilt in the Cass shop.[88]

During the first few years the skidders were in use, the choker men would occasionally ride in on the logs at the end of the day saving themselves a mile or more walk over the rough terrain. The ride was dangerous and not often done. On one occasion a man, riding logs in, was stranded high in the air during a breakdown and almost froze to death. E. P. Shaffer heard of this incident and gave orders to fire the next man caught riding the lines.[89]

The use of steam skidders was a very destructive practice. The logs being hauled in knocked over and uprooted many of the small trees not suitable for cutting. The wheel-like patterns of skid roads radiating from a skidder set were clearly visible from the air many years after the skidding was done.[90]

The use of steam skidders evidently reflected a fundamental decision on the part of the company to opt for a short-term, large-scale removal of timber instead of a sustained yield effort that would greatly cut back on lumber and pulp production but give a better chance for long-term operation.

In 1920, James D. Lacey and Company of New York was hired to study the Cheat and Elk River holdings, estimate the amount and kinds of timber remaining, and make recommendations for operation of the properties. Their report stressed the advantages of skidding with horses instead of steam skidders with respect to far less damage being done to the land and to young trees by horses. The report strongly recommended that horse skidding be used whenever possible on these lands. As we have seen, this recommendation was not followed, and preparations for extensive skidding by steam skidders was initiated in 1922 just after the report was made.[91]

The steam skidders were set up and taken down time after time until the last set was made on Bald Knob in 1959. By late spring of 1960, the Bald Knob area was cut, and the skidder was moved to Old Spruce where a spur was built to log the excellent second growth spruce in that area. However, the closing of the mill on June 30 ended those plans, and the skidders, loaders, and many of the flatcars were taken to Cass and junked.

Winding Down

One of the innovations introduced by the Mower Lumber Company was the replacement of "permanent" camps by camp trains. This allowed for much more flexibility in moving camps and, in the long run, was more economical.

At least one of Mower's camps, in 1952, was made up of blacks. The *Pocahontas Times* reported that this camp was one hundred percent on the Cancer Drive.[92]

Mower had two camp trains with a total of seventeen camp cars. Bunk cars each held twenty men. They had double bunk beds. Two men slept on the bottom of each bed and two on top. A typical train had a supply car, a kitchen car, a dining car with room to serve forty-two men at one time, a lobby car, and four to five bunk cars. There were also several shanties for coal and supplies, and a pit toilet. The foreman, leverman, filer, and one or two others slept in one end of the supply car. The cook and cookee slept in the kitchen car. The remainder of the camp slept in the bunk cars.[93]

Camp cars were built by Guy Tallman, Roger Dickenson, and Russell Clarkson beginning on November 15, 1944, with assistance of a crew of workers including Harry Gum and Johnny Varner.[94] They were "built by eye" without detailed plans.[95]

Snow was often a factor in the logging efforts. On December 7, 1944, it started snowing at 6:00 a.m. and by 11:30 a.m. it had snowed thirty-six inches. It kept snowing and blowing for several days until drifts reached the second-floor windows on the boardinghouse at Spruce. Mrs. Walter Good ran the boardinghouse at the time. They had bedrooms for fourteen people and were stuck with twenty men and two women. They ran out of several items of food and had to "scratch the bottom of the barrel" to survive. The company put two engines together to plow the snow off the tracks.[96]

During the storm, the skidding efforts were moved to Rock Run. The only way they could find the logs was to find the stump, by the hump in the snow, then dig down and see which way the tree was felled and hunt the log out. There were more logs left than were skidded in. The bellboy built a fire which melted its way down into a hole so that he was standing four to five feet above it.[97]

One big snow was on the headwaters of Cheat in 1947. There were four or five teams of horses there, and they ran out of hay. The horses ate the ropes they were tied with. Finally, when the snow stopped, about eighty men shovelled the tracks out to get the train there with feed for the horses. The first day they didn't get the hay in, and the horses were tied with chains from the log cars.[98]

On one occasion, the snow was so deep on Fool's Knob that skidding was stopped, and the men came out eight to twelve together, taking turns breaking the path through the snow. It was drifted about shoulder deep.

One of the last woods foremen under the West Virginia Pulp and Paper Company was Saul McNeely. He was followed by Jimmy Carson for a short time. Okey Kale from Rainelle was woods foreman when Mower first took over. He was replaced by Clark Phillips who ran the woods operation until April, 1957,[99] when Rocky Fisher took the position.[100]

IX
THE TOWN OF SPRUCE

After the railroad was completed to the top of the mountain in 1901, the cutting and shipping of pulpwood from Cheat increased and the number of men working multiplied. Camp 2 was built on Cheat River near where the train reached the top of the mountain. Camp 3 was built about one mile up Cheat River from Camp 2 and Camp 4 was built further upstream. The men working on the mountain were obliged to stay in camp all week and could ride the log train to Cass Saturday night. They returned Sunday afternoon on another train. For men with families, this arrangement proved unsatisfactory, and the idea of building a town on top of the mountain was conceived. We read that as early as April 24, 1902, "Messrs. Hunter, Taber, Gerow, Williams have said they will remove their families to Cheat Mtn., if the Company builds houses. Mr. Shaffer thinks this would be a good move, as it would do away with running the engine down here on Saturday evenings and returning on Sunday evening. There are a number of men in the habit of coming along down on these trips and loading up with liquor, which would be done away with if the men who have families living here remove to the mountain."[1] In response to this on April 29, 1902, Shaffer wrote, "will commence building houses on the mountain as soon as we get the lumber."[2]

The location chosen for these houses was near the "low place" where the railroad crossed over the mountain. It was named Spruce.[3] Before the logging operations, a single cabin was in the vicinity. Reputedly, this was inhabited by a Civil War soldier who left the fighting for the solitude of Cheat Mountain.[4]

A post office was established at Spruce (Old Spruce) on August 25, 1902, with E. P. Shaffer listed as postmaster.[5]

As the amount of pulpwood shipped from the top of Cheat increased, much of it was shipped unpeeled. They soon learned, however, that when these logs were peeled at Covington and the bark burned, a feathery ash came in the windows and contaminated the pulp, sometimes ruining rolls of paper.[6] Also, considerable space was required for the peeling operations at Covington, which cut down on the amount of peeled wood that could be stockpiled.[7] Peeling all of the pulpwood on Cheat Mountain before shipping was then resorted to, and hundreds of men were employed peeling the logs with axes and spuds, a very expensive and inefficient operation because of the weather and the necessity of housing the men.

These reasons induced the company to build a rossing (peeling) plant on Cheat close to the supply of pulpwood.[8] In 1904, a new town, also called Spruce, was begun about one and three-tenths miles from the original town of Spruce, henceforth called Old Spruce.

In addition to the rossing mill, the new town had a hotel of forty rooms, a branch of the Pocahontas Supply Company Store, a school and thirty-five dwelling houses.[9] The post office was moved from the original location at Old Spruce to the new town. The town's location, at 3,853 feet above sea level, made it one of the highest towns in the eastern United States. At this elevation, frost sometimes occurred during the summer months, but many residents of Spruce supplemented their budgets with gardens.[10]

Spruce was unusual in having no highway access. All materials for the community were brought in by rail, and visitors and townsfolk alike rode the log train to and from Cass, a distance of eight and one-tenth miles, or, in later years, to Mace on Elk River. Some persons owned motorcars, adapted to ride on the railroad. These were used for transportation to and from the mountain.[11] Spruce has no cemetery; bodies of deceased persons were brought out by train. The company controlled what materials entered Spruce. Consequently, there were no saloons there.

The rossing mill at Spruce initially cost about fifty thousand dollars. It started operation about the middle of February, 1905, and operated almost continuously until 1925.[12] It was designed to handle spruce logs fifteen inches or less in diameter. These were dumped into a "hot" pond heated with steam to prevent freezing in the winter months. They were then floated to a "jack slip," which consisted of an inclined plane up which the logs were pulled by means of cleats on a heavy "bull chain." On the main floor of the rossing mill, the logs were cut into 24-inch blocks by a swing cutoff saw. The blocks were then conveyed to the rossing machines.[13]

There were eighteen rossing machines in the plant each requiring seven men to operate. These machines consisted of heavy metal wheels with radial knives. The blocks were held against the rossing head and knives removed the bark in a few seconds. The bark fueled the steam boiler, which supplied power to run a 400-horsepower steam generator.[14] Larger blocks were split to accommodate handling. The barkers or peelers were made by the Holyoke Machine Company of Holyoke, Massachusetts, and by the Waterville Iron Works of Waterville, Maine. The splitters were made by the Carthage Machine Company of Carthage, New York, and by the Waterville people.

After rossing, the blocks were conveyed to the loading dock and loaded into railcars. Open cars were used at first but cinders from the locomotives fell on the peeled logs and spoiled the paper.[15] This induced the use of boxcars. Six cars could be loaded from the mill at one time.[16] Laborers for the pulpwood operation were mostly Austrians, who were preferred for their hearty, cheerful, and contented nature. In the winter of 1905, there were about 480 men employed in the pulpwood operations and an additional force was expected in the spring. They were mostly engaged in cutting the smaller timber from the area cut over by the timber crews. All trees down to 4-inch diameter were felled and processed in the peeling mill.[17] During the period of 1905 to 1925, from twelve to sixteen carloads of pulpwood, each car holding ten to fifteen cords of wood, were shipped daily from Spruce six days a week. These loads were augmented by edgings and other scrap from the sawmill at Cass to make an average of twenty-two cars of pulpwood each day for the grinders and digesters of the mill at Covington. This production continued from 1909 to 1925.[18]

Polk's Directory for 1904-05 lists business personnel in Spruce as follows:

Population 50
E.P. Shaffer, postmaster
E. Cruikshank, train dispatcher
O.G. English, express and tel. agent
J.L. Ervin, shoemaker
Amos Lyons, blacksmith
Robert Newcomer, proprietor Hotel Spruce
B.W. Watson, clerk, Pocahontas Supply Company
L.B. Smith, blacksmith
O.B. Sprague, blacksmith
D.J. Taber, lumber superintendent[19]

After the mill opened, the population of Spruce in 1906 was listed as 300.[20] Changes in personnel in 1906-07 included the addition of W. F. Anderson, mill superintendent, Lanabelle Gillespie, schoolteacher; R. S. Fitzgerald, physician, and C. Z. Sellers as hotel proprietor.

Spruce was not long spared the violence common to lumber towns of the day. Sunday, August 26, 1906, was marred by tragedy when L. H. Cash, mill foreman of the pulpwood peeling mill at Spruce, shot and fatally wounded William Davison.

Earlier in the day, Davison slapped over a younger brother of Cash and beat him up some. He later picked a quarrel with Cash, which ended in a fight during which Cash whipped Davison. Davison then went to the hotel.

An Italian gave Cash a pistol, which he carried with him when he later also went to the hotel. There he was accosted by Davison who invited Cash to come up the steps and be killed. Cash tried to ignore him and went to the office, where he was followed by Davison. Cash fired three warning shots near Davison and, when the latter continued advancing, Cash shot him.[21]

The year 1906 was an eventful one for the town of Spruce. The large number of men working in the peeling mill and in the surrounding pulp and lumber operations, as well as the families of many of these men living in Spruce, made the hiring of a doctor there imperative. A young man, born in 1881 at Arbovale in Pocahontas County, graduated from the Medical College of Virginia at Richmond in 1906, returned to Pocahontas County, and was hired as company doctor at Spruce. Thus began a long career of service for Dr. Uriah Hevener Hannah, who stayed at Spruce until 1914 when he moved to Cass and practiced there until his death in 1943.[22]

Tragedy struck at Spruce again on Sunday, May 31, 1908, when a band of nine Italians attacked the office of the West Virginia Pulp and Paper Company. In the ensuing fight, Walter Alvis, aged about twenty-four, was killed and Joe Hannah, superintendent of the peeling mill, was badly hurt. The trouble arose when a number of Italians, who had been discharged, stormed the office thinking they had not drawn as much money as they deserved.[23]

Justice was swift in those days and one week later the *Pocahontas Times* reported that four of the culprits had been sentenced to eighteen years each at Moundsville State Prison.[24]

The next few years brought about several changes. Spruce was incorporated in 1909. In 1912, Lanabelle Gillespie was replaced by Anna Ervin as teacher. Samuel L. Clark assumed the duties of postmaster on January 24, 1912. In 1914, Dr. U. H. Hannah moved to Cass and was replaced at Spruce by Dr. H. W. Neal. G. M. Brice was hired as railroad express and telegraph agent, and S. B. Nethken and Company at Cass supplied meats.

It was the practice for the company to keep a certain amount of cash on hand at Spruce to pay workers who quit and wanted their money. They also served as a bank and kept money for workers. The company owned a safe, shared by the post office, in which the money was kept. On September 16, 1915, the safe was pried open by means of two brake shoe keys and $1,000 in stamps and money was stolen. Five hundred dollars of this was in stamps, $250 cash was owned by the Pocahontas Supply Company, and $250 was owned by laborers who had asked the company to keep the money for them.[25] I have found no record that the robbery was ever solved.

After 1913, Spruce was the junction point for the Greenbrier, Cheat and Elk Railroad where logging trains were dispatched along Elk River and along Cheat River to Bemis. Log trains from these points were made into smaller units at Spruce and dispatched to Cass. Coal trains from the Elk River mines were dispatched to Bemis with occasional cars to Cass as needed.[26]

Elmer Duncan moved to Spruce in 1916 and was employed as a store clerk. On October 31, 1919, Clark was replaced as postmaster by Ellet C. Smith. Clark was made manager of the Spruce store of the Pocahontas Supply Company. Clinebell was superintendent of the pulp mill.[27] J. M. Cope (or Cofer) was physician and Frank Francilli was harness maker. The population was listed as 350.[28]

By 1920, Spruce had a two-room school. One room held grades one through three and the other room grades four through eight.

No permanent minister was stationed in Spruce. However, the Presbyterian minister at Cass visited periodically to encourage the flock.[29]

In 1925, the pulp peeling mill at Spruce closed and the town rapidly declined. Many of the workers and their families moved to Cass or Slatyfork and continued employment with the company. On August 31, 1925, the post office closed and Spruce was officially dead, although several families continued to live there.

On March 3, 1927, the Cheat and Elk branches of the Greenbrier, Cheat and Elk Railroad were sold to the Western Maryland Railroad Company. The West Virginia Pulp and Paper Company retained the right to use the tracks, at a set rate, for hauling lumber and coal and made some use of Spruce for assembling trains to Cass.[30]

By 1939 the town of Spruce consisted of nineteen houses, an engine house, and a boardinghouse, all operated by the Western Maryland Railroad. Eight Western Maryland locomotives were kept at Spruce. Two engines left Spruce in the morning with empties for Mine No. 4 and Hickory Lick. Two helpers ran light to Bergoo to pick up the loaded train. One engine could pull twenty-five cars from Bergoo to Laurel Bank but at Laurel Bank three or four additional engines were picked up making six to eight engines over the hill to Spruce from Laurel Bank. There were usually ten loaded cars per engine or eleven under favorable conditions. There were two trips daily or about 150 cars out during a 24-hour period.[31]

A school was maintained at Spruce until 1950.[32] Louise Brown and Ruth Blackhurst of Cass were two of the last teachers. They rode to Spruce from Cass on Monday morning in a motorcar and returned on Friday afternoon.

The vicissitudes of time have all but obliterated signs of habitation at Spruce. No houses are standing and, in the future, all traces of man will be gone except the Western Maryland Railroad which forms a large loop at the townsite.

New interest in the Spruce area arose when the Western Maryland line from Elkins to Durbin was abandoned in 1984, leaving Cass without a rail connection to the outside world. Plans were made to connect the Cass Scenic Railroad to the CSX (formerly Western Maryland) line running between Elkins and Webster Springs. The most logical location for such a connection was between the Cass Railroad near Old Spruce and the CSX line at Spruce. Federal funds were obtained to assist in the construction. An environmental impact study was required which included an archeological study of the site of three homes that were in the path of one of the proposed routes for the connection. The archeological study was done in the summer of 1988 by Dr. Charles Hulse, Dr. Phillip Simpson, and fifteen students from Shepherd College.[33] Construction on the connecting line was begun in the spring of 1990.

X
THE LUMBER OPERATIONS

Building and Operating the Original Mill

Building the lumber railroad to the top of Cheat Mountain, in order to reach the vast spruce stands there, was top priority during the summer of 1900. It was imperative that pulpwood shipments to Covington begin as soon as possible. However, sight was not lost of the second reason for the railroad, that is, a large sawmill to be located at the mouth of Leatherbark Run. Early in 1900, Slaymaker and Shaffer were busy planning the new mill and in May, Slaymaker sent a sketch of the layout of the mill and yard to David L. Luke. The preliminary sketch was approved and a search for the best deal on the purchase of a mill was made.[1]

Preparations for building a dam and pond began immediately. On July 6, 1900, J. G. Luke wrote that "O'Connell has made arrangements with the St. Lawrence people with reference to timber for the dam."[2] This refers to the dam to be built across the Greenbrier River. On July 20, 1900, he mentioned that work on the mill was getting underway.[3] (This referred to site preparation only.) Shaffer mentioned on August 2 that two teams had been bought and were put to work hauling timber for the dam.[4] Again, on August 5 he wrote, "We commenced to clear away for the dam and pond."[5]

A man named Noon was placed in charge of building the dam. He advised that a dam ten feet high would be perfectly safe.[6] The spikes for the dam arrived on August 23, and by September 4, there were eighteen men working on it, with three teams hauling stone and timber.[7] By September 20, the crew was cut down to ten men who were putting on "sheating" (sheathing) and cleaning out the pond above the dam.[8] Despite the good beginning, on November 14 the dam was still not finished, and Shaffer complained the "Work on the dam seems to be dragging some. Mr. Noon is getting too old for this kind of business."[9] Not long afterward, the dam was completed at a total cost of $561.88 of which $108.08 was listed as merchandise.[10]

Numerous investigations concerning used saw mills were made by Slaymaker. One offer from W. H. H. Smith Company of Toledo, Ohio, was to sell the complete mill inventory including sawdust burner, smokestack, wire, rope, guys, sprinkler apparatus, and unspecified machinery for nine thousand dollars.[11] Another was with L. F. Seyfert's Sons who, on November 21, 1900, described a mill that was in first class shape having been used for only about thirty-six days. It was a Sterns 8-foot band mill with twenty feet of carriage, three 40-inch self-receding headblocks, 30-foot "Prescotts" steam feed, haul-up rig and three 11-inch saws. A filing room outfit consisting of two anvils, automatic filing machine, energy stand and brazer was also included. The price was fifteen hundred dollars including one hundred dollars commission for Slaymaker if he sold it.[12] This is evidently the sawmill at Camden, West Virginia, as this is referred to in a later letter.[13]

During the spring of 1901, work began on the mill buildings. The Edwin P. Allis Company of Milwaukee, Wisconsin, secured the contract to construct the buildings and H. S. Mitchell, architect for this company, personally brought the plans to Cass. The main building was 76 feet by 192 feet.[14] Work on the mill buildings was pushed and on June 20, 1901, the *Pocahontas Times* reported that the frame of the big mill was to be raised that week.[15]

By December 1, 1901, the mill buildings were completed and Shaffer reported that, "We have left all the mill carpenters go."[16]

The engine room was built of brick. Four masons arrived on the night of October 17, 1901, and were getting along nicely with the foundation.[17] A car of brick for the ovens arrived October 21.[18]

Red brick was obtained from Charles Muffett at Covington; fire brick from the Union Mining Company (locality not given). Bad weather held up the brick work several days in late November but by December 7, there were six bricklayers at work.[19] By Christmas there were only three masons remaining on the job and they were laying brick for the walls of the powerhouse.

Machinery and other equipment arrived during late 1901. William Collum was in charge of installing the stacks, boilers, engine and other equipment. By November 8, the engine bed was finished and work was going well with the ovens.[20] The boilers were obtained from the company's Piedmout paper mill. They had been in use there for several years and were being replaced because of a change in processing. The boilers were sixteen feet long, sixty inches in diameter, with 4-inch tubes. They were rated at eighty horsepower each and were capable of carrying 125 pounds of steam.[21] The crews commenced to install the boilers on November 15.

By December 8, two stacks had been completed, and a third was well on the way.[22] Stacks were three feet in diameter and fifty feet tall.

The Luke's policy was to use new equipment whenever possible and a new Allis Telescopic Mill was purchased in September, 1901, from the Allis-Chalmers Company of Erie, Pennsylvania. This was an 8-foot band saw with a 12-inch wide saw. The freight bill for this shipment was $7.73.[23] The cost of the mill could not be determined.

The mill machinery was pretty well in place before Christmas, and on Christmas Day, Shaffer wrote that Collum was putting the pipe together that connects the boilers and was ready for the men to put the belts on.[24] On January 8, 1902, steam was put in one of the boilers, and a man arrived to put the engine together.[25] Two days later, they had enough steam to blow out the engine "and Mr. Collum and the engineers say that will start the machinery in the mill on Monday."[26] By January 14, all of the machinery, except the band saw, was running.[27]

Much of the machinery of the Dewing Mill at Point Marion, Pennsylvania, was moved to Cass. On October 25, reference was made to the planer from Point Marion "along with the other machines that you intend bringing from there."[28] Other equipment came from the J. L. Rumbarger Lumber Company at Dobbin;

one example was the dust collector, which was shipped on September 26.[29]

Experienced men were brought in to fill key positions in the mill. William F. Anderson was brought from Horton (Parsons Pulp and Lumber Company) to be mill superintendent. A man named Frazer was hired as saw filer, a key position.[30] and Beebe was hired as setter.[31]

On January 24, 1902, Shaffer informed Slaymaker that the sawyer arrived on January 23, and that they were going to try the mill that afternoon.[32] However, a letter dated January 25, 1902, said that due to the breaking of the ratchet that tightens the saw on the band mill, no lumber was cut the previous day.[33] A telegram of the same day[34] informed Slaymaker that "Mill men have arrived. Mill is running all right this afternoon"[35] and so the first run was made. On January 28, Shaffer wired Slaymaker, "Would like to have orders for lumber. Mill is running."[36] In a letter of the same date, he said one planing mill was ready to run and on January 30, he reported, "the planing mill is running and we are in shape to get our tongue and groove or slip-tongue orders." The first orders were received from a Mr. Lippencott, but they were for "such small stuff" that Shaffer didn't think much of them.[37]

The first orders from the New York office (orders No. 1 and No. 2) were received on January 30, and the new mill was in business.[38]

Things did not go well, however. The first inkling of problems was in a letter to Slaymaker in which Shaffer complained that they were only able to cut from fifteen to twenty thousand board feet per day, which he thought very good to start with but he had expected to be cutting at least forty thousand per day by the date of the letter (February 1, 1902).[39]

One problem was that the weather was very cold and ice on the logs hampered the sawing a good deal as the dogs would not hold the logs firmly on the carriage.[40]

Lumber cut over the next few days was meager in amount: 16,946 feet on February 7; 12,356 feet on February 8; 22,217 feet on February 10; and 17,542 feet on February 11, and poor in quality being "nearly all thicker at the one end than the other."[41]

Finally, on February 12, Shaffer decided that before they would be able to get lumber that was marketable, they would have to get a new sawyer and filer. Mr. Ellis was hired to replace Frazer as filer, and things improved somewhat. In the next letters Shaffer reported 27,589 feet cut on February 12; 23,102 feet on February 13; and 25,284 feet on February 14; and the quality was pretty fair.[42]

The first four railroad cars were loaded on February 14. Shaffer sent a wire to Slaymaker on February 15, "Mill is working better send us more orders."[43]

Poor quality continued to plague the new mill, although the cut increased to 34,108 feet on February 20, and 32,863 feet on March 3. Shaffer was filling some orders, but he experienced difficulty in getting enough good quality lumber. On March 4, he wrote, "You will notice from our letters that we are running the mill nearly every day, but owing to the bad condition of the lumber turned out, we are unable to ship as soon as we should. We have on our books the following unfilled orders: RCL order No. 3537; orders No. 6, 7, 10, 11, 8, 14, 15, RCL 3548 and 16 and 17."[44] Lumber that was too poor in quality to ship was used for building the lumber docks and for other uses around the mill and town. The new camp on Cheat, Camp 3, was also built with lumber from the new mill.[45]

Clearly another change in sawyer and a new filer was necessary. On March 6, Mr. Ellis (the filer who had taken Frazer's place) and the sawyer were let go, and the mill shut down because of snow in the pond and to await a new mill crew.[46]

The new filer and sawyer arrived on March 9, and on March 10, the cut was 24,882 with a "decided improvement in the condition of the lumber sawed. The new filer reports the saws as being in very bad shape."[47] The next day's cut was 37,303 feet in ten hours, and the quality was much better.[48]

The cut continued to improve and, on March 25, amounted to 48,938 feet. In addition, 12,500 lath were cut that day.[49] Shaffer advised that another band saw be ordered that was ten inches wide instead of twelve inches.[50]

The next problem appeared to be a shortage of railroad cars to ship lumber in. During the latter part of March and early April, Shaffer wrote numerous letters complaining about this and, on April 28, he said the dock was pretty well filled up with orders ready for shipment, awaiting cars.[51]

Excess bark and slabs were carried by conveyor to an area

near the dam and burned, setting the dam on fire twice.[52] Shaffer decided to haul the slabs by wagon and use them to fill up the low places between the stable and mill.[53] A "consumer" (burner) for excess sawdust and slabs was planned next to the river but it was feared it would get washed away during floods.[54]

Key persons were being placed in various parts of the operation during the early part of 1902. William T. Anderson was working well as mill foreman.[55] For fifty dollars a month, R. L. Rose was placed in charge of the lumberyard and Shaffer said he was "away head of the last man in efficiency."[56] Stuart B. Nethken was sent to various other lumber jobs to recruit capable and skilled workers. One of these men, Joe Graves, was recruited by Mr. Nethken from the Horton job. Graves later became foreman of the lumberyard. J. Hobbs Rose was also foreman of the lumberyard for a time. Nethken was also in charge of securing horses for skidding on the mountain and was given responsibility for supplying meat to the company camps.[57] In 1902, he organized S. B. Nethken and Company which supplied meat to the town as well as to the woods crews.

By the end of April, 1902, most of the problems concerned with the new mill were being worked out, and the operation became one of improvement, expansion, and development. The docks were extended further south, and an order for sufficient 25-pound rail to lay four hundred feet of track on the docks was placed.[58] In June, 1902, Shaffer decided to close the mill for a few days until some repair work could be done. Braces were put in the slasher and, since the timbers had dried out throughout the mill, the crews were set to tighten all bolts.

On January 29, 1903, the *Pocahontas Times* reported that the West Virginia Spruce Lumber Company expected to add another mill to the works at Cass.[59] The expansion would increase their capacity from eighty thousand feet daily to one hundred fifty thousand feet and would require three additional camps in the woods, giving employment to seven hundred men. At that time, the mill had run steadily all winter, running eleven to sixteen hours every twenty-four hours.[60]

The mill, with its many saws and other moving machinery, was a dangerous place to work. Safety measures were taken but occasional accidents were bound to happen. The first fatal accident on the new mill took the life of Elliott Hiner. On August 18, 1903, a board became caught in a saw and flew out, striking him on the head and crushing his skull.[61]

Production continued to improve and by September 8, 1904, the mill broke all previous records by cutting, with one Allis Telescopic Mill, 95,438 feet of spruce lumber in ten hours twenty-three minutes. J. B. Hannah was sawyer; Oscar Sarson operated steam set; U. L. Nichols was edgerman; and J. H. Lantz was trimmer man.[62]

The Cass mill ran almost continuously until a temporary business slump occurred in December, 1907, when four hundred men were laid off because of a tightness of money and a shortage of railroad cars.[63]

E. P. Shaffer was a keen observer of the entire operation. When constructed, the mill had an ordinary burner for disposal of excess waste wood. The setup was such that slabs, edgings and trimmings from the sawmill were carried into a peeling shed by a conveyor belt where stock suitable for pulpwood was picked off and the remainder went to the burner. This required extra handling of the pulpwood. An inspection of the slabs left to go to the burner revealed that much good pulpwood was left on the conveyor thus reducing the work of the "pulp pickers."

Shaffer had the setup rebuilt so that all refuse passed through the peeling shed and had to be handled whether good for pulp or not. The change greatly increased the pulpwood production, with only the bark and unsound wood sent to the hog for grinding and feeding to the furnaces.[64]

Two practices insured that only the highest possible grade of lumber was produced: (1) the smaller timber, under fifteen inches in diameter, was utilized as pulpwood, thereby giving the sawyers large, high quality logs with which to work, and (2) the logs were heavily slabbed because the slabs were worth as much as pulpwood as they would be if manufactured into lumber.

Cheat Mountain spruce became the standard in the industry for high quality. This reputation, combined with Slaymaker's efficient sales organization, insured that West Virginia spruce was used throughout the world. For example, a request was received from the Wright Cycle Company, 1127 West Third Street, Dayton, Ohio, dated March 5, 1904, for about 500 feet of the finest possible spruce for use in constructing flying machines. This order was filled, and on November 29, 1905, a check for fifty dollars was written by the Wright Cycle Co. to S. E. Slaymaker and Company for "Spruce." Apparently this spruce was used by the Wright brothers to construct the "Wright Flyer No. 3," which logged the most number of flight hours of the Wright aircraft.[65] Cheat Mountain spruce became the mainstay of the builders of flying machines. It was used almost exclusively by the French government in the years before World War I.[66] Other foreign markets developed: for example, in 1908, seventy-five carloads of lumber were shipped from Cass to South America.[67]

By 1910, the mill, now consisting of two band mills, was averaging about one hundred twenty-five thousand board feet of lumber a day. This amounted to about three million feet per month and an annual production of about thirty-five million feet. Approximately the same amount of pulpwood was also produced.[68]

During May, 1910, the company shipped 1,149 cars or an average of a little over forty-four cars for each of the twenty-six days of the month. Shipments were frequently in excess of one thousand cars per month. These figures included pulpwood, lumber and laths.[69]

This level of activity was maintained during the years leading up to World War I except for a business slump in March, 1915, when five hundred men were temporarily laid off in the woods and mill.[70] The timber supply was plentiful, and new areas were opened up on Elk and Cheat Rivers when needed.

Wages for laborers around 1910 were $1.85 a day but increased business after World War I began, allowed an increase to $1.95 per day.[71]

In 1914, Charles W. Luke moved to Cass and was placed in charge of all wood procurement and timbering operations. He worked directly with E. P. Shaffer and learned the logging and wood procurement profession.[72] Recognizing that an adequate local wood supply was the secret to continued successful operations, Charles W. Luke transferred from Cass to the New York office in 1921, to develop a vigorous, new woodlands and procurement organization for all the company mills. He had received an excellent education in the economics of logging and the value of good men and timber while working with Shaffer. He soon developed one of the outstanding timber resource departments in the paper industry.

One of the far reaching decisions by Charles W. Luke was the hiring of a professional forester. On September 29, 1919, Herman Work, a graduate of Penn State University with a Bachelor of Science degree in Forestry in 1910, and a Master of Science degree in 1914, was hired.[73] The forestry profession was new in America and reforestation was almost unheard of. The West Virginia Pulp and Paper Company had experimented with replanting cottonwood trees near its Tyrone, Pennsylvania, mills as early as 1898, but no extensive, consistent reforestation had been done.

In the summer of 1920, the James D. Lacey Company of New York was engaged by the WVP&P to complete a timber survey of the remaining virgin timber stands on the company lands on Cheat and Elk watersheds supplying the sawmill at Cass and the Pulp and Paper Mill at Covington. The study included the amounts of standing timber as well as species reproduction. The report contained a description of cover types on both the Cheat and Elk River drainages and the location and extent of each. A map was included that showed uncut, cutover and burned-over lands.[74]

On June 1, 1921, a second professional forester, Sam Sweeney, was hired by the WVP&P. Sweeney was a graduate of Cornell University (B.S., 1918; M.S., 1920), and had worked for the James D. Lacey Company during their study of the WVP&P Company lands in 1920-21. During that time, he often saw Charles W. Luke riding on the GC&E in a motorcar. Sweeney paid Luke a call at the company's New York office and convinced him that an expanded forestry organization within the company would save a great deal of money on cruising and other forestry jobs. Duke Kaynes, another former Lacey employee, was also hired into the WVP&P forestry organization.[75]

After the war, the mill continued at its usual pace until the early morning hours of February 24, 1922, when fire was discovered in the planing mill. When the fire appeared to be out of control, Shaffer called Sam Waugh at Spruce and said, "Sam, this is E.P. Shaffer. The mill is on fire in Cass and I want you to run down the mountain as fast as you can so we can pull cars in the millyard clear of the fire. I don't want you to run so fast as it is dangerous though."[76] Waugh started immediately on Shay No. 8 and reached Cass twenty-seven minutes later—the fastest run ever for the eight and one-tenth miles[77] from Spruce to Cass.[78] Sam Waugh with Shay No. 8 saved much of the lumber in the yard by moving loaded railroad cars and by pulling over lumber piles in front of the fire creating a firebreak of sorts.

"Million Dollar Fire" ran the headlines in the *Pocahontas Times* the next week, and the following account of the fire was given:

> The big mill, storage house, planing mill, and dry kiln of the West Virginia Pulp and Paper Company, at Cass, was burned last Friday morning, February 24. The loss entailed perhaps a million dollars. There is some insurance.
>
> The fire originated in the planing mill, spreading to the big band saw mill, to the big storage house and then to the drying plant. After a time the pumps were put out of commission by the fire, and the lumber in the immense yard was saved by hard and effective fighting. The cause of the fire is not known.
>
> The mill had not been running at the time of the fire on account of a temporary shortage of logs.
>
> In the storage house was about a hundred carloads of the finest kind of finished hardwood lumber, mostly flooring. This was one of the largest items of the loss.
>
> The planing mill was equipped with modern woodworking machinery, all new, and a great deal of it only installed in the past few months. Some of it was put in just the day before the fire.
>
> The dry kiln was a new building of steel and concrete construction and filled with the best of hardwood lumber. It was an immense structure, and had been but recently completed.
>
> A more disasterous fire to Greenbrier Valley could not well be imagined. It was the biggest of our industrial plants and running full and extra time. It was the permanent lumber operation of the valley and in the past year or two had been equipped throughout with up-to-date machinery. For over 20 years the mill has run steadily.
>
> The company has not made public its plans for future as regarding the rebuilding.[79]

There was much speculation concerning the cause of the fire, but nothing definite was determined.

BUILDING THE NEW MILL

No time was lost in clearing up the burned mill. A Marion steam shovel, owned by the company, was brought in to help clean up the area. Most of the machinery was junked although any useful parts were salvaged; for example, 6- and 8-inch gate valves were sold to the Forest Service for use in fish hatcheries at Berkeley Springs, Petersburg and Edray, West Virginia.[80]

Rebuilding a new mill began immediately. Lumber was cut by the Warn Lumber Company at Raywood from logs that were brought off Cheat Mountain by the GC&E, and the new buildings began to take shape.[81] The main mill building was 188 feet long and 56 feet wide. It was 30 feet high on the side and 42 feet high at the ridge. It consisted of two floors, the ground floor was 16 feet high, and the mill room on the second floor was 14 feet high. The saw filing room was 23 feet above the sides, making that part of the building 53 feet high at the ridge. A walkway 88 feet long and 4 feet wide extended from the saw filing room to the rear of the mill 14 feet above the mill room floor. The mill was equipped with two 8-foot Allis-Chalmers band sawmills. It had a resaw, edger, trimmer and slasher. A hog was installed to chip the edgings, slabs and scraps which were then carried by a conveyor to the top of the boiler room where they were stored until fed to the furnaces by gravity.

The bullpen, where lumber was sorted after leaving the mill, extended seventy-five feet from the mill building to the boiler house. It was forty-five feet wide and fourteen feet above ground level. The bullpen had fifteen loading tracks each of 30-inch gauge. The grading deck was eleven feet three inches wide and three feet high. A transfer table, ten feet wide, ran the length of the bullpen on 6-foot gauge tracks.

Adjoining the bullpen was the boiler house which was fifty-six feet long, fifty feet wide, and sixty-four feet high. Four tubeless boilers provided steam for the engine. Fuel was largely sawdust and chips, although some coal was burned when wood was scarce. Two large cyclones (fans) were located on the roof.[82]

The brick enginehouse was fifty-six feet long, fifty feet wide and twenty feet high. It contained a 500-horsepower engine, which ran a flywheel that measured eighteen feet in diameter and was thirty-six inches wide. The flywheel drove a leather belt that was thirty inches wide and over two hundred feet long. The belt, in turn, drove the line shaft located in the basement of the mill one hundred feet from the engine.[83] Machinery in the mill was driven by belts from the line shaft.

Eight feet from the boiler house was one stack base, of concrete, 15 feet square and 35 feet tall. This stack was 6 feet in diameter and 152 feet high or, counting the base, 187 feet tall. The other stack was five feet in diameter, and the same height. Both were made of steel ¼-inch thick. In 1944, the second stack was shortened to 105 feet high. It had gotten too hot and was bulging near the base despite bands that had been placed around it by the shop crew.[84]

A 48-foot space between the boiler house and the dry kiln contained transfer tables for the dry kilns. The dry kiln area was 182 feet long, 68 feet wide, and 14 feet high. The nine kilns were made of brick with a concrete roof. On the front and back of each was a door 18 feet wide and 12 feet high. Two tracks entered each door. The dry kilns were heated by steam and had automatic controls. **Each kiln had a capacity of 36,000 feet, making a total capacity of 324,000 feet per run. The kilns contained eleven miles of steam pipe, nine motors, nine control units, and forty-five 42-inch fans.**[85]

A two-story planing mill, 96 feet by 224 feet, was built. It contained forty-five electric motors that ran the following machinery:

1 Yates A7 Flooring Machine Disc-head
4 End-Matchers
1 Yates 95 Surfacer
1 Molder (American #26-A, 12″ – Cost $2,450.00.)[86]
1 Sander
2 Resaws
1 Double gang rip saw
1 Chain belt feed rip saw
1 Dimension rip saw
6 Cut off saws
1 Square edge flooring unit
2 Large elevators each with a capacity of 5,000 feet
1 Large double fan with a 100 H.P. motor to pick up all shavings and sawdust and blow them to the boiler room 300 feet away through a four-foot pipe

A large, two-story, flooring storage building called the ware room was 50 x 224 feet. The structure and the basement of the planing mill could store 3,000,000 feet of flooring. These buildings were supplied with a sprinkler system. A 16-inch thick brick fire wall separated the planing mill and the ware room.[87]

Since pulpwood was an important concern of the company, a pulp shed twenty-eight feet wide and one hundred feet long was constructed on the west side of the dry kiln along the tracks. Peeling machines were installed. The pulpwood mill at Spruce was closed in 1925, and the entire pulpwood operation was moved to An open pulpwood yard extended southward an additional 126 feet. The pulpwood shed was protected on the dry kiln side by a brick fire wall seventy feet long, thirty-four feet high, and sixteen inches thick.

South of the planing mill and wareroom, three lumber docks were constructed. The dock nearest the railroad was 1,350 feet long and was made of concrete for a distance of 400 feet along the dry kiln and wareroom, where its width was 10 feet; for the remainder of it length it was 16 feet wide and made of wood. It was used for dimension stock at the upper end and for spruce the remainder of its length. The second dock was 1,100 feet long and 12 feet wide and was used primarily for spruce lumber. The third dock was 800 feet long and 12 feet wide and was used for hardwood lumber. Turntables, 6 feet in diameter, were used to take trucks from one dock to another and to enter the wareroom and the planing mill.

MILL OPERATION

Loaded log cars were set in on the track beside the pond by one of the Cass Hill locomotives each morning. Thirteen loads were placed, with the first load beside the unloading ramp. The two unloader men then chopped almost through the stakes holding one tier of logs. The lower chain, which crossed the car about one-half way down the tier of logs, was knocked loose by a long (twelve to fourteen feet) handled hammer. The top cross chains were pulled loose by use of a long chain, and the logs rolled off the car, down the ramp, and into the pond.

On the pond, one or two men, using long pike poles and walking on floating walkways, sorted the logs and brought them to a third man, who fed them to the submerged end of the jack slip. There they were caught by cleats welded on the bull chain and were conveyed to the mill.[88]

At the top of the jack slip, just inside the mill, a scaler measured the board feet in each log using a Doyle log scale. He noted the species and measurement in his records. The scaler controlled the movement of the bull chain.[89]

Logs were "boxed" out of the jack slip by a kicker onto the log deck. This was inclined toward the carriage. Logs could be kicked to either side of the double band sawmill. The scaler controlled the kicker.

The logs were held on the deck by short projections and when ready, the steam "nigger" flipped the log onto the carriage. The "nigger," under control of the sawyer, turned the log on the head-blocks of the carriage until placed to the best advantage against the carriage knees. The dogs, heavy teeth designed to bite into the log and hold it in place, worked in a groove in the knees and securely held the log on the carriage. They were controlled by the dogger, who rode on the carriage. The sawyer, by hand signals, instructed the setter, who also rode on the carriage, how far to set out the log in order to make a cut of the desired thickness.

After the log was dogged and set out, the carriage carried it past the saw where a cut was made. At the end of the feeding trip of the carriage, one slab was cut off. The carriage was automatically offset to prevent the log from striking the saw on the return or gigging trip. All decisions as to thickness of cut, when to turn the log, etc. were made by the sawyer through hand signals to the dogger and setter on the carriage. The skill and experience of the sawyer controlled the quality of lumber that was produced.

Lumber sawn by the headsaws was sent by conveyor chains to the edgers, where the edges were trimmed off. As the log got too thin for sawing on the headsaw, it was sent from the edgers to the resaw for the final cuts.[90]

After passing through the edger and to the resaw, if necessary, the board was conveyed to the trimmer or cutoff. The trimmer consisted of a number of circular saws suspended above the conveyor. They were spaced at the proper distances to allow the cutoff man to saw the boards at standard lengths in order to get the best grade from them. The cutoff saws were counterbalanced and were controlled by ropes pulled by the operator.

A Wicks gang saw with thirty-six straight saws, each thirty-six inches long, was installed in 1927 or 1928. These saws were in a rigid frame and were keyed on top for tightening. The gang saws ran in a reciprocating vertical motion. The idea was to heavily slab the logs with the headsaw and put the squared-off timber through the gang saw for sawing into boards. Although the gang saw was expected to increase production, it did not run satisfactorily, and in 1937, it was replaced by a resaw.[91]

As lumber left the cutoff, it was graded by the lumber grader, who marked the grade on the lumber with chalk. The lumber was also tallied (recorded by board foot, species, and grade) as it entered the "bull pen." It was then sorted by men in the "bull pen." The trucks (pushcarts with flanged wheels) were loaded with the appropriate kind and grade of lumber in such a way that they could be taken down the correct dock, unloaded, and piled in the proper pile. Turntables and cross tracks allowed trucks to be taken to the planing mill or to the various docks. Lumber for the dry kilns was taken directly from the "bull pen" to the pilers for the kilns by means of short tracks and the "cross over."

For air drying, two men set out the loaded trucks to the track leading to the proper dock, where they were picked up by the truckers. The truckers unloaded the lumber at the proper pile, piling it on the dock temporarily or left the truck for the pilers to unload onto a pile. Trucks were stopped at the proper spot by sticking a heavy piece of wood, the "chock," into the spokes of one truck wheel. This jammed against the truck frame and caused the wheel to skid, acting as a brake. The docks were on a slight downhill grade and the "chock" was also used to slowdown a truck if it ran too fast.

Crews, of two lumber pilers each, moved from pile to pile stacking the lumber for drying. The crew member working on the pile wore a heavy, long leather apron, leather gloves and a heavy square piece of leather for each hand, the "hand-leathers." By grasping a board with the slick "hand-leathers" and allowing it to slide between them and the leather apron, heavy lumber could be easily let down from the dock to the pile as much as twenty feet lower. Stacks were sixteen feet long and twelve or sixteen feet wide. Single layers of hardwood lumber were separated by four 1-by-4-inch spruce or hemlock stickers, each twelve feet long. These were placed across the pile at each end and at a distance four feet in from each end. This allowed lumber of any standard length up to sixteen feet to be stacked. Two-inch spruce was piled in double layers and was often "stuck" with the material being piled.

When a stack was completed to a distance of about ten feet

above the dock, a roof of projecting and overlapping boards was put on, the date was marked on the pile, and it was allowed to dry for two months or more or until it was shipped.

After being rebuilt following the fire, the mill continued to run two 11-hour shifts per day and on April 23, 1923, a general raise in wages of ten percent on common labor was announced.[92]

In 1925, a lath mill (U.S. Machinery Company, location not known) was installed at a cost of $546.94 for the mill and $156.05 for the installation.[93] It was located between the pulp shed and the flooring warehouse. Hemlock and low-grade spruce were the main sources of lath.[94]

However, harder times loomed, and the mill was shutdown temporarily in 1925. During the latter part of 1927, the night shift was discontinued never to be reactivated,[95] and the workday was reduced to eight hours.

During these years, accidents in the mill were surprisingly few. On November 7, 1918, the second fatal accident in the long history of the mill occurred when Noah A. Cline, edgerman, was struck by a board and sustained injuries from which he died.[96] In June, 1924, a foreign workman (name unknown) caught his leg in a log chain resulting in a log crushing his leg so badly it had to be amputated.[97] A man named Keyser lost an arm in a pulpwood peeling machine at Cass shortly before Christmas, December, 1924.[98] R. W. McCormick was injured on the Cass Mill early in 1926.[99] In May, 1929, Ashby Smith lost fingers off his left hand in the planing mill. They were caught in a cogwheel.[100] On May 15, 1932, James C. Copen was killed on No. 2 dock in the yard when a slide board broke, threw him off a lumber pile and broke his neck.[101]

A blow to the entire operation occurred when E. P. Shaffer's health began to fail in 1928. In 1933, he was forced to retire and went to his former home in Bryn Mawr, Pennsylvania. The Cass operation was never the same.

Sterrett D. "Steve" Huff took over as superintendent when E. P. Shaffer left. Huff had been head of the office force and assistant superintendent for some time. He was an office-oriented man and knew little about the working end of the logging and lumber operations.

During the early 1930s, hardwood timber became available in areas that could not be reached by the railroad, and contracts were made to bring logs to Cass by truck. To facilitate this, a railroad spur was built north of the shops to the first Leatherbark Bridge.[102] A steam loader was spotted there, and a log dump built on the Back Mountain Road. For several years logs were dumped over the hill from the road and were loaded onto flatcars and taken to the millpond. Later, in the late 1930s, a road was built along the east side of the planing mill to an unloading dock directly on the pond, making the trucking of logs a much more economical venture.

S. F. Slaymaker and Company continued as lumber sales agent for the West Virginia Pulp and Paper Company until December 3, 1936, when the stockholders held a meeting at 230 Park Avenue, New York. The resolutions to discontinue S. F. Slaymaker and Company and surrender the charter to the state were passed. The resolutions were signed by Charles W. Luke, president, WVP&P Company.[103]

Major breakdowns and long shutdowns were rare on the Cass mill, a tribute to the intense efforts of E. P. Shaffer and the entire mill and shop crew. However, one such accident occurred at 1:15 p.m., June 24, 1940, when the 18-foot (diameter) wheel that ran the power belt for the mill flew apart. Pieces knocked a gaping hole in the wall of the engine room and, of course, closed all operations in the mill. The shutdown lasted thirty-nine and one-half days until repairs could be made.[104]

World War II provided a demand for lumber that kept the mill running ten hours a day, six days a week. Many workers volunteered or were drafted into the armed forces and others moved to Baltimore, Maryland, Canton, Ohio, and other centers of war production. It was difficult to maintain a work force, and many youngsters, including this writer, found work on the mill at the age of seventeen before becoming eligible for the draft.

August 20, 1943, marked the beginning of a new era for Cass. On that date, the entire remaining holdings of the West Virginia Pulp and Paper Company at Cass, between sixty and seventy thousand acres of land, mill, town, remains of the extract plant, machine shop and all equipment, were sold to the Mower Lumber Company.[105] The rolling stock, tracks, and mill were badly in need of renovations; however, there was an enormous inventory of lumber and flooring in the yard and wareroom at Cass, which made the purchase profitable.

New ownership led to new management of the holdings. Fred Weber, who had begun working for the Meadow River Lumber Company at Rainelle at age fourteen and had worked his way up to yard foreman, was asked to be superintendent of the operations.[106] He took the job and moved to Cass, living in the Huff house.

Other new supervisors were:

James "Jim" Osborne   — lumber yard foreman
O.H. Shriver   — mill foreman
Robert "Bob" Ervin   — assistant mill foreman
Russell Clarkson   — dry kiln foreman
Forrest Haptenstall   — shop foreman, followed by
Leonard Long   — and later by
Grover "Jughead" Wright
Flosten Sampson   — planing mill foreman followed by
Gilmer Zopp

From the spring of 1946 to April, 1953, Louis H. Camisa was hired as forester or as truck logging superintendent, depending on the situation. He was in charge of the purchase and logging of all the trucked timber and logs for Cass (about five million board feet annually) and made needed surveys and other work on the seventy thousand plus acres of land owned by Mower. He was replaced by Chester "Chet" Kenny.

Mower bought and logged timber from Deerfield, Virginia to Glenville, West Virginia and from Parsons, West Virginia to Hillsboro, West Virginia. Most of the logging and trucking was by contract although Mower had six or eight trucks and three loaders involved in the trucking activities.[107]

UNION ACTIVITIES

The independent nature and job mobility of the lumberjack did not readily lead to the formation of labor unions. Men freely moved from job to job and when at work, maintained their own code of conduct.

The mill men were considerably more settled, and unionization efforts centered on them. In the early 1900s, the International Woodworkers of the World formed a group at Cass. This was more of a lodge than what we today consider a labor union. Even among the laborers, the IWW was belittled and paraphrased "I Won't Work." Calling a man an "IWW" was fighting words, particularly in the woods crews.

By 1911, the Mechanical Workers of America had established thirteen camps in Pocahontas County, including a camp at Cass with twenty-eight members.[108] This also had little effect as a union.

E. P. Shaffer and other management personnel made every effort to discourage unionization at Cass. However, an interest in forming a labor union there persisted. A meeting for that purpose, held in March, 1925, was attended by over three hundred people. The company resisted the organization of a union and the effort failed. By 1932, the Junior Order United American Mechanics were recruiting members in Cass.[109]

The retirement of E. P. Shaffer in 1934, gave new impetus to attempts to organize a union. In the fall of 1934, these attempts led to a strike of the mill that lasted over three months.[110] Nevertheless, the union was largely ineffectual and considered by many to have no real influence.[111]

Labor unions do not give up easily, however, and on October 26, 1936, a huge rally was organized at Cass during which W. M. Rogers, past president of the State Federation of Labor, was the main speaker.[112]

The union was not an important force at Cass until after World War II, when many of the men who were in the armed forces or who had worked away during the war returned. These men had been exposed to unions elsewhere and were prepared to increase the influence of the union at Cass. Conditions were ripe for a change in the summer of 1951 when a representative of the Woodworkers of America arrived in Cass and began discussions with Chester Shrader, then president of the local union. A series of meetings and discussions began, concerning the advisability of joining the Woodworkers of America and of striking, if necessary, to obtain higher wages and better working conditions. Not all workers were in favor of the new union. Much hard feelings ensued with such terms as "yellow dog" and "company man" being used to describe the non-union dissenters.

Finally, in late April, 1952, a secret ballot was taken and a majority of the men voted to join the new union. This included the timber cutters, skidder men, and trainmen who Webber, general superintendent of the job, had been certain would not vote to join.

The election was followed immediately by a general strike to force the company to accept the union. Not all of the men were in favor of the strike, and the term "scab" was used to describe those who wanted to work or attempted to break the strike. After the strike had lasted about a month, it was decided that the union would demand a five-cent per hour raise. The company finally agreed, and after seven weeks, the strike ended on September 22.[113]

Webber spread the word that he was "tickled to death," that if the workers had held out one more week, the company would have given a quarter raise. This rumor did much to lessen the union victory and helped weaken the organization.[114]

The Woodworkers of America continued to represent the workers at Cass and did much to improve safety and to establish a seniority system for assigning extra work, layoffs, etc.

THE LAST YEARS

One factor that influenced company output and profits greatly was the steadily diminishing supply of timber. By 1936, the virgin forests of Cheat River and Elk River had practically all been cut. Only second-growth timber was left in the former wilderness lumbered by the West Virginia Pulp and Paper Company. Furthermore, the oldest second growth was less than fifty years old and lacked the size and quality of a mature forest.

The Monongahela National Forest, first established by a presidential proclamation by Woodrow Wilson on April 28, 1920,[115] and expanded by later proclamations, had made extensive purchases of timberlands throughout Randolph, Pocahontas, and Webster Counties. In May, 1951, the Monongahela policymakers entered into their first venture into long-term timber sale contracting. A. H. Anderson, forest supervisor, was instrumental in preparing and advertising the sale. Mower Lumber Company was the highest bidder and the contract was signed on May 29, 1951. This provided for a 13-year cutting period lasting until August 14, 1964.

This contract called for fifty million board feet of saw timber and eleven thousand cords of pulpwood to be cut on twenty-seven thousand acres of National Forest lands. Approximately sixty miles of roads were to be built by the purchaser on these lands. Timber, cut under this contract, was hauled by truck to Cass and to another Mower-owned mill at Dailey, West Virginia. After the Cass mill closed in 1960, the remainder was sawn at Dailey. Mower Lumber Company operated under the contract until November 21, 1961, when it was taken over by the Pioneer Lumber Company who completed it.[116]

Changes made in the mill by Mower included the removal of the resaw operations, tearing down part of the pulp shed, and a great reduction in the amount of pulpwood shipped.

West Virginia Pulp and Paper Company had installed a slanting conveyor leading from a railroad siding to the boiler house. It was used to unload coal to keep the fires going during the periods of deep snow in the winter or at other times when wood for fuel was low or when pulpwood was badly needed at Covington. The conveyor was discontinued by Mower, and when deep snows came, it was difficult to keep steam up. During one of these snows, Shay No. 5 was taken behind the boiler house to attempt to keep up enough steam to prevent damage from the freezing of pipes. Fires in it were allowed to get low and the cylinders froze, cracking a cylinder block.[117]

A scarcity of good quality timber continued to slow production. One after another, the steam skidders on Cheat completed their last set and were brought to Cass where they were used for parts, to keep the remaining skidders operating, or were junked.

As flatcars needed repairs and were put out of service, they were sometimes shoved to the end of a spur line and allowed to sit and rot or were brought to Cass and burned. The scrap was used in the foundry or was allowed to accumulate and was sold for junk.

The general decline of operation was also evident in the mill. For years there was little preventive maintenance, and things were kept operating on a day-to-day basis. The machinery was getting worn out, the carriage wheels were almost completely gone on the short side, and those on the other carriage were badly worn.[118]

The mill and related operations at Cass had remarkably few fatal accidents during its operation. This record was marred on April 15, 1955, by the tragic death of Dewey Elliott Hiner, aged fifty-five years, from injuries received in a fall from a lumber dock at Cass. Mr. Hiner had worked for many years as a trucker on the lumberyard. The accident was caused by a truckload of lumber that tumbled, knocking him off the 25-foot high dock and resulting in fatal injuries.[119] This was the last fatality on the Cass operation. Ironically, Dewey Hiner's father, Elliott Hiner, was the first man killed on the mill on August 18, 1903.[61]

The mill continued to run somewhat sporadically. F. Edwin Mower, owner of the Mower Lumber Company, died on December 11, 1956. The Charleston National Bank handled the estate with The Charleston National Bank and Don Mower as executors. Directors of the company were Dorothy Mower, Don Mower and Charlie Love.[120]

The company continued operations with increasing periods of shutdown due to a decline in business and the lack of a good supply of high quality logs. Finally, on June 25, 1960, the following succinct notice was posted on company billboards:

JUNE 25, 1960
N O T I C E

DUE TO CONDITIONS BEYOND OUR CONTROL,
IT BECOMES NECESSARY THAT ALL OPERATIONS IN
CONNECTION WITH THE CASS PLANT BE
CLOSED DOWN EFFECTIVE AS OF JUNE 30, 1960.

EMPLOYEES, WHO ARE ELIGIBLE FOR A VACATION, WILL
RECEIVE THEIR VACATION PAY ON JUNE 30.
THE MOWER LUMBER COMPANY[121]

This was fifty-eight years, five months and five days after the first cut was made on January 25, 1902.

Even though rumors of the job closing had abounded for years, many persons believed the notice was a ploy of some kind by the company and that in a month or so the mill would resume running. Many of the workers had spent their entire working years on this job and found it hard to believe that it would close after almost fifty-nine years of continuous operation.

The fact that, after June 30, one furnace was kept fired and the planing mill continued working until July 31, 1961, added strength to the rumor. However, no logs were sawn after June 30, 1960.[122]

For months after closing, rumors surfaced that the mill was sold to other operators who would soon revitalize it. In fact,

J. W. Harrell, an attorney from Jacksonville, Florida, became interested in the town and mill and formed a partnership, presumably to reactivate the mill. One of the partners, Charlie Love, an attorney from Charleston, West Virginia, retained an interest after Harrell bought out the other partners. Love often visited Cass, arranged for some maintenance on the houses, and took care of other local details. His visits often stirred up rumors concerning the restarting of the mill. Slowly, scrapping operations began, and harsh reality set in. Many persons left to obtain work elsewhere, some to the National Radio Astronomy Observatory developing at Green Bank; some to industries in nearby towns; others, remembering their wartime jobs, went to Baltimore and other cities.

The capital stock of the Mower Lumber Company at Cass was sold to Walworth Farms, Inc., an affiliate of Grace Steamships Lines.[123] The Ritter Lumber Company bought the complete inventory of 8,700,000 feet in the Cass planing mill warehouse and lumberyard.[124]

The physical components of the entire holdings were contracted to the Midwest-Raleigh Steel Company for dismantling and sale as junk. Tom Hayes was placed in charge of the salvage operations and equipment and men were moved in to do the job. Dismantling started at the end of the track on Cabin Fork. Rails were loaded onto flatcars and moved to Cass by Shay No. 4. Clyde Galford was engineer. The rails to Bald Knob were next removed, then those from Old Spruce to Spruce.[125] A single former Mower employee, Ivan O. Clarkson, was kept in the shop and helped maintain equipment.

Finally, on October 14, 1962, the last load of lumber was loaded and left town the next day. Workers loading the last load were Puzo Cassell, Warren Slavin, Woodrow Swisher, Caleb Haislip, and a Tyson.[126] The docks themselves were next torn down, and by May, 1963, all that remained were the railroad spurs.[127]

In late summer and fall of 1960, events took place that resulted in the purchase of the railroad, shop, and rolling stock and the eventual development of the Cass Scenic Railroad State Park by the State of West Virginia. A new era for the town of Cass began.

The town itself, the company store, and the mill were not included in the purchase agreement and were retained by the Don Mower Lumber Company.

In August, 1966, the stock in the Don Mower Lumber Company, belonging to the Mower Estate, was sold to a Florida interest represented by J. W. Harrell. The sale included about seventy houses in Cass and the mill property and water services. The rumor that the mill was to be reopened surfaced again.[128]

The carriages and much of the machinery of the mill had been removed, however, and the buildings had steadily deteriorated. The planing mill collapsed during the winter of 1974-75. A final blow came when fire was discovered in the planing mill building on Sunday, August 20, 1978. The fire engulfed and destroyed both the planing mill and the flooring wareroom. Only valiant efforts of the Cass, Bartow-Frank-Durbin, Green Bank Observatory, and Marlinton fire departments prevented the fire from spreading to the sawmill and powerhouse areas. The cause of the fire was suspected to the arson.[129]

The sawmill building itself was not to be spared long. On February 14, 1982, at about 2:30 a.m., fire was discovered in this building. Again, men and equipment from surrounding fire departments were called in, but the mill building was beyond saving and their efforts were concentrated on protecting the C&O water tank. The fire was under control by 4:00 a.m., but all that remained of the mill was a twisted mass of pipes, shafts, wheels, and other parts.

The sixty-year-old structure was completely destroyed except for the powerhouse, boiler house, the smokestacks, and part of the dry kilns.[130] Even the smokestacks were soon leveled when they fell during the spring of 1988.

XI
THE
MACHINE SHOP

Most lumber jobs of the early 1900s were located far from sources of supply. Such isolation necessitated a self-reliance akin to that of pioneer communities of an earlier century. If a shaft or cog broke on one of the engines, on the mill, or on the many other mechanical devices used, days or even weeks could be lost in attempting to obtain a replacement from a far-distant supplier, even if such a part could be obtained at all.

Provisions for a repair facility were paramount. This need was met at Cass with the construction of a machine shop along Leatherbark Run north of the C&O water tank. Its single inside track could hold two Shay engines. To provide castings for certain parts of machinery, a foundry was built across Leatherbark Run, connected to the shop area by a footbridge.[1]

The combination shop and foundry was to serve the Cass operation well and, as experience was gained, the shop crew was able to make or repair almost any part of the locomotives, skidders, loaders, rolling stock, and sawmill machinery.

E. P. Shaffer's ability to judge and hire good men was demonstrated in 1904 when he brought E. J. "Herb" Shafer to Cass as master machinist. Herb Shafer was the epitome of a master craftsman. Resourceful, imaginative, hardworking and dedicated, he later became shop foreman and directed repair operations for many years.[2] To him and to the crew of skillful machinists, blacksmiths, foundrymen, and others go the credit for keeping the mill and woods operations running with little time lost due to breakdowns.

In 1921, a new shop was built between the railroad and Leatherbark Creek north of the original one. It was constructed of surplus fabricated steel purchased from the Army. It was moved into in October, 1922.[3]

The new shop was powered by an overhead line shaft that drove belts which, in turn, ran the various pieces of equipment. It contained three fully equipped blacksmiths' forges; two drill presses, one large, one smaller; one thread machine with dies and both bolt and pipe heads; three lathes including one that took 14-foot stock; a hydraulic press; two grinders; one key-way machine, inside; one key-way machine, outside; a milling or boring machine; one band saw; one planer for metal; one shaper for metal; two electric welding machines; acetylene torches; one power hacksaw; one rolling mill for sheet metal; hoists and cranes.[4]

A new foundry was built along Leatherbark Run north of the shop. A railroad spur ran alongside for easy unloading and loading of materials. Cast iron and brass were poured in the foundry. Iron used was obtained from 100-pound pigs and from scrap.

Two men worked in the foundry full time with an occasional extra man when needed. When they were ready to pour, extra men were borrowed from the shop. Allen "Farmer" Blackhurst and Roy Cook were the regular foundrymen for many years.

A "heat" or "pour" was made three times a week with four thousand pounds of cast iron. One heat made sixty-four brake shoes. When preparing a pour or heat, one and one-half days were required to set up the molds, using wet sand and wooden patterns. After the sand was dried, the metal was melted and poured into the molds. Pouring one heat took about forty-five minutes. The molds were allowed to cool and were then broken apart to loosen the product. In addition to cast iron brake shoes, wheels and other items, a large amount of brass was poured to make parts for engines, loaders, skidders, and the mill.

The foundry also made parts for neighboring lumber companies and for townspeople and farmers. Stove grates were items in great demand by these latter persons.[5]

A heavy steel building, used to store dynamite, sat along Leatherbark north of the new shop.[6]

The shop crew roster and wages for April, 1914, read:

E.J. Shafer	—	$4.50 per day
W.J. Hall	—	3.75 per day
Eugene Powers	—	3.00 per day
Charles Fallen	—	3.00 per day
Howard Dickerson	—	3.00 per day
George Madson	—	2.75 per day
S.L. Seitz	—	2.64 per day
John Loury	—	2.65 per day
H.B. Fudge	—	2.25 per day
C. Canfield	—	2.00 per day
W.A. Painter	—	2.35 per day
Italian #484	—	1.90 per day
Italian #292	—	1.90 per day
Italian #247	—	1.90 per day
Italian #226	—	1.90 per day
Italian #37	—	1.90 per day
W.D. Dickson	—	2.45 per day
William Lowery	—	1.90 per day
Monroe Phillips	—	2.50 per day
Charles McCarthy	—	2.75 per day
J.R. Meadows	—	1.90 per day
L.H. Deem	—	2.25 per day
Harry Wooddell	—	1.35 per day
Oscar Slavin	—	1.90 per day
H.L. Trout	—	2.00 per day
J.F. Blakenship	—	2.75 per day
D.F. Jordan	—	1.90 per day
D.F. Clifford	—	1.90 per day
John Carey	—	1.90 per day
M.B. Jones	—	1.90 per day
Clyde Hardin	—	2.00 per day
J.A. Hartman	—	2.31 per day
Roy Glidewell	—	1.90 per day
O.F. Burford	—	2.75 per day
S.L. Waugh	—	2.00 per day
H.S. Sprouse	—	1.90 per day

D.C. Reed	—	2.50 per day
Kyle Steel	—	1.90 per day
W.A. Phillips	—	1.90 per day
D.F. Clifford		
Floyd Moupr	—	60.00 per month
M. Cottrill	—	2.75 per day
Charles Winans	—	2.50 per day
Roy Siple	—	1.90 per day
Frank Bloum	—	1.90 per day
S.F. Rose	—	2.00 per day
H.W. Osborne	—	1.90 per day
W.A. Phillips	—	2.00 per day
Jess Williams	—	1.90 per day
H.D. Marshall	—	2.25 per day
C.E. Ripley	—	1.90 per day
George Shay	—	1.90 per day
D.C. Reed	—	2.50 per day
H.P. Neal	—	1.90 per day
Moris Dolan	—	1.90 per day
C.P. Hite	—	1.90 per day

Almost all of the men worked eleven hours a day. The large number of men listed indicates that a night shift was also working.[7]

Numerous changes of personnel were made and during July, 1920, the following were listed:

E.J. Shafer	—	Wages not listed
P.E. Warner	—	$.82 1/2/hour
C.E. Kirkpatrick	—	.66/hour
L.E. Bowling	—	.66/hour
W.E. Galusha	—	.55/hour
C.R. Shrader	—	.69/hour
C.F. Norris	—	.66/hour
R.C. Siple	—	.44/hour
L.L. Dodson	—	.66/hour
Willie Simmons	—	.45/hour
Wm. Gragg	—	.55/hour
George Gum	—	.49 1/2/hour
G.W. Friel	—	.55/hour
C.E. Kincaid	—	.49 1/2/hour
Robert Newman	—	.49 1/2/hour
Lacy Bird	—	.70/hour

R.O. Crowley	—	.50/hour
Roy Myers	—	.50/hour
Roy Cook	—	.55/hour
J.A. Porter	—	.49 1/2/hour
William Cassell	—	.45/hour
Carl Ryder	—	.49 1/2/hour
G.V. Blackhurst	—	.45/hour
W.H. Houff	—	.50/hour
J.S. Smiley	—	.45/hour
Walter Shafer	—	.20/hour
M.C. Smith	—	not listed
W.P. Helmic	—	not listed
W.T. Larue	—	not listed
A.J. Blackhurst	—	.60/hour
Grover Craddock	—	not listed
Ed Wolverton, Locomotive 4 Engineer	—	not listed
Ben Cameron, Locomotive 4 Fireman	—	not listed
Italians		
#200 Jim	—	.60 1/2/hour
#1867 Fred	—	.49 1/2/hour
#1857 Tony	—	.49 1/2/hour
#1859 Ben	—	.49 1/2/hour
#1854 Mike	—	.49 1/2/hour
#1804 Ernest	—	.49 1/2/hour
#1888	—	.49 1/2/hour
#1899	—	.45/hour

The workday had been cut to ten hours although a couple of men worked twelve hours a day. The average number of days worked was twenty-four a month or six days a week.[8]

In July, 1931, the Shop Time Book listed the following. No wages were shown.

A.J. Blackhurst	Albert Hedrick
L.E. Bowling	H.H. Halterman
J.C. Butters	A.E. Harouff
A.E. Butters	J.C. McCalpin
Roy Cook	O.S. McKisic
William Cassell	Jack Mays
E.L. Duncan	W.R. Nichols
John Grogg	J.A. Porter
Charles Galford	C.D. Ryder
F.J. Haptonstall	E.J. Shafer

C.R. Shrader   Clifton Wolfe
Norman Shrader   Italians
R.P. Stanley   #1984
Harry Smith   #1968[9]
P.E. Warner

During the 1930s, shopworkers not on the above roster included Claude Halterman, Chester Shrader, Ivan Clarkson, Guy Tallman, F. W. Holiday, Henry Queen, Charles Galford, and D. L. Collins.[10]

The shop crew roster during the period January 1, 1940, to December 31, 1942, showed the following:

A. J. Blackhurst—Foundry Floor, Moulder
Roy Cook—Foundry Floor, Assistant Moulder
William Cassell
Ivan Clarkson—Machinist (absent for service in the U.S. Army
                July 10, 1942, to June 10, 1946)
Elmer L. Duncan—Shop Clerk and Supply Man
J.M. Grogg (left August 3, 1942)
Charles Galford—Motorcar Operator
Albert E. Harouff—Machinist
Forrest J. Haptonstall—Floor Work and Boiler Repairman
H.H. Halterman—Blacksmith
Claude Halterman
F.W. Holiday
Jesse C. McCalpin
J.A. Porter—Floor Work and Boiler Repairman
Carl D. Ryder (left July 20, 1942)
E.J. "Herb" Shafer—Master Machinist
C.R. "Dugan" Shrader—Welder
P.E. Warner—Machinist
Louie Savich
Ernest Halterman
Ed Howell
George Howell
Henry Queen[11]
Additions in 1942 included:
Paul Bradley[12]

From December 31, 1942, to July 1, 1943, the roster included the following in addition to the above.

Harper Gum
Frank M. Eary
Osborn Hill
G.C. Barkley
Cornie Cross
*Clyde Galford
*Walter Good
George Sullivan

*Clark Phillips
*John Varner
Grover Wright
Henry Gibson
George Conier
Helbet Payne
Porter Moore
Woods Gaylor

*Indicates train crews temporarily working in the shop.

From August, 1944, to September 1, 1945, the roster read:

A.J. Blackhurst – Moulder
Roy Cook – Assistant Moulder
Russell Clarkson (left October 9, 1944)
E.L. Duncan – Shop Clerk and Supplyman
Charles Galford – Motorcar Operator
Harper Gum
A.E. Harouff – Machinist
F.J. Haptonstall – Floor Work and Boiler Repairman
H.H. Halterman – Blacksmith (left February 12, 1944, returned later)
J.A. Porter – Floor Work and Boiler Repairman
Andy Portolese (left February 7, 1945)
E.J. Shafer – Master Machinist
C.R. "Dugan" Shrader – Welder
Louie Savich
John Varner
Grover Wright
A.E. Parsons
W.L. Ralston – Motorcar Operator
Albert Brown
Henry Wanless
Guy Tallman (left February 12, 1945; died June 3, 1945)
Luther Fowler
Dennis Grimes
Ralph Lowe (left April 17, 1945)
John Mitchell
T.A. Burdette
Robert A. Wooddell
R.R. Dickenson
Woods Gaylor[13]

Additions to the list above during the next year, September 1, 1945, to October 1, 1946, were:

J. Thompson	Dewey Galford
Woods Gaylor	Frank Varner
Huffman Summerfield	Bruce Nelson[14]
Melvin Good	

After the Mower Lumber Company bought the operation, Forrest Haptonstall was made foreman. He was followed by Leonard Long and later by Grover "Jughead" Wright.[15]

On July 18, 1957, a fire destroyed the foundry and pattern house.[16] Over twelve hundred patterns were lost. The fire was especially harmful because much of the mill machinery and rolling stock of the company were badly in need of replacement parts. Another great loss in the foundry fire was the diary of Allen Blackhurst that he had maintained since 1909.[17]

The shop continued its important work through the Mower years. Equipment was getting old and required a great deal of maintenance. It and surrounding land were purchased by the State of West Virginia on June 20, 1962. It then performed an essential function for the Cass Scenic Railroad.

On July 23, 1972, a disastrous fire destroyed the shop and machinery and parts it contained. Climax engine No. 9 was damaged but Shay engine No. 3 was pulled free without damage. A temporary shop was established to get through the summer season; then a new shop was built. While lacking the historical interest of the old shop, it serves well in keeping the rolling stock in good repair.[18]

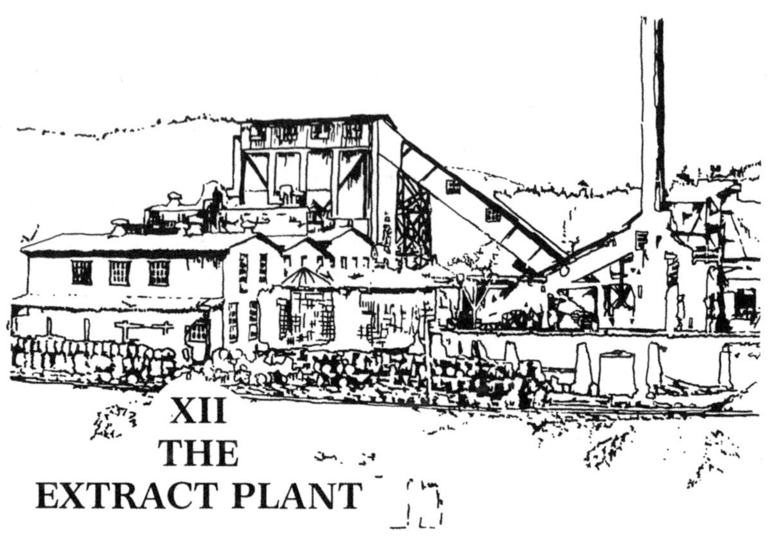

XII
THE
EXTRACT PLANT

During World War I, the market for chemicals greatly increased. Since the West Virginia Pulp and Paper Company had extensive experience in chemical production of pulp, they decided to enter the lucrative chemical market. The pulpwood mill at Spruce was producing large quantities of bark from which tannins could be extracted. To capitalize on these chemicals, the company built a plant at Deer Creek, one mile south of Cass. This venture became known as the Extract Plant.

Construction of the facility was started in November, 1913, and was apparently completed in December, 1914.[1] A subsidiary, the Industrial Chemical Company of New York, was formed to do research in chemical manufacture and utilization. On March 29, 1915, the company purchased 579 shares of the Robeson Processing Company.[2] Both of these companies were involved in operating the Extract Plant.

The site included several bark storage sheds with firebrick walls, a powerhouse, chipping house, shipping room, pan and autoclave house, scale house, two-story office, and several tanks for the extraction process.[3]

Building the extract plant cost at least one life. On April 29, 1914, while excavating for one of the pits, Clyde Weiford was killed instantly by a premature blast when an Italian, working the battery, touched the key before the men were clear.[4]

The Extract Plant was designed to utilize waste bark of spruce and hemlock along with American chestnut and oak bark and wood to produce extracts for use in tanning leather.[5] These trees were peeled in the woods, the bark was stacked on end, dried, and then it was shipped to the extract plant. In addition, chestnut and oak slabs and edgings were purchased from the lumber companies in the vicinity and from as far away as Rainelle, West Virginia.[6]

As the United States became involved in World War I, the Extract Plant was used to produce both liquid and powdered extracts used in dyeing olive drab cloth for military uniforms. Osage Orange wood, used as a source of the dye, was shipped in by the trainload from the south and midwest.[7]

Two rows of houses were built south of the C&O wye to provide homes for the workers on the Extract Plant. These houses were mostly two-story, constructed on the same plan as the company houses built earlier in Cass. A larger house for the superintendent of the chemical department, Arthur Moulton, was built along the C&O tracks at the mouth of Cold Run. This area of houses became known as "Slab Town," a name still used by local residents. The Moulton Hole located here in the Greenbrier River was a favorite fishing spot.

Danger lurked in all phases of the work. A fatal accident occurred about 1920 when an autoclave exploded and scalded Emmanuel Tyson to death.[8]

In processing bark for the removal of tannins, a silo was used to store finely ground bark before it was fed, by gravity, to the autoclave and digestors. On April 21, 1926, Clarence Tacy, nineteen year old son of Charlie Tacy, was working at the top of the silo and sometime later he appeared to be missing. The flow of ground bark from the silo was shunted away from the autoclave and in a little while his body came out the chute. It was thought the bark dust in the silo had partly emptied out, leaving a crust on the top, and he had stepped on the crust, caving it in. An examination by the undertaker, J. B. Sutton, showed his lungs to be packed full of the fine dust.[9]

The Extract Plant continued operations until 1926, when it closed.[10] The workers were mostly absorbed into the main company work force. In 1929, the equipment was advertised for sale.[11] During scrapping operations, the buildings were accidentally set afire and burned.[12]

A sample record of freight bills of the Extract Plant in May, 1920, follows:[13]

Chemical Department—A. Moulton, Supt.

Dist. of C&O Freight Bills—	5/04	5/18	5/27
Spruce Bark	$ 20.10	$ 26.79	$ 6.70
Hemlock Bark			6.70
Coal	20.10	13.39	13.39
Barrels	13.40	234.22	109.94
Chestnut wood	608.22	143.06	99.49
orange wood	746.63		
repairs	12.93		1.28
express		21.52	
construction		6.70	

XIII
THE POCAHONTAS SUPPLY COMPANY

The practice among lumber companies, mining concerns, and others establishing a new industry in a sparsely inhabited area, was to incorporate a store where supplies could be bought by the workers. Such establishments, built, supplied, and run by the company, were universally called the "Company Store." Company stores were often the only store available to the town's inhabitants and were accused of controlling prices and of unfairly charging their "captive" customers. Actually the Company Store filled a need that otherwise would have been sorely vexing to the townspeople. In many cases, the company was the only source of the necessary capital, the business knowledge, and the interest needed to supply the people. It is surprising that, in most cases, they took so little advantage of their powerful position.

When the initial activity associated with the developments at Cass started in 1900, there was a small country store there owned by J. S. Matthews. It was apparent that a larger supply base was needed, and on July 6, 1900, Shaffer telegraphed Slaymaker "have commenced commissary."[1] The store was a small building located near where the C&O Railroad Station later was built.[2]

Meanwhile, the officers of the West Virginia Pulp and Paper Company met in June, 1900, and established a subsidiary, the

Pocahontas Supply Company, with a capital stock of ten thousand dollars, to handle the retail business of workers and their families. A large building was constructed and on November 28, 1900, Shaffer took inventory of stock in the Cass Commissary and transferred the business to the Pocahontas Supply Company.[3]

Harry Moore was named first manager of the new store. On looking for ways to increase the business, he saw that if supplies for the lumber company itself were ordered through the store at a fixed percent profit instead of directly from the vendor, a huge increase in store business would result. C. F. Moore related this idea to Slaymaker and appropriate action was taken.[4]

In addition to the main store, a large warehouse for the storage of hay, grain, and other bulk items was completed in January, 1901.[5] Hay, in large quantities, was purchased from F. W. Brown and Daiden Company and from others. For instance, in November, 1900, 21,908 pounds of hay at 90¢ (a bale) were purchased from W. C. Ward at Huttonsville, West Virginia.[6]

Under the direction of Robert S. Hickman, manager from 1902 to 1947, the Pocahontas Supply Store expanded to become one of the largest company stores to operate in the country. On October 24, 1905, the executive board of the company increased the capital stock of the Pocahontas Supply Company from ten to fifty thousand dollars. It was now operating two stores, one at Cass and the other at Spruce. Later, additional branch stores were opened at Cheat Bridge, Laurel Bank, and Bemis.

The main store at Cass was a phenomenal operation. It carried almost every item that was needed by the working force, the townspeople, and the surrounding agricultural trading area. It sold work and dress clothing for men, women and children, fabrics, jewelry, furniture, dishes, all kinds of household wares, coal, hay, groceries, books, drugs, toys at Christmas, flowers at Easter, and sent dry cleaning to Baltimore. Such staples as canned goods, feed, nails, fencing, and loggers' boots were bought by the railway carload. As many as four carloads of condensed milk were purchased at one time. The store is reported to have done over one million dollars worth of business annually for many years.[7]

One of the biggest problems, in the days before refrigeration, was providing fresh meat. Poultry was easily taken care of.

Chickens and turkeys were kept in a pen north of the store, and when ordered, a live bird was selected, the feet were tied and the fowl was handed to the customer, who did his own preparation. Beef was slaughtered in a slaughterhouse located along the tracks above the machine shop. The preparation and selling of meat was handled by S. B. Nethken and Company.[8]

The store was a center of activity in the town. Here, in winter, people gathered around the large iron Burnside stoves for the latest gossip and conversation. In summer the front steps were lined with people waiting for the C&O passenger train to arrive with the mail, looking over newly arrived passengers, or just passing the time talking.

The store was remodeled several times and eventually was increased in size to a building three hundred feet long by sixty feet wide, with a full second story and basement. The company office was originally located in a building south of Nethken's Meat Market. It was later moved to the north end of the first floor of the store along with a drugstore and soda fountain. The post office, with an outside door, was also on the north end of the building.[9] Jewelry was displayed in the south end of the store as was bolt cloth. Clothing filled the central area. The post office was later moved to the south end in back, and the company office was placed in the front part of the south end. Still later, the post office was moved to the building that was formerly Nethken's meat market.

Most business, done at the store, was on a charge basis. Employees and other persons with good credit could charge their purchases, at least to a reasonable limit. Bills were written on small billing pads which included a carbon copy. The bills were accumulated and the totals subtracted from the worker's pay each payday.

The store was open from 8:00 a.m. to 8:00 p.m. People congregated in the store in the evenings to listen to popular programs and special events such as prize fights (boxing) on a radio in the furniture department.[10]

Scrip, which played an important part in the business in many lumber and coal companies, was not used at Cass although some scrip was minted for the Pocahontas Supply Company.[11]

Loggers often came to town and spent their paychecks on drinking and other pursuits. In order to obtain additional cash, they charged items such as shoes in the company store, carried them outside, and sold them at a reduced price to obtain a new cash supply.

Considering the all-wood construction and the amount of inflammable material in the store, it is surprising that fire was not a greater problem than it was. The only serious fire in the Company Store occurred on Monday, March 19, 1918, when "the big store of the Pocahontas Supply Company at Cass was burned. The fire started in the second story and was put out before it reached the first floor. How the fire started is not known. The immense stock was greatly damaged by fire and water. The loss is fully covered by insurance."[12] The store building was enlarged to its present size after the fire by extending north and south into the area formerly occupied by Nethken's Meat Market. The meat market was moved closer to the company office.

The Company Store had free delivery of feed, hay and other bulky items. Coal was a special item since many of the townspeople and surrounding farmers changed from wood to coal for much of their cooking and heating needs.

During the 1930s, the company contracted to furnish and deliver coal to Green Bank District Schools. Trucks often got "hung up" on the roads while supplying the rural one-room schools of the district. The last school deliveries were made in 1936.[13]

In 1933-34, the company won the bid to supply coal to the courthouse and jail in Marlinton. Coal was brought from the Baldwin mines by rail and loaded onto a 1933 V-8 Ford for delivery by Charlie Sheets.[14]

For many years George Oliver, John Kane or Crawford Gum, employees of the Company Store, came to each house in town to take orders for meat, groceries, feed, hay, coal, etc. At night, they filled orders for the next day, swept the floor, and restocked shelves. Orders were delivered next day by Ben Conner, Ed Jackson, Joe Urbanick or Floyd Wright using a horse-drawn dray wagon, and in later years by a truck driven by Sam Waugh and still later by Charlie Sheets.[15]

An ice machine was put in the space behind Nethkin's meat market. Ice was pulled down a slide to the delivery truck in front. Ice was delivered to the homes of townspeople every other day by Joe Nethken, Clarence Nethken, and later Charlie Sheets.

A drugstore was located near the center of the store on the

west side. Prescription drugs as well as a profusion of patent medicines could be purchased there. Dr. Ayers, Dr. Harry Hill and Dr. Wilhide were druggists at various times. A soda fountain and ice cream bar were located in front of the drugstore.

To give an idea of the variety of items carried by the store and their cost, the following inventory of the Laurel Bank store is given:

Pocahontas Supply Company
Inventory of the Laurel Bank Store[16]

5 gal. tomatoes @ .60	3.00
1 doz. beets	2.53
28 jars mustard @ .23	6.44
1 doz. St. beans	1.85
1 doz. Sw. potatoes	2.50
60 # lard	15.60
1 doz. No. 2 berries	2.25
40 cans Salmon @ .30	12.00
1 cs. V.C. Hominy	3.30
45 # D.S. Side @ .24	10.80
17 sm. Catsup	2.46
1 cs 1 gal. tomats booths [sic]	7.20
100 # rice	19.00
90 pass G. Dust 5 3/4	5.17
1 cs. Gold X milk	5.50
60 ft. wire cloth	5.40
1 meat saw	2.10
1 butcher steel	1.00
10 – 100 # soup beans 9 1/2	9.50
6 bu potatoes 5 1/2#	19.80
1 bbl. flour	14.50
1 cs. matches	7.50
1 bbl. oil	12.50
2 shovels No. 2	2.50
6 mattocks	6.60
1 hand saw	2.10
1 hatchet	.50
1 spalding hammer	1.00
1 roll roofing	1.70
1 No. 3 scoop	1.65
1 pitchfork	.65
1 Sk. Bran	3.50
1395# hay	29.99

6 sm. bags salt	.24
10 beds @ 5.50	55.00
10 springs @ 6.00	60.00
10 army blankets @ 2.25	22.50
10 cotton blankets @ 3.15	31.50
20 pillows @ 1.15	23.00
5 coffee pots @ .70	3.50
2 wash boilers @ 3.25	6.50
3 fire shovels @ .15	.45
11 bracket lamps @ 1.25	13.75
4 sets knives & forks @.85	3.40
4 sets table spoon @ .40	1.60
1 egg beater	.20
1 can opener	.25
2 wash boards	1.50
154# grindstone at 2 1/2	3.85
6 cant hooks @ 3.50	21.00
70 cakes laundry soap @ .07	4.90
8 cakes Ivory soap @ 8 1/2	.67
5 pkg. oats large @ .35	1.75
88# coffee	34.76
3# chocolate @ .40	1.20
5 pkg. yeast	.18
4# Rumf. B. Powd	1.00
17# corn starch	.94
15 Pa. Mace	1.65
14 Pa. noodles	1.54
26 Pa. Raisins	5.72
	524.64

The manager of the Company Store during most of the ownership by the West Virginia Pulp and Paper Company was Robert S. Hickman. Burke McCarty was assistant manager. When the Mower Lumber Company took over, the store managers were Henry Mabe, followed by H. H. Thompson and later Robert Wright. Many of the clerks worked years for the Pocahontas Supply Company. In later years, hiring town youngsters resulted in a rapid turnover of clerks.[17]

The Company Store continued in business until, on September 1, 1960, the Mower Lumber Company Store advertised a quitting business sale during which the entire inventory was sold.[18]

The building was empty until 1963, when the Cass Country Store was organized by Warren E. "Tweard" and Stella Blackhurst, Jessie "Brown Beard" Powell and others. The store has continued to prosper and has a wide variety of souvenir items as well as a small restaurant and soda foundation.

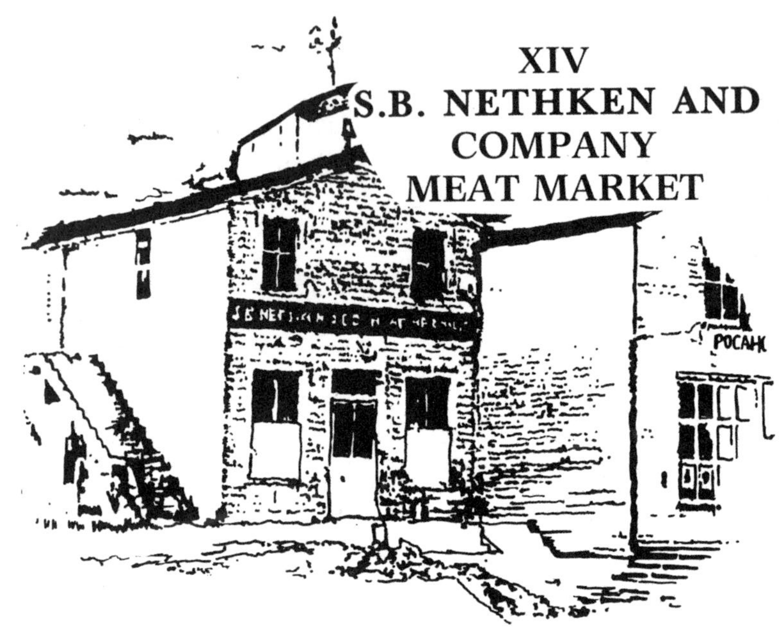

XIV
S.B. NETHKEN AND
COMPANY
MEAT MARKET

A major problem in boarding a large work force of men was supplying them with food and other necessities. At Cass, the formation of the Pocahontas Supply Company and the building of the Company Store solved the dilemma in part.

Since meat was a major item of the diet, the organizers of the company realized that tremendous savings could be made by buying live animals in quantity and keeping them on hand for butchering as needed.

To assist in this endeavor, the talents of Stuart B. Nethken were called upon. Nethken came to Cass in January, 1901, from Horton, West Virginia.[1] He assisted in recruiting men and purchasing horses as well as supplying meat to the camps and town.

Stuart Nethken was an excellent horseman and traveled entirely by horseback, never by buggy or wagon. His energy and ability are illustrated by the following sequence of events:

On April 12, 1902, he was in Zenda, Virginia, reporting that he was starting home with seven horses and would pick up others at Zenda and West Augusta.[2] He arrived at Cass on April 13, informed the company he had purchased a carload of cattle,[3] and expected to leave the following day for more horses. He requested that two thousand dollars be sent to him at Mt. Crawford, Virginia, by the end of the week.[4] Again on April 30, the request for twelve thousand dollars "for Nethken to purchase cattle" was forwarded to the main office.[5] Numerous similar transactions are noted in the company records.

S. B. Nethken and Company "Dealers in Fresh Meats" was located in a building adjacent to the south side of the Pocahontas Supply Company.[6] Here townspeople could purchase fresh meats and related items. Nethken's main responsibility was to supply meat to the company's working force and numerous vouchers show the shipment of meat to various camps on Cheat Mountain and Elk River. An example of one month's billing (June, 1919) follows:[7]

```
Camp 10
     June  2      Beef              111 lbs.
           5                        157
           9                        164
          12                        147
          16                         83
          19                        147
          26                        114
          30                        143
                                   ─────
                        1066 lbs. @ $.25 − $266.50

Camp 11
     June  2      Beef     112 lbs. @ $.25 − $ 28.00

Camp 16
     June  2      Beef              115 lbs.
           5                        253
           9                        318
          12                        285
          16                        130
          19                        263
          23                        249
          26                        245
          30                        263
                                   ─────
                        2121 lbs. @ $.25 − $530.25

Camp 46
     June 12      Beef              368 lbs.
          12                        157
          16                        135
          19                        295
          23                        274
```

26		272
30		122
		1623 lbs. @ $.25 — $405.75
2	Liver	28 lbs.
19		24
		52 lbs. @ $.25 — $ 13.00
2	Hearts	15
19		19
		$.35 each — $ 3.15
		$421.90

Camp 48

June 2	Beef	462 lbs.
5		154
12		142
16		94
19		296
23		276
26		239
26		29
29		253
		1945 lbs. @ $.25 — $486.25
2	Liver	28
16		23
23		22
29		10
		83 lbs. @ $.25 — $ 20.75
3	Hearts	$.35 each — $ 1.05
		$508.05

Camp 49

June 2	Beef	336 lbs.
12		288
16		183
19		283
23		304
26		379
29		400
		2173 lbs. @ $.25 — $543.25
2	Liver	21
12		22
19		15
		58 lbs. @ $.25 — $ 14.50

2	Hearts	11		
19		10	–	2.10
				$559.85

Camp 51

June 2	Beef	341 lbs.	–	$ 85.25

Camp 53

June 2	Beef	463 lbs.	–	$115.75

Camp 55

June 2	Beef	154 lbs.	–	$ 38.50

Big Run

June 5	Beef	141 lbs.	
9		168	
12		151	
16		136	
19		116	
23		138	
26		111	
30		159	
		1120 lbs. @ $.25 – $280.00	
2	Liver	25	
26		22	
30		12	
		59 lbs. @ $.25 – $ 14.75	
30	Hearts	10 lbs.	.70
			$295.45

In the early years, a slaughterhouse and barn were located along the tracks north and west of the machine shop at Cass. Cattle were shipped in by the carload and were held in pens located north of the slaughterhouse. A house for storing corn for the cattle was located near the foundry. The butchers were Jim Parker and Ollie Davis.[8] Meat was wrapped and brought down to Nethken's Meats on a handcar. From here, it was sent directly to the camps on Cheat or sold to townspeople.

It became apparent to the company that, in order to economically supply meat to the lumber camps and to handle the quantity needed, local farms would be advantageous.

A large acreage on Deer Creek, three miles east of Cass, was purchased from George and Brassie Siple in 1919. This became known as the "Company Farm." A large barn was built there by

Frank Ervin who submitted a bill for the job for $499.45 on October 20, 1919. The lumber was furnished by the company.[9]

Another farm was established later on Elk River just below Laurel Bank (where the present Western Maryland Railroad yards are located). Slaughter pens were located adjacent to the farm in an area since known as "Slaughter Pen Hollow."[10]

Two other farms, the Sharp and Meeks Farms, were mentioned in the Pocahontas Supply Company bills.[11]

The slaughterhouse in Cass was closed in 1929 and torn down in 1932 or 1933.[12]

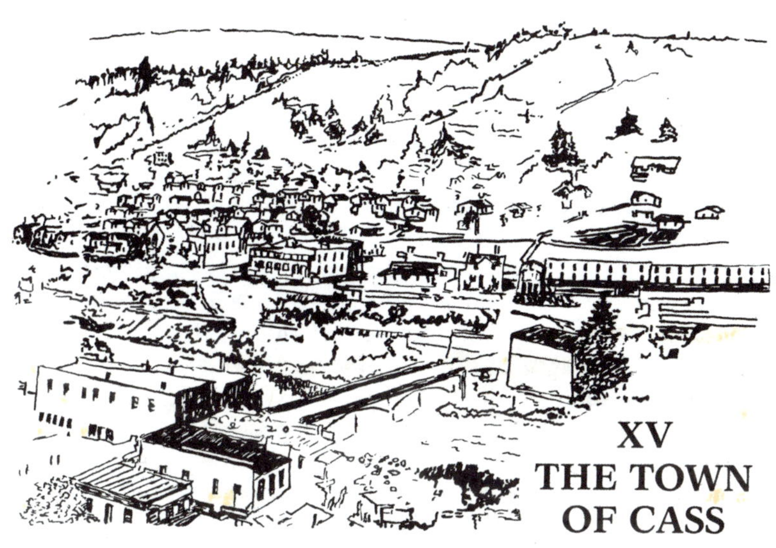

XV
THE TOWN
OF CASS

The locale of our story is in Pocahontas County, West Virginia, along the Greenbrier River at a location formerly known either as Leatherbark or Leatherbark Ford. Here Leatherbark Run tumbles down from Back Allegheny Mountain and enters the Greenbrier from the northwest. Nearly a mile further south, Cold Run empties in from the southwest. Between the two stream mouths the Greenbrier is bordered with strips of bottomland, hemmed in by steep hills. The land originally was part of a patent to Jeremiah Knox on November 18, 1799.[1] By the mid-1800s, the land was owned by Isaiah Curry and by 1876, several hundred acres of the Greenbrier Valley and surrounding hills were owned by Robert Curry, Isaiah's son. Eighty acres east of the river were sold by him to Allen Craig Burner on December 28, 1876.[2] On March 10, 1882, Robert Curry and his wife, Elizabeth, sold 150 acres along the Greenbrier River to their son Charles Z. J. Curry for one dollar.[3] In 1889 Charles Z. J. Curry and his wife Ida C. (Burner) Curry sold 56 acres on the west side of the river near the mouth of Cold Run to Allen Galford.[4]

By 1890 there were three farms located in this narrow valley on the lands described above. One farmhouse, owned by Charles Z. J. and Ida Curry, was located at a spring near the present Company Store and within a stone's throw of the present depot.[5] Another farmhouse, owned by Allen Craig Burner, was near a spring east of the Greenbrier River;[6] and the third, owned by Allen Galford, was located west of the Greenbrier near the mouth of Cold Run.[7] Other scattered farms lay on the lower slopes of Back Allegheny Mountain west of the Greenbrier, both north and south of Leatherbark.

A road, known as the Back Mountain Road, meandered north-south connecting these farms.[8] A one-room school known as the Cold Run School, was located west of this road on a branch of Cold Run.[9] The school served families within several miles along the road in each direction. Most students attended only the first three or four grades before needs at home kept them away. They received a strong background in reading, writing and arithmetic using McGuffie's Reader and Ray's Arithmetic. Memory exercises such as learning the alphabet backward as well as forward were practiced.[10]

A sash sawmill, powered by water, was constructed by Allen Galford on Leatherbark Creek near where the Back Mountain Road crossed. A second water sawmill, owned by James Cassell, was located near the present Bill Simmons' place, on Mill Run, a tributary of Leatherbark.[11] A flat rock above this mill was a favorite place for gambling and drinking. Two small circular steam sawmills owned by the Robertson Brothers were also located along Leatherbark Creek.

A road connecting Leatherbark with Green Bank crossed Little Mountain east of the Greenbrier at a point north of the mouth of Leatherbark Creek and came downstream to cross the river near where the cement bridge across the Greenbrier now stands. The farms in the Deer Creek Valley were connected to the Back Mountain Road by a winding road that came down the stream, forded the Greenbrier River at the mouth of Deer Creek and went up Cold Run.

To accommodate the scattered farms, a small store, run by George D. Oliver, was established before 1900 at Leatherbark near where the present Cold Run Road levels off after coming down the mountain.[12]

The Curry farm consisted of 136 acres. It encompassed the land later occupied by the shop, the mill, the Company Pasture and most of the incorporated part of the town. On January 26, 1892, this farm was sold by Charles Z. J. Curry and his wife, Ida, to Jacob N. Gum for eight hundred dollars.[13] The property was conveyed to Nancy E. Gum, Jacob's wife on October 18, 1894, for the sum of four hundred dollars.[14] On April 3, 1899, Jacob N. Gum and Nancy E. Gum resold the property to John G. Luke for the sum of one thousand dollars.[15] The property was finally transferred by John G. Luke to the West Virginia Spruce Lumber Company on July 31, 1901, for the consideration of five dollars.[16]

Shortly before 1900, residents of the community of Leatherbark had cause for excitement as the building of the Greenbrier Division of the Chesapeake and Ohio Railroad began. This line was to follow the Greenbrier River from Whitcomb in Greenbrier County northward to near the present location of Durbin. It would pass by the farms located at the mouth of Leatherbark and would bring about changes that could not have been imagined by the local residents.

A New Town is Born 1900-1909

During the late 1800s, John G. Luke, representing the Lukes' interests, began buying timberlands in the Leatherbark area and in the Cheat River country atop Cheat Mountain to the west and north. Rumor had it that a sawmill and town were to be built. The old Curry farm, mentioned above, would provide land for the millsite and related activities and for a town to house the officials and workers connected with the mill operations.

Early in 1900, Emory P. Shaffer, a young, experienced lumberman then working at Whitmer, West Virginia, and Sam Slaymaker, a lumber dealer from Philadelphia, arrived at Leatherbark. Slaymaker and Shaffer began making preparations for building a camp to house Italian workers, who would prepare the millsite and the grade for a lumber railroad up Leatherbark Creek and into the Cheat Mountain country.

Lumber for the camp, designated as Camp 1, was obtained from the Robertson Brothers' local circular sawmills, and a rough building was erected west of the present depot where the coal bin and scales were later located. The first meal served in Camp 1 was on the Fourth of July, 1900.[17] The camp was completed July 6, 1900,[18] but was not moved into until early in August.[19] Supplies were hauled in by wagon from Stanton, Virginia. Ed Jackson, who settled at Cass, was one of the original teamsters.[20] A small commissary was placed nearby to provide for personal needs of the workers. The commissary was soon found to be partially on land owned by the C&O and designated for their railroad station. On September 21, Mr. Hawkins, chief engineer for the C&O, notified Shaffer of this and asked him to move it by the spring of 1901.[21]

Company headquarters were established at Green Bank where access to the other company officials was possible. Green Bank had telegraph and mail services that were lacking at Leatherbark. The return address, Green Bank, was used for the next two years on company letters.[22]

The circumstances surrounding the naming of the new town are not known. The name, Cass, was decided on before May 24, 1900. The first publication of the name was in the Covington *Sentinel*. In an account of the work being planned at the mouth of Leatherbark, it stated simply, "The place will be known as Cass."[23] The first letter in the company records using the name, Cass, is from Shaffer to Slaymaker dated August 2, 1900. References to the town prior to that time used the name Leatherbark and Shaffer used the return address, Green Bank, on his letters.[24]

The name was in honor of Joseph K. Cass, a native of Coshocton, Ohio. Mr. Cass was owner of Morrison and Cass Paper Company of Tyrone, Pennsylvania. A merger of this company with the West Virginia Pulp and Paper Company of West Virginia during the summer of 1899 provided needed capital for the new lumber and pulp venture.[25] Mr. Cass was vice-president of the newly formed West Virginia Pulp and Paper Company of Delaware and was an incorporator of the West Virginia Spruce Lumber Company.

As the town was planned, the need for a better road to provide access to Green Bank and points east became evident. The original road from Green Bank led over Little Mountain north of the town site. It was too steep in places for heavy wagon traffic. Shaffer, on behalf of the company, offered the Pocahontas County Court five hundred dollars and the services of Mr. Boal, a company surveyor, if a road would be built down Deer Creek Valley thus avoiding crossing over the hill.[26]

Mr. Boal and Harvey Cromer began locating the road in September, 1900, but by September 25, the county court had still not made a decision. The local residents were in favor of a good wagon road to Cass except for Mr. Hughes, who lived on a farm east of Cass and did "considerable kicking."[27] In September, 1901, $342 was charged to "Making County Road" by the West Virginia Spruce Lumber Company.[28] Once the Greenbrier Division of the C&O was completed in 1901, practically all transportation to and from Cass was by rail, and a good road to Green Bank was of less importance for a time.[29]

In October, 1900, one of the problems of the new company was solved when a telegraph line was completed to Cass.[30] Until that time, telegraph messages had to be taken by horseback to Green Bank and sent from there.

Telephone service reached Cass during the week of October 18, 1900, via a branch of the Pocahontas Telephone Company's line, from Ronceverte to Elkins, which ran through Green Bank.[31] The lumber company developed its own telephone system with phones at the main office, the superintendent's house, the doctor's house, and the trainmaster's house. Lines were later extended to Spruce, Slaty Fork, and Bemis.

One of the many important details involved in setting up the new town was established a post office. J. G. and D. L. Luke initiated the Twentieth Century by arranging a meeting with Senator Stephen B. Elkins in Washington on January 19, 1901, and were assured that the post office at Cass would be established as soon as the necessary paper work could be done.[32]

The establishment of a lumber town was a carefully planned affair. On March 7, 1901, R. H. Boal was given the task of surveying the main residential section of the town, and the building of houses commenced soon afterward.[33]

Three north-south streets were laid out and named Front Street, Main Street and Spruce Street. Luke, Emory and Short Streets intersected these.[34] The general layout was to have the houses in three series of two rows except Front Street which had one row of houses. Each row of houses faced a street. An alley extended between the rows separating the backyards. Streets were planned fifty feet wide and the alleys were fifteen feet wide. A woodshed and an outside toilet in the backyard of each home lined the alleys. Running water and electricity were supplied to each house by the company.[35]

Work on the first group of six houses progressed rapidly. They were located on the slope above the Chesapeake and Ohio Railroad. The street was known as Railroad Avenue at first, but the name was soon changed to Front Street. William M. Siple and his family moved into the first house built. The second house was used to house workers who boarded at the Siple home for a time.[36]

The first houses built had four rooms, two upstairs and two downstairs. The front rooms were fourteen feet by fifteen feet and the two back rooms were ten feet by fourteen feet. A hall and stairs were on one side of the house.[37] Surviving documentation shows that, in early October, 1901, a check to a Mr. McClintic for three hundred dollars for plastering the houses was sent to Shaffer.[38] The plasterers were boarded by A. M. Oliver.[39] Leases for renting the houses were prepared in the New York office in late October, 1901.[40]

Most later company houses were built on a simple plan with a large living room, kitchen and dining room on the first floor and three bedrooms on the second floor. The rooms were plastered over wooden lath. Wallpaper and other improvements were usually added by the renter, using material supplied by the company.[41] The houses were built on lots that were fifty feet by one hundred feet.

Two powerful social forces were early at work in the rapidly growing town. One, Christianity, was formally introduced by Rev. Henry McLaughlin on January 13, 1901. The *Pocahontas Times* reported as follows:

> Rev. Henry W. McLaughlin, [whose regular charge was Liberty Presbyterian Church near Greenbanks and Baxter Church at Stony Bottom],[42] preached in the Company dining room Sunday evening, January 13, to a congregation composed of five women and forty or fifty men. His text was John, XIII 34, 35.[43] He has the honor of having preached the first sermon at this place. Cass will undoubtedly become a city, and then it can be said that the first sermon in this city was preached in the camp dining room on the second Sunday of the Twentieth Century.[44]

He preached a second sermon at Cass on Sunday, February 10, and planned to return March 10.[45]

The other social force, "John Barleycorn," drew considerably more adherents. Most of the land lying east of the Greenbrier River was not initially purchased by the company, and directly across the river from the company-owned town, private interests developed businesses including speakeasies and hotels. This section of town was called Brooklyn for several years and was later known as East Cass.[46] Brooklyn was connected with company-owned West Cass by a wire suspension footbridge that crossed near where the present highway bridge stands.[47] Wagons, supplies, and horseback riders forded the river just below the suspension bridge.

Drinking, brawling, and violence plagued East Cass. The first published indication of things to come was in the *Pocahontas Times* of March 7, 1901, which stated, "It looks as if intoxicants were sold in great quantity in the neighborhood. It seems that proof could easily be found should it be desired," a week later it stated, "drunkenness and disorder are on the increase in Cass."[48]

The first accidental death of a workman in the vicinity of Cass occurred on November 23, 1901, when Chesapeake and Ohio Railroad locomotive No. 85 collided with a handcar, killing William Walker, a C&O employee. The accident occurred at a curve above Cass.[49]

Drunkenness was the cause of a particularly common and insidious accident. Sometimes a man started walking back to camp along the railroad after a weekend of drinking and carousing in Cass, often taking a good supply of spirits with him. He became tired and sleepy, sat down to rest, and went to sleep on the tracks, only to be sent to his eternal resting place by the next train.

The first victim of such an accident was David McDonald, who was run over by the log train in January, 1902, as he was lying in a "drunken stupor" on the tracks.[50]

Drunkenness became an increasing problem to the town. On February 21, 1902, Shaffer reported to Slaymaker, "There are two more speakeasies in the course of erection below here, and think we will soon have to do something to put a stop to it, as the place is today full of drunks."[51] Again on February 25, 1902, he wrote that "Slavin and Durbin have purchased a lot from Burner – 'to run a feed store,' but you can imagine the kind of feed store."[52]

Attempts at law enforcement were ineffectual. On February 26, 1902, Shaffer wrote, "Squire Hudson held court to the sorrow of two speakeasy proprietors. One was held in $100 bail and the other, Mr. Hevener, under $600."[53] On March 24 he wrote, "The proprietors of the speakeasies were arrested this a.m."[54] A few days later he reported, "The speakeasy men, Geiger and Hevener, were jailed but are back in Cass today. Slavin was not taken at all and is doing as much business as ever. Kincaid was in custody of Constable Gum and succeeded in getting him drunk and made his escape. Looks as though the only effectual way of breaking up speakeasies is with dynamite."[55] An injunction in favor of John R. Hevener against Andrew Geiger and others for maintaining a nuisance in the form of a speakeasy at Cass was granted in August, 1902.[56]

Provisions for fighting fire were among the first things accomplished in the new town and by September, 1901, a gang of Italians were putting in a large reservoir at the top of the hill near the mill to store water for fire fighting. Hydrants to connect with 6-inch pipe were ordered from R. D. Wood and Company, Philadelphia.[57] They were spaced along the main street of town and at the mill and yard. The fire hydrants were later enclosed in small locked buildings known as "valve houses," which also contained fire hose, wrenches, etc. R. D. Wood and Company furnished 350 feet of 6-inch pipe, 400 feet of 8-inch pipe, 300 feet of 10-inch pipe and 150 feet of 12-inch pipe, at $27.40 per ton.[58] To complete the basic fire fighting equipment, a 1,000-gallon Knowles Steam fire pump was purchased for $750.00.[59]

The lack of skill and care in the erection of some of the early buildings, especially those not owned by the company, caused the first fire in Cass when the building occupied by J. H. Bird's Feedstore and Cash Grocery in East Cass was burned to the ground on February 7, 1902. Shaffer wrote, "There was no air stirring or it would have been 'goodby Brooklyn.' The fire was caused by a defective flue."[60] The fire was discovered by the crew of a C&O engine across the river, and numerous shrill blasts from the engine's whistle brought streams of men and boys who crossed the new wire suspension bridge from the main part of town. They prevented spread of the fire to J. K. L. Dysard's store and other buildings.[61]

Building of the company-owned part of town continued at an accelerated pace during 1902. Work had commenced on the hotel on February 27, and it was under roof by April 23. Laths for the hotel were among the first cut by the new mill and were largely culls.[62]

A company store, The Pocahontas Supply Company, was formed in 1900. In 1902, a large building to house this store was constructed west of the C&O depot. Another building adjacent to the Company Store was built to accomodate S. B. Nethken & Company, a store that supplied meat to the lumber camps and the town. By September, 1902, a two-story office, located south of Nethken's Meat Store, and several additional houses were under construction.[63]

Dr. Julian D. Arbuckle, a native of Greenbrier County and a graduate of the Richmond School of Medicine, came to Cass in 1901 to serve as a doctor.[64] He was joined in late 1901 by his brother, Dr. J. A. Arbuckle, who stayed until 1903 when Dr. Henry Ward Randolph, also a graduate of Richmond Medical College, came to Cass.[65]

Dr. Randolph related that on his first day in Cass he performed a caesarean operation, using the kitchen table as an operating table with one scalpel, one pair of scissors, two forceps and just enough silkworm gut and catgut to sew the patient up. Next he had to operate on a man for appendicitis. This operation was performed on the front porch using a shutter placed on two barrels for an operating table. People sat on the rail watching and a woman was present to keep the flies away.[66]

On another occasion, a teamster who had fallen on a stump was brought to Dr. Randolph. The man's heart was beating but no pulse was evident. Dr. Randolph put two quarts of salt water in his veins, operated, tied off the ruptured splenic artery, and put in two quarts more of salt water. The patient lived.[67]

In 1903, the company built a two-story hospital on Main Street, on the hill behind the Company Store. The lower floor had a kitchen on one side separated by a hall from the dining room on the other side. There was space for twelve beds on the upper floor.[68]

In addition to their town and lumber camp duties, Drs. Arbuckle and Randolph traveled through much of the surrounding country to deliver babies and to attend the sick and injured. Babies were almost always delivered in the home, usually with the aid of a midwife. Travel was by foot, on horseback, buggy, or by rail on the train or on a foot-powered speeder which had flanged wheels to allow travel on the railroad track. Dr. Randolph recalled walking thirteen hours in a snowstorm at ten degrees below zero to get from Durbin to Cass.[69] Frequent trips to the logging woods were made. If possible, they rode the log train; if that wasn't feasible, the speeder was called into action. Going up the mountain on a speeder was hard work, but the speeder was light and could be lifted off the tracks if a train was met or if cars, loaders, or other obstructions needed to be by-passed.[70]

The method of payment of the doctor was similar to that used in many other company towns. The doctor's dues, of seventy-five cents per month for a single man and one dollar for a married man and his family, were deducted from each employee's pay. The fee allowed the employee and his family unlimited office visits. In many cases, medicine was dispensed by the doctor without additional cost. The practice led to much abuse on the part of some families, and numerous unnecessary visits to the doctor were made.

A similar check-off system of hospital dues was used. After the hospital was discontinued at Cass, a similar plan with the Greenbrier General Hospital at Ronceverte was worked out. Dues were $1.25 per month for family coverage.

Dental needs of the new town were taken care of by Dr. C. L. Austin who also owned the Cass Drug Store in East Cass and by Dr. Ernest B. Hill. In addition, Dr. Jarrett, a visiting dentist from Marlinton, set up an office in Cass one day each week. By 1903, Dr. M. Stout periodically spent a week or ten days at Cass. He alternated his Cass visits with visits to Durbin, Collins (Hosterman), Clover Lick, Academy (Hillsboro) and Marlinton. He advertised "All kinds of modern dentistry including gold crown, bridge work, and artificial teeth mounted on plates of every description known to the profession."[71]

The first school in Cass, with one room, was located on Main Street. Miss Emma Burner, the first teacher, opened school there in 1901 with about sixteen pupils.[72]

Organization of town government at Cass was accomplished with an incorporation election on August 2, 1902. The results were 38 for incorporating and two against.[73] The town was incorporated on August 15, 1902. A copy of the incorporation order follows:

At a Special Term of the Circuit Court of Pocahontas County, West Virginia, held at the Court House thereof on the 15th. day of August, 1902, the following order was entered of record:

IN THE MATTER OF THE INCORPORATION OF CASS:

A certificate under oath of Chas. A. Fletcher, Jas. K. Jackson and Harry J. Scott, was this day filed showing that a majority of all the qualified voters residing in the following boundary, to-wit: Beginning at an apple tree at the south end of the lumber dock 65 feet from the center of the railroad S. 81-45 E 200 feet to a white oak on the bank of the River by a large red oak, N. 73 E 390 feet crossing the River to a red oak above the County road corner to the lands of Allen E. Burner with his lines, S 60-30 E 470 feet to two chestnut saplings, Burner's Corner, continued same course 198 feet to a leaning chestnut on side of a ridge, N 88 W 720 feet to a stake in a bottom, thence about N 35 W 2542 feet to a stake, N. 50 E 3250 feet to a stake on Leather Bark Creek, thence down the same about S 35 E 960 feet to a sugar in the bottom of said creek S 7-30 W 1180 feet to a stake 21 feet from the center of railroad on the east side of said railroad S 30 W 850 feet to a stake S 55-30 E 27 feet to the point of beginning, containing 162 acres; have been given in due form of law in favor of the incorporation of the Town of Cass, in the County of Pocahontas, bounded as herein set forth. And it appearing to the satisfaction of the Court that all the provisions of Chapter 47 in Code of West Virginia, have been compiled with the applicants for said corporations, the said town is duly authorized within the corporate limits aforesaid to exercise all the corporate powers conferred by said chapter from and after the date of a certificate of incorporation which the Clerk of this Court is directed to issue upon application by said petitioners. And it is further ordered that C.A. Fletcher, Jas. K. Jackson and Harry J. Scott be and they are hereby appointed commissioners to hold the first election of officers in said town.

A TRUE COPY

TESTEE:

____
                                          Clerk.

By ____
                                   Deputy Clerk.

W. T. Newcome was chosen first mayor.[75] (a record of town officials from 1902-1985 is found in Appendix X).

Following is a listing of town businesses and public figures in 1902-03:[76]

Population 350. Stage to Green Bank, Arbovale, Boyer and Traveler's Repose.

J.S. Matthews, postmaster
J.D. Arbuckle, physician
C.L. Austin, dentist
Brown & Ruhl, saw mill
Cass Drug Store [owned by C.L. Austin]
Cass Jewelry Company
B.F. Conrad, notary
Samuel Cooper, general store
G.O. English, railroad express
A.S. Gillespie, notary
Cass Hotel, Robert R. Mason, proprietor
Jasper S. Mathews, insurance
W.T. Newcome, mayor
George D. Oliver, general store
Pocahontas Hospital, Dr. J.D. Arbuckle in charge
Pocahontas Supply Company
H.W. Randolph, physician
Ware and Hide, restaurant
WV Spruce Lumber Company, sawmill
Ernest Hill, dentist [visiting from Marlinton 5 days each month][77]

In February, 1903, the company was "putting down some good plank walk in Cass," and the suspension bridge had been rebuilt and made safe.[78]

Brooklyn (East Cass) was the stereotype of an early logging town. Here were located speakeasies, boardinghouses and gambling places that lured the hundreds of loggers when they came to town after long weeks or months working in the woods. Whiskey was shipped in regularly, and in 1902, G. O. English, C&O freight agent at Cass, stated, "There has not been a time in the last six months that there has been a consignment of whiskey in the depot for parties whose purpose is to make illegal sale of same."[79]

Fights among the loggers or between them and townspeople were too common to be recorded in the county paper but the frequent arrests, murders and fatal accidents were usually reported.

In 1902, Elmer D. Burner was appointed Town Sergeant and began largely ineffectual attempts to bring things under control. He was soon nicknamed "King Brady" after a dime-novel policeman of that name.[80] In September, 1902, he raided a house in East Cass where a poker game was going on and arrested Grant Hullihan and a man named Cross. Mayor Anderson fined them each ten dollars and costs. Laws providing such light punishments had little effect in deterring lawbreakers.[81]

Sergeant Burner was kept busy, and on September 5, 1902, he arrested four woodsmen for "flimflamming" R. S. Mann of Hinton out of a one hundred dollar watch and a twenty-five dollar gun. The four men arrested, Rider, Stern, Phillips and Kelly, were locked in a boxcar, because the jail at Cass was not yet finished. They set the boxcar on fire and got a good smoking before anyone noticed it burning.[82]

In addition to the unsavory establishments in East Cass, other legitimate businesses were started there. One of the first businesses, a clothing store owned by Samuel Cooper, was located along the road east of the bridge. It was sold in February, 1903, to Mike Finger, a "wide-awake merchant from Horton." Finger immediately had a half-price sale featuring such things as:

$2.50 for suits and overcoats reduced from	$ 5.00
5.00 for suits and overcoats reduced from	10.00
7.75 for suits and overcoats reduced from	15.50
9.25 for suits and overcoats reduced from	18.50
1.75 for shoes reduced from	3.50
.75 for shoes reduced from	1.50
.50 for shoes reduced from	1.00
.25 for shoes reduced from	.50[83]

The year 1902 ended on a pleasant note when "The first wedding in the town of Cass was celebrated at Hotel Moore, December 31, 1902, when Mr. James B. Sutton and Miss Charlotte Friel was [sic] made man and wife by Rev. J. W. McNeil." After the wedding, the bride and groom were served a nice dinner by waiters at the hotel. Afterward, the newlyweds left for Green Bank where they made their home for a time.[84]

In February, 1903, one of the first barbershops, run by John Will Carpenter, was opened.[85]

In an attempt to control the drinking problem, two additional special policemen, C. L. C. Burner[86] and Allen Eugene Burner, were hired. On April 23, 1903, C. L. C. Burner shot G. L. Osborne in the leg after Osborne had fled with a man who had resisted arrest by Mayor Newcome. There was considerable doubt as to the necessity of the shooting and both C. L. C. Burner and Allen Burner, who was with him at the time, were charged with felonious shooting and were bound over to await the action of the grand jury. The charges were dismissed.

This was C. L. C. Burner's third shooting scrape during the five or six years he had been a lawman. The report in the *Pocahontas Times* blamed Burner as being too quick with his gun and he promptly sent in a contrasting report putting all the blame on Osborne.[87]

Tragedy struck at Cass in July, 1903, when George Galford, a woodsman employed by the West Virginia Spruce Lumber Company, attempted suicide. He was taken to the hospital at Cass where Dr. Randolph rendered surgical assistance. Galford was then taken to Hinton for X rays where he lived three weeks before he died. His suicide was attributed to the effects of "pig's ear liquor."[88]

Frequent efforts to control the sale of whiskey by the Town Sergeant or other police officers were made. Raids, in response to warrants by local citizens, were frequent. The Burners were prominent in such efforts. For example, Miss Emma Burner, the first schoolteacher at Cass, dressed as a man and went to establishments in East Cass, saw alcohol being sold in several places and bought alcohol herself at one place. She, along with her brother, Allen E. Burner, swore out warrants and the "principal business of Cass other than the lumber business was raided." Officer Paris D. Yeager arrested Gratz Slaven, James Sizemore, J. W. Graham, James Benson, Arthur De Nio, Joe Griffith, and John Herbert for illicit sale of intoxicants.[89] No account is given of the disposition of these cases, but the usual punishment was a fine of twenty-five to one hundred dollars.

Other, more virtuous, groups began to organize in Cass as the social structure materialized. On November 12, 1903, Riverside Lodge No. 124, Ancient Free and Accepted Masons was chartered. The first lodge meetings were in the Austin Building in East Cass. On February 7, 1907, the West Virginia Spruce Lumber Company deeded a plot of land to the lodge.[90] It was located on Front Street across Luke Street from the Mountain Inn Hotel. A lodge hall consisting of a two-story building, 24' by 24' by 48', was later built at a cost of fifteen hundred dollars.[91] A list of masters and secretaries in this lodge is found in Appendix K.

Adjoining the Masonic Hall on the south was the Cass Presbyterian Church, convened on March 12, 1905, by the Rev. Asa

Watkins[92] and Ruling Elder J. S. Matthews. Officers of the new church were J. S. Matthews and Dr. Ward Randolph, ruling elders; Dr. J. D. Arbuckle, James Kirkpatrick and B. F. Conrad, deacons.[93] The original membership was fifteen persons.[94] The bell was donated by the West Virginia Spruce Lumber Company.[95]

Directly behind the Masonic Hall, across the alley, the town hall and jail was erected in late 1902. The jail with four cells, barred windows and an iron door with a massive outside lock was placed on ground level with the council room and mayor's office above it. On the west side of the jail was a pen known as the lockup where cows, caught roaming the town, were placed.[96]

An Odd Fellows Hall was built along Main Street south of the original schoolhouse.[97]

Local hauling of freight, feed, etc. was done by horse or mule-drawn drays. Jimmie Sevoy and Ed Jackson were the first dray-men.[98] The stable for mules and dray horses was located on the hill along Main Street near the hospital. Horses that were injured in the woods were also kept in this barn. In warm weather, they were allowed to roam in the company pasture until they recuperated.[99]

A slaughterhouse was placed along the tracks north of the machine shop. When the logging was in full swing, about twenty-six head of cattle and roughly the same number of hogs were butchered each week. They supplied the meat for Neth-kin's Meat Market which provided enough meat for the logging camps on Cheat Mountain.[100] A camp of one hundred men could eat a beef and a couple of hogs in a week's time.[101]

An icehouse, thirty-five by forty-five feet in size, was built by the company along the west bank of the Greenbrier River just north of the bridge.[102] It had a double-walled construction with about a foot of sawdust between the walls. Ice was cut from the river in winter and stored in the icehouse for use during the following summer. Ice was harvested usually in late January or February when it was about ten inches or more thick.[103] Sawdust was piled over and between the layers of ice for insulation. Ice was used by the company to keep meat cold for use in the lum-ber camps and was sold by the Company Store to town residents, as long as the supply of ice lasted, which was usually the middle of the summer. Ice was then brought in from Ronceverte by box-car loads.[104]

"Man killed at Cass" read the headline in the *Pocahontas Times* on May 5, 1904. The story reported the first of many homicides that would occur in the growing town. A man named David Green was walking up the steps of the Cass Hotel when he met Walter Smith and his brother, Joe Smith. There was bad blood between Green and Walter Smith, and a quarrel ensued. Smith hit Green on the head and the latter drew a pistol and shot Smith through the heart. Green was tried and acquitted on the basis of self-defense.[105]

Violence in the many lumber towns along the Greenbrier was common. August 14, 1905, was an especially disastrous day for Pocahontas County. On this day, eleven persons met violent deaths in the county.[106] The largest number of these, killed in a single incident, were eight Italians who were blown to "Kingdom Come" by dynamite exploding under their cabin at Dunlevie, West Virginia.

There were two theories concerning this explosion. One held that the Italians had stolen the dynamite and had hidden it under their cabin. It was supposedly detonated when someone inside, probably drunk, fired a bullet through the floor.

The second, more plausible, and widely believed theory, was that the Italians were murdered, by persons unknown, who objected to foreigners taking jobs from Americans. This theory was supported by the report that an attempt had been made to blow up an Italian shanty on Cheat Mountain several weeks before.[107]

It was evident to all that a tough man was needed to keep order in the town of Cass and in 1905 such a man was obtained when Lincoln S. "Link" Cochran was appointed constable. One of his ploys was to secretly engage several deputies, ride with them out of town on the train, stop the train a couple of miles away and walk back to surprise lawbreakers. One such raid in January, 1906, netted Joe Griffith, Jack O'Brine [sic], Bill Craver and Les Kennisen and resulted in the confiscation of ten barrels of beer.[108]

Renewed efforts to control drinking at Cass were made as a result of the death of Fry Bird in January, 1906. This was reported in the *Pocahontas Times* as follows: "Fry Bird, 50 years old, was killed by a train at the Galford's Crossing. He had been drinking and sat down on the tracks and went to sleep. The view of the track was obscured by a curve that prevented the engineer from seeing him."[109]

Another violent death was attributed to alcohol when a lumber-jack named Jack Brown was hit at Cass by a C&O passenger train on February 11, 1906. Both legs and one arm were cut off by the train. He had been drinking and sat down close to the tracks.[110]

Violence again erupted in July, 1906, when Town Sergeant C. L. C. Burner shot and wounded Jim Phillips, who attempted to run when arrested for theft of jewelry.[111]

In August, 1906, warrants were issued and sent to the town sergeant, C. L. C. Burner, to raid the "Pig's Ear" run by E. H. Ayers at Cass. He found only a small amount of booze. However, another warrant was sent to Pat Simmons, who was raiding Dunlevie, twenty miles north of Cass. He returned to Cass and his first victim was Sergeant Burner. In Burner's wareroom adjoining Ayers' "Pig's Ear," he found one hundred cases of whiskey of three gallons each and a large amount of Mumm's Extra Dry.[112]

Not being satisfied, Simmons obtained another warrant and additional help and raided E. H. Ayers' place and captured three barrels of whiskey, 12,600 bottles of beer and another lot of Mumm's Extra Dry. Ayers was also accused of having gambling tables in his establishment.[113]

John Barleycorn extracted his toll again on September 23, 1906, when "A man named Donahue, while under the influence of liquor, was killed while attempting to board a morning train at Cass. . . . The wheels passed over him and he was almost cut in two but he lived several hours."[114]

Fire is always a threat in a town made almost entirely of wood and on Sunday, December 30, 1906, "One of the worst fires ever experienced in the Greenbrier Valley wiped out the Brooklyn section of Cass. . . . The fire originated in Jacob Cooper's department store and spread to adjoining buildings with incredible speed and within a short time eleven houses were on fire and very little of their contents could be saved."

Cooper lost his entire stock of dry goods and general merchandise, valued at $15,000. Another building, known as the Drysard Building owned by Samuel Sheets, was burned. It was valued at $2,000. Adjoining Cooper's were the Byrd and Slavin buildings owned by Dr. Austin. They were both destroyed with a loss of $3,000. Also burned were Finger's General Store, Cross' Restaurant and J. W. Graham's store, all owned by Elmer Burner and valued at $3,200; other losses were: C. L. Hamilton, barbershop, $1,000; Joe Griffith, household goods, $2,500; W. B. Cross, restaurant, $1,000;

S. B. Rosewell, restaurant, $900; John Herbert, barbershop with a value of $250; personal losses of J. W. Graham were $500 and David Finger lost $9,000 in merchandise. This fire left no building standing in Brooklyn (East Cass) except a few dwelling houses.[115]

Rebuilding began almost immediately with most of the former businesses surviving for a time. Additions soon after the fire of 1906 were Max Curry's General Store, W. A. "Shorty" Brill's Restaurant and a store owned by Siegel. Curry's General Store was at the end of the bridge on the north side of the road, Brill's was on the south side. Brill's was of brick construction, one of only two brick buildings in Cass. The Siegel building was built of cement blocks manufactured by the Miracle Hollow Block Company.[116]

Floods were a frequent threat to parts of the town. The Greenbrier River is usually a lazy, low-water stream; however, during an occasional flood, it becomes a raging torrent. Floods are especially apt to occur in the spring when the ice goes out. The "ice going out" presents an unforgettable experience. Large chunks of ice ten to fifteen inches thick and as much as ten feet square churn, grind, and flip down the rapidly moving stream. These chunks are crowded out on the banks where they lay for weeks after the ice floe. Occasionally, an ice jam occurs, which increases danger from the flood.

During the winter of 1907-08 snow piled and drifted for weeks in the headwaters of the Greenbrier until there was an accumulation of five feet. In February, 1908, a sudden warm rain fell in torrents, and a warm south wind began melting the snow. Within a few hours, the water rose and the ice began to break up in the Greenbrier. The dam at the mill at Cass checked the flow for a time as the ice piled up behind it.

The railroad north of Cass, which was twenty feet higher than the river, was blocked by large chunks of ice. Eleven telegraph poles set along the tracks were knocked down. In clearing the way, an engine had its head lamp torn off by the ice. At 5:00 p.m. on February 14, the fastenings of the milldam broke, and for several hours the river ran full from side to side with ice, timber, and treetops. The business section of East Cass was flooded with several feet of water, but the ice chunks did not do any damage to the town.[117]

On November 3, 1907, an incident at Wanless, five miles north of Cass, resulted in the death of Howard Galford, age twenty-three years. He and Amos Cassell had been quarreling over a young lady they were both interested in. During the quarrel, Cassell reached up on the wall and took down a gun. When Galford moved toward him, Cassell turned with the gun and shot, killing Galford instantly.[118]

In 1907, a Methodist church was built on a rise along the Back Mountain Road about one mile southwest of Cass. It served the people who lived within several miles along the road. It was built on land owned by Joe McLaughlin and became known as the McLaughlin Church. The Reverend Harry Blackhurst preached the first sermon in this church.[119]

The population of Cass was steadily increasing and the need for a larger grade school was evident. In 1908, a new, three-room school was built on Spruce Street. The first principal of the new school was Burley B. Williams; C. F. Hull was primary teacher.[120]

Violence continued to trouble Cass. In September, 1908, a young Negro woman, wife of Jack Tyson, took a shot or two at her husband during a quarrel. She was locked up in the town jail and after a time she set fire to the contents. When the fire was discovered, she was dead from smoke inhalation.[121]

In 1909, a second Cold Run School was built on Cold Run near the McLaughlin Church. It served the farm families along the Back Mountain Road in that area. It had one large room and was heated by a wood- or coal-burning stove.[122]

A school serving families on the Back Mountain Road north of Cass was the Olliver School, built in 1904-05 and closed in 1938-39.[123] It was located in the turn in the road above the present Bill Simmons' home.

A CRESCENDO OF ACTIVITY:1910-1919

The second decade of the century at Cass began quietly. The grade school held its first graduation in 1911 with a class of seven: Lena Anderson, Maude Jackson, Esty Sharp, Bess Oliver, Alice Blackhurst, Albert Harouff, and Allen Blackhurst.[124]

The social event of the decade occurred on May 11, 1911, when the job superintendent, Emory P. Shaffer, and Pattie V. Hannah were married at Arbovale by Rev. J. S. Kennison. After a week or so, they returned to reside at Cass. For a short time they lived in rooms upstairs in the company office building. The hospital, which had closed, was renovated as a dwelling for them.[125]

Lawbreakers continued to plague the town. Cocaine as well as whiskey and wine were pushed by unscrupulous dealers and the *Pocahontas Times* for August 7, 1911, reported that the jail at

Marlinton was being filled with these men and noted that three sellers were brought from Cass. [126]

Also, in 1911, the Back Mountain Road was connected to Cass by a road that entered the town west of the Company Store. It met the old Back Mountain Road near the farm of Andy McCloud and the Olliver School. [127]

On April 1, 1912, a much-needed professional set up business in Cass when Dr. Frank C. Nickell, veterinarian, accepted an engagement with the company. [128] In addition to his duties as company veterinarian, Dr. Nickell treated the many cows, hogs and horses of the people in the neighboring countryside. His favorite diagnosis of a sick cow was "hollow-head and wolf-in-the-tail."

The county elections in 1912, brought about a change in law enforcement in Cass when L. S. "Link" Cochran was elected county sheriff, thus interrupting a successful and colorful career as town constable. He was succeeded as constable by Luther M. Foster. [129]

Dr. J. D. Arbuckle had a narrow escape on the Cass-Green Bank Road in December, 1912, when his horse "began to play" and stepped over the steep bank. The doctor escaped by jumping off over the horse's head but the horse (valued at $750) was killed. [130]

On December 5, 1912, another fatal accident involving the train at Cass occurred when Randolph Wees was killed. He was driving a dray wagon and the horse became frightened by the train. Mr. Wees was thrown under the train as he attempted to control the animal. [131]

Cass continued to prosper and many businesses were established in East Cass. A portent of things to come, however, occurred on February 7, 1913, when the wooden cab of a freight engine caught fire and burned, while the crew was warming at a nearby house. [132]

Less than a week later, on February 13, East Cass again suffered heavy loss by fire. It started in J. H. and Allie Griffith's boardinghouse and restaurant, spread to the barbershop and dwelling of J. W. Carpenter, then to the large store of Max Curry. Losses were estimated at five thousand dollars to Griffith, twenty-five hundred dollars to Carpenter and fifteen thousand dollars to Curry. In each case, insurance covered most of

at PETERSCREEK grade school all kids
drank out of same long handled dipper.
we were taught to put lip of dipper
under lip of mouth. Still do this

the estimated loss.[133] The damaged buildings were quickly replaced and business continued as usual.

A step forward in public health was taken in April, 1913, when the common drinking cup in public places was abolished by the State Legislature.[134]

On July 24, 1913, the east side of Cass came near to being burned out again. Odey Harouff was going home at 1:00 a.m. and discovered a fire in the rear of a building owned and occupied by Italians named Tony Sagatone and Jasper Maune. An alarm was given and the fire was put out.[135]

At 4:00 the same morning, another fire was discovered in the rear of an adjoining poolroom. An Italian named Rome was seen running from the building and was arrested. He was not convicted of the arson attempt. It is interesting to note that, at that time, setting fire to a building at night was a capital offense.[136]

January and July were sale months in the local department stores in Cass. On July 26, 1913, Jacob Cooper's Department Store ran a full-page ad in the *Pocahontas Times* offering prices as follows:

	Men's Clothing	
	regular price	*sale price*
suits	$ 8.00	$ 5.40
suits	10.00	6.60
suits	16.00	11.98
suits	20.00	14.40
trousers	2.00	1.19
trousers	3.00	1.80
trousers	6.00	3.98
	regular price	*sale price*
trousers	$ 3.00	$ 1.80
trousers	6.00	3.98
handkerchiefs	0.10	0.03
socks	0.15	0.07
shoes	4.00	2.98
dress shirts	0.75	0.39
work shirts	0.50	0.36
hats	1.25	0.89
	Ladies' Clothing	
shoes	$ 2.00	$ 1.39
shoes	2.50	1.89
corsets	1.25	0.89

Today when drinking out of a cup of unknown cleanliness I am still thinking of what I am doing.

Dry Goods

calicoes	$.035/yard
ginghams	.05/yard
India linen	.075/yard
floxon	.18/yard
lenaire	.135/yard
woolen goods	.79/yard
woolen goods	.39/yard
corset cover	.20/yard
flouncing/45 inch	.48/yard

At the same time J. Hamed and Brothers sale in their Cass store had even better bargains.[137]

Mens

Regular	$1.50	pants for	$ .98
	3.50	pants for	1.95
	4.50	pants for	2.95

All wool blue serge suits, regular $15 for $9.90
Oxfords, White House brand, patent leather, lace or
   button: regular $3.50 for $2.79
            regular   4.00 for 2.98

Ladies

Regular	$ .10	hose for	$0.07
	.25	hose for	0.19
	.50	hose for	0.38
	.75	petticoat	0.45
	1.50	petticoat	1.15
	1.00	gown	0.60
	.50	gown	0.39
	1.50	princess slip	0.98
	.75	white waists	0.39
	1.00	white waists	0.79
	1.50	maiden blouse	1.10
	1.00	ladies' washable skirt	0.79
	3.00	parama	1.69
	1.25	ladies' dresses	0.85

Ladies' oxfords, gun metal, tan and patent leather, lace or
   button:

Regular	$3.00	for	$2.19
	2.50	for	1.98
	$1.25	children's oxfords	$0.90
	1.50	misses' oxfords	1.19

2.00	boys' oxfords	1.48
0.25	skirts and blouses	0.19
0.25	children's caps for	0.13
$0.29	bleached turkish towels for	$0.10
0.60	bleached sheeting	0.42
0.15	pillow cases	0.10
0.25	yard oil cloth	0.18
1.50	lace window curtain	0.98
0.07	calico/yard	0.05
0.08	apron gingham/yard	0.05½
0.12	½ percale	0.09
0.20	fancy drape	0.18
0.50	all wool 36″ wide serge	0.39
0.35	worsted 34″ wide	0.23
0.40	linen 36″ wide	0.29
1.00	linen sheeting 90″ wide	0.84
0.50	corset	0.39
0.75	corset	0.45
1.00	corset	0.85
0.25	good roasted coffee	0.19
	7 cakes Octagon soap	0.25
0.25	can peaches, apricots, pears	0.17
	3 cans Silver Cow milk	0.23
0.10	can sourkraut	0.08
0.40	broom	0.24

A. A. Cutter shoes, the type favored by woodsmen, trainmen and millmen could be ordered from J. A. Hoover, Clothier at Marlinton, to be delivered by mail COD as follows:[138]

Genuine A. A. Cutter shoes, No. 40,	
heavy weight, delivered	$7.15
same, caulked	7.75
No. 39 middle-weight	6.15
same, caulked	6.25
No. 39 ½ middle-weight, 18″ tops	7.40
No. 50, heavyweight	8.15
No. 220, low top	3.80
No. 125, low top, tan	4.50

In 1915, a Ford touring car cost $570, a Ford Runabout cost $520. In addition, Henry Ford personally guaranteed a $50 rebate on every new car purchased. A Hupmobile cost from $950 to $1,400. A five-passenger Maxwell touring car cost $750. This price included a convertible top, a "Full 25 Horse-Power Engine (4 cylinders), Speedometer, all four tires the same size, Four Springs, Tire Holder, Presto Light Tank, High Tension Magneto, Three Speed Selective Transmission, Worm and Sector Steering Gear and Standard Brake Drums—all features of a high priced car." For the wealthy, a Chandler Six convertible could be bought for $1,295. This was a six-cylinder car that developed 50 horsepower and had "genuine hand-buffed leather seats— luxurious stream-lined body and a Golde patent one-man top, covered with Jiffy curtains."[139]

The year 1914 brought a devoted doctor to Cass. Dr. Uriah Hevener Hannah had gone to Spruce as a physician for the West Virginia Spruce Lumber Company in 1907, following his marriage to Laura Susanna Bock. The need for a doctor at Cass allowed them to move there in 1914. They purchased the large house and office built by Dr. Arbuckle near the hospital. Dr. Hannah became a legend in and around Cass. He had a widespread private practice throughout the town and countryside in addition to his duties as company doctor. House calls were the general rule for country doctors and he was kept busy visiting the sick or delivering babies in the homes. For many years Emma Susan "Granny" Bird,[140] a well-respected midwife, assisted in the delivery of babies. In addition, Dr. Hannah visited camps on Cheat, when necessary, to administer medical services. Dr. Hannah opened an office in a small building near his home and held regular office hours. Many drugs (calomel was a favorite) were given free to the patients.[141]

Prescriptions were filled at the drugstore located in the Company Store. The druggist[142] not only filled prescriptions but had a full line of patent medicines as well. A common practice was to buy back "ounce-bottles" (bottles marked off in ounce measurements) from youngsters in the town. They collected them from neighbors or eagerly searched for them in the Company Store trash pile located in East Cass. Five- to ten-ounce bottles could be sold for one cent each while larger bottles (twenty to twenty-five ounces) brought a nickel each.

During this time, a dental office was opened by Dr. Hammond in a small back room of the Masonic Hall. He was succeeded in about 1926 by Dr. Gregg of Durbin. Dr. Gregg's office was upstairs in the back of the Masonic Hall. He visited Cass two or three days a week.[143]

The Death Angel made many violent visits to the vicinity of Cass. On September, 1913, Layman Channell, aged nine years, ran in front of an engine in the lumberyard of the Deer Creek Lumber Company at Deer Creek. Two engines were traveling, one close behind the other. When the first passed, the youth ran across the tracks and was struck by the second.[144]

Almost a year later, on November 13, 1914, Robert Burns, aged twenty-four years, was killed at Stony Bottom while attempting to catch a freight train.[145]

"Mother and Children Burned" ran the headlines of the following story in the *Pocahontas Times,* February 4, 1915.

"One of the saddest occurrences in the whole history of the Greenbrier Valley was the burning to death of Mrs. George Doyle, her little daughter aged nine, and her son aged four, when their home at Cass was burned early Wednesday morning, February 3. Mr. Doyle was awakened by smoke and found the house to be afire. He let two of the children out of the window and then jumped out, but his wife was overcome and could not let the other two children out to him. By the time he got a ladder, the house was entirely on fire." The bodies were unrecognizable and all three were buried in the same coffin.[146]

The Doyle home was located on Main Street beside the moving picture theatre. Mrs. Doyle was about thirty years old and the daughter of P. S. Cutlip of Riverside, near Marlinton. The house belonged to Dr. J. W. Price of Marlinton.[147]

The spectre of fire was never long absent from the town. On February 25, 1915, the *Pocahontas Times* again ran the headlines "Fire at Cass." This concerned the burning of two buildings in East Cass belonging to Max Curry.[148]

On February 24, the fire started on the second floor of Curry's Department Store and quickly spread to the adjoining building, also owned by Curry. It was occupied by the Cass Jewelry Store, a pool hall and a residence. A third building, the barbershop of John W. Herbert, was badly damaged, and the store buildings of J. W. Brill, Finger-Siegel Company, and Jacob Cooper, all of which stood across the street, received some damage. A fire hose was stretched from across the river, and the fire was brought under control.[149] Loss in the fire was expected to reach twenty thousand dollars, part of which was covered by insurance.[150]

The above fire led to the unfolding of a bizarre story that would have sold in any dime novel of the day. The story begins in the late 1800s in Lincoln County, West Virginia, where a girl grew up by the name of Mattie Curry. She became a schoolteacher and opened a store at Dingess, Mingo County. Within a few years, the store burned and Mattie moved away.

Soon after 1900 she went to Cincinnati, had an operation performed, and thereafter Miss Mattie Curry became Mr. Max Curry. He later married and came to Pocahontas County to live. He and his wife first opened a store, along the railroad south of Cass, at Clover Lick, but then moved to Cass where he built a large store in East Cass and opened business.

On February 13, 1913, fire broke out in a hotel adjoining his store and both buildings, along with others, were destroyed. Curry collected about fifteen thousand dollars insurance, rebuilt his store and built some dwelling houses.

Curry then began an elaborate scheme. He imported to Cass a young man named William Kitchen, from Portsmouth, Ohio, and represented him as a businessman. He had a sales contract executed to show that Kitchen had bought one of his stores for two thousand dollars cash.

Kitchen had been married shortly before coming to Cass to an adopted sister of Max Curry's wife; however, at Cass, he paid court to Miss Maud Jackson, posing as a single man. Curry made a disastrous mistake by concealing the fact that Kitchen was already married and on January 19, 1915, Kitchen and Maud Jackson were wed.

Kitchen's first wife was young, but not naive. She began a search for her missing husband — a search that ended with Kitchen being jailed for bigamy.[151]

In questioning Kitchen about his relations with Curry, officials learned that Curry had told Kitchen that he had hired a man to burn his store in the 1913 fire. Further investigation brought to light a man named Arch Dilley, who confessed that he had been hired by Curry in 1913 to burn his store. Curry was to pay him $750 of which only $65 was paid two years later.

Curry was arrested for arson and at the trial in Circuit Court in April, 1915, yet another person, J. Henry "Peg-leg" Rider, testified that Curry offered him the 1913 arson job. He refused but put Curry in touch with the above-mentioned Arch Dilley who confessed he had done it. Rider was paid twenty-five dollars for his part in the deal.

The jury's verdict was like a "Crack of Doom." Curry was found guilty of "procuring his store burned in 1913 for the purpose of defrauding the insurance company" and was sentenced to six years in the state penitentiary. Max Curry carried his case to the State Supreme Court, and in June, 1915, that body refused a writ of error and he began a six-year penitentiary term.[152]

Arch Dilley was sentenced to three years in the penitentiary. "Peg-leg" Rider was also sent to the penitentiary for his part in the case.

Max Curry's wife, Lillian, was charged with setting fire to the store in 1915 but was acquitted of having any knowledge of the affair.[153]

The years 1913-14 were years of expansion for the town of Cass. In November 1913, construction of an extract plant at Deer Creek began. It was completed in 1914[154] and was operated by a West Virginia Pulp & Paper Company subsidiary known as the Industrial Chemical Company of New York. Tanning and dye extracts were made there.

In order to house workers for what became known simply as the Extract Plant, eleven houses were built along the bank of Cold Run south of Cass. This area soon became known as "Slab Town." The largest house in this addition, located near the mouth of Cold Run, was occupied by Arthur Moulton, superintendent of the Extract Plant.

These houses were supplied with electricity by the company. Water was supplied by wells and hand pumps. Several houses used a single well. There was no inside plumbing.

Business establishments in the company-owned part of town, lying west of the river, were dominated by the Pocahontas Supply Company Store located on the hillside above the C&O depot. The Cass Hotel, later called the Mountain Inn and also owned by the company, was south of the Company Store along the main road. The first proprietor, C. A. Fletcher, was followed by Amos Gillespie and then by Robert R. Mason.[155] In 1903, Jimmy Kirkpatrick, a highly esteemed cook at Camp 3 on Cheat, was brought to Cass to run the hotel.[156] It was later run for many years by John E. Cruikshanks.[157]

Permanent guests at the Mountain Inn were mostly mill and train workers. The $1.00 to $1.50 per day charge was withheld from the worker's paycheck and included board as well as the room. After 1920, the hotel boasted four indoor bathrooms. The men's bathroom was at one end of each hallway, the women's at the other end. A pitcher, washbowl, and towel were supplied with each room. Rooms also had a "slop-jar" (a two-gallon metal chamber pot) and a spittoon. Guests supplied their own soap.[158]

Competition with the Mountain Inn for the weekend lumberman's trade was successfully provided by three hotels in East Cass, the River View Hotel, the Central Hotel, and the Loggers' Home.

The River View Hotel was located a short way north along the old Green Bank Road on what became known as "Dirty Street." The River View had two floors. The first floor had four large rooms; a kitchen, dining room, a lobby, and living quarters for the manager. Guest rooms were on the second floor.

The River View was not blessed with inside plumbing. Outhouses were located across the road along the river. Men had merely to cross the road and walk a short distance. Women had to cross the road, walk through a coal and woodshed and through a covered area to reach the outhouse. At night the trip was made by hand-held coal oil lantern or by candlelight, for there were no electric lights.

Guests could obtain a drink in the kitchen from a water bucket and a common dipper.[159] A pitcher of water could be taken to their rooms for drinking and for washing in the morning. A washbowl or pan was provided in each room.

One "outstanding" feature of the River View Hotel was a "park" located across the road next to the river. This was a platform about 24 by 24 feet with wooden benches but no roof. Shade was provided by a large cucumber tree.[160] The River View Hotel was run by John Peter Cross, and then, for a time, by James Breakiron and later by Sid Church.[161]

The Central Hotel, located on the east side of the Green Bank Road where it bends southward, was owned and operated for many years by John Peter Cross. Like the River View, it also lacked any type of plumbing. There were two outhouses on the hillside behind the hotel. These were reached by a 50-foot catwalk that led from the second floor. It was twenty feet off the ground. A semblance of light was provided by a 25-watt light bulb at the end of the catwalk. Power was provided by a 32-volt gasoline Delco generator.

The Central Hotel had a kitchen, a dining room, and a lobby on the first floor. Two buckets of water and a dipper provided drinking water for customers. Buckets were refilled when needed from a pump located at the River View Hotel.[162]

Directly across the road from the Central Hotel was the largest building in East Cass. This four-story hotel was known as the Loggers' Home and soon became known as the "White Elephant." It was built around 1907 by Elmer D. Burner. He and his family operated it and lived there for a time. Like the other buildings in East Cass, there was no plumbing. Outhouses were outback and reached by a walk.

Like the River View and the Central Hotel, the Loggers' Home was heated only by a coal and wood stove in the lobby and the cookstove in the kitchen. Fires were allowed to burn out by about 10:00 p.m. and were kindled again about 4:00 a.m. It took two hours to get the lobby warm. Guest rooms were unheated, and ice would freeze in the water pitchers on cold nights.[163]

The Loggers' Home had a nice restaurant. It was lit by eight hanging gasoline lamps whose mantles gave off a brilliant white light.[164]

Other establishments along the main street of East Cass included Samuel Cooper's (later Jacob Cooper's) General Store; David Finger's General Store, by 1917 Finger-Siegel Company; Old Home Restaurant in the basement of the Siegel building; G. B. Slaven's boardinghouse; Byrd's boardinghouse; C. L. Hamilton's barbershop; Joe Griffith's household goods; W. B. Cross' restaurant; S. B. Rosewell's restaurant; John Herbert's barbershop; J. W. Graham's; and Shorty Brill's restaurant.[165] Brill's had a continuously burning cigar lighter. Youngsters sometimes roasted marshmallows over it when business was slow.[166] Punchboards were popular items in stores and restaurants. ⓘ

The local reporter to the *Pocahontas Times* wrote on June 17, 1915, that the town of Cass boasted of having the largest sawmill, the largest preacher (Rev. Harry Blackhurst),[167] and the largest colored girl in the county. The same writer stated that the population of the town was in part Caucasian, Italian, Russian, Mongolian, Creole, etc. and that an abundance of "garden sass" was being grown by townspeople.[168]

As the town and surrounding community grew, the need for a larger school building became pressing. In 1915, a four-room grade school building was built on Main Street near the southern corporate limit of town. The first principal in the new school was Graham La Rue. This building, which became known as the North Wing, was soon too small and in 1916 the South Wing of four rooms was added. Henry Overholt was in charge of the construction.[169] Enrollment was about four hundred.[170] A sound education in the "three R's" was provided by the competent and dedicated teachers. The daily school routine was interrupted periodically by lice and itch inspections by the principal. Students found infected with lice were sent home where the usual treatment was shaving the head and scrubbing down with coal oil (kerosene).[171] *HAD This Done in 1944 — passed*

The year 1915 saw other changes in the town. In late fall two large new store buildings were erected. One, in East Cass, was owned by F. Hamed who already had a store at Arbovale. The other, near the C&O wye west of the river, was built by Brown Gum.[172]

The Cass Theatre Company, owned by Ada Doyle and George W. Doyle, was established in 1915.[173] It was located in a building on Main Street beside the Cass 5 and 10 Cent Store, which was in the lower level of the Odd Fellows Lodge building.[174] On November 4, 1915, the "Trey O' Hearts," a silent motion picture drama produced by Universal Film Company, was shown. A novelized version of this film had been running for several weeks in the *Pocahontas Times*. The advance advertisement caused great interest in the film necessitating multiple showings.[175] Walter L. Ralston ran the theatre for a time in 1916-17.[176]

By 1915, the road to Green Bank had been widened and improved but was not yet a paved road.[177]

In response to the growing population in the Blackhurst Addition in East Cass, on December 16, 1915, a swinging footbridge was completed across the Greenbrier River. It crossed the river near the town's southern boundary and allowed easy access to the school and the lower part of West Cass to those families who were building houses in the Blackhurst Addition east of the river.

The original swinging bridge was built by William M. Siple and his sons.[178] It was supported by two heavy upright poles sunk in the ground on the riverbank at each side of the river. Heavy cables ran between them, one near the top of each pole at a height of about fifteen feet from the ground and one about eight feet high. The cables were secured at the ends by "dead men"[179] buried in the ground. The upper and lower cables were fastened together by wires running from the bottom cable to the top one. Fence wire was stretched between these to form sides to prevent people falling off. The bottom cables had two-by-eight-inch spruce boards as cross members between them. The floor made of rough one-by-ten-inch lumber was placed on the cross-pieces.

The 200-foot long swinging bridge reached only across the river. It was further extended on the west end by a walk 140 feet long supported by posts.[180] This connected the bridge to the railroad track embankment. Repairs of the swinging bridge were a community effort of the people living on both sides of the river. The company provided cables, lumber, wire, etc.

During floods, the river overflowed in a slough, which cut off most of the Blackhurst Addition from the swinging bridge and forced residents to walk around to the cement bridge in order to get to school. A footlog was placed across the slough when the water was not too high but this frequently washed out. Three homes owned by James "Jim" Belcher, Walter G. Clarkson and Allen J. "Farmer" Blackhurst were located on the island formed by the slough and river. During floodtimes, the only access to these homes was by the swinging bridge. The northern part of the island was owned by the company and contained the pest-house and a large garden plot.[181]

Spring, 1916, saw the organization of the Cass baseball team. In order to raise funds, an oyster supper, minstrel show and motion pictures were held at the Cass Theatre on March 4. They netted ninety dollars and were considered a great success.[182]

The Baseball Club promoted a huge Fourth of July celebration in 1916. The main attraction was a game between Cass and Bemis. Cass won, 2-1. Other events were:

High jump. Won by H. Hamrick – prize – $5 given by Dr. Hammond.

Broad jump. Won by H. Hamrick – prize – one-month pass to Cass Theatre.

Junior 100-yard dash. Won by Frank Jackson – prize – one pair $5 shoes given by Finger-Siegel Company.

Senior 100-yard dash. Won by C.C. Clendenin – First prize – one pair $5 shoes given by Pocahontas Supply Company.

Second prize. Won by J.D. Davis – watch chain given by Cass Jewelry Store.

Junior 50-yard dash. Won by Buzz Heaster – prize – $2 watch given by Dr. C.W. Kramer.

Potato race. Won by J.D. Davis – prize – one silk shirt given by Jacob Cooper.

Pie eating contest. Won by Willie T. Morgan – prize – one silk cravat given by F. Hamed & Brothers.

The Honorable Michael King of Elkins gave a talk and there was an old-time platform dance.[183]

Baseball games were played at a field adjacent to the bark piles at the Extract Plant at Deer Creek. The bark piles served as bleachers. In later years this field was occasionally used for school field day competitions.[184]

One of the townspeople, Miss Lena Anderson, daughter of the mill superintendent, William Anderson, had an excellent soprano voice and would often entertain at club meetings or other semiprivate occasions.[185]

In 1916, Charles Luke married Mary Elizabeth Hannah, youngest daughter of Mr. and Mrs. S. B. Hannah of Arbovale. They built a summer residence at Cass. After Mrs. Luke died in 1921, Charles turned the summer home over to E. P. Shaffer and his family. It later became known as the Club House.[186]

The first recorded news of 1917 included the report, in Justice Court, of quite a few cases of "bootlegging," a common crime. In early February, 1917, Sheriff William Gibson arrested five bootleggers as they got off the Western Maryland train at Durbin to transfer to the Cass train. Arrested were two blacks, Lee Jackson and John Crews, two Italians, and one Austrian. They had been under suspicion for some time of selling "wet goods" in Cass. About "90 quarts of cheap, fighting whiskey" were confiscated. The usual sentence for bootlegging at the time was a fine of one hundred dollars and a jail sentence.[187]

About a week later, on February 7, an Italian, whose name is not known, shot himself at Cass. He had been working as a laborer on the tracks on Cheat and lived in a shanty with a number of other Italians. He had recently received a letter from his wife in Italy upbraiding him for not sending her more money.[188]

Early in 1917 a new business, consisting of a pool hall, restaurant, and beer parlor, run by Page Hamrick, opened in East Cass. It was located in the building at the end of the bridge on the north side of the road.[189]

Opportunities for entertainment steadily increased in the area. For example, those persons with business in Marlinton in March, 1917, or those few who could afford a special trip, could view the premiere showing of "The Trail of the Lonesome Pine" in the Imperial Theatre.[190]

Flooding was a continuing problem at Cass. In late February, 1917, the east side was overflowed again by floodwaters.[191]

April, 1917, brought good news when the state road department advertised for bids for the removal of the old steel bridge that connected East Cass with the remainder of town and the construction of a cement bridge "of two spans 60 feet each, 18 feet wide, and one six-foot overhang side walk."[192]

Construction of the new bridge across the Greenbrier progressed, and by the middle of July, 1918, the foundations were poured and it was ready for the framework for the arches. It was completed later in the summer.[193]

The townspeople of Cass were shocked by another killing on May 7, 1917, when Thaddeus Hall, C&O brakeman on the Greenbrier Division and well-known all up and down the valley, came to his death by a shooting at Cass. Hall had been on the Greenbrier run for the past thirteen years and lived at Ronceverte where his wife and three children resided. The run for his train was between Ronceverte and Cass, staying alternate nights at each place. On Monday night he had completed his run to Cass and had gone to a house near the end of the swinging bridge.

At about 9:20 p.m., "Bill and Charlie Johnson, living near the C&O wye, heard shots and went to investigate and found Hall lying dead. He had been killed by four shots from a .32 automatic pistol. One of the shots was through the heart, one in the neck, one in the arm and one in the back.

"He was 33 years old.

"An inquest was held over the body on Tuesday by Justice Smith and Prosecuting Attorney W.A. Bratton. After the inquest, George 'Piney' Williams, of Cass, was arrested and charged with the shooting and brought to jail Tuesday afternoon. Williams had no statement to make. . . ."[194]

George "Piney" Williams was one of the oldest and most-valued employees of the West Virginia Pulp and Paper Company. He was forty-five years old at the time and had been with the company for sixteen years. He was engineer of Shay No. 8 and had made the Cass Hill run since it first began.

At the trial the fireman on No. 8 testified that "Piney" never left the engine at the time of the shooting. He was found "not guilty" and the case was never solved.[195]

World War I stimulated production at the mill and assured a ready market for all the lumber and pulpwood that could be supplied. The mill ran full time night and day.

When the United States entered the war in 1917, many townspeople went marching off to the tune of *Over There* and *Pack Up Your Troubles*. Some, like Albert E. "Sam" Harouff, came back with lungs damaged in the trenches by chlorine gas; others, Charles N. Gum, Edgar E. McMillion, and Elbert Messer were to sleep eternally in "Flander's Field," but for the most part, the war meant greater prosperity and security for the town.[196]

Among the men serving in World War I from Cass and Spruce were: Henry Anderson, Joseph A. Ayers, Henry O. Blackhurst, Robert Bolding, Warren G. Bragg, Claude L. Burwell, John Callen, Houston D. Carpenter, John Carrington, Kemp Lambeth Carter, Acey E. Cassell, Frank Cassell, John B. Cassell, Robert Cassell, William B. Cassell, Charles Coe Clendenin, Thomas Coles, George W. Cosby, Ervin C. Cunningham, Parker L. Curry, Leonard F. Cutlip, Dominico Dandrea, Herbert Darnell, Mack Davis, Sidney Davis, Jacob Dean, Elkins Dowell, William A. Fertig, Wincuncas Gaunlas, Arnold H. Gladwell, Charles N. Gum, Mack Gum, Albert E. Harouff, Frank B. Herbert, Harry Hill, Jasper Hinkle, Clyde House, Hampton H. Hunter, Joseph K. Knight, Arthur Kounce, Giarrusso Lalvatore, Fred Lynch, John Lyons, John Mayton, Jacob H. McCloud, Page C. McCloud, Edgar E. McMillion, Thomas O. McQueen, R. H. Mitchell, Howard Pawley, Jessie Perkins, Wallace D. Phillips, Frank J.

Rager, Everett W. Rodernick, Danas Scott, Charles Simmons, Oden D. Siple, Charles S. Smith, G. A. Sparks, Clarence L. Tabor, Louis W. Taylor, Frazier O. Thomas, Russ Wainwright, Paul Wakulohik, George A. Wanless, Harry Wanless, and John M. Wood.[197]

The need for secondary education was beginning to be felt by local residents of Cass but there were few opportunities for most people to go beyond the eighth grade. The more affluent families sent their children to private finishing schools, but most families could not afford them. In 1916, there were only ten high school graduates in all of Pocahontas County—the highest number to that date. The single high school in the county was at Academy (Hillsboro).[198]

People in the upper end of the county began pushing for a high school as early as 1913 and on September 24, 1917, Green Bank High School was opened with twenty-seven pupils. W. P. Haught was principal. Three years of high school were offered. Residents of Green Bank and Arbovale offered to furnish boarding for the students. Enrollment slowly grew and by November 1, the high school had thirty-six pupils.[199]

The high school had great and permanent effects on residents of Cass. No longer was the town isolated from outside contact. Young people met others, of similar background and social standing, from other towns. Contact was greatly increased when the football and basketball teams, the "Golden Eagles," were organized and games were played with schools outside of the immediate area. Interest in sports gave a new sense of unity to the town and to the upper end of the county.

In 1917, the grade school at Cass had about three hundred pupils. Miss Lutie Cunningham was principal and also taught the eighth grade. The honor roll and teachers for December were:

First grade—enrollment 38—Jessie Willetts, teacher—Robert Anderson, Linnie [Lennie] Church, Porter Dodson, Oscar Dill, Carl Galford, Carl Guthrie, Alvin Hamrick, Goldie Kline, Hubert Williams, Virginia Henegan, Josephine Jackson, Anne Louise Moulton, Virginia Pleasant and Virginia Williams.

Second grade—enrollment 26—Evelyn Graham, teacher—Edmond Dill, John Guthrie, Sidney Heaster, Bernell Henegan, Bennie Jackson, Julian Puffenbarger, Basil Siple, Grover Wright, Maud Jackson, Margaret Moulton, Hazel Stitzinger and Vivian Anderson.

Third grade – enrollment 28 – Ruth Kline, teacher – Earl Brice, Raymond Hines, Arnold Hevener, Frank Kane, Ted Moulton, William Pleasants, Edwin Puffenbarger, Hazel Brown, Bessie Church, Vergie Cline, Irma Marshall, Georgia McCloud, Zoe Kirkpatrick and Olive Mick.

Fourth grade – enrollment 33 – Beulah Moore, teacher – Paul Jackson, Olen Hiner, Jasper Matthews, Curtis Henderson, Joe Graves, Walter Shafer, Hubert Matthews, John Moulton, Domineck Reda, Lyle McPherson, Audria [sic.] Dill, Lelia Doyle and Olive Gunning.

Fifth grade – enrollment 18 – Nina Curry, teacher – Ted Guthrie, Harry Kerns, Wallace Dill, Bennie O'Brien, Francis Stitzinger, Gretchen Williams, Beulah Guthrie, Beryl Marshall and Edith McClung.

Sixth grade – enrollment 25 – Warren Moore (Miss McGraw after January 1918), teacher – Omer Brill, Julian Marshall, Adolph Cooper, Judson Heaster, Samuel Jackson, Ola Doyle, Naomi Dill, Vida McLaughlin, Grace Graves, Ernestine Hall, Lola Taylor, Frances LaCome and Verna Siple.

Seventh grade – enrollment 17 – Anne Correll, teacher – Harry Ervine, Edwin Doyle, Carl Nottingham, Virgie Lytton, Thelma Conrad, Ethel Ervine, Annie Richards and Thelma Kiess.

Eighth grade – enrollment 15 – Lutie Cunningham, teacher – Teddy Cooper, Fred Menefee, Theodore McClung, Beulah Brill, Lelice Heaster, Sallie O'Brien, Inza Ball, Esther Stitzinger and Florence Nethken.[200]

As the war progressed, an appeal was made by the Red Cross for bandages and other similar items. In January, 1918, women of the town held a meeting in the dining room of the Mountain Inn. It was decided to set up a Red Cross bandage sewing room in the front room of the Masonic Temple. Townspeople were to donate old tablecloths, bed linens, etc. for the bandages. The response to the plan was enthusiastic.[201]

Fire struck at Cass again on March 11, 1918. This time the big store of the Pocahontas Supply Company was partially burned with great damage to the stock. Robert S. Hickman was manager of the store at the time, and Harry Hill ran the drugstore located in the store building.[202]

The Pocahontas Supply Company opened temporarily in the Odd Fellows building after the fire. A huge fire sale was held on April 16.[203] The post office and company office, both of which were in the Company Store, were relocated temporarily to the front room of the Masonic Temple.

The Red Cross bandage room was moved upstairs to the Masonic Lodge room.[204] They were now making various items. By the end of March, they had sent in 800 gauze wipes, 160 many-tailed bandages, 55 four-tailed bandages, 140 T bandages, 30 abdominal bandages, 24 napkins, 44 pillowcases and dozens of knit sweaters and socks.[205]

People at home supported the war effort in various ways. For example, in May, 1918, the Raywood Auxiliary presented a play at the Cass Theatre for benefit of the Second Red Cross War Fund. The people of Cass donated $2,726.25 to the fund.[206]

On May 12, 1918, Rev. Fred W. Gray, the new minister of the Presbyterian church, preached his first sermon at Cass.[207] The Reverend Mr. Gray was to become a leading figure in the religious life of the town for the next eleven years.

The Reverend Mr. Gray's chief concern was his work as a minister, for which he was highly regarded. His hobby was botany with special interests in lichens, mosses, liverworts, and ferns. He collected thousands of plant specimens from the hills surrounding Cass and added greatly to the botanical knowledge of the area.[208]

One day he was weeding an obnoxious plant from his garden when one of his parishioners walked by. The man said, "Parson, what is the name of that weed you are having so much trouble with?"

Without hesitation, the Reverend Mr. Gray answered with some irritation, "It's called Devil's Delight. It would make a preacher cuss." The plant has since been known locally by that name. This is the only common name of a plant known to have originated at Cass.[209]

The Reverend Mr. Gray was also somewhat of a mathematical whiz. Occasionally he would appear at school assemblies where he fascinated the children with his ability with numbers. He sometimes sponsored flower shows at the Masonic Hall and gave as prizes tulip or gladiolus bulbs that he grew as a hobby.[210]

During July, the Radcliff Chautauqua, sponsored by the government to keep up morale, was in Cass. The motto was "Keep the Home Fires Burning." It was held in a tent on the flatland in front of the Presbyterian church. There were both matinee and evening performances.[211]

The year 1918 closed out with several sad events at Cass. On July 23, a twelve-year-old Italian boy named Pacifico was killed at Deer Creek when he tried to jump the C&O train and fell under the wheels. Joe Pacifico, his father, had been killed about a year before on Big Run.[212] In October the influenza epidemic swept across the country. In a single issue, the *Pocahontas Times* reported six deaths in Pocahontas County from the flu.[213] November brought word that Charles Gum, son of Mr. and Mrs. J. N. Gum, had been killed in action in France on October 25.[214]

The year ended with another murder in town. Saphronia James and Eliza Crawford, both black women, "fell out" over the disposal of rubbish. The resulting dispute ended with James woman being charged with shooting and killing the Crawford woman.[215]

The police themselves were not exempt from getting into trouble. On March 24, 1919, L. M. Foster, sergeant at Cass, was brought to the courthouse at Marlinton by some special officers. He had been engaged in an argument with Burke McCarty and S. L. Clark and used his gun to add weight to his remarks. A bystander, Dice Winenot, stepped up behind the chief and got a lock on his gun arm. Pretty soon the chief was in his own cooler. The *Pocahontas Times* recorded this as follows:

> The Chief of Police of Cass was brought to the courthouse Monday morning by some special officers. He was charged with a number of counts all having something to do with remoulding of his city more after his heart's desire.
>
> The trouble as usual can be lain at the door of John Barleycorn. As near as we can make out, the Chief arrested some Italians late Saturday who had in their possession some sixteen pints of liquor of the kind that would make your maiden aunt roar like a lion.
>
> The next morning (the Chief) was in no mood to stand any trifling. He came to breakfast and made gestures to emphasize his remarks. The gestures would not have been so notable had it not been for the fact that he had a full grown pistol in his hand. It easily made him the autocrat of the breakfast table.
>
> Going on his rounds, the Chief took a kind of notion that a prominent wood-hick, who is universally esteemed, was an I.W.W. and to call a man an I.W.W.[216] is fighting words in this part of the country. So the Chief fought the woodsman up a while and left him for the good Samaritans to gather up.[217]

April, 1919, brought to light one of the most publicized murders to occur in Cass when the body of Bascomb McFall, a young lumberjack from Greenbrier County, was found in a laurel thicket north of Cass. The body was found by Frank Smith who lived on a nearby island in the river. McFall had been missing since December 20, 1918.[218] The crime was not solved for two years (see page 225).

Despite these events, things were looking up in many respects in the late teens. On August 2, 1919, at 7 p.m. in the cornerstone of the remodeled Presbyterian church was laid by the M. W. Grant Lodge, AF & AM of West Virginia.[219]

Living conditions steadily improved at Cass, and in 1919, W. H. Kelinger was putting inside plumbing in the Luke house and the Hill house.[220] In December, 1919, A. O. Baxter and John Hull worked for two days at three dollars per day on surveying sewer lines.[221] Other houses in the company-owned section of town received plumbing soon afterward. Sanitary sewers emptied directly into the Greenbrier River at several places.

Water was supplied free by the company to the company houses and some adjoining private homes. Water was obtained from Leatherbark Creek and pumped to a storage tank north of the town by a pump located at the mill. The water ran over beds of gravel, then beds of sand. Samples were sent each week to Charleston to be checked for bacteria. After a heavy rain the town water would be quite muddy. To help alleviate the need for clean water on these occasions, a town pump was located in the second block of Main Street.

An American-LaFrance fire engine was purchased by the company in 1919 to enhance the fire fighting ability.[222]

LEGACY OF WORLD WAR I: 1920-1929[223]

By 1920, Cass had reached its zenith. The mill was running two 11-hour shifts, six days a week. The Extract Plant also was running full time. The population of the town had reached its highest point — 1,195 in the incorporated part of town, by official census figures, plus an estimated nine hundred persons living mostly south of the unincorporated area on both sides of the river. By this time, the social structure was well established, and the town was divided into well defined and, to a large extent, mutually exclusive areas.

The largest houses in the town had been built on the hillside west of the Company Store. At one time or another, these homes were occupied by Charles Luke (summer only), E. P. Shaffer, Dr. U. H. Hannah, Joe Graves, Stuart B. Nethken, George S. Graham, Jasper S. Matthews, Joe Hannah, Capt. William Anderson, Robert Hickman, A. S. Gillespie and Robert Hivacks. These persons were all associated directly with the company.

Day laborers and their families looked at this part of town with mixed feelings of awe, envy and artificial disdain. It is little wonder that the appellations "Big Bug Hill" and "Quality Hill" were applied.

Immediately north of "Big Bug Hill," across a hollow, several houses were built and a community of immigrant Italians, Hungarians, and others developed. Many of them worked on the section gangs, others in the mill or elsewhere on the lumber job. Having no social relations with their affluent neighbors and separated from the rest of the town by the Company Store, this group remained mysterious and separate, and their part of town became known as "Bohunk Hill." In time the fathers and children became accepted because of their work and school interactions. The mothers retained much of their native habits and language. Families of Frank Taliercio, Joe Urbanic, Gyursic, and others lived there.

After the mill at Spruce shut down, several blacks moved into houses northwest of the Italians. They were Myers, Stewart, Henry Jackson and Lee Jackson. On the upper side of the road in a little shack lived an elderly black named John Henry Crewe, who worked at odd jobs and did gardening for the Shaffers, Hannahs, Grahams, Nethkens, and Hickmans.

East of this section, in houses owned by the C&O Railroad, lived J. E. Brice (telegraph operator), Bill O'Brien, Harry Ray, and Charlie Woolwine.

The main part of the town was located south of "Big Bug Hill," along Front, Main and Spruce streets. Most of these persons were white protestants and considered themselves the mainstay of the town and the "Salt of the Earth." Here most of the mill, planing mill, shop, and train crews lived and raised their families.

It was the largest section of town and was known as "Uptown" or simply "Town." Long-term employees raised their families there and lived sometimes in the same house for forty years or more. Rent was twelve dollars per month including electricity and water. Prominent families were: Ira Coyner, Lacy Bowling, Lake Miller, Jess McCalpin, Grant Eddy, Gilbert Dahmer, Phil Church, Homer Slavin, Charles "Blacky" Calhoun, Ed Cassell, Forrest Haptonstall, Floyd Wright, Norman Smith, James Porter, Joe Wooddell, Roscoe "Pie-Belly" Ervine, Harry Hill, Timothy Kenealy, Elmer Duncan, Russell Richard, Joe Vint, Cliff Wolfe, Carl Ryder, R. P. Stanley, Sam Waugh, Ralph Holsaple, Luther Jones, Roy Seitz, Charlie Fuhrman, George Lewis, Cary "Red" Stanley, Joseph Nethken, Burke McCarty, Hobbs Rose, Ray Fox, Paul Warner, Kenny Puffenbarger, Calvin Stover, Connell Gillespie, Howard Fulks, O. S. McKisic, James Arbogast, Delbert Loudermilk, Jack Laurie, Sam Clark, Ernest O. Dill, Merle Ervine, Harry Shaw, Chalmer "Dugan" Shrader, E. J. "Herb" Shafer, George "Piney" Williams, Tom Brown, George Harry Norris, John Jack, Sid Keyser, Oscar Hertig, Guy Stanley, Ed Moore, James Moyer, Peer Hill, Emsley Martin, Fred Blanchard, Ollie Meeks, Alfred P. "Butch" Vering, John Hannah, Noah Ervine, William M. Siple, Hamrick, George Oliver, Homer Brown, John Kane, Dick Lewis, L. S. "Link" Cochran, Guthrie, Crawford Gum, Wallace Dill, Henegan, Mike Milan, John Slaven, Guy Tallman, and Burdenclint. Ed Jackson, Walter Ralston, William Bible, and Rev. Timothy Pharr lived adjoining this area on the south. They owned their own homes, except Pharr who lived in the Presbyterian manse. They were supplied water and electricity by the company.

West of town was a hill, Chestnut Ridge, known as the Company Pasture.[224] It was cleared and used as a pasture field for cattle waiting slaughter by the company and for sick or injured horses from the woods operations. Townspeople were allowed to pasture their milk cows there for one dollar a month. On the flat behind the Luke house a tennis court was made for the Graham girls.

Further south beyond the C&O wye were eleven houses built for workers at the Extract Plant. These houses were in two rows, one row on each side of a street roughly paralleling Cold Run. The homes were built by the company along the same plans as those in the main part of town. Two additional small cottages were later built along Cold Run. For some unknown reason, this area was known as "Slab Town."

At one time or another the following families lived there: Clifton Lyle, Perrin Lawrence, Owen Curry, Bill Nichols, John Smith, Glen Moss, Calvin Neighbors, Caleb Haislop, Randolph Galford, Lewis Seldomridge, Jesse Tacy, Jesse Cassell, Roger Dickenson, Clarence Gum, Ed Lyle, Frank Gray, Lon Rexroad, Homer Hoover, Chester Neighbors, Ralph Wykles, John Phillips, Kale White, Gutshaws, Dolly, and Wade Morris. The superintendent of the Extract Plant, Arthur Moulton, lived in a large house overlooking the river at the end of these rows of houses.

"Slab Town" and "Uptown" were connected by the highway along which the Cass Graded School was located. Families living in this section were Levi Galford, Harry Thomas, Bernard Hamrick, Boyd Meeks (these latter two ran a store along the road near their homes), Tom Chestnut, Brown Gum (home and large store), Hoxie Meeks, Harper Gum, Frank Varner, Aggie Galford, Burbon Niceley, Frank Slaven, Ollie Tacy, John Cassell, Clarence "Peg-leg" Gum, Paul Doyle, Ollie Cassell, Lucy King, Lola Addington, Emsley Martin, Alice Wade, Grace Gailor, Ed Cassell and Fred Cassell.

On the east side of the road lived Bill Hodson, Goodwin, Henry Hudson, George Gilbert, Sam Jackson, Tony Scitone (Scitone ran a store, boardinghouse and diner in a large building across from the Cass Graded School; this house was later the home of Ellis "Chipmunk" Ervine), Ed Cassell, Harrison Pusey and Warren Shifflett.

About one-half mile south of "Slab Town," the unincorporated town of Deer Creek was strung along the west side of the C&O tracks. The Range Lumber Company built Deer Creek to house the workers on their mill located there. Its railroad crossed the Greenbrier River at the piers still standing in the river and continued up Deer Creek to the Green Bank area. After the tracks were removed this was a popular Sunday hiking area. After Range cut out and moved, these houses were mostly occupied by workers on the Extract Plant.

Among the families living in Deer Creek were those of: Laban Wolfe, George Friel, Joe Smith, James Swisher, Harmon and Lily Galford, Ambrose Tyson, Domineck Pacifico, Roy McLaughlin, Stomling, Philips, Dean, Jack Mayes, Walter Nelson, Kale Whites, and Chester Neighbors. A boardinghouse was run by Stitzinger. A small store was located east of the tracks.

On the eastern side of the Greenbrier, the cluster of businesses leading from the end of the cement bridge eastward along the highway was known as East Cass.

Starting on the north side of the road at the end of the bridge was Page Hamrick's pool hall and restaurant;[225] next was Kirkpatrick's restaurant run by Jimmy and Hattie Kirkpatrick,[226] the upper floor contained the Moose Lodge meeting room; the next building contained Dale and Grace White's grocery store with living quarters upstairs;[227] this was followed by MacDonald's men's clothing store which sat on the corner.[228]

On the south side of the road starting at the bridge was Brill's clothing and dry goods store, a brick building, with living quarters downstairs and, in the back, upstairs;[229] a stairway was located between Brill's Store and the next building, the Siegel Building. The latter housed dry goods and clothing upstairs with the Old Home Restaurant downstairs;[230] an open lot was between Siegel's and the Jacob Cooper's Building which contained a clothing store downstairs and living quarters upstairs;[231] the building on the corner was the largest building in East Cass. Four stories high, it contained the Logger's Home Hotel. It was known as the "White Elephant."[232]

A street branching northward off the highway at the sharp curve became known as "Dirty Street." Here were saloons ("pig's ears"), gambling establishments, and hotels.

The northernmost building on this street, on an island above the mill, was the home of Frank "Hog Island" Smith; south of his home and east of the street was the River View Hotel, one of the most popular hotels for wood hicks in town for the weekend. South of the River View Hotel, between the road and the river, was Lee Queen's house;[233] east of the road were Burbon Niceley's barbershop, followed by the Central Hotel, later known as Belle's Place, run by John Peter Cross and his children, Ward, Lee, and Belle;[234] south of the Central Hotel was John Reda's store, followed by John Reda's garage,[235] a grocery store[236] and the home of Sid Church;[237] across the road was a store that was used later as a church, where Rev. Harry Blackhurst preached for a time.

This part of town was the mecca of many wood hicks, who, after spending weeks in the woods, came in on the log train, drew their pay at the company office, and headed "in a bee line" across the bridge for "Dirty Street." Drinking, endless fights, and an occasional murder made "Dirty Street" off limits to most residents of the other parts of town. Many a logger spent weeks of hard-earned wages in a wild weekend (or longer) fling on "Dirty Street." Or, worse yet, imbibed too much whiskey, went "skidded," and while asleep, was "rolled," only to wake up later with his remaining money stolen.

When prohibition began on January 17, 1920, the *Pocahontas Times* declared "John Barleycorn Dead."[238] However, the visitors to "Dirty Street" hardly knew the differnce for bootleggers kept them well supplied.

Directly south of the business section of East Cass between the highway and the river were two rows containing a total of eleven small houses, ten homes and a school-church, built and owned by the company. These homes were occupied by blacks and the area was called "Nigger Bottom." The term "Nigger" was used universally with reference to blacks. There was no disrespect intended by the use of the term and it was accepted by blacks in like manner. Blacks and whites worked side by side in similar jobs on the mill and other parts of the job and there was very little conflict. Like the immigrants on the other side of the river, the blacks were isolated, both in space and in social interactions, from the remainder of the town. They had their own one-room school, which doubled as a church, and spent most of their non-work time within their own group.

The families of George Holly, Jim Parker, Margaret Brown, Tom Myers, Walter Brown, Oliver Tyson, Boyd Myers, Ralph Boggs, Lizzie Mann, George Holly, Virginia Brown, and Ether Tyson lived here. Jim Parker and George Holly were butchers for the company.[239] The other men worked at various jobs on the mill or section crews.

When originally built, these houses were sixteen feet wide and twenty-five feet long with a 6-foot wide porch extending along both the front and back. The houses were divided into two rooms, one for cooking and eating, the other for sleeping.[240] Several persons added one or two additional small rooms as their families grew. The homes were heated by a coal-burning stove in the back room and the cookstove in the front room. There were no chimneys—the stovepipe went directly through the side of the house. This caused several fires over the years.

These families carried their drinking water from a well on "Dirty Street" several hundred feet away. Water for washing clothes and bathing was carried from the river which was nearby. A coal shed and an outside toilet sat behind each house. All these "luxuries" were provided by the company for $2.50 per month rent.[241]

Teachers in the one-room black school were Hattie K. Holley, Sydney Goodwin, Marie Goodwin and Ida Choice. It closed in 1956 and black students attended Cass Graded School.[242]

Church was held on the second Sunday of each month in the schoolhouse. Visiting ministers preached the sermons. Among these were Rev. Isaac Goodyn from Marlinton, West Virginia; Rev. P. A. Barmer from Davis, West Virginia; Rev. H. B. Womack from Elkins, West Virginia; Rev. George Jett from Morgantown, West Virginia; and the Reverends Mr. Cook and Mr. Hale from Fairmont, West Virginia. The church was known as the First Baptist Church.[243] Baptisms were held in the river closeby.

On May 23, 1951, the black community purchased the Northern Methodist Church in East Cass and held regular services there. The Reverend Mr. Jett from Morgantown held some of these services. Through the years members of the community such as George Gilbert and Ambrose Tyson served as lay ministers.[244]

There were two parcels of land east of the river, south of the black community. One, the Allen E. Burner Annex, was bounded by the Green Bank Road on the east, company land on the north and west and the Blackhurst Addition on the southwest. The other, the Blackhurst Addition, lay southwest of the Burner Addition between the river, the Green Bank Road and the Burner Addition.[245] Further expansion of housing east of the river was accelerated when an auction sale of lots in the Blackhurst Addition was announced. The auction, on May 26, 1915, was highly advertised. A brass band was on hand, and twenty dollars in gold was given away. Auctioneer, Captain C. B. Swecker, cried the sale. Sale agent of the owner was the American Company of Charleston, West Virginia.[246]

In the Blackhurst Addition, there were mostly one-story homes of mill, planing mill and railroad workers. It was a source of pride to many of these people that they owned their own homes, despite the fact that they had no running water, no plumbing, and no electricity. Outside toilets, containing large buckets for waste, served the needs of the populace. These were surreptitiously emptied at night into the slough or river during floodtimes. It seems like an uncivilized practice until one remembers that, after 1920, the more sophisticated, company-owned side of town with running water and inside plumbing also dumped their raw sewage into the river. Carrying it down neatly enclosed in pipes somehow seemed so much more dignified. This part of town was known as "The Blackhurst Addition," "unincorporated East Cass" or commonly called "The Street." Persons living here interacted socially with the residents of the main part of the town and were accepted as more or less equals.

Families of men such as Ellis "Chipmunk" Ervine, Walter Vint, Henry Blackhurst, Dr. Frank C. Nickell, Dewey Hiner, William "Bill" Blackhurst, Paul Pennington, Thomas W. McFerrin, Webster Cross, Kenny James, Markwood Gum, Clarence Petts, Jones, "Tuckahoe" Smith, Neely Gragg, Earl Rosewell, Ingraham Smith, Jesse Warwick, Houston Carpenter, Forrest Wilfong, Ida Curry, Charlie Sheets, John Nelson, Newton "Newt" Gum, Dane Scott, Amos Wooddell, McClung, Emma Burner, George W. Litton, John Kane, Kline Gilliam, Ernest O. Dill, Roy Stewart, Albert E. Harouff, Roy Cook, Edgar Shinaberry, Roy Vint, Lyle McPherson, Willy Sampson, Andrew Sisca, Sid Church, Clyde Kritzen, Cooper Irvine, Flosten Sampson, Jake Mauzy, Wylie Church, Allen Richards, F. D. "Denny" Flynn, Allen "Farmer" Blackhurst, Walter G. Clarkson, James "Jim" Belcher, Oney Plyler, Maggie Tallman, Benton Ervine and Ted Blackhurst lived in this part of town.

Along the Green Bank Road, in East Cass, was located the Methodist Episcopal Church, commonly called the Northern Methodist Church. The original Allen Craig Burner home[247] (still standing) and James B. Sutton's home and embalming parlor were nearby. The latter was the only brick home in town.[248] The remaining homes were made of wood.

A large house located on a small hill at the southern end of "The Street" was the home of the Reverend Harry and Lou Blackhurst and their family. The Blackhurst family was one of the largest and most respected families in Cass.

The bottomland adjoining their home became known appropriately as "Blackhurst's Bottom." It was used for ball games, school Easter egg hunts, bonfires, and similar events.

The town swimming hole was located south of "Blackhurst's Bottom" on Deer Creek at its junction with the Greenbrier River. Dozens of town youngsters made a daily trek to the swimming hole on pretty summer days to spend a delightful afternoon in the water. The rhododendron thicket on the bank next to the river made a convenient dressing room for the boys and an over-hanging oak tree served as a diving board.

The swimming hole provided a place where blacks and whites alike received spiritual rejuvenation through total immersion baptismal services. A deep hole in the Greenbrier River below the highway bridge also served this purpose at times.

Another swimming hole was located, on Deer Creek, along the Green Bank Road east of Cass. It was known as Sheet's Swimming Hole.

The hill due east of Cass was owned by Elmer D. Burner and was known as Burner's Hill. The large home he built about 1913 on top of the hill dominated views eastward from the town. The road leading to Burner's house from the county road along the west slope of the hill provided one of the best sled runs in town. Robert Wimer and Jesse Moore lived in houses on the hill east and north of Burner's hill.

The stringent social stratification found in Cass appears strange to us now, but in 1920 it was very real and few persons attempted to challenge it.

The most conspicuous feature of the town was wood. Almost every house was wood frame with wood weatherboard. The white painted homes were accentuated by white picket fences enclosing almost every yard. Wooden walkways connected the house with the coal shed and outhouse in back. Wooden sidewalks ran the full length of the town on each side of the main streets, with the exception of Front Street, which had a cement sidewalk in later years. Wooden steps connected the houses on the hill behind the hotel with the Company Store area. A trestle walk went from the road across to the Graves, Nethkin, Graham, Matthews and Gillespie houses. A wooden turnstile was placed at the road end of this walk. A similar turnstile was placed at the end of the walk leading from the road to Main Street. The turnstiles prevented cows from getting on the walk. A trestle walk also went from Dr. Hannah's house over Luke Street to the Joe Hannah house.[249]

Life in Cass was dominated by the mill. Daily, except Sunday, at 5:30 a.m., the mill whistle blew a long, loud blast. This served to awaken the town residents and remind them that another working day was about to begin.

The first chore was to build a fire in the wood or coal-burning cookstove, take out the ashes from yesterday's fire and prepare to cook breakfast. In cold weather, fire in the heating stove in the living room was kindled, and the house slowly started to warm. The older children were awakened. In winter they came out near the stove to dress. Everyone wore long underwear so modesty was no problem.

By about 6:15, breakfast was ready and the family sat down to a hearty meals of eggs, ham or sausage, fried potatoes, and fresh baked biscuits or similar fare. Oatmeal, cornmeal mush and pancakes were popular. By 6:30 the husband was off to work and the wife was busy getting the children ready for school, cleaning house or preparing for one of the many chores she had to do. At 6:50 the mill whistle blew to tell the men to get ready to start to work when the starting whistle blew at 6:55.

A short blast of the mill whistle at about 9:30 a.m. signaled time to change saws (putting on a newly filed saw) and a second blast sounded when this task was completed and the mill was ready to run again.

The mill whistle sounded again at 12:00 to signal the noon hour; at 12:50 the warning whistle blew and at 12:55 the signal to start work for the afternoon, was given. The saws were changed again at 3:30 in the afternoon and at 6:00 the whistle signaled the end of the day shift. During the many years a night shift worked, the procedures were repeated during the night.

The day ended one hour earlier on Saturday. However, to make up the hour, work started five minutes before the hour each morning and noon.

Any prolonged blowing of the mill whistle, at times other than those scheduled, was a dreaded sound. It signaled a fire. When fire occurred, all the men of the town came running to man the hoses, carry out furniture, or to help in any way possible.

The school bell could also be heard throughout the town and on school mornings at 8:50 it was rung to signal that school would start in ten minutes. It was rung at 9:00 to start school, 10:30 for a 15-minute recess and at 12:00 to signal lunch. The same procedure called the students at 12:50, started school at 1:00 signaled recess at 2:30 and dismissed school at 4:00. Early dismissal at 3:30 on Friday were eagerly anticipated all week. Before school and at recess, the students were very active playing marbles or such games as Lost-Turkey and Ring-A-Le-Vi-o and on the Giants-Ride, swings and seesaws.

Weddings were special events not only for the bride and groom but also for the townspeople, who used the occasion for a rousing wedding-night serenade for the newlyweds. The celebration included a crowd that surrounded the home where the newlyweds were spending the night. They rang bells, shot guns, beat on pans, and yelled; stopping only when the bride and groom appeared on the porch of the house to hand out cigars and candy.

Deaths also involved the entire community. The body was embalmed by either J. B. Sutton at Cass or Ed Smith at Marlinton[250] and returned to the home where it was "viewed" for two days or more. Here relatives and neighbors gathered bringing large amounts of food, to console and to grieve with the bereaved family. A "wake" was held each night during which a few persons sat up the entire night.

On the appointed day, the body was removed to the church for the funeral or, in many cases, the funeral was held in the home. If a church funeral was held, it was often preceded by slowly tolling the church's bell one ring for each year of the deceased's life. Burial was usually at Arbovale Cemetery, Olliver Cemetery, Wanless Cemetery, McLaughlin Cemetery, or in a family cemetery if one was available.

Recreation was not lacking in the town. Frequent oyster suppers, cakewalks, dances, picnics, box suppers, poundings, and other socials were held by the local Odd Fellows, Loyal Order of Moose, the Masonic Lodge, church groups, etc.[251]

In winter, skating on the river and sled riding on Burner Hill, Ralston Hill, the Company Pasture, and the Back Mountain Road were popular. Youngsters of the town banded together to play softball, Hide-and-Seek, I-Spy-Hit-the-Can, Fox-and-Geese, Go-Sheepy-Go and Andy-Over. Crimping food cans over the bottoms of shoes and walking on them and walking on stilts were fun activities as was making "bombs" by adding water to carbide in a can, sealing on the lid, lighting it and letting it explode. Fishing in the upper Cheat River, Greenbrier, Leatherbark and Deer Creek and hunting in the surrounding hills occupied many a leisure hour and provided an occasional meal.

By the 1920s, entertainment had reached a peak in the vicinity of Cass. The Pocahontas County Fair at Marlinton was off to a strong start giving several days' diversion in the fall of each year.

Admission was fifty cents for adults, twenty-five cents for children and fifty cents per auto. "Sparks World-Famous Shows" was touring the country and appeared in Marlinton in early summer. The Amusu Theatre at Marlinton had a full billing showing such classics as *A Connecticut Yankee in King Arthur's Court* starring Harry Myers and Pauline Starke; *The Four Horsemen of the Apocalypse* starring Rudolph Valentino and Alice Terry; *Way Down East* with Richard Bartholomew and Lillian Gish; and Buster Keaton in *The Paleface*. Selected shows appearing in Marlinton were shown on Saturday nights at the Cass Theatre.[252] A bulletin board, located between the meat market and the company office, advertised the weekly offerings. As in most movie houses a piano was played by one of the many young ladies of the town. Mary Elizabeth Ralston played, at Cass, for several years in the late twenties.[253]

An extensive Chautauqua was held at various times during the summer in a large tent at Marlinton. In 1921, offerings included the Mendelssohn Orchestral Club, the Dunbar Male Quartet and Bell Ringers, a play called *Nothing But the Truth* and a lecture entitled "The Magic Circle." Season tickets cost $2.50[254]

Touring shows, smaller than those at Marlinton, annually set up tents in East Cass, or at the C&O wye. An example was "Campbell, Bailey and Hutchinson's Combined Circus, Menagerie and Wild West Show."[255] An animal parade through town highlighted these events.

Ordinary activities such as berry picking, gardening, hunting and milking the cows, cooking, cleaning, washing clothes, washing dishes, taking care of the hogs and chickens, cutting wood, carrying coal and wood in and ashes out, carrying water and many other household chores kept leisure hours to a minimum for many of the town inhabitants, however. Practically every house had a small vegetable garden.

The company took every opportunity to buy land or buildings in East Cass. In July, 1920, they purchased the Joe Hamed building for $4,000. At the same time, a mule cost $235 and a pony $160.[256]

The year 1920 ended on a tragic note when Harry Grimes, of Raywood, killed his wife and then committed suicide.[257]

January, 1921, saw the going-of-business sale of Finger-Siegel Company, a store that had been in East Cass for over fifteen years.[258]

Great excitement was created in the town on February 24, 1922, when the big mill burned. The workmen all rushed to help fight the fire while the rest of the townspeople watched from a safe distance. A detailed account of this fire is found in Chapter 10.

April, 1922, brought more violence to the town. Three blacks, Ray Morris, Ruben Coles and John Brown, who worked for the company at Spruce, came to Cass for payday and went to Brown's shanty in East Cass for a "friendly" poker game. Some liquor was drunk and a falling-out occurred. Brown went to a neighbor's house, borrowed a shotgun, and returned. He shot Coles in the leg and Morris in the head. Sergeant Warwick and Constable Cochran arrested him and took him to the county jail at Marlinton.[259]

In November, 1922, Constable L. S. Cochran arrested Pete Kelley and charged him with killing George Mallory at Cass in July, 1913. Kelley was under suspicion at the time of the murder but there was not enough evidence for an arrest and Kelley left town. In 1922, he returned, was arrested and lodged in the Cass jail. During the night, some confederates took the bolts out of the hinges of the outside door of the jail and released him. He left for parts unknown and was never brought to trial.[260]

Finally, in December, 1922, the full story of the Bascomb Mc-Fall murder four years before was told when William Dudley and Samuel Davis were held by the grand jury and charged with the killing.[261] A black man named Charlie "Jellyroll" James was also indicted. James was already in prison by this time for the murder of Eliza Crawford at Cass on December 20, 1918. Eliza Crawford knew of James' part in the McFall murder and was killed by James to prevent her telling of the event.[262]

The story that unfolded was: on December 19, 1918, McFall came down from the Cheat Mountain woods to Cass, drew his pay and had a roll of several hundred dollars. He fell in with a bad gang and was not heard of until the first week in April, 1919, when his body was found hidden in a laurel thicket on the old abandoned road from Cass to Green Bank. His throat had been cut.

At the grand jury hearing, a man named Horton Johnson testified he had seen McFall in the company of the accused men, had heard struggles, had seen bloodstains in a room near the one he occupied at the Breakiron Hotel (River View Hotel), and had seen men carrying what looked like the body of a man downstairs.

Frank Smith testified that on the morning of December 20, 1918, he had seen a trail of blood leading from the east side of Cass to a point opposite from where he found the body months later. Elmer Burner also testified seeing the trail of blood. Saphronia Carter testified she had seen McFall with the defendants on the evening of December 19, 1918.

William Dudley was found guilty of murder in the first degree with a recommendation by the jury of a sentence for life in the state penitentiary.

Davis was scheduled for trial in the June, 1923, court. The case was continued until the October, 1923, term and again continued at that time. Dudley appealed his case to the Supreme Court of Appeals and in the June, 1924, Circuit Court the case against Dudley and Davis was nullified.

James was expected to be a witness at Dudley's trial, but he went insane while in prison and was committed to the asylum. He was never tried for the McFall murder.[263]

During the summer of 1922, a boy named Kemp Taylor was admitted to the Marlinton Hospital with a bullet embedded in his heart. It was successfully removed, and he recovered. The story of the shooting involved four boys, Romeo Rose, Buzzard, Kellison and Kent Taylor, who were playing cards under a hemlock tree on "Dirty Street" in Cass.

Rose and Kellison went farther up the river, and when they returned, Rose whipped out a pistol, and holding it at his hip said to Taylor, "Damn you, dance" and pulled the trigger. When Taylor fell over screaming, Rose threw the gun away in astonishment, crying he had not meant to shoot. Rose gathered up the victim and took him to his home, where he sat up with him all night before notifying the authorities the next morning.

A justice sentenced Rose to six months in jail for carrying a pistol and while serving that sentence, he was charged with malicious wounding. During the trial, the defense argued that the gun had been cocked accidentally upon removal from Rose's pocket and that the shooting was accidental. The jury was convinced, and Rose was acquitted.[264]

In June, 1923, the Chesapeake and Ohio Railroad contracted to have the overcrowded freight and passenger station at Cass replaced with a larger building. The new depot was in service by September.[265]

Many adventurous Sunday afternoons were spent by town youngsters prowling around in the woods surrounding Cass. In the fall, chestnuts, black walnuts, butternuts, and hickory nuts were gathered for cracking during snowbound winter nights. Occasionally a group would decide to explore the McLaughlin Cave,[266] a well-known limestone cavern on land then owned by Joe McLaughlin. The cavern was a source of adventure to some, a place of fear and awe to others.

The aura of fear of the cave was heightened in August, 1923, when word was received that on or about July 21 a man had committed suicide in the cave. The story appeared in the *Pocahontas Times* as follows:[267] Clarence Wamsley, a 45-year-old man whose home was in Ridgeway, Pennsylvania, had gone into the cave, sat down on a paper in which a gun had been wrapped, and shot himself. He was afflicted with a cancer on his tongue. Doctors had told him that, without an operation, the cancer would kill him in about three months, but by removing his tongue he possibly would live a year.

He had written a letter from Elkins to his brother, enclosing a will and a check for what money he had in the bank. He wrote:

> I have decided not to have an operation, and will take the matter in my own hands and end it all. I know of a place about 100 miles from here where I can get about 50 feet underground. This will be a kind of burial for me. Break the news to mother some way. You look after her and see that her bills are paid for she will forget them. Get her pension check for her. I will never be back in Ridgeway, Pennsylvania. Tell the folks I have gone to Norfolk, Virginia, for my health.

On July 21, Clarence Wamsley came to Cass, bought a money order for fifty dollars and enclosed it in a note to his brother. It said:

> Dear Floyd—I have about 6 miles to walk up a mt.
>
> Clarence."

Upon receipt of these letters, Floyd Wamsley and a Mr. McGeehin came to Cass and, upon showing the local people the letters, it was decided to search the McLaughlin Cave.

Sergeant L. S. Cochran and U.S. Deputy Marshall Beasley went with them to make the search. They found the body about

150 feet inside the cave sitting with the back against the wall, the right hand still holding a small .42 caliber pistol. About a half-inch directly in front of the right ear was a bullet wound. The bullet had penetrated the brain.

The body was brought to Cass, where an inquest was held. The jury rendered the verdict that Wamsley had come to his death from a self-inflicted gunshot wound. The body was taken by truck to Elkins and then by rail to Ridgeway for burial.

The deceased was a man of good character and good education. Some sixteen or eighteen years previous to the time of his death, he had been employed on a sawmill owned by D. D. Hazeltine, who cut lumber on the McLaughlin farm near Cass. Thus, he knew of the cave.

Fall was a dreaded time of year for Cass residents in the years before 1923. For, in the fall, diphtheria began its annual ravages of children. Many graveyards show tombstones of several children in the same family whose deaths occurred a few days or weeks apart. The stones usually record the effects of diphtheria. The *Pocahontas Times,* on August 30, 1923, carried news that diphtheria could be prevented and advocated diphtheria vaccine for everyone, especially all children.[268] Within a couple of years the scourge of diphtheria was a thing of the past.

At about the same time there was a case of smallpox in town. Dr. Hannah and his assistant, Dr. Miller, went from house to house giving smallpox vaccinations. One woman was washing clothes at the time and washed the vaccine off with a wet cloth. She was the only person to take smallpox that summer.[269]

L. S. "Link" Cochran, town constable, kept close tabs on persons in the town, and in November, 1923, he arrested Frank Spinks. Squire J. B. Sutton fined Spinks fifty dollars and six months in jail for carrying a gun and one hundred dollars and sixty days in jail for having a quart of booze.[270]

Townspeople took a great interest in the town government, with many of the leading citizens running for office. The January election of 1924 had the following results:

Mayor:	J. Hobbs Rose
Recorder:	George S. Graham
Councilmen:	Dr. U.H. Hannah, J.C. Graves, W.F. Anderson, Robert Hivick, J.B. Sutton, J.A. Belcher, J.A. Kirkpatrick, Sidney Church[271]

As the town's population grew, the need was felt for an additional church. Money was subscribed for and the First Methodist Episcopal Church was built in 1924 on the east side of the river next to the Green Bank Road northeast of J. B. Sutton's undertaking establishment. This church became known as the Northern Methodist Church.[272]

J. P. Smith, Henry Blackhurst and A. J. Hardeburger were confirmed as trustees of the Cass Methodist Church by the Circuit Court in April, 1924. The Reverend Harry Blackhurst was chosen minister.[273]

A large congregation attended this church, including most of the persons east of the river. Pearl Harouff, Henry Blackhurst, and William "Bill" Blackhurst were among the dedicated Sunday schoolteachers. Pearl Harouff's class sold homemade potato chips and doughnuts to townspeople and to men working on the lumberyard and mill. They made enough money to buy rugs for two Sunday schoolrooms.[274]

When automobiles became common, a gas tank was installed between the Company Store and the depot. Here gasoline was pumped by hand from the tank to a glass storage and measuring container above the pump. It was then let into cars by gravity. The amount purchased was shown by the drop in level in the glass container.

Increased use of the automobile brought about inevitable accidents. One of the first in the area near Cass was at First Bar Ford east of Cass. In January, 1921, Clyde Nickell and Hunter Adams, both local men, wrecked there, throwing Nickell to the railroad grade one hundred feet below the highway. Adams was unhurt but Nickell was terribly bruised, although he recovered.[275]

By 1924, the list of businesses and professional people in Cass had grown to the following:

S.F. Clark, postmaster
Lena Anderson, music teacher
Rev. H. Blackhurst (M.E. Church North)
James Breakiron, hotel
G.M. Brice, express & Tel. agent
Walter A. Brill, dry goods and notions
Cass Meat Market and General Store
Cass Motor Company (George W. Baker)
Cass Theatre (C.E. Carpenter, Manager)

Citizens Band of Cass
Link S. Cochran, Constable
Herber E. Conant, mechanical engineer
Jacob Cooper, general store
Mr. J.E. Cruikshank, prop. Mountain Inn Hotel
Amos S. Gillespie, City Treasurer
Greenbrier Cheat & Elk RR Company (E.P. Shaffer, Manager)
Rev. F.W. Grey (Presbyterian)
B.M. Gum, general store
W.A. Hammen [*sic*] Hammond, dentist
Hannah Brothers, livestock
U.H. Hannah, physician
H.B. Hill, druggist
Industrial Chemical Company (A. Moulton, Superintendent)
J.A. Kirkpatrick, restaurant
V.M. McCarthy, barber
Dan McGuire, hotel
Wm. L. Miller, physician
Mountain Inn Hotel
S. B. Nethken and Sons, meat
C.B. Niceley, barber
F.C. Nickell, veterinarian
Edith Pitts, school principal
Pocahontas Supply Company, general store and drugs
W.L. Ralston, garage, blacksmith
Rev. J.W. Rasenberger (M.E. Church South)
John Reda, general store
C.V. Rosewell, restaurant
E.P. Shaffer, General Manager, West Virginia Pulp and Paper
Leona C. Shephard, public stenographer
Andrew Sisca, tailor
J.B. Sutton, Justice of the Peace
Andrew Taylor, shoemaker
West Virginia Pulp and Paper Company[276]

Roy Vint hauled scrap flooring for firewood to homes in town. He used a dray horse and wagon.

The spectre of violent death was not long absent from Cass. "Three Persons Killed" announced the story in the *Pocahontas Times* for April 10, 1924. The account was terse; Tiny McCoy shot and killed his wife, Mrs. Hallie Totten McCoy (age twenty-one years), his mother-in-law, Mrs. William L. Totten (age forty-five years), and his brother-in-law, Hobert Totten (age nineteen years), at Deer Creek, near Cass, on Sunday afternoon, April 6. He then shot himself in the forehead. The bullet ranged up, and although he had a fractured skull, he was not seriously hurt. He ran away after the shooting but was apprehended at Sitlington, two miles south of Cass.

McCoy and his wife had not been getting along well together. She had left their home at Durbin and returned to the home of her parents at Deer Creek. McCoy had been trying to get her to go back with him and had been forbidden to go to the Totten home. On Sunday he came down from Hosterman to see his wife and found her at the home of a neighbor, Laban Wolfe. Mrs. Totten and her son Hobert soon came over to the Wolfe house.

After some controversy, McCoy apparently prepared to leave and asked his wife to come outside and bid him good-bye. As she was coming out the door, McCoy shot her in the head with an automatic .32 caliber pistol. Mrs. Totten then came to the door and was also shot in the head. Hobert Totten tried to grapple McCoy and was shot twice. All three died almost instantly. McCoy then shot himself in the head but the shot grazed off. Mr. Wolfe and Calvin Neighbors, who were then on the scene, tried to disarm him. He tried to shoot them but the weapon jammed. McCoy then made for the river, swam it and made his way to Sitlington where he was stopped and held by Charles P. Adams until the officers arrived.

The bodies of the slain persons were laid out on the bed. Townspeople, men, women and children, flocked in to see the scene of the murder and filed by to see the bodies.[277]

The courts acted swiftly. The above events occurred on April 6, 1924. Tiny McCoy was indicted by the Grand Jury on three counts of murder and on June 11 and 12 he was tried for the murder of his young wife and found guilty without a recommendation for life imprisonment. Judge Sharp then pronounced the death sentence, setting September 12 as the date of execution.

Before leaving for the penitentiary, McCoy sent the following confession to the *Pocahontas Times* for publication:

> Marlinton, W.Va. – I, Tiny McCoy, do hereby acknowledge that I murdered my wife, brother-in-law and mother-in-law, but I am sorry of my crime and ask all who are affected thereby for forgiveness as I believe that God has forgiven me. As I go to pay the just penalty of my deed I want people to know that I go trusting ab-

solutely, solely and only in the atoning blood of Jesus Christ, the Savior of sinners, to justify me before God. Having accepted Jesus Christ as my Personal Savior and received Christian Baptism, I have no hatred nor ill will in my heart toward any. I ask Christian people everywhere to pray that I may meet my end with Christian fortitude and my God and Savior with joy. Sincerely, Tiny McCoy. June 16, 1924, Witnessed, W.A. Eskridge.[278]

"May god bless us all, and take us to Heaven on the Day of Judgement." Thus spoke young Tiny McCoy, twenty-three years old, ten seconds before he met death by hanging at the Moundsville State Penitentiary at 4:66, Friday afternoon on September 12 just 160 days after the murders.[279] The year 1924 was a year of violence in and around Cass. The following year was one of revival and conversion. The Ku Klux Klan played an important role in this. In January, 1925, a film entitled *The Fifth Horseman* was shown twice to packed houses at the Cass Theatre. This movie was billed as "exposing the inside workings of the Klan." A review of the movie said the Klan was shown to be "the most powerful organization known for the betterment and upbuilding of unfortunate, poverty stricken homes, and for the breaking down of the bossism practice of crooked politicians and crooked officers . . . the Ku Klux Klan is exerting a mighty influence for [sic] to make the world better as the days go by. J.B."[280] During the summer of 1925, the Knights of the Ku Klux Klan burned crosses on the Company Pasture hill west of Cass and on Burner's Hill east of Cass. The rallies aroused a great deal of interest in the Klan, and many solid citizens of the town joined. The Klan inspired several couples, who were living together without the benefit of wedlock, to get married and brought about other beneificial changes in the town.[281] On Thanksgiving night, 1925, the Klan presented an American flag to the Cass School. They had previously erected a flagpole in front of the school. The Klan was highly recommended as "an influence for good that will grow stronger down through the ages. . . ."[282] The spirit of revival was accentuated by special meetings held at the Cass Presbyterian Church in February by Dr. Trigg Thomas of Kansas City. In addition to preaching to overflow congregations each evening for two weeks at the church, he spoke, to men only, from 12:30-12:40 at the Pocahontas Supply Company Store.[283]

As a result of these meetings, while the congregation sang "Just As I Am," "Almost Persuaded," "Softly and Tenderly" and other moving hymns, 227 conversions, 400 reconversions and 20 letters of transfer to the Cass churches were made.[284] At this time Cass contained a Presbyterian church, the Northern Methodist Church, and a Negro Baptist Church, which met in the one-room Negro school.

Not long after this, in 1926, a second Methodist church was built along Spruce Street on the southern edge of the main part of town. Dedicated on June 12, 1927, it was known as the Methodist Episcopal Church South or Southern Methodist. This church had large congregations from both sides of the river.[285]

Further expansion of the Cass School occurred when the junior high department was begun in the early 1920s. Miss Edith Pitts was the principal. Two additional classrooms were made by partitioning the auditorium with folding doors. Also, in 1921, a furnace generating steam heat was installed to heat both buildings of the school, replacing the dangerous coal stoves previously used to heat the classrooms.[286] A library was created in the school in the early 1930s by partitioning off part of the wide hallway in the upstairs south wing. There was also a small library in the back hall of the junior high department. The West Virginia Pulp and Paper Company contributed books to these libraries.[287]

One of the big events of the year at Cass during the 1920s was the commencement exercise for the junior high department of the school,[288] a week-long event with much fanfare. For example, in 1926, commencement exercises began on Friday, May 21, with a musical recital by Miss Yost's music pupils. On Sunday, a sermon was preached at the Presbyterian church by Dr. F. W. Thompson, president of Greenbrier College for Women.

Monday night was set aside for stunt night for the lower grades.

Tuesday night, a recital was scheduled by Miss Yost.

On Wednesday night, the senior play *Bashful Mr. Boobs* was presented.

Finally, on Thursday evening, Dr. M. P. Shawkey, president

of Marshall College, gave the commencement address and presented the diplomas.[289]

Teachers for the 1928-29 school term were: Cass Graded School – T. A. Reed, principal, Alda Haught, Mayo Beard, Marguerite Carter, Virginia Beard, Claire Warwick, Madeline Fuhrman, Opal Gum, Arlene Judy, and Lotus Butcher. Cass Colored School – Hattie K. Holley. Cold Run – Mary B. Bowers.

In October, 1928, a home talent show was presented by the young people of the community to raise money to buy a school piano.[290]

For several years during the 1920s a subscription series of cultural programs were presented in the school auditorium.[291]

Later an operetta put on by Mildred Pritchard became the highlight of the school year. When Elizabeth Woodell took over as music teacher the tradition was continued.

During the 1920s, students attending high school at Green Bank were transported in a truck owned and driven by James "Jim" Belcher. Difficulties of the driver were emphasized when he announced that "if occupants of said truck find it convenient to scuffle again they will be set at liberty to walk home."[292]

In February, 1926, continuous telegraph service started at Marlinton and Durbin with two shifts of eight hours each at Cass.[293]

In May, 1926, an unusual accident occurred on the northbound passenger train on the Greenbrier Division when J. E. Brice of Cass, express messenger, was buckling on his .45 caliber pistol, as required by regulations, dropped the gun, and was shot in the leg.[294]

The heyday of Cass, like most lumber towns in West Virginia, was during the years 1909-1925. Soon after that time, the depression struck and unemployment was rife. The residents of Cass were fortunate, for those who wanted could have a garden. Even the company houses had room for a small garden in back. Plowing was done by local farmers such as Ward and Pearly McLaughlin, Griffie Sheets, Walter Vint, Bernard Hamrick, Levi Galford, and others. Persons who lived in Cass during the late 1920s to the 1940s will remember Bernard Hamrick and his team of oxen "Amos" and "Andy." He made the air turn blue yelling at the team. He always ate dinner (midday meal) and oftentimes supper with the family for whom he was plowing. These meals stretched into hour long affairs as Mr. Hamrick entertained the family with tall tales.[295]

Many residents owned one or more milk cows. These were allowed to graze on the Company Pasture or through the town and surrounding lands in summer. The company charged one dollar per month in winter and two dollars in summer for pasture.[296] Later, cows were not allowed in the incorporated part of town except in the pasture. Cows found roaming through the town were put in the lockup adjacent to the jail. Persons from east of the river often drove their cows down the river and across to the old Extract Plant land.[297] Hogs for butchering in the fall and chickens for eggs and meat throughout the year were raised by many residents.

Silent motion pictures were popular in the mid-1920s and such titles as *Richard the Lion Hearted* starring Wallace Beery; *That Royal Girl* with W. C. Fields and Harrison Ford; *Sally of the Sawdust* with Carol Dempster and W. C. Fields; *The Everlasting Whisper* with Tom Mix and Tony the Wonder Horse; *Durant of the Bad Lands* with Buck Jones; and *The Man in the Saddle* starring Hoot Gibson were shown. Admission was fifteen and thirty-five cents.[298]

In any group of people there are those who are less gifted mentally than others. Such was the case with "Rich" McLaughlin. Rich lived on the Back Mountain Road south of Cass and frequently walked to town, sometimes carrying a lantern at midday. He struck some people as strange, but the fact is, it was sometimes dark before he arrived back home. An unfortunate aspect of Rich's character was discovered when someone started the rumor that he had consorted intimately with sheep on his farm. Rich heard the rumor and exploded in a stupendous display of wrath. Thereafter, hecklers, including many youngsters of the town, made his life miserable by calling out, "Baa," as he went by and running away as he turned in anger to chase them, amidst gales of laughter from onlookers. His nickname soon became "Baa Rich."

The grade school and junior high continued to flourish under the guidance of T. A. Reed, principal. In 1928, the teachers were Alda Haught, Marguerite Carter, Mayo Beard, Virginia Beard, Claire Warwick, Arlene Judy, Lotus Butcher, Madaline Fuhrman, and Opal Gum. The Cass Colored School was taught by Hattie K. Holley and the Cold Run School by Mary B. Bowers.[299]

A change in merchants in East Cass occurred on September 1, 1928, when Cooper's Department Store moved its entire stock to Durbin after twenty-four years of operation at Cass.[300]

The late 1920s saw the rise in popularity of the radio. The Atwater Kent radio was a popular marvel that could be had in either battery-operated or electric models.[301] Jasper Matthews was the first person in Cass to own a radio.[302] Radios were owned by only a few people, and neighbors came in droves to hear the radio debut of John Philip Sousa and his band in April, 1929, during the "General Motors Family Hour."[303] Homes with radios became social centers during the ensuing years when "Amos 'n' Andy," the "Joe Lewis Prizefights," and other popular events were aired.[304]

During the Reverend Mr. Gray's ministry a girls' circle at the Presbyterian church was organized which continued until the church closed. Also, a young people's organization was started. They met each Sunday night and from time to time had programs and social events.[305]

A change of ministers at the Cass Presbyterian Church occurred in 1929 when Rev. Fred Gray was replaced by Rev. T. H. Pharr.[306]

The year 1929 was another year of tragedy at Cass. In February, the body of Dave T. Corbett of Washington, D.C., was found on the tracks below the Extract Plant at Deer Creek. He had been run over by the freight train.[307]

Later in the year, on August 13, the railroad claimed another victim, Albert O'Brien, a native of Cass. Following a common practice, he had ridden the freight to Durbin. Unfortunately, he slipped under the train when he tried to get off.[308] His father had been killed by being run over by a train in the Cass yard about twenty-three years previously.[309]

In October, Clark McCloud committed suicide on Back Mountain. J. B. Sutton, undertaker at Cass, prepared the body for burial.[310]

There were also numerous cases of typhoid fever in the town.[311] It was a common belief that typhoid was imported from the South by watermelons since the season for these two events coincided. It is surprising that typhoid was not more widespread, for the town sewers opened directly into the Greenbrier River at several places.

Another noteworthy event at Cass in 1929 was the establishment on June 1, of Cass Chapter No. 124, Order of the Eastern Star. The first Worthy Matron was Ruth (Mrs. Ray W.) Fox.[312] A list of successive Worthy Matrons is given in Appendix L.

THE DEPRESSION YEARS: 1930-1939

The stock market crash on October 24, 1929, had an inevitable effect on Cass with the mill cutting back almost immediately, although it continued running at reduced hours.

A change in passenger service on the C&O was made on November 27, 1929, when the steam locomotives were replaced by gas-electric motorcar trains utilizing one of the new Brill engines, No. 9055, and a coach trailer.[313] Further decrease in business caused the cancellation, on July 21, 1930, of the morning and evening passenger trains, Nos. 141 and 144, on the Greenbrier Division.[314] These runs were never made again.

Many families in Cass, especially those without a large garden, chickens, a cow, hogs, etc., were hard hit by the depression. In order to help the most needy, Mack H. Brooks, principal of the school, set up free lunches for those without food. Persons who were working supplied beans, vegetables, and bread. Many of the more prosperous townspeople took turns supplying a meat dish. The ninth grade students helped prepare the food.[315] Many hobos left the train at Cass to "bum" a meal from the generous housewives.

On April 24, 1930, an exciting development took place in the entertainment area when the first sound talking picture was shown in Pocahontas County at the Seneca Theatre (formerly the Amusu Theatre) at Marlinton. A Vitaphone Production, billed as an all-talking picture, it was entitled *The Girl from Woolworths* and starred Alice White, Jack Delaney, and Wheeler Oakman. Matinee admission was fifteen to thirty-five cents and evenings twenty-five to fifty cents. The Seneca Theatre advertised having the best sound in the Greenbrier Valley.[316]

Nineteen thirty was a year of drought. The treetops left in the woods dried out more and more until the late summer when there were vast areas on Cheat that were as inflammable as kindling wood. The West Virginia Pulp and Paper Company made every effort to suppress fires and was fairly successful; however, by August, fires burned in many places along the Western Maryland Railroad, and hundreds of men went from Cass and Durbin to fight them.[317]

The town was again saddened in late August, 1930, when news was received of the death of Lyle Elmer Houchin, fourteen-year-old son of Elmer and Mattie Houchin of Back Mountain. He had accidentally shot himself while trying to cross a fence with a gun.[318]

In 1931, a Russian, known in the town only as Felix, shot himself at his home on "Bohunk Hill." He had lost a leg in an accident in the mill and was demoralized by the thought of having to spend the remainder of his life with a heavy wooden peg leg.[319]

"Army Aviator Lost." This headline in the *Pocahontas Times* for December 31, 1931, announced an event that caused great excitement at Cass. An army plane piloted by Lieutenant E. H. Bobbitt, Jr., aged twenty-four years, was last seen on Christmas Day, starting to cross over Cheat Mountain from west to east. Lieutenant Bobbitt was flying from Detroit to Hot Springs, Virginia. He landed at Uniontown, Pennsylvania, refueled, and proceeded on his way. He was traced to Mace, Pocahontas County, where he was seen heading eastward over the mountain. When he did not arrive at Hot Springs, a search commenced.

Hundreds of men from Cass and from the lumber camps on Cheat searched the woods for days. A half-dozen army planes searched the area from Marlinton to Randolph County.[320] These planes flew low and provided the first real look at an airplane for many residents of Cass. The wreckage and Lieutenant Bobbitt's body were not found until several months later. The plane had crashed on the side of Sharp Knob and burned. It then became hidden under snow until the spring thaw, when it was found by a woods crew. Souvenir pieces of the plane were taken by the dozens of people from Cass who rode the train up the mountain to view the wreckage.

Sometime during the 1920s, a telephone exchange was established in the second floor of Nethken's Meat Market. The first operator was a Mrs. Taylor.[321]

In February, 1932, floodwaters again did a great deal of damage to the businesses of East Cass. Several buildings were flooded on the first floor. Some residences in the Blackhurst Addition to East Cass were flooded and Walter G. Clarkson was hired to move the houses of F. D. Flynn and Clyde Kritzen to higher ground.[322]

The cement bridge across the river was damaged by the flood. Soon afterwards, the eastern end of the bridge cracked and the northern half of that end fell into the river. The Pocahontas Construction Company was in charge or repairing the span.[323] They did a good job of tying the new part of the bridge in, and it is still standing.

In 1930, Cass hired a new town constable who was to serve for many years. Joe "Uncle Joe" Wooddell had been a former trainman and lumberman on Cheat Mountain and was conductor on the log train before becoming town policeman.[324]

The early 1930s were quiet in and around Cass. On May 8, a beautiful pageant, *Silver Threads,* was given in the Cass Presbyterian Church in honor of Mother's Day. Music was presented by the Cass Junior Choir under the direction of Lena Anderson. Solos, duets, and quartets were handled beautifully by Alice Hannah, Genevieve Moss, Mary Shafer, and Bertie Lee Huff. Speaking parts were directed by Madeline Fuhrman.[325]

In 1932, the grade school had an enrollment of three hundred.

> The principal was Mack Brooks. Teachers were: Zoe Kirkpatrick, Pearl Carter, Alice Friel, Mildred Pritchard, Laurie Arbuckle, Mayo Beard, Lotus Butcher, Madeline Fuhrman, and Claire Warwick. The teacher at the Cass Colored School was Hattie K. Holley.[326]

In 1933, the schools closed on March 3 due to a shortage of funds; however, the dedicated teachers at Cass continued to teach one month without pay.[327]

Receiving diplomas in the Cass Elementary School in 1933 were:

> Marvin Dill, John Taliercio, Pearl Ryder, Earl Copen, Adam Taliercio, Alma Bowling, Catherine O'Brien, Delores Wright, Ruby Grimes, Eva Bowling, and Virginia Bible.[328]

In the early 1920s, school busses (trucks with a canvas cover) were used to haul students to Green Bank High School and from outlying areas to Cass Graded School.[329] At first, these busses were driven by high school seniors. Charles Lightner, Austin Lightner, and Margaret Lightner were among the early drivers.[330] Jim Belcher then took over the bus. The drivers owned their own busses. Mr. Ashford then started driving a separate bus for girls.[331] Pearl Kessler started driving the bus in the late 1930s from Back Mountain north of Cass. He brought all students from Back Mountain to Cass then continued to Green Bank, hauling girls only. Pinkney Doyle brought students to Cass from the Stony Bottom and drove the boys' bus to Green Bank.

In the early 1930s, movies shown at the Cass Theatre featured Buster Crabbe in *Tarzan the Fearless;* Mae West in *I'm No Angel;* Buck Jones in *The Lone Rider;* and Wallace Beery and Clark Gable in *Hell Drivers.*[332] Admission was ten and twenty-five cents on weekdays and thirty cents on weekends. In addition, occasional live entertainers, such as the singing group Cap, Andy and Flip, were very popular.

During the difficult economic times of the late 1920s and early 1930s, religion was a strong force in many people's lives. Attendance in the churches at Cass soared. On January 15, 1928, the attendance at Sunday school in the three white churches at Cass were 474 persons. In July, 1932, more than 500 persons attended the Candlelighting Pageant service held by the Cass Presbyterian Church under the big willow trees on the riverside lawn of W. A. Brill in East Cass.[333]

The surge in religious fervor brought wandering preachers and their families to Cass. They held services in tents at the C&O wye or in East Cass. Sometimes they occupied one of the vacant buildings in East Cass. Townspeople became caught up in the spiritual euphoria and supported the visitors. Most of these groups were of the Apostolic religion and depended on arousing the congregation to a high emotional pitch when a general outbreak of "speaking in tongues," quaking, shaking, dancing and sometimes falling to thrash on the floor would come about. These activities earned them the name "Holy Rollers." Numerous townspeople were "saved" at these meetings and gave repeated "witness" to their salvation.

After radios became more common, many people listened to such religious programs as E. Howard Cadle's "Hour of Prayer" broadcast from the Cadle Tabernacle in Indianapolis. The broadcast was carried on station WLW, Cincinnati each morning and on Sunday. Mrs. Cadle's introductory song, "Sweet Hour of Prayer," caught and held the attention of listeners.

Spiritual renewal was obtained by baptisms held in the river below the cement highway bridge or at the swimming hole at the mouth of Deer Creek. Here a large crowd formed, singing "Shall We Gather at the River," and "Washed in the Blood," to watch as the minister led one convert after another into the stream and totally immersed them to "wash their sins away." The Cass Baptist Church, the Pentecostals, and other religious groups held baptisms at the close of special revival services.

Churches also developed strong youth programs in an attempt to attract and hold the young people and to develop leadership for the church. Starting in the late 1920s boys and girls from the Cass Presbyterian Church were sent to Lewisburg as delegates to the Young People's Conference. In 1936, those sent were Sarah Hannah, Betty Hannah, Alice Hannah, Wilbur Kenealy, William Viering, Bob Nickell, Polly Ralston, James Moyer, and Dolores Wright.[334]

Small traveling shows and circuses periodically set up tents at the C&O wye or more often in East Cass. They featured melodramas, comedies, minstrels or circus acts with animals. They were poorly done by today's standards but were highly enjoyed by the townspeople, who had little other access to these types of entertainment.

During the years preceding the depression, the company had a doctor at Slaty Fork or Bergoo to take care of the men in that part of the operation. For years Dr. Cofer served in that capacity. The depression made it impossible to employ him and Dr. Hannah made the trip to Slaty Fork twice a week. He went by way of the CCC road after it was completed. He always carried an axe and a shovel to clear the road of fallen trees or to dig the car out of a snowdrift.

The 1930s brought about a significant change in the physical appearance of Cass. In about 1932, the main road through town was paved. Rocks for the road base were hauled in in a solid, rubber-tired truck by Kyle "Catty" Neighbors and were napped by hand with sledgehammers.[335]

The Prohibition Amendment was repealed on April 7, 1933, and was followed by repeal in Pocahontas County in June, 1933.[336] There was slight effect seen in the amount of drinking at

Cass, for whiskey had been readily available all along to those who wanted it.

In 1933, Congress provided funds to establish the Civilian Conservation Corps (CCC) to provide employment for hundreds of thousands of the nation's young men. The CCC resulted in a vast array of worthwhile projects. A CCC camp, Camp Randolph, was established in 1933 or 1934 at the top of the hill on the Cold Run Road where it met the Back Mountain Road about two miles southwest of Cass.[337] The main project of the men at Camp Randolph was to build a road from the above intersection across the southeastern flank of Cheat Mountain to Linwood. This road was completed by about 1936 and has since been known as the CCC Road.

Many young men from Cass were in the CCC at Camp Randolph, Camp Seneca at Seneca State Forest, Camp Watoga at Watoga State Forest, or at Camp Thornwood near Durbin.

Movies, with sound, brought to entertain the CCC boys were open to the public, and many persons went from Cass to see them.[338]

On April 21, 1934, David Luke, president of the West Virginia Pulp and Paper Company died of a heart attack in New York. His death was followed on May 31, 1934, by the apparent suicide of his son, Alexander M. Luke, who reportedly leaped from an airplane near Richmond, Virginia.[339] The latter had lived at Cass for about two years in 1927-29.

The depression brought about a rise in labor unions, which had not been popular with lumbermen in general. There had been a camp of the Mechanical Workers of America in Cass since the early days of the operation there. In 1911, the Cass camp had twenty-eight members and was one of the thirteen camps in Pocahontas County.[340] It was more of a social organization than a labor union. By 1934, however, the unrest produced by the depression catalyzed a strike that closed the mill at Cass for more than three months.[341]

During the next few years, at least two unions were established at Cass. The first of these, the Junior Order of United American Mechanics, was present by 1935. John Jack was councilor and Owen B. Curry was financial secretary.[342] In 1937, the United Timber and Sawmill Workers was recruiting members at Cass.[343]

The Cass Lumber Council, a group of employees of the company but not a labor union, instituted an annual employee picnic in the 1930s. The outing was held at Cass or at one of the other company towns. All employees and their families were invited. Transportation was provided via the log train, and there was a large attendance. In 1935, Bill Keyser and George Howell comprised the Transportation Committee. Entertainment included a square dance, baseball game, tug-of-war, greasy pole climbing, greasy pig catching, fat men races, three-legged races, and motion pictures. Prizes were given the winners.[344]

During WPA days, a playground was built on the Company Pasture northwest of Cass. An area of several acres were leveled and a ballfield established. Level land at Cass was at a premium and Sunday softball games were played on this area for a number of years despite the fact that there were no shade, no water, and no other conveniences located there.

The location picked for the ballfield was formerly a potter's field where several persons were buried. These persons had no known relatives and included foreign laborers whose metal number tags were found with the remains. The disinterred remains were buried at the cemetery near Deer Creek.[345]

For many years, the *Pocahontas Times* published a popular feature, a "Top Notchers" list. It was a list of pupils in each county school who had an average of ninety percent or more for a grading period. The "Top Notchers" for the Cass Grade School on January, 1935, were:

Albert Church, Norman McLaughlin, Augusta Pharr, Freda Bowling, Pat McKisic, Beatrice Blackhurst, Pauline Cosner, Arden Curry, Leonard Galford, Josephine Hannah, A.C. Hill, Dewey Hiner, Jack Hoover, Ruth Lawrence, Warren Shifflett, Howard Wilfong, Marie Dill, Billy Ervine, Thurmond Cosner, Harry B. Hill, Bertina O'Brien and Aretta Phillips.[346]

Two long-standing businesses in East Cass are still remembered by people who lived there during and after the depression years. One such business was "Buck" Hamrick's place. Buck took over the restaurant and pool hall run by his brother, Page, in the building in East Cass at the end of the bridge on the north side of the road. In 1940, this building burned and Buck moved across the road into the Siegel Building. Still later, he moved into the brick Brill building, where he operated for many years. The family lived downstairs and in the back rooms upstairs. "Buck" sold his business in May, 1961, to Charles Gum who operated it until June, 1969.[347]

The other business was Kirkpatrick's Restaurant on the ground floor of the Moose Lodge Building. Affectionately known as "The Greasy Spoon," Kirkpatrick's, run by Hattie and Jimmy A. Kirkpatrick, was a plain place where young people gathered to talk, dance to a jukebox, and have a Coke. This was later taken over by Joe and Maggie Vint.

In the 1930s, residents of Cass joined other "sportsmen" of the state in cruel and misguided attempts to increase game fish and animals by holding Varmit Killing Contests. These contests, sponsored by local sportsmen's clubs, assigned points for each designated "varmit" killed. Examples of points assigned were: Panther 10,000, Wildcat 600, Weasel 400, Red or Gray Fox 400, Mink 400, Eagle 300, Owl 200, Hawk 200, Wild or Hunting House Cat 200, Kingfisher 200, Crow 200 and Red Squirrel 100. The panther was further singled out with a reward of fifty dollars for the first one killed in Pocahontas County. To claim points, the head or skull of the "varmit" was presented to a judge. The pelts were retained by the owner.[348]

The number of animals killed was astounding. Nearly 200,000 were killed in 1933-34 in twenty-six participating counties in West Virginia and almost 300,000 in 1934-35 in the forty participating counties. One year's kill, 1933-34, was distributed as follows: 3,007 hawks, 1,892 hunting house cats, 79,481 snakes, 13,497 water dogs, 9,438 crows, 1,430 weasels, 1,451 gray fox, 15,370 turtles, 1,030 kingfishers, 34,475 rats and mice, 87 garfish, 4,417 terrapins, 321 mink, 59 German carp, 399 red squirrels, 8,089 chipmunks, 954 owls, 3,985 starlings, 311 wildcats, one timber wolf (coyote) and 1,907 English sparrows.[349]

The *Marlinton Journal* reported on September 8, 1932, that "Master 'Bobby' Fox, the interesting young son of Mr. and Mrs. Ray Fox of Cass, celebrated his eighth birthday with a porch and lawn party assisted by little Miss Evelyn Fox. Favors were toy trucks filled with lollipops. Guests were: Emory Shaffer, A. C. Hill, Pat McKisie [*sic*] McKisic, Nim Ralston, Buddy Geiger, Nelson Lewis, Clyde Gilliam, and Junior Oliver."[350]

In February, 1933, Cass lost one of its prominent citizens

when Samuel Lake Clark died with a heart attack. Lake Clark was born in Greenbrier County on March 2, 1884. He operated the store at Spruce before he and his wife, the former Virginia Gillespie moved to Cass. He was a longtime Sunday school superintendent at the Presbyterian church, served on the town council, and held a responsible position in the Pocahontas Supply Company. He was in his third term as postmaster when he died.[351]

Also, in 1933, a great loss to the lumber operation occurred when E. P. Shaffer retired. He had been in poor health since about 1928.[352]

In the late 1920s, a 4-H club was established at Cass under the leadership of G. Pearl Carter. Since there were originally twelve female members, it was called the Lucky Dozen 4-H Club. Within a few years the membership had grown to thirty. The name was changed to the Handy Andy 4-H Club and Zoe Kirkpatrick became leader. From 1932 to 1939 Margaret Hannah was the leader and the club reached its greatest membership, thirty-five. The club's name was changed to Cass Work Faster 4-H Club and in a year or so, to A.W.W. 4-H Club. In 1939, Elizabeth Wooddell became leader. In a few years the membership was down again to twelve.[353]

The drums of progress slowly began to beat again at Cass in the late 1930s. In September, 1936, officials of the West Penn Electric Company met with interested persons to discuss the possibility of extending an electric line from Marlinton to Durbin. In December, the decision was made to make such an extension and to build a line from Dunmore to Cass.[354] The line was surveyed by a crew headed by Jennings Bradford.[355] The following summer, the residents of the southern part of the East Cass, as well as private homes west of the river and in the surrounding farms and communities, were treated to the conveniences of electricity.

The year 1937 was another year of tragedy for the people of Cass. In late January, Albert Ray, who operated a store and filling station in East Cass, shot and killed himself.[356] Further violence erupted at Cass when a man named Armentrout, an escaped convict from Virginia, was reported to have been seen in Durbin, walking down the C&O tracks toward Cass. Lawmen from Cass immediately headed up the track and waited in ambush at the curve above the mill. When Armentrout came by, they called for his surrender, and when he ran, they shot him.[357]

On March 19, the town was saddened when Joseph Knight, aged forty-nine years, was instantly killed in an accident in the Cass lumberyard. Knight, a brakeman on the log train, fell under a loaded car of lumber while shifting cars in the yard. The engine was Shay No. 13 with Guy Stanley at the throttle. Knight was the husband of Neva Galford. A World War I hero with nine months of front line service, he had been awarded several medals for bravery in action. The remains were taken to the Sutton Funeral Home at Cass where the funeral was conducted by Rev. H. Blackhurst.[358]

Shortly afterward, on March 24, Stanley Roberson fatally shot his wife, Vivian. Roberson was found guilty of murder in the second degree by the October Circuit Court and was sentenced to eighteen years imprisonment.[359]

On July 5, 1937, Mack H. Brooks, the prominent young principal of the Cass Graded School, was appointed assistant superintendent of Pocahontas County Schools. He was temporarily replaced at Cass by C. E. Flynn.[360]

The effects of training youth of the more affluent families for religious leadership were evident in 1938, when Miss Alice Hannah, daughter of Dr. and Mrs. U. H. Hannah, went to the Belgian Congo to teach for three years in a mission school.[361] Her letters, describing conditions in the Congo, appeared in the *Pocahontas Times* for many months thereafter.

The Senior Girls' Circle of the Cass Presbyterian Church met at the home of Miss Catherine Blackhurst, Thursday evening, July 1, 1937. Refreshments were served to the following members: Mrs. E. J. Shafer, chairman; Nadine Eddy, Polly Ralston, Kathryn Wright, Mary Shafer, Molly Anderson, Mary Ruth Richard, Louise Richard, Sara Lee Ralston, Jane Shaffer, Roma Roy, Catherine Blackhurst, Betty Hannah, Margaret Gum, and Genevieve Moss.[362]

In 1938, the Durbin Theatre began bringing movies to Cass on Friday night, replacing the movies that had been shown at the CCC camp. The first showing, on July 22, was *Snow White and the Seven Dwarfs*.[363] Movies were shown in the auditorium of the grade school and later in the Siegel Building. Mr. Summerson had the franchise at Cass.

The Handy Andy 4-H Club sold popcorn and suckers at the movies to make money to send members to Jackson's Mill State 4-H Camp and to the Pocahontas County 4-H Camp.[364]

October 30, 1938, will be remembered by many as the night of the "Invasion from Mars." The now-famous Orson Welles radio show, "War of the Worlds," was received in Cass, where it caused the same panic that occurred nationwide. Several residents who heard the broadcast went immediately to get their families from church to prepare for the inevitable. Faces were red when the truth became known, but the fear of the moment was very real.

On November 1, 1938, Joseph K. Cass, for whom the town of Cass was named, died. This event went largely unnoticed by Cass residents, for he had not been there for many years and was practically unknown by the townspeople.[365]

A concentrated effort to revitalize the religious life of the town was made in March, 1939, when revival services were held simultaneously in all churches. Minister of the Presbyterian church was Rev. J. T. Pharr; Rev. Harry Blackhurst was leader of the flock at the Northern Methodist Church in East Cass; Rev. A. C. Bell was pastor of the Southern Methodist Church, and George Gilbert was lay minister of the Cass Baptist Church.[366]

The Cass Grade School received new leadership in 1939 when J. Kermit Arbogast was named principal. Teachers were: Edmonia Gibson, Louise Hull, Elizabeth Wooddell, Mary Warwick, June Riley, Laurie Arbuckle, Margaret Hannah, Mayo Beard and Madeline Fuhrman. Sidney Goodwin was teacher at the Cass Colored School.[367]

"Top Notchers" were:

Cass Colored School—Aylea Jackson, Trellis Tyson, and Beatrice Jackson. Cass Graded School—Joanne Shrader, Alice Keyser, Gertrude Blackhurst, Patty McPherson, Dorothy Dickenson, Norman Loudermilk, Letha Cassell, Virginia Gray, Julian McLaughlin, Tommy Meeks, Edward Plyler, John Slaven, Theodore Wymer, Alyne Gum, Doris Miller, Freda Rexrode, Marie Smith, Abbie Tacy, Dorothy Taylor, Betty Jean Tumblin, Edwin Lee Doyle, Charles Miller, Eugene Moore, Phyllis Brice, Madeline Gum, Frances Keyser, Marietta Lester, Virginia McLaughlin, Imagene Shifflett, Mary Jo White, Jimmy Addington, Russell Cassell, Lewis Shinaberry, Marie Burris, Nina Mae Fuhrman, Ruth Lewis,

Francis Sheets, Anna Mae Smith, Junior Loudermilk, Ted Shinaberry, Mary Ann Gillespie, Henrietta Ralston, Genevieve Carpenter, Thurmalee Cassell, Mary Hunter Gum, Mable Mauzy, Ruby Miller, Mary Etta Nelson, Anna Plyler, Velma Ray, Gaynelle Rexrode, Janet Rose, Marilee Ryder, Catherine Sheets, Nadine Shifflett, Maxine Shinaberry, Berdeen Simmons, Jewel Sutton, Maxine Webster, Glenna White, Norman Dickenson, Bobby Fuhrman, Lee King, William Moore, Roy Nickell, Julian Sampson, Oliver Tacy, Leonard Wilfong, Tressie Cassell, Roy Clarkson, Katherine Hendley, Buddy Keyser, Ayleene Kesler, Gay Miller, Gertrude Moss, Susan Porter, Lucille Rexrode, Bernard Shifflett and Ruth Taliercio. Spruce School — Lemuel Powers.[368]

Eighth grade graduates in 1939 were:

Cass, Colored — George Steward. Cass, Graded — Roy Arbogast, Madeline Bennett, Edith Bradley, Clinton Cassell, Delbert Cassell, Dale Cassell, Albert Church, Isabel Church, Beulah Copen, Lila Gum, Hilda Hamrick, Raymond Haptonstall, Donald Haptonstall, Joe Holiday, Ruby Houchin, Nelson Lewis, Franklin McCalpin, Norman McLaughlin, Calvin Miller, Naomi Miller, Junior Moats, Augusta Pharr, Dale Ryder, Roma Ryder, Lucy Gray Scott, Marshall Shinaberry, Rhoda Summerfield, John Tacy, Lillian White and Maggie Wymer.

The school benefited by the hot lunch program initiated during the 1938-39 school year. It provided the best meal of the day for many children.[369]

On July 23, 1939, word was received that Charles W. Luke, aged fifty-one years, had died. He was one of the founders and vice-president of the West Virginia Pulp and Paper Company. He and his family had a summer house in Cass for a number of years before 1920.[370]

In October, 1939, three of the Taliercio boys, John, Adam and Sam were in an automobile wreck when their car plunged into Knapps Creek near the Minnehaha Bridge. All received injuries, especially Sam who was badly injured, but, fortunately, all survived.[371] They were the sons of Frank Taliercio.

The year 1939 was not the most promising year to start a new business in Cass. But, with firm faith in the future, John M.

"Deacon" Kane did just that. He opened the Cass Grocery Store in the Odd Fellows building on Main Street where the Cass 5 and 10 Cent Store formerly was and where "Tex" Blackhurst had operated a store. His store provided direct competition to the Company Store, where he had been a clerk and meatcutter for many years. Many people thought he would go under; however, by good business practices and a lot of luck, the business survived and eventually expanded, using the old Cass Theatre as a warehouse.[372]

A practice instituted by "Deacon" Kane when he first opened his store was that of charging groceries. Records were kept on small books with carbons between the pages so that a copy of each transaction could be given the customer. When the bill was paid each month, a treat of a bag of candy was invariably given. It was the only candy many families had during the hard times preceding World War II.

WORLD WAR II TAKES ITS TOLL: 1940-1949

The year 1940 started with another fire in East Cass. Buck Hamrick ran a beer parlor on the ground floor of the building at the east end of the bridge on the north side of the road beside Kirkpatrick's Restaurant. The family lived upstairs. On January 9, a fire destroyed the living quarters. Buck moved his beer parlor and family across the street to the ground floor of the Siegel building. The family lived on the same floor.[373]

A popular event, anticipated throughout the year, was the Pocahontas County Fair, held annually in August at Marlinton. Citizens from throughout the county thronged to see the sideshows, races, stock and vegetable displays, school exhibits, rides and other attractions.

On the way home from the fair on August 21, 1940, a truck driven by Clifton Lyle of Cass, went off the road south of Dunmore. The truck, carrying thirty-eight children and adults, was returning home from the fair in a dense fog. Homer Hamrick, four-year-old son of "Buck" and Mae Hamrick, was so badly hurt in the wreck that he died on August 23. Homer was a favorite of many people in town and his tragic death anticipated the mood of the war years ahead.[374]

Events in Europe during the years immediately before 1940

led to the peacetime draft. In October, 1940, the following Cass residents were registered:

Frank M. Sutton	Flosten M. Sampson
Stanley W. Barkley	Alvin H. Richards
Earl Woodrow Belcher	Leonard James Long
Warren Cross	Roscoe Galford
Wallace Lee Dill	Frank L. Taylor
Roy Allen Barkley	Walter Brooks White
James Russell Waugh	Lloyd F. McLaughlin
Earl Hampton Copen	Joseph J. Vint
Merle William Ervine	William Fred Lawrence
Grover Wm. Wright	Clyde Joseph Tallman
Lyle Gilmore Sharpe	Alfred Garfield Gum
Clifton Isaac Lyle	Chester H. Neighbors
Berton Bernell Gum	Jerald Gerome Teter
Byrd F. Shrader	Earnest Lee Halterman
Virgil Leebert Taylor	Samuel S. Jackson
Ed. J. Barkely	Porter L. Sheets
Earl Elmer Cosner	Carnie Carles Cross
Woodrow W. Hamrick	James Edward Hall
Richard B. Blake	Emmett Ray Loudermilk
Ollie Marten Sheets	Robert Lee Ervine
Edward Edmond Howell	Joe Allen Hamrick
Earl Stanley Kisamore	Carl Emory Cosner
Rudolph Urbanick	Charles Marvin Moss
Carson Casper Nelson	Luther B. Wilfong
Clarence Orsbin Lyle	Roland C. Swisher
Ralph Julian Cassell	Paul James Brake
Roy Cassell	Henry Walter Adams
Floyd E. McLaughlin	Frank G. Puffenbarger
James Earl Brice	Snowden Glenn Galford
Kenton W. Halterman	Walter Eugene Perry
Paul Clayton Bradley	Burley Berton Fowler
Theodore W. Jackson	Arnold Hevener Sheets
Huffman Summerfield	Claude W. Halterman
Clarence Roy Taylor	George Smith
Harlow Cassell	Jesse Ward Tacy
James Garfield Walker	Stanley Nathan Lovelace
Oliver Rail Tyson	Frank Andrew Varner
Clyde Lee Wilmouth	Leland Leroy Ervine
William H. Fulks	Lester Robert Cook
Frank Hopkins Gray	Earl Wilson Ralston
Walter Brown, Jr.	Myrl William Cassell

Robert Kyle Slaven
Albert N. Smith, Jr.
John Phillip Varner
William H. Gillespie
Lonza F. Rexroad
Carl Hannah Rose
William Jason Gore
Raymond A. Cosner
Laban M. Foe
John M. Taliercio
James William Sutton
Nile W. Gainer
Jesse David Tumblin
Hubert O. Williams
James R. Pusey
Lyle W. McPherson
Charles A. McPherson
Ether J. Tyson
Hughes M. Cook
James Wilson Friel
Carl John Galford
James P. Cook
Marvin Hannah Dill
William F. Viering
Carl Hunter Gumm

Dale H. White
Ollie Joseph Tacy
George A. Duncan
Boyd Myers
William Lester Begley
John Bert Friel
Guy Julious Gum
John Ballard Cassell
Charles Stanley Mayes
Oscar George Sill
Bedford C. Chestnut
Graham G. Tallman
Bruce Edward Nelson
Arthur Lemual White
Benjamin N. Jackson
Johnny E. Sheets
Ivan O. Clarkson
Ralph M. Tallman
Hilton W. Church
Jack Pusey
Kyle J. Neighbors
Arlie G. Carpenter
Claude A. Stimeling, Jr.
Pearl C. Ryder

J.B. Bear, Chmn. Selective Service Board, R.W. Fox, Secretary.[375]

Life went on as usual. A class of thirty-nine students graduated at the Cass Grade School Commencement, Wednesday, May 7, 1941. It was held at the Presbyterian church. The speaker was Dr. R. T. L. Liston, president, Davis and Elkins College.

Graduates were:

Irene Arbogast
Carl Beverage
Audaline Carpenter
Genevieve Carpenter
Beulah Cassell
Hazel Cassell
Thurmalee Cassell
Norman Dickenson
Roy Nickell
Albert O'Brien

Ruth Hamrick
Lee King
Mable Mauzey
Ruby Miller
Bobby McLaughlin
William Moore
Marietta Nelson
Ruth Nethken
Nadine Shifflett
Maxine Shinaberry

Anna Plyler
Gaynelle Rexrode
Janet Rose
Marilee Ryder
Julian Sampson
Catherine Sheets
Mary Alice Sheets
Bobby Fuhrman
Evelyn Galford
Mary Hunter Gum

Berdeen Simmons
Patricia Slaven
Jewel Sutton
Russell Stanley
Oliver Tacy
Ray Thomas
Peggy Wanless
Maxine Webster
Glenna White[376]

The rumblings of war grew louder and louder in 1941. During September, a brilliant display of northern lights was interpreted by many as an omen that war was inevitable.[377] The attack on Pearl Harbor confirmed their fears and Cass, like communities across the land, prepared for the long, bitter struggle.

Another victim of John Barleycorn, Roland Swisher, was killed on December 16, 1941, as he lay on the C&O Railroad track sleeping.[378] This accident occurred just below the Cold Run Bridge at Slab Town.

World War II had two contrasting effects on the town of Cass. On the one hand, the continued demand for lumber stimulated business, and assured long work hours for the workers, and good profits for the company. On the other hand, the town was decimated by the number of volunteers and draftees who went to war and the other men and women who left Cass for war-related jobs in Baltimore, Akron, Dayton, Cleveland, Detroit, Charleston and other cities.

This latter exodus was speeded up by the United States Employment Service, under the War Manpower Commission, which brought in representatives to interview townspeople for jobs in crucial war industries.[379]

Practice blackouts, rationing, long work hours, Movietone newsreels at the theatre, and Lowell Thomas with the evening news on the radio brought the realities of war close to the folks at home; however, nothing quite prepared them for the shocking news of sons, friends, and close comrades killed in action. As each telegram was delivered to the next of kin, the entire town felt the loss deeply. Among those to give their lives in battle were: Marshall G. Shinaberry, son of Mr. and Mrs. Albert Shinaberry and popular manager of the athletic teams of Green Bank High School during his high school years; Letcher Lee King,

Lucy King's son and Eugene King's brother; Garland Moore, foster son of Mr. and Mrs. J. B. Sutton; John H. Mathews; Frank Burris, son of Mrs. Mable Burris, was killed in action in Germany; "Dutch" Haptonstall, son of F. J. Haptonstall, died on board the U.S.S. *Leyte*; Floyd Edwin McLaughlin was killed in action; James Garfield Walker was killed in Germany.[380]

All news was not bad, however. One Cass native, Harold E. Bird, U.S.N.R., received the Distinguished Flying Cross for heroism in the Pacific.[381]

Other, prominent townspeople fell to the "Grim Reaper" during the war years. On February 26, 1943, E. P. Shaffer, former superintendent and moving force on the Cass operations, died.[382] The same year, Squire James Byron Sutton, mortician, carpenter, and justice of the peace, succumbed on August 23.[383] Dr. U. H. Hannah died in October, 1943, after twenty-nine years in practice at Cass. On November 23, 1943, Bernard B. Hamrick, who is remembered for his tall tales and his team of oxen with which he plowed the local gardens, died.[384]

The war years also saw a tragic killing in Cass. The town policeman, Joe "Uncle Joe" Wooddell, arrested a man named James "Jim" Adams and put him in the old town jail. Officer Wooddell either didn't place him in a cell or the cell wasn't locked. When Wooddell entered the jail later, Adams attacked him and Wooddell had to shoot in self-defense.[385]

August 20, 1943, was an eventful day for Cass. The town, mill, timberlands, and all other holdings were purchased by the Mower Lumber Company from the West Virginia Pulp and Paper Company. Almost immediately, an infusion of new administrative officials and their families moved to Cass. The Company Store was revamped inside. The company office replaced the post office, which was moved into the former Nethkin's Meat Market building adjoining the store.

On September 25, 1944, the home folks were startled when a low-flying Army fighter plane zoomed down Leatherbark Hollow and over the town. An exciting air show followed during the next half hour. It was not until later it was learned that the flyer was Lt. Harry K. "Buz" Blackhurst, who was passing nearby and couldn't resist the opportunity to "buzz" the town.[386]

Kirkpatrick's "Greasy Spoon" remained open during the war years and was a haven for high school students. Nightly dancing to "In the Mood," "Always," "I'll Be Seeing You," "Sentimental

Journey," and other sentimental tunes helped pass the time until the boys were old enough to enlist or be drafted, and the girls could get into war production work.

Buck Hamrick's Place in the Brill building provided pool, beer, and companionship for those who were not yet in the service.

Bell Cross' Place was also open as a hotel and beer parlor. On July 7, 1945, Merle Lee Kelly killed himself in Bell's Place.

The basic nature of Cass was different after World War II. A large number of the populace had been exposed to the outside world for the first time. Many of them were now dissatisfied to remain in the small, isolated town and work on the sawmill or in the woods as their fathers had done. Some, like Earl Belcher, stayed in the armed services until retirement; Calvin Galford stayed in the Army but died on August 6, 1947, from injuries received while working on a telephone line.[387] The GI Bill opened educational opportunities to many who could not otherwise afford them. Young men left to attend college to become doctors, dentists, teachers, professors, lawyers and other professionals. Other people remained in the cities where they had gone to work during the war years.

A building in the Blackhurst Addition along the Green Bank Road, owned by Willis Cassell, contained a garage run by Glow Sampson. In 1940, it was purchased by Oney Plyler. Oney converted it to a skating rink, with a small store in front. After two or three years, he built an addition on the side in which he operated a garage and converted the skating rink into living quarters.[388]

December 31, 1946, marked the demise of Stuart B. Nethken, former operator of Nethken's Meat Market.[389]

Mrs. Ollie R. Ervin and Mrs. Shears began operating the Cass Boardinghouse in 1948. It was located in the old hospital on the hill above the Company Store. (After the hospital closed the E. P. Shaffer, Joe Hannah, and Sid Keyser families had lived there.)[390] Reasonable room rates and home-cooked meals made the boardinghouse a popular place for workmen on the train and mill. Many mill and lumberyard workers ate lunch there.

The need for additional social life was felt by some townsfolks and the ladies organized the Cass Rebekah Lodge No. 91 which was instituted on August 31, 1949. Ernestine Clarkson was chosen Noble Grand; Irene Doyle, Vice-Noble Grand; Beulah Dahmer, secretary; and Edythe Davis, treasurer. Margaret "Sis" Jackson and Myrtle Cook were chosen Noble Grand during the following years. The lodge was discontinued after four or five years due to the low membership.[391]

A gymnasium was added behind the grade school in 1949 giving Cass students opportunities for basketball and other indoor sports. A full lunch program was also begun in 1949.

A popular entertainment event during the 1940s and 1950s was donkey basketball. Donkeys were equipped with special foot coverings and the games were played in the gymnasium at Green Bank. Local teachers or other well-known persons mounted the bareback animals and attempted to play basketball. The game was enlivened by the liberal application of electrical shocks to the donkeys to make them run, buck, etc. much to the merriment of school children and friends as the teachers and others were bucked off or otherwise made to look ridiculous.

THE END OF AN ERA: 1950-1959

A pall of gloom fell over the town on April 9, 1951, when news arrived that one of the town's favorite sons, Capt. Harry K. "Buz" Blackhurst, who had provided the excitement of an air show to the town in 1944, was killed in a plane crash. "Buz" was one of a party of Air Force personnel en route to Charleston, West Virginia, from Godman Air Force Base in Kentucky, where they had attended the funeral of a fellow officer. The toll of the April 8 crash was twenty officers. Other Cass natives who died in the armed forces during the Korean War were John Thomas Geiger and Hubert Earl Thomas.[392]

The Northern Methodist Church, where the Reverend Mr. Blackhurst had been minister for twenty years, had closed during World War II because of a lack of attendance, and the congregation moved to the Southern Methodist Church. The building was sold on May 23, 1951, to the Cass Baptist Church for two thousand dollars.[393]

The mill continued running through the 1950s with an occasional interruption for a breakdown of one kind or another. The machinery was getting old, and repairs were becoming more difficult. The foundry burned in 1957, destroying hundreds of molds and further reducing the ability to repair broken or worn-out parts.[394]

Some local excitement occurred in January, 1953, when the liquor store at Cass was robbed. Randy Taylor, a clerk, was knocked unconscious.[395]

During this decade, enrollment at the Cass Graded School had dropped. Only six teachers and a principal were hired. In 1955-56 they were: F. Wilmer Ruckman, principal; Glenn P. Tracy, Ruby Gum, Gertrude B. Wooddell, Louise Brown, Lynn Kerr and Ruth F. Riley. Allen J. Blackhurst was custodian. Only eight students graduated that year.[396]

The Cass Colored School was still a separate one-room school taught by Ida S. Choice. Students there received high quality education and, in 1953, the West Virginia Golden Horseshoe Award for excellence in knowledge of state history and government was won by Samuel Tyson.[397]

During the 1950s and later years, a well-known figure around Cass was Eugene King. Eugene spent his days at the Company Store, the depot, or at Kane's Grocery where he assisted in work being done and talked to visitors.

In the 1950s, movies were popular and the Durbin Theatre had showings at Cass on Monday and Friday nights. *Operation Pacific* starring John Wayne and Patricia Neal; *Two Flags West* starring Joseph Cotton and Linda Darnell; *Appointment with Danger* with Allan Ladd and Phylis Calvert; *West Point Story* with James Cagney and Doris Day; and *Dallas* starring Gary Cooper and Ruth Roman were among those being shown.[398]

The Company Store steps made an ideal place for unemployed or retired persons to sit and talk and to wait for the passenger train to arrive. Toward train time a faithful group gathered there and moved down to the station to see who might be arriving or leaving when the train pulled in.

There was a new topic for conversation in 1954 when a Cass native, Warren E. "Tweard" Blackhurst, well-known teacher at Green Bank High School, naturalist, homespun philosopher, Sunday schoolteacher, taxidermist, and local authority on many things, published a book, *Riders of the Flood*, depicting the life and times of the men who made the log drives down the Greenbrier River before the turn of the century.[399] Blackhurst had heard tales all his life about the river drives. He had talked to participants in those exciting events. His book skillfully retold those tales in novel form, weaving in historical events in an accurate and interesting fashion. Tweard's book was an instant success, a tribute to the talents and knowledge of this extraordinary person. *Riders of the Flood* did much to awaken local people to the great historical legacy hidden in the recesses of the minds of former workers in the lumber operations in the regions.

The year 1956 saw a major change that would affect future developments at Cass. The U.S. Postal Service, on March 8, began carrying mail by truck to the upper Greenbrier Valley from Lewisburg. For fifty-five years, mail had been carried by rail. In 1956, total revenues for the train, exclusive of the mail, were $5,739 while operation costs were $39,170.[400]

The year 1956 was a year of rejoicing as the vaccine for polio became available. This controlled a disease that blighted the lives of many and filled the summer months with fear and dread.[401]

Other changes in 1956 included the death of Rev. Harry Blackhurst on November 24. The Reverend Mr. Blackhurst was eighty-six years old. Sixty of those years were spent as a Methodist minister. He was known and loved by everyone in the town.[402]

During the same year on December 11, F. Edwin Mower, aged fifty-seven, owner of the Mower Lumber Company, died leaving the company and therefore the town with a somewhat uncertain future.[403]

The death of Mower, along with a general decline in business, forced the closing of the mill for several weeks in the early part of 1958. On March 6 of that year, the Cass area was declared an emergency area by the governor. Immediately thereafter, representatives of the State Commodity Distribution Division came to Cass to take information concerning the need for commodities. Mayor P. F. "Bus" Long and Jack Kane, owner of Kane's Grocery and a member of the board of education, also took requests for commodities. Flour, meal, rice, powdered milk, and cheese were soon distributed to needy townsfolk on a weekly basis.[404]

The Greenbrier Division of the Chesapeake and Ohio Railroad served the people of Cass well for fifty-seven years. Reliable passenger, mail, and freight services were of great importance to the town, particularly in the days when highway travel was inconvenient and unavailable to many. On July 1, 1953, the first freight train on the Greenbrier, powered by a diesel locomotive, went through Cass. It was a token of things to come. Although steam engines were used during the next year, the last steam-powered freight train on the Greenbrier line ran to Durbin on Friday, June 25, 1954, and returned to Ronceverte on Saturday, June 6.[405]

The last regular passenger train pulled by a steam engine had run earlier in 1954 when, on January 16, 18, and 19, No. 1058 made the round trips from Ronceverte to Durbin. The last steam engine used on the Greenbrier in regular service was No. 992, which powered a work train on December 19, 20, and 21, 1955.[406]

On December 24, 1957, the C&O Railroad petitioned the Public Service Commission to discontinue the passenger run to Cass. Public Service Commission hearings revealed that No. 143 carried a daily average of 1.9 passengers per mile and No. 142 carried 1.5 passengers per mile. The petition was approved, and the last motorcar passenger trip was made on January 8, 1958.[407]

The End and a New Beginning: 1960-1969

Considering the slow business and irregular workdays experienced by the company in the late 1950s, it should not have been a shock to people when the final notice was posted that the mill was to close effective June 30, 1960.[408]

However, reality is not always easy to recognize and the habit of years is not easy to break. Months later, people were still waiting, eagerly grasping at rumors that the mill would reopen. The news that the capital stock of the Mower Lumber Company at Cass had been sold to Walworth Farms, Inc., an affiliate of Grace Steamship Lines, fueled these rumors for a time.[409] When the Company Store closed and the Ritter Lumber Company bought the complete inventory at the Cass planing mill and lumberyard, the townspeople became more pessimistic. The tracks and equipment of the lumber railroad were sold to the Midwest-Raleigh Salvage Company, which sent crews to the far end of the tracks to begin tearing up the rails. As the extensive stacks of lumber were loaded and the lumber docks were torn down, the reality that the mill was closed forever sank in.

The curtain had rung down on Cass as it had on so many other logging towns along the Greenbrier River. North of Cass, the sawmill towns of Wildell, Gertrude, May, Burner, Braucher,

Boyer, Olive, Madeline, Winterburn, Dunlevie and Nottingham had all flourished for a time, supported by sawmills, only to fade into oblivion when the mill cut out and closed. Southward, Deer Creek, Raywood, Cloverlick, Stillwell, Watoga, Seebert, Denmar, Locust, Spice Run, Renick, Spring Creek, and Anthony's Creek had met the same fate.[410]

A sense of deep pessimism fell on the people of Cass, and those who could find jobs elsewhere began to leave. One local job prospect was the National Radio Astronomy Observatory (NRAO). Located at Green Bank because of its remoteness, the lack of radio interference, protection by the surrounding hills and a variety of other reasons, the NRAO promised to catapult the region into the twenty-first century. Ground was broken for the NRAO on October 17, 1954. The first major telescope was completed, and observations were underway by the fall of 1959.[411] The NRAO continued expansion and provided jobs for many Cass natives, some of whom continued to live at Cass; others moved to Green Bank or Arbovale to be closer to their new jobs.

Then, a new hope appeared when the state showed an interest in purchasing the lumber railroad, shop, and rolling stock for a tourist attraction. As these plans developed, former track workers, trainmen, shopworkers, mill workers and others who had devoted years of their lives to activities involved with hauling logs from the heights of Cheat and cutting them into lumber now started working just as diligently toward preparations for hauling tourists up the same ancient tracks, with the same antique locomotives. The townspeople were not optimistic about the probable success of the new venture, but it provided employment for some and confidence gradually grew.

June 15, 1963, was a red-letter day for Cass. On that day the first official passenger trip on the Cass Scenic Railroad was made. The initiation of regular passenger service brought an influx to Cass of thousands of persons on weekends and lesser numbers during the week. During the first year, sandwiches were prepared and sold by the women of the local churches in Cass. These were sold in the old Company Store building and were also hauled by truck to the train terminus at Whittaker.

In 1963, another book about the local lumber industry was written by Tweard Blackhurst.[412] *Sawdust in Your Eyes* was a novel but it contained much about the lives and times of early Cass.

By the next year, the Company Store was leased by a group of local persons. They opened it as the Cass Country Store, under the management of Jesse Brown Beard Powell.

Tweard and Stella Blackhurst prepared a Wildlife Museum, featuring mounted specimens of local animals. Tweard was a taxidermist and for years had maintained a display in the big attic of the Blackhurst home at Cass. A hightlight in many a Cass youngster's life was a visit to the Blackhurst attic to see Tweard's stuffed animals. These specimens were moved to the warehouse adjacent to the Company Store and set up along with various, interesting local items.

Good attendance on the Cass Scenic Railroad the first year of operation encouraged further developments at Cass. In 1964, Jack Kane purchased a railroad dining car for a restaurant and opened the Shay Inn. It was placed on a sidetrack north of the old C&O station, which served the Scenic Railroad as ticket office and provided rest room facilities.

The same year Kyle "Catty" Neighbors and his wife, Ina, established a Civil War Museum adjacent to the Wildlife Museum. In 1973, it was expanded to include a logging-lumbering-railroad collection called the Cass Historical Museum.

The renewed interest in state history sparked by the State Centennial Year celebrations, in 1963, was reflected in another book by a Cass native, Roy B. Clarkson. *Tumult on the Mountains—Lumbering in West Virginia 1770-1920* was an attempt to record the events involved in one of the most exciting times in our history. In addition to general descriptions of methods used in lumbering and the way of life of the woodsmen, short descriptions of several lumber towns, including Cass, were given. Over 250 photographs were included to illustrate many phases of the lumber industry. The book also contained a bibliography of 266 items.[413]

In 1965, Tweard Blackhurst wrote another book concerning life in and around Cass.[414] *Of Men and a Mighty Mountain* has a fascinating style. It consisted of short chapters in which various residents of the town speak. The book provides an excellent insight into how the people in Cass lived. It is required reading for anyone who wants to understand Cass or any similar lumber town.

Momentary excitement was generated in February, 1965, when Marlene McLane, daughter of movie star Barton McLane, visited Cass and announced plans to buy and restore "Dirty Street" to early 1900s condition and also spoke of acquiring the mill.[415] These plans were never carried out.

The Cass Grade School had continued to decline in numbers of students and by 1966 there were only nine graduates. That fall there were 108 pupils in the school.[416]

The continued popularity of the Scenic Railroad led to further business adventures by various persons. A successful stagecoach ride was operated many years by William Tyler and later by a Taylor and still later by Hoxie Meeks. The ride left the parking lot of the Cass Railroad just north of the Cement Bridge, forded the Greenbrier River when the water was low enough, made a circle down through the lower part of East Cass and returned.[417]

In 1969, Mr. and Mrs. John S. Benjamin, producers of the Greenbrier Repertory Theatre at Lewisburg, opened a theatre in East Cass in the former Siegel building. They produced old-time melodrama and variety shows several weeks in the summer.[418]

The following year, on August 12, one of ten special TV programs on "American Heritage" was taped at the depot at Cass. The show featured country stars Oscar Brand Odetta, the Leon Bibb Singers, Merle Travis, and Bill Monroe and the Bluegrass Boys.[419]

A DREAM DEVELOPS: 1970-1979

The year 1970 marked the end of an era at Cass when the Cass Graded School was phased out. That year there were seventy-five students and five teachers. The school was merged with the Green Bank Grade School. The Cass School had operated for sixty-nine years, fifty-five of those in the present school buildings.

In 1970, Tweard Blackhurst wrote yet another book based on life in and around Cass.[420] *Mixed Harvest* was primarily about the lives of pioneer farmers and how their lives were changed when a sawmill came to their part of the country and a town was established.

Tweard's pen was silenced forever on October 5, 1970, when he died. A last book, *Afterglow,* containing his unpublished writings, was published by his wife, Stella, in 1972.[421] His books continue to give us pleasure and insight into life in Cass.

The first notable event of 1971 was the robbery of the liquor store in February. During the robbery, Clarence "Tony" Ware, who ran the store, was beaten. Money stolen amounted to $90.67.[422]

An announcement in May of the same year created much excitement in the town. The Greenbrier Railroad Company, Ronceverte, West Virginia, announced plans for eight steam rail excursions on May 30, July 11 and 25, August 1 and 8, September 5 and October 10 and 17. The largest operating steam engine in the United States at the time, Reading Railroad's No. 2102, would pull a train on the Greenbrier Division from Ronceverte to Durbin and return. Over three hundred railfans from thirty-two states rode the initial trip. Operating as the Greenbrier Scenic Railroad, these successful tours were continued through 1973, when seven tours were held, and 1974 with eight tours.[423]

Regular operations of the C&O continued to be curtailed, however. In September, 1972, the C&O reduced services on the Greenbrier Division to two freight trains a week—up Monday, down Tuesday and up Thursday and down Friday.[424]

An event announced in 1973 that would greatly effect the Cass area was the development of the Snowshoe recreational facility in the headwaters of Shavers Fork. Developed primarily as a ski resort, Snowshoe proved immensely popular. Jean-Claude Kiley acted as consultant in planning the ski runs.[425] The high altitude and resultant low temperatures enables Snowshoe to have a longer season than many other area ski facilities. Opened for skiing on December 13, 1974, Snowshoe proved to be one of the most successful skiing facilities in the East. By February, 1975, when the official opening was held, a resort center complex, two administrative buildings, four and one-half miles of ski slopes served by three triple chair lifts, a $1 million snow-making system, a tertiary sewage plant, and 6.1 miles of access road had been completed.[426] Additional plans were to make this a year-round resort.

Snowshoe has continued to be popular with an average of about three hundred thousand visitors each year.[427] During the fall of 1983, a permit was issued to Snowshoe by the West Virginia Department of Natural Resources to remove coal on seven acres on the mountain to the north of the Snowshoe access road, the first step in the construction of an airport to serve the facility. The runway was planned to be between 4,500 and 5,000 feet long.[428]

In 1974, the Presbyterian church in Cass was donated to the town by the Greenbrier Presbytery for use as a community center. Teen dances, family nights, square dances, reunions, and other events were held there. Music by Carl Davis, Thurmond Cosner, and "Lefty" Meeks was a popular feature of some of these events.[429]

Cass senior citizens were active during this period. They met at various homes to complete a community quilt and to work on other projects.[430]

Another fire occurred in Cass on May 5, 1975, when the former C&O depot used by the Cass Scenic Railroad burned.[431] Fire continued to plague the town and, on January 4, 1976, a company house, rented by Frank Eary, burned to the ground.[432]

The town was shocked on February 6, 1976, when Gene Allen Crist died of self-inflicted gunshot wounds.[433]

On July 1, 1976, the dream of many Cass natives seemed to be coming true when U.S. Senators Jennings Randolph and Robert C. Byrd announced the approval of a $896,000 grant to help provide funds for acquisition of 685 acres of land in and around the town of Cass including the company-owned homes and the Company Store. It was the first step in a long-range plan to restore the town to the condition it was in about 1920. These funds were to provide the means to relocate seventy-nine families and to renovate thirty-eight dwellings.[434]

In addition to the above grant, the Bureau of Outdoor Recreation of the U.S. Department of Interior approved $308,000 for the project and the state agreed to furnish $301,000 for a total of $1,505,000.[435]

The deed for the Town of Cass was recorded in the county clerk's office at Marlinton on January 18, 1977. Title to this land, along with various other tracts, was conveyed by the Mower Lumber Company to the State of West Virginia for the sum of $669,611.[436]

A small book, *Do I Want to Go Home*, relating memories of his early years at Spruce and Cass, was written by Harry E. Duncan and released in the spring of 1977.[437]

Fire struck yet again in 1977. A house on Spruce Street burned in the early morning and set fire to two additional houses. All three were destroyed.[438]

The McLaughlin Cave, now known as Sheet's Cave or Cass Cave, claimed its first victim in September, 1977, when Reginald V. White, aged twenty-one years of Akron, Ohio, died from effects of a climbing accident while descending the 140-foot high waterfall. During the descent, he became loose from his chest harness and was suspended upside down in the waterfall. Death was caused by hypothermia.[439]

On August 10, 1978, the town of Cass was nominated to the National Register of Historical Places as the Cass Historic District. The Cass Scenic Railroad was already listed on the National Register.[440]

Violence occurred again at Cass on October 26, 1978, when Delnor "Del" Wilson Cassell, aged thirty-eight years, was shot to death at his home by two blasts of a shotgun.[441] It was ruled justifiable homicide and no arrests were made.

The Greenbrier Division of the Chesapeake & Ohio Railroad had declined in usage until an application to abandon the line was filed with the Federal Trade Commission and approved. On December 28, 1978, a train, pulled by engine No. 2311, made up of four hopper cars, loaded with wood chips, one with coal, five empty boxcars, and a boxcar of railroad material followed by a yellow Chessie System caboose, made the last trip from Durbin to Ronceverte. The line was officially abandoned on December 29, 1978.[442]

The West Virginia Department of Natural Resources purchased the section of track from Cass to near Durbin in order to have rail access to the "outside." Rails were removed from Raywood, two miles below Cass, to North Caldwell and the right-of-way was donated to the state by the C&O. It was developed as The Greenbrier Hike, Bike, and Ski Trail. The state purchased the rails from Raywood to Cass for use on their line at Cass.[443]

A near tragedy occurred in June, 1979. While they were fishing from the cement bridge at Cass, David Eary, aged fifteen years, and Scott Cassell, aged twelve years, were hit by a car driven by Roy L. Cain, Jr. Both boys were seriously injured.[444]

On October 6, 1979, a new wrinkle was tried by the state in an attempt to get some of the town houses renovated. The state offered 20-year leases on five houses. The homes were to be fixed up by residents with materials sold by the state. The exteriors were to be restored according to strict specifications to conform with the original design. The minimum permissable bid was two thousand dollars. In addition it provided for a 20-year lease at a cost of one hundred dollars per month. There were no takers of this plan, and the task of renovation remained entirely with the state.[445]

In his State-of-the-State Address in January, 1979, Governor Jay Rockefeller asked for two million dollars to speed up the renovation of Cass; however, his proposal was not passed by the legislature and renovation has gone at a snail's pace.[446]

WHAT NEXT? 1980-?

The first phases in renovating the town were to upgrade the water system and to install a sewage treatment system. Public meetings were held concerning the sewage system, and a decision was made to build settling tanks on the west side of the Greenbrier between Cass and Deer Creek. Total estimated cost of the sewage system was $1,537,000. Funding came from the Environmental Protection Agency, the Appalachian Regional Commission, the state, and the local share through Farmers Home Administration. The sewage treatment system was completed early in 1982.[447]

Bids on improvements to the water system were opened on December 4, 1980. Plans called for a small impoundment in Leatherbark near the shop, a new water treatment plant to be located next to the impoundment, and new waterlines.[448] A storage tank was situated on the old ballfield in the Company Pasture west of Cass. This provided gravity flow for the town water supply. This project was estimated to cost seven hundred thousand dollars.

A milestone was passed in February, 1981, when the Cass Historical District was placed on the National Register of Historical Places. Included were ninety-six surviving buildings representative of a 1910-20 lumber town.[449]

Business activities in the town in 1982 included the Cass Country Store and Restaurant, Kane's Grocery Store and Amoco Station, Kane's Shay Inn, Lefty Meeks' Barber Shop, Back Mountain Crafts, the Wildlife Museum run by Stella Blackhurst Miller, the Cass Historical Museum run by Ina Neighbors, the Cass Scenic Railroad, the Alpine Lodge and Restaurant, the Golden Whistle, the Cass Inn run by Tammy Cosner, and Charley's Place run by Charlie Gum. The population was 173 persons.[450]

Interest in the natural beauty of the area became evident when the Greenbrier River was included in a study by the United States Forest Service for Federal Wild and Scenic River designation.[451] The study was done under the direction of the Monongahela National Forest. Much opposition to such a designation was expressed by landowners in the lower Greenbrier Valley. The Forest Service study found the river suitable for inclusion in the wild and scenic system either for scenic or recreational status. Most of the river above Caldwell was included in a bill approved by a subcommittee of the Interior Committee of the House of Representatives. Excluded from wild and scenic status for three years was a section between Marlinton and Cass that was being considered as the location of a flood control dam.[452] The Greenbrier was not included in the Wild and Scenic River Bill.

The early 1980s saw a resurgence of interest in Cass. Frequent reunions of graduating classes from Green Bank High School and of families were held. The largest family reunions were those of the Blackhurst-Burner relatives held in the community building. These were attended by large numbers of family members and friends.[453]

During the summer of 1983, construction began on a second ski resort in the headwaters of Cheat River. Known as Silver Creek, the new 2,700-acre facility was bounded by Snowshoe to the south, Cheat River to the east, the Western Maryland Railway to the north and the top of the mountain to the west. The property included the drainage of Black Run and Mace Knob. Long-range plans called for a $500 million year-round resort with a mountaintop ski lodge, indoor-outdoor pool, indoor ice skating rink, and twenty-four summit-to-base ski slopes with seven to nine triple chair lifts. Also planned were an 18-hole golf course, tennis courts, horse stables, riding and hiking trails, indoor and outdoor playgrounds and game rooms. The golf course was planned for use in cross-country skiing in the winter.

The project developer was American Resort Services, Inc. of Columbia, South Carolina, whose president was John Kruse. Leonard Jackson was a fellow developer. The lodge was to contain nine floors. The first floor would have lounges, ski shops, restaurants and health clubs. The other floors would contain 450 one- and two-bedroom condominium units in the $50,000 to $185,000 price range. The complex was designed by Sno-Engineering of Lyme, New Hampshire. It was estimated that full development would require ten years.[454]

Silver Creek was officially opened on Monday, December 19, 1983. The core building and ten ski slopes with three lifts were in operation at that time.[455]

A potentially significant meeting was held in the Cass Shop on May 22, 1982, during which the Mountain State Railroad and Logging Historical Society was established. The Association was concerned with railroad and logging history throughout West Virginia. Plans called for the preservation and display of artifacts from the two industries as well as historical research and writing. A journal called *The Log Train*, to be published at least quarterly, was planned.

First officers of the new organization were:

President – George Deike, Cass, WV
Vice-President – Richard Sparks, Alexandria, VA
Secretary – William Olson, Worthington, OH
Treasurer – Fred Bartels, Cass, WV
Principal Directors – John Bledsoe, Huntington, WV
    E.E. Burrus, Charlottesville, VA
    William P. McNeel, Marlinton, WV
Directors-at-large – Richard Dale, Cass, WV
    Benjamin Kline, Lancaster, PA
    William Bell, Kensington, NJ
    Roger Mower, Philadelphia, PA
    Tony Koester, New Jersey
    Ralph Glover, Charleston, WV
Ex-officio Directors (or their representatives) –
    Don Andrews, Chief of Parks, WVDNR
    John Killoran, Executive Director,
     WV Railway Maintenance Authority
    Norman Fagan, Director, WV Department of
    Culture and History
Editor – Max Robin, Denville, NJ
Archivist – George Collins, Williamsburg, VA
Publicity – Michael Allen, Brighton, MI[456]

In 1983, the Department of Natural Resources purchased the Cass Graded School building from Odessa Kane. They planned to develop it as a museum and display area.[457]

Violence was common in the old days at Cass, and occasionally headlines still attest to violent acts there. The latest was in the *Pocahontas Times* of January 6, 1983; "Arrest Made in Glenn Corbett Death." Glenn Corbett was found in his truck at Cass on May 24, 1980, with a serious head wound. He was dead on arrival at the hospital.[458]

One of the landmarks of Cass was destroyed in 1983 when the Cass Theatre building was torn down. It had been used for many years as a warehouse for Kane's Grocery.[459]

On July 3, 1983, a reunion of former Cass residents was held at the community building. This event was very successful with an attendance of hundreds of persons.

A new idea for utilizing the state-owned houses at Cass was announced on April 26, 1984, by Department of Natural Resources Director Willis H. Hertig, Jr. Six of the original houses had been totally refurbished by Department of Natural Resources' Division of Parks and Recreation and were to be rented as 6-person "cabins" on the same basis as cabins in the other state parks. Completely furnished for housekeeping, the houses feature modern bathrooms, fully equipped kitchens, cooking utensils, tableware, linens, blankets, towels and dishcloths. Energy efficient wood stoves and electric bathroom heaters provide heat. The houses are open year-round.[460]

In August, 1984, a change in the postmaster at Cass was made by the replacement of Evelyn Lightner by Maude Moore.

October 1, 1984, marked the change of ownership of a long-standing business at Cass when Kane's Grocery was sold to Benny Simmons. The business had been in Kane's family for forty-five years. The business closed in July, 1986, leaving Cass without a grocery store or gasoline station.[461]

The popularity of the Cass Cave resulted in the death of a second young spelunker on December 1, 1984. Mitchel Gubkin, aged twenty years, died in an accident similar to one on August 28, 1977, which also claimed a life. In each instance, the caver was making the 150-foot vertical drop into the main room of the cave from a ledge near the waterfall. In each case, his climbing gear became fouled, hanging the victim in the waterfall and trapping him until death resulted from hypothermia.[462]

The general malaise stifling the town government of Cass foreshadowed its end when only one person attended the town meeting in March, 1985.[463] On July 1, 1985, the town charter was surrendered to the secretary of state, and the town government was officially ended.[464] The existence of a town government is not essential for the town to continue, however, and the future of Cass is assured because of the Cass Scenic Railway State Park.

There have been several floods over the years that have flooded the first floor of businesses in East Cass, primarily in 1908, 1913, 1917, and 1932. However, none of these compared to the flood of November 4 and 5, 1985.

During the last days of October and the first days of November, hurricane "Juan" moved from the Gulf of Mexico, making landfall near Mobile, Alabama. The circulation of air around "Juan" forced warm tropical air northward over the southeastern United States. This air mass remained intact as the weakening remnants of "Juan" moved up the Mississippi Valley.

At the same time, a low pressure system moved slowly north through the southeastern states to center in northeastern West Virginia. A flow of air was created, bringing abundant moisture from the Atlantic Ocean and causing heavy, widespread rainfall. The soil became nearly saturated by November 3. The onset of heavy rain on November 4 quickly saturated the soil forcing the additional heavy rainfall into streams in northeastern West Virginia. Rainfall may have exceeded twelve to fourteen inches in the headwaters of the Greenbrier and in the South Branch of the Potomac Rivers.[465]

As a result, almost all of East Cass was inundated. There were four business buildings, former Brill's, Siegel's, Cooper's, Granny's Restaurant, and a post office trailer located in the business part of East Cass. All were heavily damaged. The Cooper building collapsed as did the rear part of the Siegel building. Granny's Restaurant, owned by George Alikakos, was completely demolished and washed away. Brill's brick building had less damage, but when the National Guard was burning the remains of the Siegel building, the Brill building also burned. It was so damaged that it had to be razed along with the remaining portions of the other buildings. The business part of East Cass was completely destroyed.[466]

Dwellings were also heavily damaged. The remaining houses for blacks south of the business section were washed a hundred yards downstream, and the remains were burned by the National

Guard. Further south, the floodwater reached over thirty inches deep in some homes and extensive damage was done to the homes lining the street.

The people living there quickly started clean-up operations. With the help of people from the unaffected part of Cass and the surrounding countryside, the homes were soon being lived in again.

Restoration of the state-owned part of town made remarkable progress during 1986-87. Eleven houses had been renovated for rental.[467] Board sidewalks and picket fences had been rebuilt along Main Street and Spruce Street. Wooden steps were constructed up the hill behind the Company Store and a wooden trestle led northward across a valley to another set of steps, not present in the original town, that connected the Cass Showcase area with a walkway on the hill.

As the work of renovation progressed, Cass began to take on the character of a prosperous, early-century lumber town. It is the goal of the State Parks and Recreation System to restore the town to the appearance it had in 1910-20 thus making Cass a unique museum of the lumber era in West Virginia.[468]

Another important development during 1987 was the establishment of the Cass Volunteer Fire and Rescue Company (CVF&RC). Organized in June the group of about thirty members soon had a charter, a constitution and elected officers.[469]

Several members took Fire and Emergency Medical Treatment courses. In November, members inspected a used ambulance and decided to purchase it for use at Cass. Donations had been received to cover the $4,000-cost of the vehicle.[470]

Attempts to purchase a used fire truck were successful in December, 1977. January 10, 1988, was designated as the first day of operation of both fire and ambulance service.[471] The CVF&RC continued training sessions on both fire fighting and emergency medical training and has become an important community organization.

During the flood of 1985 wells in East Cass were ruined. In response to this, plans were formulated to supply East Cass with running water. A grant from the Appalachian Regional Commission was obtained for eighty percent of the cost of the project.[472] In 1987, a waterline was placed under the Greenbrier River and plans for completing the system were made. Bids for the remaining work were opened on December 6, 1988. The Triple H Construction Company of Beverly was the lowest bidder.[473]

In May, 1988, a boating company under the name Whistlepunk Raft and Ducky Company set a building south of the end of the cement bridge. Their idea was to rent rafts, boats, etc. for rides on the Greenbrier River. This was removed in 1990.

A "Bed and Breakfast" was established on Spruce Street by Gil and Mary Willis. It was located in the house formerly lived in by S. D. Huff and later by Fred Weber.

The possibility of improved highway access to Cass surfaced in June 1988 when the Senate Interior Subcommittee approved a request by Senator Robert Byrd for $1.25 million in the 1989 budget for upgrading the CCC Road from Cass to Rt. 219 near Linwood. The work was begun in May 1990, and is expected to be completed in September 1990. The road, when completed will have a beneficial effect on Cass as well as on the Snowshoe and Silver Creek resorts.[474]

The Second Cass Homecoming was held July 2-3, 1988, in the community center (former Presbyterian church) with about two hundred in attendance. Honored senior guests were Mrs. Pearl Cassell, Mrs. Oney Plyler, Mrs. Nola Dahmer, and Harry Wanless. On Sunday morning Kevin McLaughlin, son of Paul and Peggy McLaughlin, preached in the church the first sermon there in eighteen years.[475]

XVI
THE CASS SCENIC RAILROAD

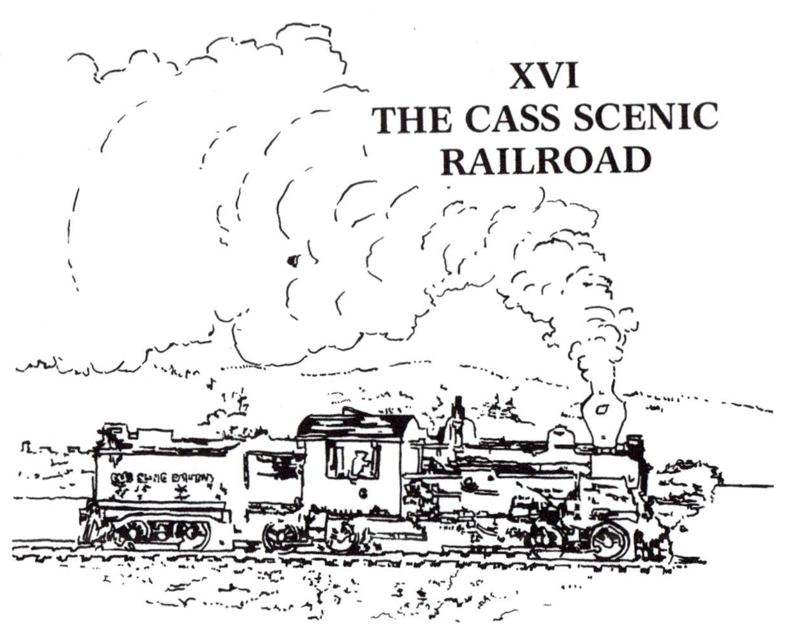

In the summer and fall of 1960, events took place that resulted in the eventual development of the Cass Scenic Railroad State Park by the State of West Virginia. On June 30, 1960, the Mower Lumber Company closed their mill at Cass after over fifty-eight years of almost continuous operation. The Mower interests were not long in disposing of their holdings after the mill was closed. The timberlands and the Mower Lumber Company name was purchased by the Wadsworth Farms, a subsidiary of the W. R. Grace and Company of New York. Don Mower set up a company to retain ownership of the town of Cass, the mill and the railroad line.[1] The rails, rolling stock and other items were sold to the Midwest-Raleigh Steel Company for scrap. A single former Mower shop employee, Ivan Clarkson, was retained to help keep the salvage equipment moving.[2] Tom Hayes was sent to supervise the scrapping operations and crews began at the far end of the line bringing in abandoned equipment and removing rails.[3] The remains of the Cabin Fork track were the first removed, then work progressed to the newer Bald Knob spur, thence to the heavy steel from Spruce to Old Spruce.[4] Loaders, skidders and log cars were brought to Cass and scrapped in the area north of the shop. Camp cars were offered to anyone who wanted them. Hayes offered to unload them with a loader at the Back Mountain Road crossing if someone would take them away. This offer was not taken up and most of the camp cars were burned at Cass.[5]

For several years, during the last phases of the logging operation, Cass, with its assemblage of Shay locomotives, steam skidders, steam loaders, the Cass Shop, and the mill, had become a mecca for steam fans, especially steam railroad fans. One of these, Russell Baum, a sporting goods distributor from Sunbury, Pennsylvania, rode one of the first scrap trains to Bald Knob and was struck with the possibility of retaining Cass as a passenger road. Baum related his thoughts to the mayor of Cass, "Bus" Long who hastily called a conference of local businessmen.

Baum also told Bill Sperry, owner of the El Poca Motel in Marlinton, about his idea and Sperry contacted Jim Comstock, editor of the *West Virginia Hillbilly* at Richwood. Baum and Sperry drove to Richwood and met with Comstock Sunday evening, October 2, 1960. "The burden of Mr. Baum's visit was brief. Something is going on in West Virginia," he said, "that was of shameful and disasterous proportions and could have lasting ramifications. . . . It was the removal of the steel at Cass."[6] Baum told Comstock that the Cass lumber railroad could mean millions of dollars to the state from tourists, who, by proper advertising, could be enticed to come into the hills of West Virginia and ride a steam locomotive.

Comstock asked Baum if he would make a further investment in time and come to the State Legislature which, fortunately, was holding a special session, and help him sell the idea. The next morning Comstock headed for Charleston, arrived there at 10:30, and went straight to House Speaker Harry Pauley's office. Waiting to see the Speaker, Comstock met J. C. Cruikshank and "unfolded the story of the Cass Railroad to him. 'Let's get going and do something about it,' Cruikshank said. Just at that minute Ralph Bean, president of the Senate, stepped in, asking if he could see Mr. Pauley, and J. C. and I [Comstock] joined forces at banging his ear with the story."[7]

Bean said that what was needed was a joint resolution put through to hold everything up until the matter was investigated. Cruikshank and Comstock went to the Resolution Office and Legislative Auditor, C. H. Koontz, had the resolution drawn up.

Next, Comstock visited Warden Lane, director of the West Virginia Conservation Commission. Lane said that he had already heard about the railroad and that "he had been thinking about the state's taking it over, but wasn't sure at all that the state could swing it even if it did prove feasible because it seemed from what he heard that the town of Cass, or the houses of the town, had to go along as a package deal with the railroad and the land on which it sits."[8]

On the afternoon of October 4, the second day of the Special Legislative Session, after the invocation, J. C. Cruikshank got to his feet to announce that he had a resolution and Clerk Blankenship read the first paragraph as he is wont to do. But Republican leader Bub Seibert suggested that the entire resolution be presented and the clerk read the following:

Providing for the Joint Committee on Government and Finance to make a study of an appropriation to authorize the Conservation Commission to acquire by purchase a railroad in Pocahontas County for its value in attracting tourist trade.

WHEREAS, the Mower Lumber Company had closed its timber operation at Cass, Pocahontas County, W.Va., and among its assets to be disposed of is a branch railroad operated by steam locomotives; and

WHEREAS, This railroad traverses the highest elevation in the east; and its tremendous value as a scenic attraction for thousands of tourists and visitors to our State is recognized and it is in the process of being disposed of for a "junk" price; and

WHEREAS, Other states, particularly the State of North Carolina, have recognized the importance of such an attraction and similar enterprises are in operation there. Now, therefore, be it RESOLVED by the Senate, the House of Delegates concurring therein:

THAT the Joint Committee on Government and Finance direct that a study of the feasibility of acquiring aforesaid railroad and its equipment be made promptly and that the study include possible cost of such an undertaking and its possible value as a tourist attraction in connection with or separate from the general parks and recreation program of the Conservation Commission;

THAT the committee be authorized to designate additional members of the Legislature to assist in such study as they deem necessary;

THAT the expenses necessary to conduct this study and to make the necessary report as early as possible be paid from the legislature appropriation for joint expenses in the 1960-61 appropriation bill;

THAT the members of the committee and the legislators so designated shall receive $25 per diem and ten cents per mile for transportation as expenses actually incurred in the discharge of their duties.[9]

J. C. Cruikshank then got up and gave an impassioned plea for the purchase of the railroad. He was interrupted by Speaker Pauley for the reading of the other resolutions. Then Pauley turned to Cruikshank who took over the Speaker's seat, and called for Mr. Baum to come before the group and tell his own story of the Cass Railroad and make his own plea.

Baum stepped to the speaker's stand and made the following historic plea:

My purpose here today is to suggest the feasibility of the state of West Virginia's purchasing and operating a segment of the Mower Lumber Co. in Cass, West Virginia, as an operating museum of railroading and lumbering—turn of the century style—for the benefit of the people of the state and as a major tourist attraction. And further, to show that this tourist attraction would pay its own way from its own revenue.

Railroads, and especially logging railroads, have for the past 15 years been my primary hobby. Through business, the military service, and vacations, I have traveled and seen most of the interesting railroads in 49 of our 50 states. Canada, and Mexico from the Cookuila and Zocateas to the White Pass and Yukon. In riding over the Mower railroad last October it occurred to me that few Railroads and none of the operating tourist railroads came close to matching the Mower in spectacular scenery. Further the most scenic part of the line is within 6 miles of Cass.

It was because of the ride that the thought kept mulling over in my mind that this definitely would be the line to preserve as an operating logging railroad to be promoted as a tourist attraction. It would be a natural for the state to include it in its Park System. This whole concept of a railroad park is not new. In 1947 the Cedarville R.R. was born in Cape Cod District of Mass. with six mile of track around a Cranberry Bog. Today it is the most successful of the tourists operations. The passengers each year are in the hundreds of thousands.

Another tourist railroad is the Tweetsie at Blowing Rock, N.C., near the Smokies but in a remote section of N.C. I was told that last year they made $150,000 net profit. This year they are adding $30,000 in superfluous additions such as the purchase of a railroad locomotive from the White Pass and Yukon in Alaska. They have a five mile circle of track. Another good example is the Silverton Line running from Durange to Silverton, Colorado. They are booked up in advance for tickets and a ride over their 45 miles of track requires a four day wait on the average. Today Durange is a booming tourist center. Hotel rates shot from $2.50 eight years ago to $7.00 today for a single, and the unusual part is that Durange is 450 miles from the nearest city of over 5,000 population and has to compete with such attractions as the Grand Canyon, Rocky Mountain National Park, and Yellowstone for the long distance tourists.

Another is the East Broad Top in Penna. It started this August with a five mile trip through some pleasant farm land. It is presently bettering expectations and Mr. Wilburn, the operating Vice President, expects to add to the line next year.

Although these other railroads are operating quite successfully, they have only one basic attraction, that is a railroad with an operating antique steam engine hauling people for an average of five miles over the track. The Mower Lumber Co. Railroad has far more to offer.

To start with, it would be the operation of a real railroad – most of the tourist lines are built for the occasion and for the historian type person, therefore lack interest.

The Mower does not merely go around in a circle or over an uninteresting stretch of land. The other lines operating in the East can come nowhere near matching its scenery. You would have the added interest of lumbering – turn of the century style – and lumbering in itself has a great appeal to many people. Today in the United States the only railroad logging by the old method of rail to logging point and skidder car and cable is the Mower Lumber Co. It travels the highest point East of the Mississippi River of any railroad. It has the best scenery East of the Rockies and is the only operational railroad east of the Sierras that would have the potential to serve as a tourist attraction.

The engines themselves are very unique in the annals of railroading. They are Shay geared steam engines complete with a real 1890 diamond stack. There are two switchbacks on the line. And I know of only two others left in the U.S.

There is an added attraction of a mammoth cave only about 50 yards from the suggested termination of the line on the hill. This cave has received innumerable write-ups in certain magazines. A cave in itself would attract numerous tourists, and the combination would make a very strong tourist attraction.

Then at Greenbank, five miles away, is a large observatory that would help attract still more people.

The Mower operation would require the operation of only five miles of track and the purchase of six miles. This would take the line through its finest scenery, and five miles is the ideal length for this sort of thing.

Because the major investment is there, the cost would not be large and no more than scrap value for rail and engines.

To summarize, none of the other railroads serve any other purpose then to memorialize steam railroads and none have operating geared engines or interesting scenery. With the Mower you have in addition the large interest in logging – the chance to show old time logging railroading at its best and a large undeveloped cave.

However, this is the last opportunity to do something about it. Unless it is stopped, the salvage company wants the tracks ripped up by time winter sets in. Building a new railroad would be prohibitive.

The highways for entering Cass from East, North, and South are very good making it readily accessible.[10]

The House voted to adopt the resolution and the Senate passed it the next day.[11] Salvage operations were suspended until a joint committee of the legislature investigated the situation.

The Legislative Committee went to Cass on Saturday, October 22, and rode the train up the Cass Hill behind Shay No. 4.[12] As they rumbled up the mountain, the prospect of developing the railroad into a viable tourist center must have appeared dim. The right-of-way from the water tower at the C&O junction at Cass to the top of the mountain was a lush carpet of weeds. Rotting ties, supported the worn rail, and alongside drooped the ancient phone line that once connected Spruce with Cass along the busy Cass Hill line. The trestles over Leatherbark creaked with age when an engine passed over them.

The area around the shop was piled high with assorted parts, equipment and junk left by the Mower Shop crew. The sidings were filled with worn-out skidders, loaders and cars waiting to be burned or in the process of being cut up after the wooden parts had been burned. The sand house was leaning and in danger of collapse and the coal tipple was in such bad condition that C&O hoppers could be pushed only partially out over its rickety wooden trestle. The lumber mill, planing mill and warehouse were in the best conditions but these too showed the effects of years of neglect. The lumberyard was well stocked with lumber, but this was in the process of being shipped out. Only the water tower, owned and maintained by the C&O and the tracks leading to the depot were in good condition.

Despite the overall decrepit condition of the operation, the committee was impressed with the potential of the proposed tourist railroad. The committee met in Charleston on Sunday, November 20, 1960. A petition bearing the names of fifteen hundred Marshall College students and numerous wires and letters were read to the 6-man group before they unanimously voted on Co-chairman Harry Pauley's motion to recommend the purchasing of about eight miles of track along with assorted equipment and facilities.[13]

When the Legislature met in March, 1961, the committee's recommendations were considered and on March 3, the House voted unanimously in favor of the purchase, and four days later the Senate also approved the purchase.

Agreeing with the recommendations of the Legislature, Governor W. W. Barron announced on April 20, that the purchase would be made. The Governor and a party of state officials rode the train on April 22 to gain firsthand knowledge of the new facility.

Details of the purchase were announced by Conservation Commission Director, Warden Lane, as follows:

The total purchase price was $142,500. Of this, Midwest-Raleigh Steel Corporation received $125,000 for twelve miles of track, three locomotives (Shays No. 1, 4 and 5), ten flatcars, a water tank and other equipment. The Wadsworth Farms received $17,500 for the right-of-way, one hundred acres of land at the top of Bald Knob and a 1.4 mile spur track connecting the tourist track with the C&O Railway Station.[14] On June 20, 1962, the Don Mower Lumber Company was paid $39,000 for the property extending from the C&O water tank to Leatherbark Creek. This property included the machine shop building, sand house, coal chute, railroad tracks, ties, switches, frogs, tool equipment and supplies then on the tract. In addition, right-of-way was purchased from the Chesapeake and Ohio Railroad, Mower Lumber Company, Floda Summerfield, D. P. Givens, Olive McLaughlin Cook, Wallace Dill, Emil Taylor, Dallas Tacy and Harry Gum.[15] The intention at the time was to lease the railroad to a private corporation to operate.[16]

Many of the natives of Cass scoffed at the state's plans to establish the logging railroad as a significant tourist attraction. Even though modest efforts had been made in the past to develop such nearby recreation areas as Seneca State Forest and Gaudineer Scenic Area, upper Pocahontas County was somewhat isolated and was not a prime vacationer's goal. Yet in the early 1960s, the Potomac Highlands Region was gaining prominence as such a goal. The nearby National Radio Astronomy Observatory at Green Bank had received national attention and was planning for an influx of visitors.

Everything possible was done to maintain interest in the railroad during the period required to settle the titles and while plans for renovation were being made. This included firing up a Shay engine and placing it on display during the period July 1 to July 4, 1961.[17]

Jack Kane, a businessman in Cass along with Bus Long, Cass mayor, and others formed the Cass Advancement Committee which conducted a vigorous lobbying and advertising effort. Through all of this, Jim Comstock had a very important role in constantly promoting the Cass Railroad in the *West Virginia Hillbilly.*

By July, 1962, the titles to the properties had been acquired by the State Department of Natural Resources.[18] A total of $189,000 had been spent.[19]

The original intent to lease the property to a private operator was dropped and the state now owned a unique park facility consisting of a 12-mile stretch sixty feet wide from Cass to Bald Knob, along with the rolling stock, repair facilities, enough land for parking and administration at Cass and one hundred acres at Bald Knob for development of an overlook.[20] Administration of the new facility was turned over to the Department of Natural Resource's Parks, and Recreation Division directed by Kermit McKeever, a native of Pocahontas County.

In-state publicity concerning the upcoming Mountain State Centennial in 1963 was generating local interest as people were urged to "Discover West Virginia" through local travel. A general increase of interest in history and cultural background of the Appalachian region was evident.

Although there was not sufficient time and money to properly upgrade the railroad and iron out operation and management problems, Kermit McKeever viewed the State Centennial as a unique opportunity to promote the new acquisition and a decision was made to make, at least, some experimental runs in 1963 and plans were made to get the track and rolling stock ready by then.[21]

A decision was reached to run trains on a short, 4.3 mile segment of the track from Cass to the upper end of a pasture, known as Gum Field, near the location of the old Italian track gang camp at Whittaker. This included two switchbacks, forested scenery along the way and a cleared overlook at Whittaker. Longer excursions were ruled out at the time because of the poor condition of the tracks and the limited time available for upgrading.

Of first concerns in getting the railroad going was insuring that excursion trains would have a safe roadbed. Cost cutbacks during the final Mower years had reduced maintenance to a minimum. Ties had rotted, ballast had washed away, spikes were loose and weeds and grass grew everywhere.

Carl Summerfield, former section foreman for Mower Lumber Company, and a crew were hired and they began upgrading the line. The grade and switchbacks, originally laid out by E. P. Shaffer and Sam Slaymaker and built laborously by their crews of Italian, Austrian and Hungarian workers in 1900-1901 using crude hand tools and used for logging for fifty-nine years, were still intact and most of the work was done in strengthening weak and washed areas.

While the section crew was slowly working its way up Cass Hill, the shop force turned its attention to refurbishing the locomotives and to building excursion cars.

Along with the purchase of the railroad, the state had received three Shays. These, like the track and other equipment, were badly in need of repairs. No. 4, last used by Midwest-Raleigh scrap trains and for three pre-purchase inspection trips in 1960-61, was in best condition. It could be in shape for use on the tourist road; however, any major breakdown would put the railroad out of business. No. 5 had been out of service since 1958 when its cylinders were cracked by freezing.

No. 1 had operated on inspection trains during 1961 and 1962, but the Interstate Commerce Commission failed to accept its worn wheel flanges for passenger hauling work.[22]

During the fall and winter of 1962, the shop crew reconditioned safety equipment on No. 4, replaced the flues and put on a new boiler jacket. As a final step, it was repainted black and lettered for the excursion line. First lettering was picturesque but cumbersome, "Cass, Greenbrier, Cheat and Bald Knob Scenic Railroad." The name of the facility was then shortened to "Cass Scenic Railroad."

For display purposes, No. 1 was repainted Chessie red and lettered with the CSRR logo. It was to be pulled down to the depot each day the train ran.

While repairs were being made on the locomotives, the shop crew was also converting ex-Mower log flatcars into excursion cars. Four of these wooden, arch bar trucked flatcars, decks splintered from years of log hauling, were chosen. The wooden, iron-topped rails on which log loaders formerly sat were removed and new floors were installed. Two cars were outfitted with sturdy wooden railing and side panels with no roof and two cars were remodeled with gaudy side panels (one blue, the other red) and sheet metal roofs. Car-length wooden benches were built back-to-back down the center of each car and along the sides. The "closed" cars protected passengers somewhat from rain and grimy cinders but were totally ineffective in blowing thunderstorms.

Another important aspect to getting the new railroad into operation was the selection of personnel to operate it. McKeever turned to the state park system in search of a qualified person for the resident administrator. After studying qualifications of numerous Division of Parks and Recreation employees, he appointed Ben H. Dickens as the Cass Scenic Railroad's first superintendent.

Within two weeks, Dickens left Lost River State Park where he had been assistant superintendent and moved to Cass. There he set up offices in his new house.[23] Totally lacking in railroad experience, Dickens immediately started locating and hiring members of the former Mower and WVP&P train and shop crews to fill key positions on the new Scenic Railroad. The roster of the crews operating the new venture could have been taken directly from Mower's payroll.

The assignment as the first superintendent at Cass was not an easy one. During his first and only year as superintendent, Dickens experienced a seemingly endless stream of unfamiliar problems ranging from bad track and broken equipment to a shortage of passenger cars, lack of sufficient motive power and insufficient parking for visitors.

McKeever was also busy drafting operational plans for the scenic railroad. He and his assistants, Jennings Boley, Milt Harr and Martin Howes, studied numerous operating proposals before deciding to run trains on a schedule of five days each week during the summer of 1963, beginning with Saturday, June 15, and closing after Labor Day weekend on September 2. The trains were scheduled for 11:00 a.m., 1:00 p.m. and 3:00 p.m. Round trip fares for the 90-minute journey were two dollars for adults and one dollar for children under twelve. Monday and Tuesday, the two "off days," would be used to make repairs that would hopefully keep the single, ancient engine running through the season. This schedule was coordinated with tours scheduled at the radio telescope observatory at Green Bank.

Finally, on June 15, 1963, the long-awaited day arrived. An atmosphere of excitement gripped the town, the C&O depot, leased by the state for use as a ticket office and for public rest rooms, throbbed with activity, reminiscent of former days when it was a gathering point for town residents. Lines of tourists formed at the small waiting room's ticket window. Cass residents mixed in, telling yarns of the bygone logging and lumbering days.

Shortly before 10:30 a.m., the noise of the crowd was interrupted by the electrifying sound of a distant whistle. Then, with a plume of black smoke catching the breeze, Shay No. 4 swung onto the C&O main line and slowly approached the depot towing the four excursion cars. Steps were lowered, the crowd was loaded on the cars and at 11:00 a.m., with seventy-five passengers aboard, Clyde Galford, engineer, tooted the whistle, released the brakes, inched back the throttle and the first run of the Cass Scenic Railroad rumbled northward along the C&O and disappeared around the turn at the water tank on the way up Cass Hill to Gum Field. Other members of the first crew were Leonard Long, fireman; Ivan Clarkson, Jesse McCalpin and Paul Bradley, brakemen; and Walter Good, conductor.

An interpretation of the history of Cass and the natural history of the area was provided by Warren E. "Tweard" Blackhurst over a primitive speaker system interconnecting the cars.[24] The schedule included a 20- to 30-minute stop at Gum Field (Whittaker) for refreshments and photography. During the early part of the first summer, sandwiches and drinks were made by local church groups and sold at hastily erected picnic tables. Later, refreshments were supplied by Kane's Grocery at Cass. These were taken to Whittaker by truck and were ready and waiting for the arrival of the train.

The Fourth of July, 1963, was a big day for the new train. Among the hundreds of riders that day were Governor and Mrs. Barron, Congressman and Mrs. Harley Staggers and their children, Hulett Smith, Bonn Brown, Senator Hans McCourt, Delegate and Mrs. Tom Edgar and other government officials. Officials were treated to a picnic at Gum Field by the ladies of the Cass churches.[25]

The same week the first mishap of the new venture occurred when Shay No. 4 broke an axle. Fortunately, Shay No. 1 was able to take over until a new axle was found in Huntington.[26]

Despite the lack of facilities and improvements ordinarily associated with West Virginia's excellent state parks, public response to the novel railroad was intense. When ticket sales were counted in mid-July, even the most optimistic supporters of the railroad were pleased. The total number of tickets sold the first month was 4,560.[27] Crowds were more than double the number anticipated. Patronage continued to spiral upward. Automobiles crowded the streets of the town and for the first time in its history, parking became a problem even though a part of the old lumber dock area had been cleaned off and was available for parking.

Various state newspapers gave excellent coverage of the Cass Railroad which fit so well into the Centennial theme of Travel West Virginia. So popular were the "Rides into History" that Shay No. 1 was called into action as a helper engine and doubleheader trains became a regular weekend feature.

Overnight facilities for visitors at Cass were almost nonexistent. Mrs. Bertha Haislop offered a limited number of rooms and board in the old Company Hotel but little publicity was given to her establishment and most visitors didn't know about it. Persons wishing to spend more than one day at Cass, or those traveling some distance, were forced to stay overnight at motels at Bartow, Marlinton, Elkins, or elsewhere in the vicinity.

Word of the new and exciting train ride spread and by August 15 the total paid riders passed the 10,000 mark with 2,423 rides during a single week, August 5-11; 1,089 of these were on Sunday, August 11.[28]

When the final train of the 1963 season unloaded its passengers on September 2, excluding children under seven and various guests, an incredible total of 23,106 tourists, rail buffs and curious townspeople had enjoyed the unique thrill of riding a rocking railcar behind a smoke-belching Shay engine.

The initial success of the Cass Scenic Railroad induced the state to improve the access road from Cass to Rt. 28 by building a short stretch connecting Rt. 28 with the Cass road just below the former Company Farm. This cut off a couple of miles of winding road and bypassed an iron bridge that was not safe for busses or other heavy vehicles.[29]

State officials were successful, in early 1964, in securing a grant from the Area Redevelopment Administration for $576,000 for further repairs and renovations to the new park facility.[30]

An administrative change was also made in the spring of 1964, with Kenneth Caplinger replacing Ben Dickens as superintendent of the Cass Scenic Railroad.[31]

The second tourist season opened May 16, 1964, with trips scheduled every Saturday and Sunday until June 15 when daily trips at 11:00, 1:00 and 3:00 were made. A pilgrimage of antique cars was made to Cass for opening day.[32]

Improvements to the parking lot, rest room and ticket sales areas had been made. A fifth, open-air, passenger car was added and Shay No. 1 was repaired and put into operating condition.

During the second season, a souvenir ticket was put on sale.

The state purchased additional land where the lumber docks had stood and increased the size of the parking lot.[33] A crew of twelve to thirteen men were employed in the shop, some working on Shay No. 5, others upgrading the railroad.[34]

Townspeople responded to the promise of tourist dollars. Jack Kane purchased a railroad dining car, placed it alongside the tracks north of the C&O depot, and opened the "Shay Inn." The Company Store was leased by a group of local persons and remodeled as a restaurant and gift shop known as the "Country Store," managed by Mrs. Jessie Brown Beard Powell.

Warren E. Blackhurst and his wife, Stella, expanded the Wildlife Museum they had started the year before in the company warehouse adjacent to the Company Store. Next to the Wildlife Museum, Kyle Neighbors and his wife, Ina, opened a Civil War Museum that was later modified to a lumber and logging museum called the Cass Historical Museum.[35]

A man named Tyler bought an old stagecoach and took passengers for a ride, fording the river above the cement bridge and continuing down the street in East Cass and back. In later years Laban Wolfe, Taylor and Hoxie Meeks drove the stage at various times.[36]

Popularity of the railroad continued to increase and, during the second season, 36,523 paid passengers took the 4-mile ride to Gum Field and back. In addition, Shay No. 4 and five cars were taken to the Mountain State Forest Festival in Elkins where 3,380 passengers took a 3-mile ride behind the belching engine on the Western Maryland tracks—3,110 of these rode in a single day.[37]

In October, 1964, the state received twenty thousand dollars from the Federal Housing and Home Administration for use in upgrading facilities at Cass.[38] During the same month, the last Shay in active duty in logging in the eastern United States was retired. This was Shay No. 7, owned by the Meadow River Lumber Company at Rainelle, West Virginia. This engine was immediately purchased by the state for use at Cass. In December Walter Good, Clyde Galford and Leonard Long went to Rainelle and brought No. 7 back under its own power. No. 7 joined Nos. 1, 4 and 5 at Cass to make an impressive assemblage of Shay locomotive power.

Shay No. 7 was built in 1920, Construction No. 3131. It is an 80-ton Class C Shay with 12-inch cylinders with a 15-inch stroke. Drive wheels are thirty-six inches in diameter. First used by Raine Lumber Company at Clover Lick in the 1920s, No. 7 had been used in hauling logs at Rainelle for twenty-nine years. It cost $21,762 to build and was sold, when new, for $24,715.[39]

Books, such as *Riders of the Flood,* and *Sawdust in Your Eyes,* by Tweard Blackhurst and *Tumult on the Mountains* by Roy B. Clarkson[40] stirred people's interest in logging history and steam engines and stimulated visits to Cass to see history come alive. The third season of the Cass Scenic Railroad utilized the four miles of track to Gum Field. However, excitement was in the air as rumors of plans to extend the railroad began circulating. In July, 1965, the

State Division of Purchasing advertised for bids to rehabilitate the existing facilities; however, all bids were too high.[41] Also, the same month, an option was taken to buy thirty-three acres of land at the Gum Field stop from Judge Muntzing, owner.[42]

Interest soared and during the 1965 season, the facilities were greatly overcrowded and on special days extra, unscheduled trips were made in order to not disappoint visitors. Special runs were also made for groups such as the National Youth Science Camp who made late evening runs to Whittaker. After eating a picnic supper, they gathered after dark on a knoll to view slides of logging history and hear commentaries by Tweard Blackhurst and Roy Clarkson. Power was supplied by a portable generator.

Studies were made and plans drawn to show the feasibility of developing an extensive logging museum centering on Cass. These included renovating the old mill, converting the planing mill warehouse into a display hall, having demonstrations of horse skidding, steam skidding and loading at appropriate locations along the tracks as well as renovating the town itself.[43]

During the 1965 season, a special passenger became a regular on the train. "Little Hobo," a nondescript dog rode each trip. He napped during most of the ride but was instantly awake when the whistle blew for a stop.[44]

The 1966 season opened with a special railfan trip on May 7. This included special photography runs and the use of double-header trains. Special night photography, using multiple-flash exposures, were featured. The machine shop, a museum in itself, was opened to inspection and photography.[45] The railfan weekend proved so popular it became an annual event.

The big news in 1966 was announced on June 30 when contracts were signed for $671,262 worth of improvements to the Cass Scenic Railroad. The first contract, for $497,476, was awarded to the Mountain State Construction Company of Charleston. This called for the rehabilitation of twelve miles of tracks from Cass to Bald Knob.[46]

A second contract, for $173,786, was awarded to Given Construction Company of Upper Glade, West Virginia, for completion of the parking lot, renovation of the depot, enlargement of sanitary facilities and the construction of two overlook areas, one at Gum Field and one at Bald Knob. The funds were part of an Environmental Development Agency-federal-state grant and loan project of state parks expansion.[47] By December, the rail had been removed from all the tracks on the line and laid aside and ballast was being laid down.[48]

December, 1966, brought about further expansion of the locomotive power at Cass. Sixty-six years before, when the railroad was first being built, the company considered buying Heisler engines instead of Shays. The decision to buy Shays resulted in the large number of Shays later owned by the lumber company. No Heisler engine ran the rails at Cass until December 14, 1966, when Heisler No. 6 was brought in, under its own power, from the Meadow River Lumber Company at Rainelle. Built in 1925 for The Hog Hollow Tile Company, at New Bethlehem, Pennsylvania, No. 6 was sold in 1934 to the Meadow River Lumber Company and had been in constant use since. No. 6 was a 120-ton Heisler, one of the largest ever built.[49]

By the time the 1967 season arrived, the lower four miles of tracks had been completely rebuilt and trains to Gum Field (now called Whittaker) were continued. The number of passengers continued to increase and 41,167 paid riders made the trip in 1967. In addition, 3,640 persons rode at two festivals; the Mountain State Forest Festival at Elkins, West Virginia, and the Strawberry Festival at Buckhannon, West Virginia, 635 underprivileged persons, thousands of children five years old or less rode at Cass and several special trips were made.[50]

The 1968 season was heralded by the announcement that the entire twelve miles of track to Bald Knob was ready for use. The official dedication of the line was held on May 25. A special trip was made and at a ceremony at Whittaker, Governor Hulett Smith, T. R. Samsell, director of the DNR, and other officials drove a golden spike to commemorate the event. A special train "The Mountaineer Limited," a sleeper, brought visitors from major eastern cities to Cass.[51]

The railfan weekend was held on May 24 in 1968 and included a special trip to Bald Knob. The regular season, featuring passenger service to Bald Knob, started on May 30 and everyone expected a record-breaking year. Attendance declined somewhat, however, with a total estimated number of riders of 53,000. The actual number of tickets sold was 47,852. Of these, 26,894 rode the short trip to Whittaker and 20,479 went to Bald Knob. The special railfan trip had 130 passengers and the Forest Festival 1,349.[52]

Administration of the railroad changed in 1969 with Kenneth Caplinger's replacement by Jim Reep as superintendent. Rolling stock at Cass was increased in 1969 when the Clinchfield Coal Company Division of the Pittston Company donated eleven items to Cass including flatcars, coaches and a caboose.[53] A nationwide advertising campaign began to pay off in 1970 and interest in the Cass Railroad mounted. In an attempt to acquire a variety of logging locomotives, a Climax engine was purchased. This was a 70-ton engine. It was used until 1960 by the Middle Fork Railroad at Ellamore—between Elkins and Buckhannon, West Virginia, and was the last Climax engine to operate commercially in the United States. This engine had been stored outside for ten years and was in very poor condition.[54]

The addition of a Climax locomotive completed a collection of major types of mountain-logging engines and gave Cass the unique position of being the only place in the world where the three types—Shay, Heisler and Climax—could be seen.

A major addition to the locomotive power in 1970 was a "Pacific Coast" style, oil-burning Shay, the first ever to operate in the East. Assigned Cass Scenic Railroad No. 2, it was purchased from Railway Appliance Research, Ltd., of Vancouver Warves, British Columbia. It was a "super-Shay" designed by Lima Locomotive Works in the late 1920s as the ultimate steam engine design. Many of these locomotives were sold to timber firms on the west coast. Built in 1928, CN 3320PC, it weighed 90.5 tons. After moderate repairs, No. 2 was put into service on the Bald Knob run.[55]

Cass Scenic Railroad No. 3, another Shay obtained in 1970, was leased from the Oregon Historical Society of Portland. This is a 90-ton oil burner formerly owned by the Mount Emily Lumber Company and other companies. It was built in 1923, Construction No. 3233.[56]

In the fall of 1970, an additional attraction was added in the Cass area when a series of steam railroad excursions were made on the Greenbrier Division of the C&O. These trips left Ronceverte at 8:30 a.m., arrived at Cass at 11:30 a.m. and continued to Durbin. The return trip arrived at Cass at 2:30 p.m. and at Ronceverte at 6:00 p.m. The schedule gave those who wished an opportunity to take the short trip on the Cass train while the excursion was going to Durbin and back to Cass. Trips were held on October 17, 18, 24 and 25 and were very successful.[57]

Excursions on the Greenbrier Division of the C&O were continued in 1971 with trips on May 30; July 11, 25; August 1, 8; September 5; and October 10, 17. The engine used was Reading Railroad No. 2102 — the largest operating steam locomotive in the United States at the time.[58]

The May 30, 1972, railfan trip was especially successful with over three hundred persons from thirty-two states riding.[59] The 1972 regular season began on May 6 with a special excursion as a salute to Michael Koch, author of *The Shay Locomotive — Titan of the Timber*.[60] About 280 persons made the trip.

That season saw the first use of Shays No. 2 and 3 in revenue service on the Cass Scenic Railroad. These West Coast, oil-burning Shays finally assured that uninterrupted service would be maintained even if one or two engines became inactivated.[61]

Equipment acquired from the Georgia-Pacific Corporation in the spring of 1972 included an overhead log skidder, a caboose, twenty-three log cars and a motorcar. These were formerly used by the Meadow River Lumber Company at Rainelle.[62]

Two nonlogging-type locomotives were acquired in 1972 from U.S. Government Surplus. One was No. 714, a small 0-4-0 saddle tank switcher, built in 1950. This was the last steam locomotive built by the Porter Locomotive Works of Pittsburgh, Pennsylvania. The other was a 2-8-0 rod engine and tender.

Things looked bright for the Cass Scenic Railroad early in 1972. There was an annual average of almost seventy thousand riders, the most impressive steam locomotive assemblage in the United States was on hand, special excursions to the Forest Festival at Elkins, the Strawberry Festival at Buckhannon and to Pioneer Days in Marlinton were made annually, and references and articles on Cass appeared frequently in popular railroad magazines. Then, on Sunday, July 23, disaster struck. At about ten minutes to 3 a.m. the hostler at the machine shop reported hearing a loud noise and then seeing the shop engulfed in flames.

Two engines were inside the shop. One, Shay No. 3, was in operating condition and was pulled from the burning building. The other, Climax No. 9, received some damage.[63]

The shop building, built in 1921-22, a museum in itself, and one of the largest steam locomotive repair shops in the United States, was totally destroyed. Many specialized tools necessary for work on Shay engines and a large inventory of rare and valuable parts were also lost.[64] Despite the loss, a temporary shop was set up and the 1972 season progressed smoothly.

A Governor's Special Tour, at a reduced rate of ten dollars, launched the 1973 season of excursions on the Greenbrier Division of the C&O between Ronceverte and Cass. These tours, seven in all, brought much attention and passengers to the Cass Scenic Railroad.[65]

Also, a new cause for excitement occurred in the late summer of 1973 when preliminary plans were announced for opening a ski resort, to be known as Snowshoe, along the slopes on the headwaters of Cheat River. Many persons felt that this development might lead to all-year-round operation for the Cass Railroad. At the end of the 1973 season, Superintendent Reep announced that riders on the Cass Scenic line totaled seventy-five thousand, an increase of about twenty-five percent over the attendance the previous year.[66]

The biggest event in the Cass area during 1974 was the opening of Snowshoe Resort on December 13. The ski slopes were appropriately named with such logging terms as "Ball Hooter," "Powder Monkey" and "Cup Run." Snowshoe was destined to become a popular ski resort. Cashflow problems, however, caused it to become bankrupt. After several yearly bankruptcies, Snowshoe was sold in 1986 to a group called Snowshoe Associates for $1,815,000.[67]

The calm of the early morning hours of Monday, May 5, 1975, was shattered by fire sirens when a fire was discovered in the C&O depot at Cass. Leonard Long and his family were awakened by the smell of smoke, discovered it was coming from the depot and Leonard sounded the alarm. The fire started in a storage room on the south side of the building and quickly engulfed the wooden structure. Loss was set at $60,000 plus $10,000 on the contents.[68] Used, since the beginning of the Cass Scenic Railroad, as an office, waiting room, ticket office and rest rooms, the loss, just at the beginning of a new season, was a blow to the tourist facility.

Trailers were quickly set up to serve temporarily while plans were formulated to rebuild the depot with authentic style and painting. The financial affairs of the state turn slowly, however, and visitors for the next three seasons were to be served by the temporary trailers.

State officials were not discouraged. Kermit McKeever, chief of the Parks Division of the Department of Natural Resources, and Lester McClung, chief of the DNR's Forestry Division, enthusiastically sponsored the idea of establishing a logging museum in the old flooring warehouse with tours into the mill and planing mill.[69]

A turning point in developments at Cass came in late June, 1976, when U.S. Senators Jennings Randolph and Robert C. Byrd announced approval of an $896,000 grant to the State of West Virginia to help provide funds for acquisition of 685 acres of land in and around the town of Cass. The grant was designated to help enable the state to restore the town to 1920 condition. Included were funds to relocate seventy-nine families and renovate thirty-eight dwellings. The total project cost was $1,505,000. The Bureau of Outdoor Recreation of the United States Department of Interior approved $308,000 for the project and the state provided $301,000.[70]

A deed for the town of Cass to the State of West Virginia from the Don Mower Lumber Company was dated December 27, 1976. This included land on which the mill and the company-owned part of the town were located, land along Leatherbark Creek north of the machine shop, several lots in East Cass, the area known as "Slab Town" and land at Deer Creek. Purchase price was listed as $669,611.[71]

The Cass Scenic Railroad received a blow in May, 1977, when Superintendent James W. Reep died of a heart attack. He had been superintendent for eight years and his loss at the beginning of the tourist season was keenly felt.[72]

A new superintendent, Richard Dale, was named in August of that year and Fred Bartels was named assistant superintendent.[73]

The 1977 season proved to be the most popular one so far for the Cass Scenic Railroad. A little over 77,000 paid passengers rode that year, an increase of about 9,000 persons over the previous year.[74]

During 1978, the Cass Scenic Railroad was listed in the National Register of Historic Places.[75]

Finally, on May 12, 1979, at 3:00 p.m., the new depot at Cass was dedicated by Governor Jay Rockefeller. He also outlined ambitious plans for the future of Cass. First of these was the construction of a sewage treatment system, which he promised would begin by July 1. Historic restoration plans he spoke about included: 1) a museum, depicting West Virginia's timber industry history, incorporating part of the old Cass mill; 2) renovation of the town hall, jail, clubhouse, country store and boardinghouse; and 3) camping and recreational facilities for visitors to Cass. The Governor noted that during the fifteen years of operation, the Cass Scenic Railroad had hauled almost 750,000 people.[76]

In addition to the annual railfan weekend in May, 1979, over six hundred people from churches throughout West Virginia rode the train on a special trip.[77]

An ongoing reconstruction effort based on the theme "Turn of the Century Cass" was initiated in 1979. It slowly gained momentum with the refurbishing and repainting of some of the old company houses.

An important addition to the locomotives at Cass was made in 1980 when Western Maryland Railway Shay No. 6 (Shop No. 3354) was leased to Cass Scenic Railroad. The idea, attributed to Lloyd Lewis of the Chessie System Public Relations Office, was to lease Western Maryland No. 6 for ten years to Cass in exchange for Cass Scenic Railroad Shay No. 1, built in 1905, and No. 714, a small 0-4-0 saddle tank switcher built in 1950 for the United States Army and acquired at Cass in 1972.

The WMR No. 6 was completed on April 30, 1945, the last and largest super-heated Shay built by Lima Locomotive Works. It was built from plans developed years earlier for West Virginia Pulp and Paper Company No. 12. The WMR No. 6 is a 3-truck, coal-fired engine of 162 tons in working order. Its cylinders were eighteen inches diameter with a stroke of seventeen inches. Wheel diameter was forty-eight inches. It cost $105,045 to build.[78]

Placed in service by the Western Maryland Railroad on the steep, 3-mile, coal mine branch from Chaffee, West Virginia, to Vindex, Maryland, it was used eight years. In 1954, it was placed in the Baltimore and Ohio Railroad Museum in Baltimore. During placement, the turntable was damaged and the first task in its removal from the museum was to repair the turntable. This was accomplished by employees of the Cass Scenic Railroad and the West Virginia Railroad Maintenance Authority with the cooperation of Chessie System officials.

After the necessary repairs were completed on August 18, 1980, a crew arrived at Baltimore from Cass and No. 6 was inched slowly onto the outside tracks. Portions of its running gears were removed to facilitate towing. A Chessie System freight engine and a special car that was provided for the crew from Cass were hooked to it and the trip began. The first leg was to Cumberland, Maryland, via the Baltimore and Ohio Railroad then over the Western Maryland tracks from Elkins to Durbin, then at Durbin it was met by Heisler No. 6 and brought via the former Greenbrier Division branch of the C&O Railroad to Cass where it arrived on August 23, 1980.[79]

Number 6 was in excellent condition but it had been out-of-service for over twenty-five years and moderate restoration was needed. During the winter of 1980-81, a new lubricator was attached to the engine, a new hose from the Shay's water tank to the injector lines was installed and new wooden beams were put on the ends of the engine.

An inspection of the firebox revealed that fourteen bricks arching across the top of the box were cracked and unusable. Since no one manufactured these special bricks in modern times, the Cass shop crew made special molds, ordered powered firebrick materials and cast the bricks themselves. Workmen also welded a crack in one of the journal boxes and replaced water glasses.

The only modification from the original designs made in No. 6 was the addition of a water siphon to allow the uptake of water from water stations along the mountain track.

As part of the original lease agreement for No. 6, "Western Maryland," was painted on the coal and water tender and a bronze plaque, signifying her loan from the B&O museum collection was attached.

On April 1, 1981, No. 6 was fired up and taken up the track toward Whittaker. She performed flawlessly. However, she was considered to be too heavy for extensive use on the Cass Hill and has been used mostly on special runs on the C&O branch between Cass and Durbin.[80]

The year 1980 saw another important addition to Cass Scenic

Railroad holdings. When the Greenbrier Division of the C&O was abandoned on December 29, 1979, special arrangements were made for the State of West Virginia to purchase that part of the line from Cass to near Durbin. The tracks on this portion were to be maintained and used by the Cass Scenic Railroad for additional tourist rides. Access to the "outside" by way of Bemis was maintained until the Western Maryland's Durbin branch was abandoned on February 15, 1984.[81]

The years 1981 and 1982 were characterized by budget cuts for all state agencies. State park employees, including Cass Scenic Railroad employees, were placed on a 32-hour week to prevent overspending.[82]

These restrictions cut into the time for making repairs and renovations; however, the passenger schedule remained the same.

Reflecting inflation, passenger fares by 1982 were:

Whittaker Station . . . .$5.50 for adults
2.50 for children
Bald Knob. . . . .$8.00 for adults
3.50 for children[83]

During the several years prior to 1983, an average of 68,000 passengers a year rode the Cass train, somewhat less than the highest usage in 1977 of over 77,000.

To keep the trains running and the tracks, buildings and other equipment in good shape, a staff of twenty-five permanent employees were required year 'round. This included six men in the shop in addition to the engineers, firemen, conductors and others of the train crews during the winter months.

During the winter of 1982, these men converted Shay No. 2 from an oil burner to a coal burner, replaced tires on Nos. 3 and 4, rebuilt trucks on No. 4, refurbished cylinders and dry pipe on No. 3, painted and rewired electrical cabinets on the 45-ton GE diesel switcher, repainted and refurbished passenger cars as needed and performed many other minor tasks.

Track workers were busy clearing trees and brush from the right-of-way and getting the tracks in tip-top shape. A large rockslide on the Greenbrier Branch presented special problems during the winter of 1982-83.[84]

The year 1983 marked the twentieth anniversary of the Cass

Scenic Railroad. The event was celebrated by a special anniversary run on Sunday, July 3, at 6:00 p.m. The anniversary trip ran from Cass to Hosterman on the former C&O Greenbrier Division line. It was pulled by Shay No. 6, the latest addition to locomotives at Cass. A record-setting crowd of 1,197 people in fourteen cars made the trip.[85] The total number of riders in 1983 was 66,033.[86]

The same year marked the completion of a study by the Monongahela National Forest staff concerning the eligibility of the Greenbrier River for inclusion in the National Wild and Scenic Rivers System. Their recommendation to designate all eligible segments of the river from the headwaters to Anthony in Greenbrier County, a total of 133 miles, was publicized and public comments sought.[87]

A step backward in development of Cass as a railroad museum center occurred in September, 1983, when the Chessie System announced plans to file an application to the Interstate Commerce Commission for permission to abandon the Western Maryland Railroad line from Cheat Junction to Durbin and the C&O Railroad line from Durbin to Bartow.[88] Arguments in favor of the state acquiring the Cheat Junction-Durbin line were made by John Killoran.[89] William P. McNeel summarized the situation in an editorial in the *Pocahontas Times* and urged that the state Department of Natural Resources immediately accept an offer by the Chessie System to donate to the state sufficient track material to rebuild the Old Spruce to Spruce connection between the Western Maryland and the Cass Scenic Railroad.[90] This would be a distance of about 1.3 miles.

The regular 1984 season for the Cass Scenic Railroad began on Saturday, May 26, with the following schedule:

Cass to Whittaker Station

May 26 through June 22 (except Mondays) – two trips daily at 1 and 3 p.m.

June 23 through Labor Day (except Mondays) – three trips daily at 11 a.m., 1 and 3 p.m.

Whittaker trains will run on Memorial Day Monday and Labor Day Monday.

Cass to Bald Knob

May 26 through September 2 (except Mondays) – one trip daily at Noon.

Fall Schedule
After Labor Day trains will operate on Saturdays and Sundays in September, Thursday through Sunday the first two weeks in October; and Saturdays and Sundays during the remainder of October.

Trains to Whittaker Station will run at 11 a.m., 1 and 3 p.m. on the Saturdays and Sundays and at 1 and 3 p.m. on the Thursdays and Fridays. One trip to Bald Knob will run at Noon on each day of the fall schedule.[91]

In addition, regular trips on the former C&O Greenbrier Division from Cass to Durbin were begun in 1984. During the spring of 1984, a section crew was busy installing new ties and in general upkeep of this track. The shop crew renovated a passenger coach for use on this line and additional passenger coaches were being sought.[92]

The annual railfan weekend on May 18, 19 and 20, 1984, was one of the most successful ever with almost 450 tickets sold. Trips were made to Bald Knob, Hosterman and Durbin. Evening programs included presentations on the development of C&O steam power, the Shay locomotive and slides taken by Ivan Clarkson during the last years of the Mower Lumber Company operations at Cass.[93] The total number of passengers in 1984 was 67,808.[94]

The Department of Natural Resources requested $1.4 million in the 1985-86 state budget for capital improvements and repairs at the Cass Scenic Railroad State Park. This included $1 million to build the rail line on Cheat Mountain to connect the Cass Railroad at Old Spruce with the Western Maryland Railroad at Spruce. This line was originally built in 1902 and was in constant use until it was removed in 1960.

Also included in the budget were:

$100,000 for renovation of houses in "Slab Town" for vacation cabins.
– Main frame for Shay #5, $20,000
– Repairs to engine #612, $20,000
– One locomotive boiler, $175,000
– Ties and rails, $65,000
– Rebuilding of a trestle on the line to Durbin, $20,000[95]

In 1985, the Cass Scenic Railroad State Park was placed in the newly created Department of Commerce. Chief of Parks,

Charles Spears, expressed his strong support for future development of Cass. He gave assurances that the track from Cass to Durbin, which had been badly damaged in the flood of November, 1985, would be repaired. The trips from Cass to Durbin were cancelled for the 1986 season. Plans were made for obtaining federal funds to help restore twenty additional houses as well as the jail and mayor's office.[96] The total number of passengers in 1985 was 65,906.[97]

Several new ideas were initiated in the 1986 season. These included Monday trips to Whittaker for the first time in several years; evening dinner trains to Whittaker on the second Saturday of each month with live entertainment and a chicken barbeque; and a special ticket was made available. For twenty-five dollars, this ticket permited an unlimited number of trips during the season.

In 1986, a new superintendent, Fred Bartels, replaced Richard Dale.

Seven company houses had been renovated to permit persons to stay overnight. These are rented as state park cabins. They have modern bathrooms and fully equipped kitchens. Renovation of additional houses was planned.

A major new attraction opened in 1986. It is called the Cass Showcase and consists of an HO gauge scale model of the former West Virginia Pulp and Paper Company mill and a large part of the town. A slide show depicts important events in the history of the town and gives visitors valuable insight to an understanding of the town. The showcase was developed by Ned Viars with the assistance of Ed White, Sam Cochran, Richard Walcomb and Joe Henson. It is located in the hay storage building behind the depot.[98]

Another development was the opening of a restaurant and boardinghouse in the old Huff house recently vacated by Richard Dale. This was run by Gil and Mary Willis.[99]

These improvements paid off in increased interest in Cass and the total number of riders in 1986 jumped to 70,661.[100]

In 1987, a new enterprise, Country Crafts, was opened. This was built by ingeniously enclosing the coal bins behind the C&O depot. Items made by West Virginia craftsmen are sold there.

The dinner trains proved so successful in 1986 that seven such trains were scheduled for 1987. These were on May 30, June 13 and 27, July 11 and 25 and August 8 and 29. Reservations were required and tickets were sold on a first-come, first-serve basis. Only 150 persons could be accommodated per trip. The Falling Branch Band provided live entertainment consisting of railroad music.[101] The dinner trains were all sold out long before their scheduled dates.

In 1987, after more than a year of effort, another Shay engine was added to the collection at Cass. Lima #2804 is a 70-ton, 3-truck engine built in 1916. It was shipped new to Alabama but soon came to the Raleigh Lumber Company at Glen Morgan, West Virginia. The W. M. Ritter Lumber Company bought the Raleigh Lumber Company and moved the engine to Oxley, West Virginia, then to Maben, West Virginia, and finally to the Brimstone Railroad in Tennessee. It was then sold to the Southern Railroad. The locomotive was bought by George Kadelak, a railfan from Indiana, and leased to the Cass Scenic Railroad for restoring and operation. It was brought to Cass on two flatbed trucks and is expected to be running in five years or less.[102]

The number of passengers who rode the Cass Scenic Railroad in 1987 was 72,844, and by the end of the 1987 season more than 1.25 million people had taken a "ride through history" at Cass.[103]

An innovation in the fall of 1987 was a special evening Halloween Train on Saturday, October 31. Train cars were decorated for the occasion, and passengers and crew were in costumes. Halloween treats were given out and entertainers strolled through the passenger cars. The event was sold out weeks ahead of time.[104]

During 1987, a West Virginia Logging Museum was proposed for Cass. The idea was well-received by Department of Commerce officials. The Mountain State Railroad and Logging Historical Association agreed to set aside one thousand dollars as seed money toward financing a planning and cost-estimating study for such a facility. The possibility of development of a national-geared locomotive museum at Cass was also discussed.[105]

In April, 1988, Ivan Newberry replaced Fred Bartels as superintendent of the Cass Scenic Railroad State Park. It was also announced in April that plans were being made for upgrading of the tracks up the mountain and building a connection between the Cass Scenic Railroad and the Western Maryland Railway at Spruce. Funds for the project came from the federal government.

The funds were initially allocated for rebuilding the rail line from Cass to Durbin after this line was heavily damaged by the flood of 1985. The state received permission to use the money for the project on the mountain instead of on the line along the Greenbrier River.[106]

The dinner train proved to be one of the most popular events at Cass. In 1988, it operated at full capacity on May 28, June 11 and 25, July 2 and 23, August 6 and 20, and September 3. A special evening train for senior citizens was run on September 10.[107] The special Halloween Train was run on October 29.[108]

June 15, 1988, was the twenty-fifth anniversary of the opening of the Cass Scenic Railroad. To celebrate, a 3-day festival was held on June 17-19. Festivities began at 6 p.m., Friday, June 17 with traditional, classic, and rock 'n roll music and storytelling. Craftspeople and dealers representing the region were housed in some of the restored homes and in outdoor booths.

On Saturday tours of Cass were guided by members of the Mountain State Railroad and Logging Historical Society. Several people, Pearl Carter, Russell Clarkson, Ernestine Hamrick Clarkson, Thurmond Cosner, and William K. "Bill" Blackhurst, who lived and worked in Cass during the boom days recalled what life and work was like in earlier times.

Regular rides on the railroad were available and short trips behind Western Maryland Shay No. 6 were made. Bicycle races, a wood-chopping event and a 10-kilometer run were held. Special activities for youngsters were available on Saturday and Sunday.

Music continued through most of the time supplied by the Falling Branch String Band, Jim Costa, Big Money, the Black Mountain Bluegrass Boys, the Joyful Noise Gospel Quartet, Delbert McClinton, John Cephas, Phil Wiggins, and Larry Gorce. Other entertainment included ghost stories by Virginia Gray and poetry by Bob Baker.

The first Cass Festival Committee consisted of:

Tom Brigham, Whistlepunk Village & Inn
Nancy Buckingham, WVDOC*
Elmer "Sonny" Burruss, MSR&LHA
Rick Davis, The Inn at Snowshoe
George Deike, MSR&LHA**
Rebecca Kimmons, WVDOC*

Richard Malcom, Cass Showcase
Robert Mathis, WVDOC*
Leslee McCarty, The Current B&B
Marty McGreal, Pocahontas Tourism Commission
Monica Miller, WVDOC*
Stella Miller, Cass Country Store
Ivan Newberry, Cass Scenic Railroad State Park
Emily Parsons, WVDOC*
Jessie Powell, Cass Country Store
'John Rossell, WV Department of Agriculture
Dondi Shears, Arbovale
Bob Sheets, Cass
Margaret Smith, Droop Mountain State Park
Mary Snyder, Cass Scenic Railroad State Park
David Tanner, Whistlepunk Village & Inn
Ruth Taylor, Pocahontas Tourism Commission
Ned and Melody Viars, Cass Showcase
Gil Willis, Elk River Touring Center

SPECIAL THANKS TO:

The People of Cass
Ernestine Clarkson
Caroline Cassell
The Weekend's Volunteers
Bill Rice, Charleston, WV
Coca-Cola of Marlinton & Elkins
The Pocahontas Tourism Commission
Pocahontas County CVB
WKKW-AM, Clarksburg, WV
FM-105, Charleston, WV
WVMR-AM, Frost, WV
Young Farmers' Association of Monterey, Virginia
Locomotive & Railway Preservation Magazine
George Collins, MSR&LHA**
Phil Rolleston
Eugene Davis, Dunmore
Rev. David Rittenhouse
Town of Marlinton
Wonderful West Virginia Magazine
Goldenseal Magazine
One Valley Bank, Charleston

West Virginia Department of Commerce
**Mountain State Rairoad & Logging Historical Association[109]

The success of the first Cass Railroad Festival encouraged planning for it as an annual affair. A corporation, the Cass Railroad Festival Committee, Inc., was formed to handle future festivals.[110]

The Cass Scenic Railroad State Park is one of the most unusual and interesting state parks in the nation. Here an individual can stand in awe beside a mighty steam locomotive, thrill to its thunderous blasts, wonder at the power smoothly transmitted by its cylinders, or, become lost in the contemplation of people and events at Cass long gone or dream of happenings yet to come.

Fig. 1—An untapped treasure of hundreds of thousands of acres of virgin red spruce timber attracted the paper makers and lumbermen to the mountains of West Virginia in the latter part of the nineteenth century. Photography by Herman. Work, 1910. *Courtesy H. E. Matics.*

Fig. 2 – Boats, horses, pikepoles, cant hooks, and men combined to keep the logs floating during a drive down the Greenbrier River. 1898.
Courtesy Ruth Beebe and the Pocahontas County Historical Society.

Fig. 3 – Log drives were made during the spring floods. Men and horses were needed to keep the logs rolled into the river and riding the flood. *Courtesy the Pocahontas County Historical Society.*

Fig. 4 – William Luke, founder and president of the Piedmont Pulp and Paper Company which evolved into the West Virginia Pulp and Paper Company, now known as WESTVACO Corporation. *Courtesy H. E. Matics.*

Fig. 5 – Samuel Slaymaker, lumber sales agent for the West Virginia Pulp
and Paper Company, had a leading role in planning the mill and
town at Cass. *Kyle J. Neighbors Collection.*

Fig. 6 – Rare picture of the men behind the West Virginia Pulp and Paper Company. Front row l. to r. David L. Luke, Emory P. Shaffer (Supt. of the Cass operations), Samuel L. Slaymaker (Sales Manager), Thomas Luke, Harvey Cromer (land acquisition and surveyor). Back row l. to r. Richard Beaston (procurement manager), M. Otley (owner of *McCall* magazine), William Luke, D. Talbott (company attorney), Allen L. Luke (in front of Talbott), and John G. Luke. June, 1909, at the Cheat Mountain Clubhouse. Four of these men were company presidents: William Luke, 1888-1905; John G. Luke, 1905-1921; David L. Luke 1921-1934; Thomas Luke, 1934-1945. *Courtesy H. E. Matics.*

Fig. 7 – The Covington, Virginia, paper mill of the West Virginia Pulp and Paper Company, early 1920s. Hundreds of millions of feet of Cheat Mountain red spruce were chipped, processed, and formed into paper here. *Courtesy H. E. Matics.*

Fig. 8 – The first house built by the company at Cass was located near the present depot. It was used to house Italian workers preparing the millsite and railroad. 1900. *Photographs from Alexander M. Luke. Courtesy Stella Blackhurst.*

Fig. 9 – Italians, Austrians and Hungarians constructed all the railroad grades with picks, mattocks, and shovels until steam shovels and ditchers took over in the early teens. The man in the right front row is Harry Craddock. *Courtesy Connell Gillespie.* Inset: metal number tags were worn by the workers for identification.

Fig. 10–On December 29, 1900, Shay No. 1 was delivered at Cass to the Greenbrier and Elk River Railroad. Weighing only forty-two tons, with a total wheel base of twenty-eight feet, four inches, 11-inch cylinders with a 12-inch stroke, 29.5-inch drivers and an 18-inch Dayton oil head lamp. No. 1 soon gained local fame by pushing fourteen loaded log cars up a grade that an ordinary locomotive could have hardly crept along. It was equipped with a straight stack when delivered. *Courtesy Kate Shaffer Hardy.*

Fig. 11 – Shay No. 1 soon became known as "Old Barney" by the train crews and loggers. Note the slanting cylinders. *From the Kyle J. Neighbors Collection.*

Fig. 12 – Second Shay No. 2 was built in 1904. It weighed seventy tons, had a total wheel base of thirty-eight feet, eight and one-fourth inches, 12-inch cylinders, 32-inch drivers and a 16-inch oil head lamp. Engineers were Robert and Charlie Hivick. 1904.

Courtesy Pocahontas County Historical Society.

pg 288 - Rode this one
see note below

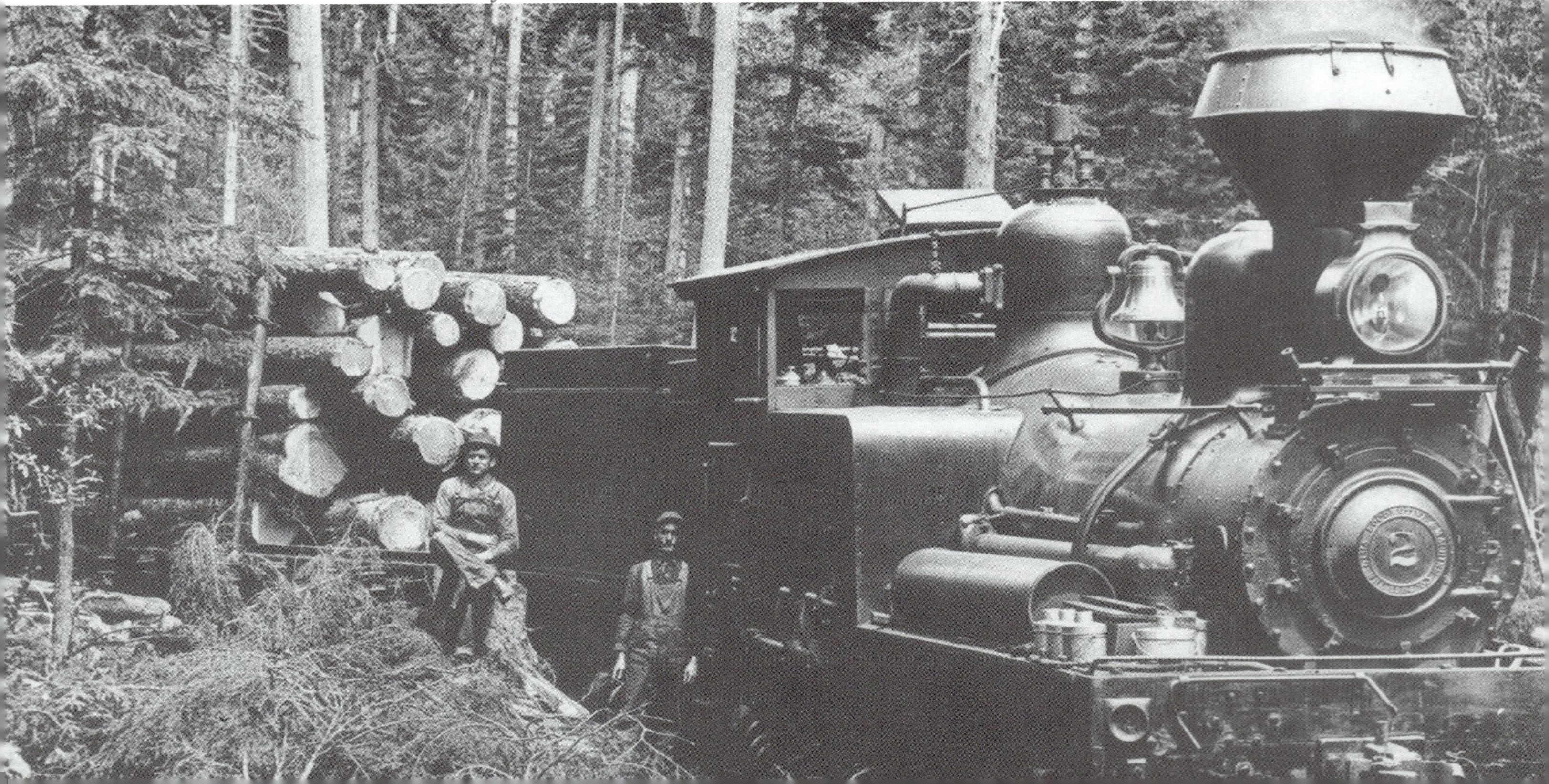

Fig. 13 – Second Shay No. 2 with supply cars at a trestle. Note the double doors on the supply car. No. 2 was in service at Cass until the late 1920s. *From the Kyle J. Neighbors Collection.*

DOESN'T MATCH WITH BROCHURE

Fig. 14 – Shay No. 3 at a log landing on Cheat Mountain, 1904. This 70-ton engine was built in 1903 and was used at Cass until it was retired in the late 1920s. The engineer shown here is Cal Bradley. *From the Kyle J. Neighbors Collection.*

Fig. 15 – Shay No. 3 and loaded train on a wooden bridge across Cheat River. Early engineers were Fred Linnan and Otts Cromer: *Courtesy Lima Locomotive Works.*

Fig. 16—Rare, left side view of Shay No. 3 with loads of logs on Cheat Mountain. The diamond smokestack contained a spark arrester to cut down on the amount of hot coals emitted. *From the Kyle J. Neighbors Collection.*

Fig. 17 – Shay No. 4 at Spruce. Built in 1904, No. 4 weighed eighty tons and had a total wheel base of forty-four feet, six inches. Cylinders were thirteen and one-half inches in diameter with a 15-inch stroke. Drivers were thirty-six inches in diameter and tractive power was 35,102 pounds. First engineers were Pat Linnan and Lewis "Pinhead" Collins. *From the Kyle J. Neighbors Collection.*

Fig. 18 – Second Shay No. 1 and No. 4 at the Spruce engine house. 1916. Preston "Springy" Galford, fireman left, and "Peg" Parker, hostler. *From the Kyle J. Neighbors Collection.*

Fig. 19 – L. to r. Shays No. 3, 2, 1, and 4 lined up at Spruce, 1905. This was the complete locomotive holding of the company of the time. No. 4 was largest of these engines and was used on the Cass Hill. The other engines were "woods engines" used mostly on Cheat River. *Courtesy the Pocahontas County Historical Society.*

Fig. 20 – On November 1, 1905, Shay No. 5 was added to the company roster. No. 5 weighed ninety tons and was the heaviest engine to that date. Engineers were George and Charlie Cromer. Shown here on Cheat Mountain in 1910. *Courtesy Lurlie Curry.*

Fig. 21 – Shay No. 5 and crew at the first switchback on the Cass Hill. Foreground, l. to r.: Merle Ervin, brakeman; Ward Hudson, conductor; Joe Wooddell, brakeman; Deffinloe, brakeman. In cab: in doorway, Craddock, fireman and in the window, George "Piney" Williams, engineer. *From the Kyle J. Neighbors Collection.*

Fig. 22 – Shay No. 5 at the shop at Cass. Built in 1905, No. 5 was in almost continuous use in lumbering at Cass for the next fifty-five years. It was purchased by the Cass Scenic Railroad in 1962 and is still in use. *Courtesy Stella Blackhurst.*

Fig. 23—Shay No. 5 near Spruce. Shays were ideal engines in snow. They could plow through snowdrifts almost as high as the headlight. Such conditions were frequent on Cheat Mountain. *Courtesy Ivan O. Clarkson.*

Fig. 24 – The first No. 6 of the West Virginia Pulp and Paper Company was a Climax. This 40-ton locomotive was built in 1904. The Climax engine had a cylinder on each side set at a 45-degree angle and geared to a drive shaft in the center of the engine. In 1908, a second No. 6 (a Shay) was purchased and the Climax was renumbered 9. *From the Kyle J. Neighbors Collection.*

Fig. 25 – In 1912, Shay No. 7, a small engine of forty-five tons with cylinders ten inches in diameter and a 12-inch stroke and with 29½-inch drivers was purchased. It was taken to the Stony River Dam for use in construction and was brought to Cass three years later. Charlie Cromer was engineer. *Courtesy Charlie Cromer from the Kyle J. Neighbors Collection.*

Fig. 26—Shay No. 8 weighed 120 tons and was the first "big" Shay purchased at Cass. It was built in 1912 with cylinders fifteen inches in diameter and a 17-inch stroke and 40-inch drivers. This Shay was used mostly on the Cass Hill. The engineer was Sam Waugh. Shown here at the Cass Yard, 1916. *From the Kyle J. Neighbors Collection.*

Fig. 27 – Shay No. 8 at the Spruce water tank. No. 8 was equipped at the factory with an acetylene head lamp. It had a steel cab with a side entrance. *From the Kyle J. Neighbors Collection.*

Fig. 28 – Shown here at the Spruce water tank, Shay No. 10 weighed seventy tons, had 12-inch cylinders and 36-inch drivers. Purchased by the West Virginia Pulp and Paper Company in 1914, it was used on the Elk River Division, Cheat River Division, and the Cass Hill. Engineers were Grover and Charlie Craddock. *From the Kyle J. Neighbors Collection.*

Fig. 29 – Shay No. 10 on Cheat Mountain. *Courtesy Jack Ryder and the Pocahontas County Historical Society.*

Fig. 30 – The size of Shay No. 11, 120 tons, 40-inch drivers, is clearly shown in the 1915 photo on Cheat Mountain. George "Piney" Williams, engineer, is left of the cab steps. Used mostly on the Cass Hill, it made more trips between Cass and Spruce than any other Shay.
Courtesy Mower Lumber Company.

Fig. 31 – Shay No. 11 and crew at the Spruce water tank, 1916. First man on left, Page McCloud, second from right, "Piney" Williams, engineer. *From the Kyle J. Neighbors Collection.*

Fig. 32 – Builders photo of No. 12, the largest Shay owned by the West Virginia Pulp and Paper Company. Built in 1921, it weighed 154 tons, had cylinders seventeen inches in diameter, with an 18-inch stroke and 48-inch drivers. It was purchased for $54,034. Engineers of No. 12 were "Piney" Williams, Cal Bradley and Walter Good. *Courtesy the Lima Locomotive Works.*

Fig. 33 – Shay No. 12 on a test run, 1921, near Mace on Elk River.
From the Phil Bagdon Collection.

Fig. 34 – No. 12 bringing a train of log cars from Slaty Fork to Spruce. No. 12 was used extensively on both the Elk River, Cheat River, and Cass Hill Divisions, making daily runs of up to eighty-five miles round trip. *Courtesy Mrs. E. P. Shaffer.*

Fig. 35 – In 1933, the Cass shop crew doubled the size of the water tank on Shay No. 12 and placed a fourth set of trucks under it. This increased its operating weight to 208 tons and allowed it to make the trip from Cass to Slaty Fork without stopping to take on water. Granville Barkley is in the doorway and Guy Stanley in the window. Taken beside the pulp shed, Cass.

From the Kyle J. Neighbors Collection.

Fig. 36 — The first Shay with four trucks bought by the company was No. 13. Built in 1906, it weighed 150 tons, had 17-inch cylinders and 46-inch drivers. The company bought No. 13 in 1923 at junk price of two thousand dollars from the C&O Railroad, rebuilt it in the Cass shop and used it until 1950. Engineers were Ben Carman and "Piney" Williams.
From the Kyle J. Neighbors Collection.

Fig. 37 – The last locomotive purchased by the West Virginia Pulp and Paper Company at Cass was Shay No. 14. This 150-ton engine was built in 1910. It had 17-inch cylinders and 46-inch drivers. It was used by the C&O Railroad until bought by the West Virginia Pulp and Paper Company in 1928, rebuilt at the Cass shop and sold to the Western Maryland Railroad in 1932. Engineer at Cass was Guy Stanley.
Courtesy of Ivan O. Clarkson.

Fig. 38—Shay No. 4 giving the Marion steam shovel water while working on the Big Cut one mile west of Spruce. The Big Cut was nearly two thousand feet long and almost one hundred feet deep. It was the largest single engineering feat accomplished by the company and probably by any lumber company in the East. *From the Kyle J. Neighbors Collection.*

Fig. 39 – The 100-ton Marion steam shovel working on the Big Cut between 1910-1914. The engineer was George Crawford. *Courtesy Robert Dean. From the Kyle J. Neighbors Collection.*

Fig. 40 – Shay No. 4 setting in empty dump cars beside the Marion steam shovel in the Big Cut.
Courtesy Mrs. E. P. Shaffer. From the Pocahontas County Historical Society.

Fig. 41 – After the Big Cut was completed the Marion steam shovel was used in making smaller cuts along the line. *Courtesy Mrs. E. P. Shaffer. From the Pocahontas County Historical Society.*

Fig. 42 – American Railroad Ditcher with crew on Cheat Mountain. Ditchers were used for grading, cleaning up slides, cleaning ditches, etc. Ditchers were modified log loaders mounted on a modified car with one set of trucks. *From the Kyle J. Neighbors Collection.*

Fig. 43 – American railroad ditcher, front view. The beam arrangement
is clearly shown. *From the Kyle J. Neighbors Collection.*

Fig. 44 – Good maintenance of tracks and equipment along with experienced workers and high safety standards made trains wrecks a rarity on the Cass operation. This wreck occurred on Deever Run, north of Cass in the early 1920s. *Courtesy of Mrs. Markwood Gum. From the Pocahontas County Historical Society.*

Fig. 45 – In 1928, the U.S. Fisheries Service arranged to have a load of trout taken over the mountain for stocking in Cheat and Elk rivers. The fish were carried in aluminum buckets and were kept cold by ice. *From the Kyle J. Neighbors Collection.*

Fig. 46 – A rare photograph of a section crew on Cheat made-up mostly of blacks. Section crews were responsible for maintenance of a specific "section" of track. *From the Kyle J. Neighbors Collection.*

Fig. 47 – Log train crew at Cass, 1950. L. to r. Elbert Galford, Henry Gibson, H. Payne, Porter Moore, Guy Stanley, Clark Phillips, Walter Good, engineer. *Courtesy Mrs. Walter Good.*

Fig. 48 – Steep mountains can be climbed by geared locomotives by the use of switchbacks. This view of the first switchback on the Cass Hill shows their construction. The track heads up the hill from Cass and into a hollow to a dead end, then emerges to head around the hill to the next hollow where the second switchback is located. *Courtesy of Forest Wooddell. From the Pocahontas County Historical Society.*

Fig. 49 – Coal mine tipple and cars of the West Virginia Pulp and Paper Company.
Courtesy H. E. Matics.

Fig. 50—Cutting crew at work felling a red spruce on Cheat Mountain. One of the knot bumpers is helping out on the near handle of the saw, while the head faller (obscured by the tree) is lending a hand on the far side. Camp 15, 1910.
Photography by Herman Work. Courtesy of H. E. Matics.

Fig. 51 – Loggers pause for a picture displaying the tools of the trade; a crosscut saw, axes for notching a tree and bumping limbs, mauls for driving wedges to assist in felling a tree or to prevent pinching of the saw, and a measuring stick for laying off logs. *Courtesy Ivan O. Clarkson.*

Fig. 52 – Two sawyers and a knot bumper with a felled spruce on Cheat Mountain. July 20, 1913.
Photograph by Samuel Gusby. Courtesy Dolly Nelson.

Fig. 53 – Teamsters and teams pose for a picture on Cheat Mountain. Horses played an important part in the logging operations. The West Virginia Pulp and Paper Company had as many as two hundred horses in the woods at one time. *Courtesy Warren E. Blackhurst.*

Fig. 54 – John Barkley, teamster, halts his team and short trail of logs on a "corduroy road." Cheat Mountain. *Courtesy Dolly Nelson.*

Fig. 55 – Well-matched teams of Belgians, Percherons, and Clydesdales were essential to skidding logs to the landing. *Courtesy Dolly Nelson.*

Fig. 56—Part of a trail of logs going into the landing, Camp 15, 1910. Logs are fastened together by grabs pounded into the adjacent ends. The camp foreman, Billie Buckingham, is on the right. *Photograph by Herman Work. Courtesy H. E. Matics.*

Fig. 57 – Log landing on Cheat Mountain. Logs were brought to the left side of the landing by teams of horses. Grabs holding the trail of logs together were knocked loose and the logs were rolled across the landing to be loaded on railroad log cars on the right. A log slide is next to the teams. *Courtesy Lacy Byrd.*

Fig. 58 – Unusual log landing on Cheat Mountain, 1910. Designed for logs to be skidded in at different levels, the logs were then rolled down successive levels to the railroad at the bottom. *Courtesy George A. Fizer. From the Kyle J. Neighbors Collection.*

Fig. 59 – Camp 15 from across Cheat River, 1910. Notice the hogs at the end of the bridge. The stable is the low, long building at the left. The other large building contains the kitchen, dining room and lobby downstairs, and sleeping quarters upstairs.
Photograph by Herman Work. Courtesy H. E. Matics.

Fig. 60—Cooks, teamsters and teams at Camp 18, Cheat Mountain. Two brothers from Franklin, West Virginia came to this camp and went to work. In less than four hours, one was dead. He helped cut a tree which fell into the fork of another. The felled tree kicked back cutting him almost in two against a third tree. *Courtesy Connell Gillespie.*

Fig. 61 – Men of one of the lumber camps on Cheat Mountain. This photo was taken on Sunday while the men were relaxing. Two men at the left front are sharpening an axe on a grindstone. *Photograph by J. A. Gardner. Courtesy H. E. Matics.*

Fig. 62–Men of Camp 15, on Cheat Mountain, 1915. Identififed men are: l. to r. First row, 1. Winters Ford, 2. Cleve Hunt, 5. Everett Sharp, 8. Harvey Craddock. Second row, 6. Floyd Branscomb, 8. Ezra Bennett, 9. Guy Ralston. Third row, 4. Wilson Darnell, 7. Lawrence Ralston, 12. Charlie Haglund. Fourth row, 10. Harry Osborne, 12. Ira Robertson. Fifth row, 1. Charles Proptst, 3. John Osborne, 7. Lenny Dean. *Courtesy Connell Gillespie.*

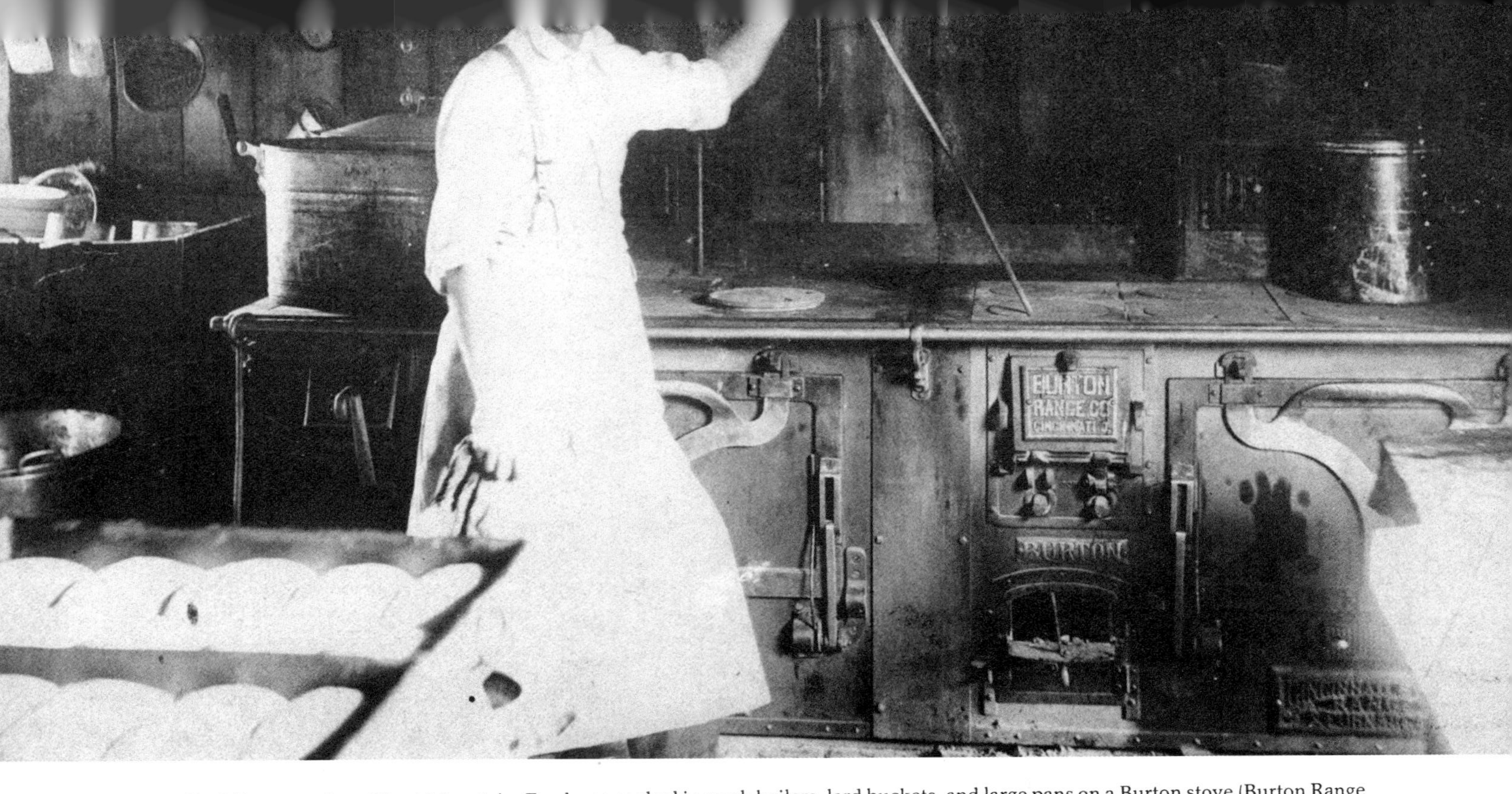

Fig. 63 – Fred Tyree, cook on Cheat Mountain. Food was cooked in wash boilers, lard buckets, and large pans on a Burton stove (Burton Range Company, Cincinnati, Ohio). The twenty loaves of bread shown at the left would be eaten in one supper. *From the Kyle J. Neighbors Collection.*

Fig. 64 – Looking from the kitchen into the dining room at a logging camp on Cheat Mountain. The cook and cookees worked seven days a week. The cook was paid $3.00 a day, the cookees $1.50 plus board and room in each case. *Courtesy Katherine Campion.*

Fig. 65 – Inside a dining car at mealtime, August 7, 1946. Mower Lumber Company. Standing, Sam Harman, cook, looking toward camera Alfred Higgins. First on left Russell "Pappy" Taylor, seventh on left, Howard Barb. Third on right row, Lester Hevener.
From the Phil Bagdon Collection.

Fig. 66 – American Log Loader Model C of the Spruce Lumber Company on Cheat Mountain, 1915.
Courtesy H. E. Matics.

Fig. 67 – Steam, cables, boom, and tongs combine to load red spruce logs on Cheat Mountain. Spruce Lumber Company Loader No. 1. *Courtesy P. E. Percy.*

Fig. 68 – Crew of log loader pose for a picture on Cheat Mountain. Note the small wheels under the loader. It can be moved from one end of the car to the other on iron-topped wooden rails mounted permanently on the car. The loader can be moved from car to car by the use of temporary rails between cars. *Courtesy Pocahontas County Historical Society.*

Fig. 69 – American Log Loader Model C No. 1 of the West Virginia Spruce Lumber Company; Greenbrier and Elk River RR car No. 38; Shay locomotive No. 2. Loader engineer, John Gerow. Shay engineer Lewis Collins, fireman, Robert Dean. *From the Kyle J. Neighbors Collection.*

Fig. 70–Shay No. 4 and log loader at a landing on Cheat Mountain, November 10, 1945. Mower Lumber Company. The men are placing stakes in pockets on the sides of the car to hold the logs on. *From the Kyle J. Neighbors Collection.*

Fig. 71 – Steam skidder on Cheat Mountain near Spruce. The intricate rigging is clearly seen as is the daredevil standing on top the tower.
Courtesy Ivan O. Clarkson.

Fig. 72 – Steam skidder on Cheat Mountain. Skidders were built on railroad flatcars and were solidly blocked underneath for stability. *Courtesy H. E. Matics.*

Fig. 73 – One of the five steam skidders to operate on Cheat Mountain from 1922 to 1960. *Courtesy H. E. Matics.*

Fig. 74 – Lidgerwood steam skidder on Cheat Mountain. *Courtesy D. Wallace Johnson.*

Fig. 75 – A Disston "beavertail" chain saw was demonstrated on Cheat Mountain, 1948. These early, heavy, bulky saws were never popular with the loggers and were used very little. *Courtesy H. E. Matics.*

Fig. 76 – The pulpwood peeling mill and the town of Spruce, 1919. The peeling mill was constructed in 1904 and the town of Spruce was built to house millworkers. *Courtesy Mertie V. Clarkson.*

Fig. 77 – Pulpwood peeling mill and woodyard at Spruce. *Courtesy P. E. Percy.*

Fig. 78 – The steam engine that powered the pulpwood peeling (rossing) machines of the Spruce mill.
Left, Scott Lockard; right, Roy Cook. *Courtesy Roy Cook.*
From the Pocahontas County Historical Society.

Fig. 79 – Main Street, Spruce, West Virginia. There was no need for a roadway since there was no highway into the town and no automobiles. Built in 1904, the town of Spruce flourished until the pulpwood peeling mill was closed in 1925, then rapidly declined until by 1960, it was completely gone. The small houses in the street were coal houses, so located as to be near the railroad which ran on the left just out of the picture. L. to r. In the early 1920s, the homes of "Denny" Flynn, train conductor; George Clinebell, mill superintendent; Elmer L. Duncan, train dispatcher; and Ellet C. Smith, store manager and postmaster. This picture was taken in the early 1900s.

Courtesy H. E. Matics. Information from Harry "Shorty" Duncan.

Shotgun houses, Rosiclade, Ill, Alcoa workers 1950's

Fig. 80 – Five local ladies pose on the porch of the company hotel at Spruce. The hotel provided room and board for workers on the mill and railroad. *From the Kyle J. Neighbors Collection.*

Fig. 81 – Out for a Sunday ride on speeders at Spruce, Dr. U. H. Hannah is on the front speeder. Mrs. E. P. Shaffer and Joe Hannah on the second. *From the Phil Bagdon Collection.*

Fig. 82 – Aerial view of the location of the former town of Spruce. Remains of the mill are shown at the left. The large wye, used by the lumber company was replaced by the loop seen here of the Western Maryland R.R. May 3, 1981. *Courtesy Terry E. Arbogast.*

Fig. 83 – Sawmill and planing mill of the West Virginia Spruce Lumber Company. These mills were built in 1901. The first lumber was cut on January 25, 1902. *Courtesy Mrs. Ica Sharps. From the Pocahontas County Historical Society.*

Fig. 84 – Lumberyard and mill at Cass, taken from above the C&O depot. *Photography by Underwood and Underwood. Courtesy H. E. Matics.*

Fig. 85 – In the late teens the mill was remodeled by adding a tall stack, an adjacent boiler room, and a pulp shed along the railroad. *Courtesy Kate Shaffer Hardy.*

Fig. 86 – The boiler room and stacks of the mill built in 1922 after the original mill burned. The sawmill is on the left, the planing mill on the right, the dry kilns in front of the stacks, and the pulp shed in the front, 1923. *Photograph by Samuel O. Sweeny. Courtesy H. E. Matics.*

Fig. 87 – Looking northward toward the new mill from across the Greenbrier River. The planing mill is the large building shown. Lumber piles are on the left. 1923. *Photograph by Samuel O. Sweeny. Courtesy H. E. Matics.*

Fig. 88 – The Hamilton steam engine that ran the mill at Cass. The engine powered the 18-foot diameter flywheel shown in the back. The flywheel ran a wide leather belt connected to a line shaft running under the mill. Various saws, conveyors, etc. were powered by belts running off the line shaft. *Photograph by R. K. Photo Laboratory. From the Kyle J. Neighbors Collection.*

Fig. 89 – Hamilton steam engine that powered the mill at Cass. The governor that regulates the speed of the engine is shown right of high center. *Photograph by the R. Kay Photo Laboratory. From the Kyle J. Neighbors Collection.*

Fig. 90 – Huge generators fill the powerhouse of the Cass mill. A permanent overhead crane made repairs on the large machinery possible.
Courtesy H. E. Matics.

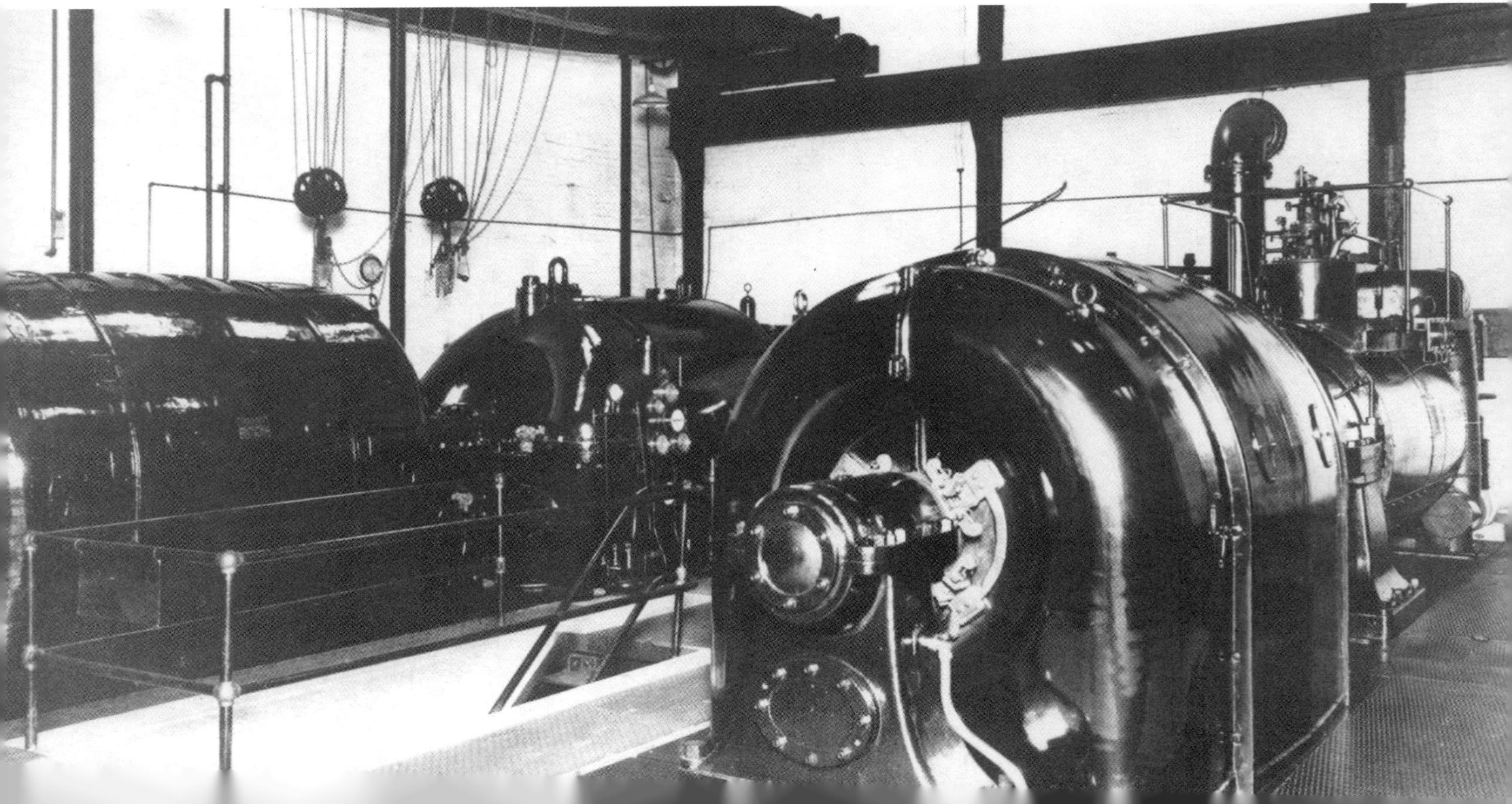

Fig. 91 – Looking from the mill northward toward the log pond and cars waiting to be unloaded. Mower Lumber Company, August 7, 1946. "Basgy" Taylor standing over the "jackslip" at right. Dennis Wade feeding the bull chain and Lyle "Peck" McPherson farthest away. *D. D. Brown Collection. From the West Virginia and Regional History Collection.*

Fig. 92—Log being pulled from the pond up the "jackslip" by the bull chain
to the entrance of the mill, Mower Lumber Company. 1960.
Photograph by the author.

Fig. 93 – Ben Jackson, scaler, measures a log as it enters the mill. A Doyle log scale enables Ben to read off the number of board feet in the log. August 7, 1945. *D. D. Brown Collection. From the West Virginia and Regional History Collection.*

Fig. 94—Band saw and carriage. The carriage has just reached the end of the cut. This is the long-side saw looking north. On the carriage: setting, Bill Simmons, far left: dogging, Olliver Tyson. Turningdown "Bean Pole" Tallman, right. August 7, 1946. *D. D. Brown Collection. From the West Virginia and Regional History Collection.*

Fig. 95 – Looking northward toward the band saws in the new mill. The rollers and conveyors carry newly cut boards from the band saws to other parts of the mill. The long-side, on the left, cut mostly spruce. The short-side, right, cut hardwoods. *Photograph by Underwood and Underwood. Courtesy H. E. Matics.*

Fig. 96 – Ether Tyson operating the cutoff saws that trim boards as they leave the mill to the bullpen where they are graded, tallied, and loaded on lumber trucks for movement to the dry kilns or lumberyard. The cutoff saws are counterbalanced by weights. The correct saw is lowered by the operator pulling the proper rope. 1956. *Photograph by the author.*

Fig. 97 – Ollie Meeks operates controls in the boiler room. The chutes feed sawdust and chips from storage above the area to the furnaces beneath the floor. Mower Lumber Company, 1956. *Photograph by the author.*

Fig. 98—John Warner operating flooring machine in the planing mill. August 7, 1946. *D. D. Brown Collection. From the West Virginia and Regional History Collection.*

Fig. 99 – Arthur "Soc" White, left, feeds flooring into an end-match machine. Marvin Moss, right, is grading flooring. August 7, 1946. *D. D. Brown Collection. From the West Virginia and Regional History Collection.*

Fig. 100 – "Alex" Duncan, left, and Sherwin·Lambert, middle, are racking flooring while Cameron Ware ties it into bundles. August 7, 1946.
D. D. Brown Collection. From the West Virginia and Regional History Collection.

Fig. 101 — Lumber was piled from the dock onto piles with stickers between the layers to allow for air circulation to effect drying. Here Marvin McLaughlin lets down two spruce boards to the piler. A heavy leather apron and heavy hand leathers allows the board to slide freely under the control of the piler. *Photograph by the author.*

Fig. 102 – After the lumber had air dried sufficiently in the lumber piles, it was loaded into railroad cars for shipment. Five men made up a loading crew; a grader who graded and tallied the lumber loaded two men on the pile and two in the car. Short leather aprons were worn to facilitate handling the lumber. This group of workers are in the Cass yard. *Courtesy Stella Blackhurst.*

Fig. 103 – Looking northward toward the lumberyard and mill of the Mower Lumber Company mill, Cass. One of the smokestakes was shortened in 1944 to about one-half its original height.

Fig. 104 – Derelict mill looking southward across the log pond. August 1, 1971.
From the Kyle J. Neighbors Collection.

Fig. 105 – Remains of the mill May 3, 1981, after fires destroyed the planing mill and flooring wareroom on August 20, 1978. *Photograph by Terry E. Arbogast.*

Fig. 106 – Looking westward across the millpond to the original machine shops of the West Virginia Pulp and Paper Company.
Courtesy Ivan O. Clarkson.

Fig. 107 – Looking northward inside the machine shop at Cass. Machinery was powered by belts running off an overhead line shaft. The line shaft was driven by an electric motor. *Photograph by Underwood and Underwood. Courtesy H. E. Matics.*

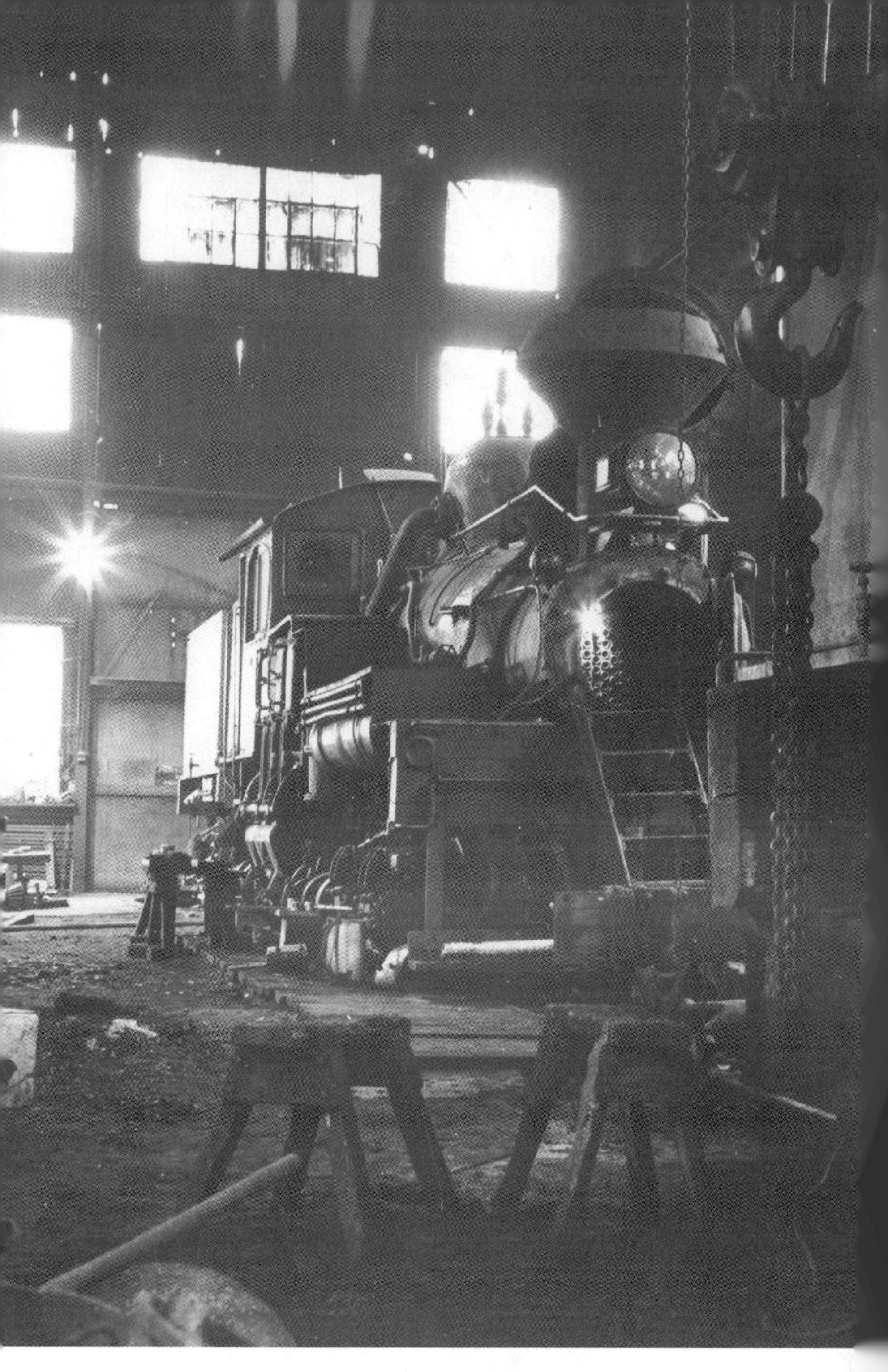

Fig. 108 – View of CSRR Shay No. 4 being repaired in the Cass shop. February 3, 1969. *Courtesy Richard Sparks.*

Fig. 109 – Making a pour at the foundry, Cass, August, 1956. L. to r. Jesse McCalpin, Huffman Summerfield, Roy Day, and Allen "Farmer" Blackhurst. Pouring one "heat" took about forty-five minutes. One "pour" used four thousand pounds of cast iron and made sixty-four brakeshoes. Brass, babbit and other materials were also used for special purposes. *Courtesy Ivan O. Clarkson.*

Fig. 110—Shop crew of the West Virginia Pulp and Paper Company, Cass, Pocahontas County. Men are: first row, l. to r.: Charlie Kirkpatrick, Clifford Wolfe, George Friel, Roy Cook, Charles Norris, Ted Campbell, Norman Schrader, and Forest Wheeler. Second row, l. to r.: William "Bill" Blackhurst, Stover Hamrick, Grover Friel, E. J. Shaffer, Carl Ryder, C. R. Shrader, M. Wheeler, Lacy Bowling, and Fred Powelle. Third row, l. to r.: Allen Blackhurst, William Nichols, Ellis Tallman, Forest Haptonstall, Paul Warner, Jim Porter, Charles King, William Cassell, two Italians—names unknown. *Courtesy Ivan O. Clarkson.*

Fig. 111 – Cass Shop Crew, September, 1947. Sitting, l. to r.: Harper Gum, Charles Cook. H. H. Halterman, Chester Shrader. Standing, l. to r.:
Roy Cook, Elmer L. Duncan, Sam Harouff, Allen "Farmer" Blackhurst, Grover "Jughead" Wright, and Paul Warner.
Courtesy Ivan O. Clarkson.

Fig. 112—Shop crew of the Cass Scenic Railroad. Kneeling, l. to r.: "Arty" Barkley, William "Bud" Cassell, Kermit Foe, Ivan Clark, Kyle "Catty" Neighbors, Robert Long. Standing, l. to r.: Jim Reep, Richard Carter, Paul Bradley, John Cassell, Robert Cassell, Paul Pennington, Stewart Swink, and "Red" McMillion. *From the Kyle J. Neighbors Collection.*

Fig. 113 – Looking northward along the Greenbrier River Valley. The Extract Plant at Deer Creek is in the foreground; the town of Cass is in the distance. *Courtesy Beatrice Blackhurst Sheets.*

Fig. 114 – The Extract Plant, Deer Creek. Built in 1914, this plant extracted tannins from bark and wood slabs. During World War I, it was used to extract olive drab dye from osage orange wood shipped in from the south and midwest. The plant closed in 1926.
Photographs by Underwood and Underwood. Courtesy H. E. Matics.

Fig. 115 – The Pocahontas Supply Company and C&O Depot. The post office was located at this time in the righthand side of the store and had an outside door. 1917. *Courtesy Jesse Pennington.*

Fig. 116 – The company office was located in the Company Store. On the left is Jasper Matthews, on the right front, Virginia Gillespie. *Courtesy Mary Clark Roach.*

Fig. 117 – Interior of the Pocahontas Supply Company Store, Cass. One of the largest company stores ever owned by a lumber company, it carried supplies for the town and the surrounding farmers as well as for the one thousand or more men working in the woods. The post office was located, at this time, in the store and is shown on the left. *Photograph by Underwood and Underwood. Courtesy H. E. Matics.* Inset: Script was minted for use at Cass but as far as can be determined was never used. *From Nodie Bascomb. Courtesy Harold Lee.*

Fig. 118—Company office located in the Company Store, 1945. L. to r.: standing far left, Joe Urbanick, seated: Beatrice Blackhurst, – – –, Jake Fulks, Howard Fulks. *Courtesy Beatrice Blackhurst Sheets.*

Fig. 119–Company Store of the Mower Lumber Company. February 14, 1947. Formerly the Pocahontas Supply Company.
Courtesy Ivan O. Clarkson.

Fig. 120 – The first couple to live on the location of Cass was Charles Z. J. Curry and Ida Burner Curry. Here they are shown in 1900 with their children. Boys, l. to r.: Harry, Parker, and Owen. Girl: Mertie Viola (the author's mother). *Courtesy Mertie Curry Clarkson.*

Fig. 121 – Allen Craig and Virginia Clark Burner founded one of the three original families at the town of Cass. *Courtesy Eugene Burner.*

Fig. 122 – Built about 1885, this house in East Cass, is the oldest surviving building. It is located north of the Baptist church (former Northern Methodist Church). It was the home of Allen and Virginia Burner. *Courtesy Eugene Burner.*

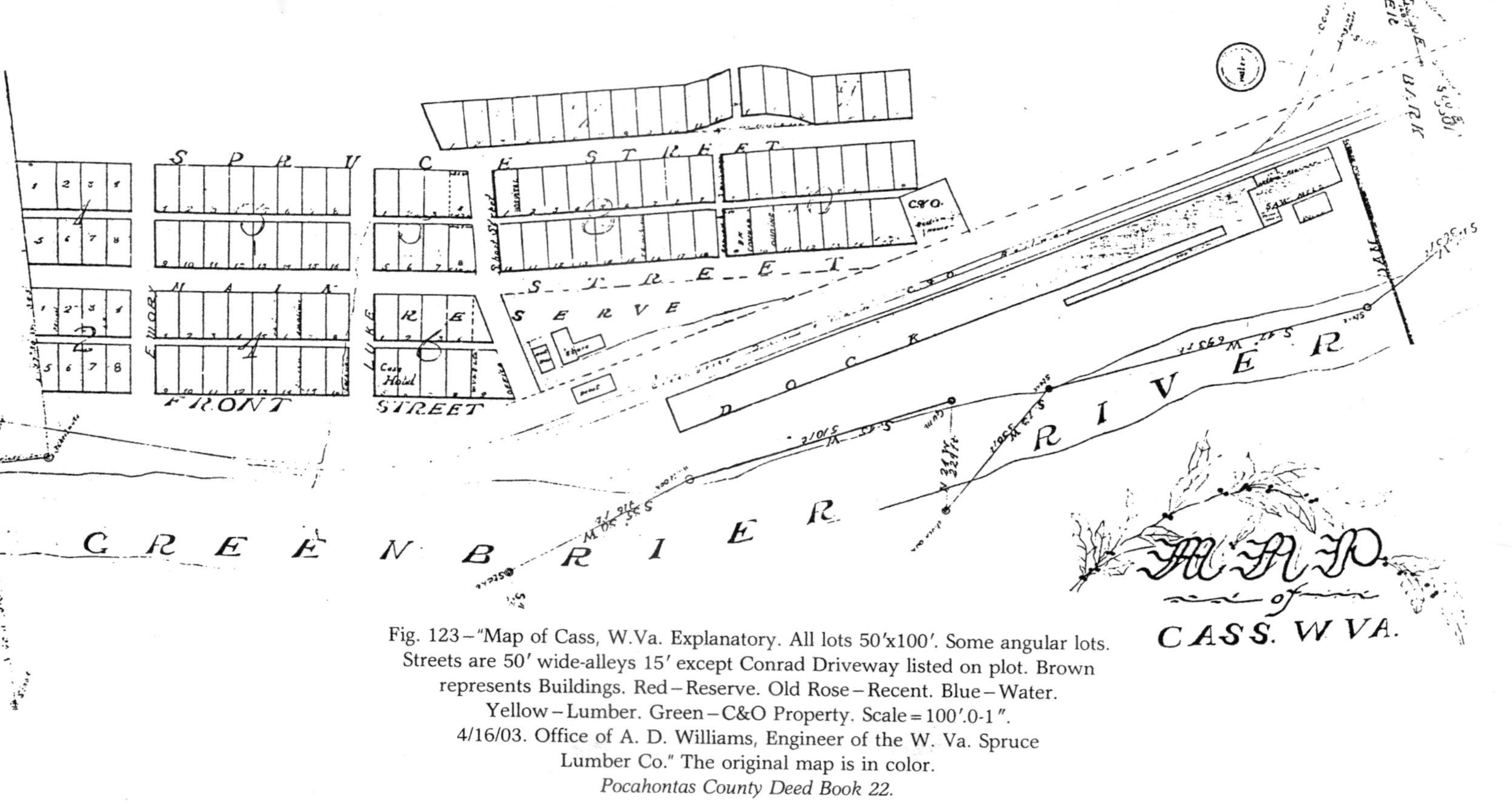

Fig. 123 – "Map of Cass, W.Va. Explanatory. All lots 50'x100'. Some angular lots. Streets are 50' wide-alleys 15' except Conrad Driveway listed on plot. Brown represents Buildings. Red – Reserve. Old Rose – Recent. Blue – Water. Yellow – Lumber. Green – C&O Property. Scale = 100'.0-1". 4/16/03. Office of A. D. Williams, Engineer of the W. Va. Spruce Lumber Co." The original map is in color.
Pocahontas County Deed Book 22.

Fig. 124 – Looking across the Greenbrier River toward the business section of East Cass. Pedestrians crossed on the swinging bridge, horses and vehicular traffic forded the stream. Believed to date before October, 1902, as there is no protective side wire in evidence on the bridge. Side wire was put on in late 1902. *Courtesy Pocahontas County Historical Society.*

Fig 125. – "Open and Ready to Sell, D. Finger." This sign, at the left of the bridge dates the picture as February 1903, when Finger purchased Samuel Cooper's store and had a one-half price sale. Looking across the Greenbrier River toward East Cass. *Courtesy Mary Roach Clark.*

Fig. 126 – Looking westward at the business section of East Cass from a vantage point on the hill east of town. The Loggers Home Hotel ("White Elephant") is on the left. The sign is advertising the opening of Jacob Cooper's store. The Cooper building is hidden behind the hotel. Other buildings in East Cass are unidentified. Across the river the Company Hotel, left; the company office, center; Nethken's Meat Market and the Pocahontas Supply Company Store, right. The swinging bridge was still in use. 1908. *Courtesy Lurlie Curry.*

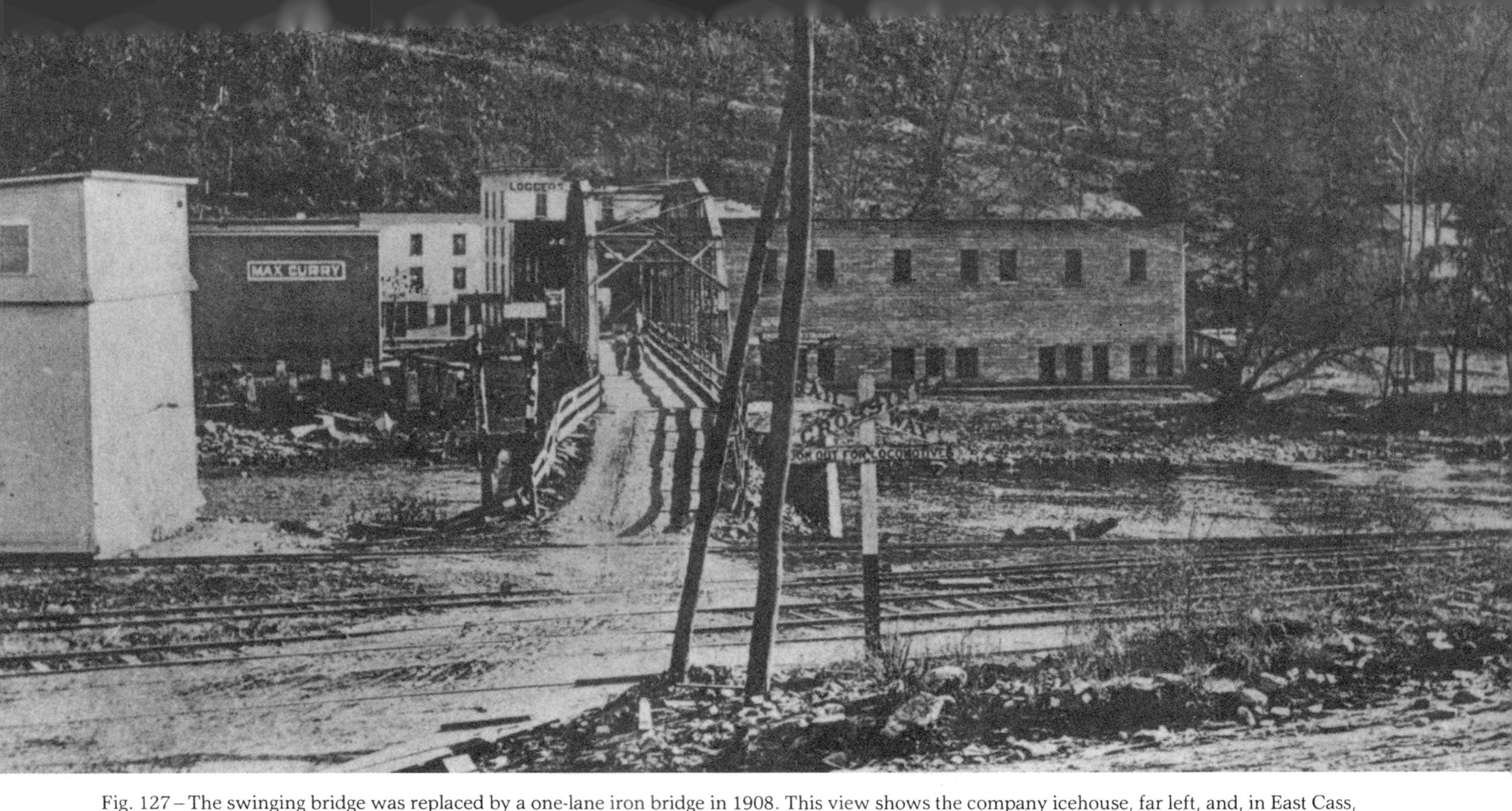

Fig. 127 – The swinging bridge was replaced by a one-lane iron bridge in 1908. This view shows the company icehouse, far left, and, in East Cass, Max Curry's store at the end of the bridge, left, and the Siegel Building, right. The Central Hotel and the Loggers Home are in the center background. *Courtesy Ivan O. Clarkson.*

Fig. 128 – Sarah Emma Poage Burner, the first schoolteacher in Cass. Emma was also a leader in the fight against the saloons in East Cass, sometimes, dressed as a man, she entered establishments, witnessed the sale of whiskey and even purchased whiskey herself. She, along with her brother, Allen, then swore out warrants against the proprietors. *Courtesy Eugene Burner.*

Fig. 129 – Elmer Davis Burner was appointed town sergeant of Cass in 1902 and soon won the nickname "King Brady" after a dime-novel policeman of that name. *Courtesy Eugene Burner.*

Fig. 130—In 1905, Lincoln S. "Link" Cochran, left, was appointed constable at Cass. One of his ploys was to secretly engage several deputies, ride with them out of town on the train, stop the train a couple of miles away, and walk back to make a surprise raid on the town saloons. This picture was taken when he was sheriff of Pocahontas County. Shown here with his bloodhound, Jim Dallas and J. J. Boggs. *Courtesy John M. Cochran.*

Fig. 131 – Aftermath of one of the several floods that ravaged East Cass. Looking west toward the Greenbrier River 1913.
Courtesy Warren E. Blackhurst.

Fig. 132 – The business section of East Cass from the hill east of town. The white building at the left is the Loggers Home Hotel ("White Elephant"), beyond it is Jacob Cooper's store, beyond that is the Siegel Building. Across the street, at this end of the bridge, is Max Curry's store. Between 1909 and 1915. *From the Kyle J. Neighbor's Collection.*

Fig. 133 – Top: The River View Hotel and other buildings on "Dirty Street" in East Cass. Bottom: Baxter Auto Sales and garage in East Cass. Located on the east side of the Green Bank Road south of the Central Hotel and John Reda's store. *Both pictures from the Kyle J. Neighbor's Collection.*

Fig. 134. – John Reda's grocery store in East Cass. It was located on the east side of the Green Bank Road south of the Central Hotel. *From the Kyle J. Neighbor's Collection.*

Fig. 135 – View of East Cass following the destructive fire of 1913. Intact buildings are, left to right: The Alpha Hotel, The Logger's Home ("White Elephant"), Cooper's store and the Siegel Building. Ruins of buildings destroyed by fire are in the right-hand portion of the picture. *Courtesy Eugene Burner.*

Fig. 136 – Looking south along Front Street, Cass. These were the first houses to be built in 1902.
From the Kyle J. Neighbor's Collection.

Fig. 137 – The Cass Hotel (later called the Mountain Inn) owned by the company, was a fashionable and popular boarding place for millworkers, trainmen, and, on weekends, loggers. Built in 1902. *From the Kyle J. Neighbor's Collection.*

Fig. 138—S. B. Nethken and Co. Meat Market, left, and the Pocahontas Supply Company Store. The steps on Nethken's market lead to the telephone exchange. About 1907. *Courtesy Stella Blackhurst.*

Fig. 139 – This barn was located on the hill near the hospital. Horses were brought in by train and kept in this barn until they were matched in pairs and taken to the woods on Cheat Mountain. Gardens in the foreground were owned by people living on the hill.
Courtesy Kate Shaffer Hardy.

Fig. 140 – Built on Front Street in 1907, the Masonic Hall is still used for lodge meetings and social events. The building is 24'x24'x48' and cost fifteen hundred dollars to build. *Courtesy Russell Clarkson.*

Fig. 141 – Main Street, Cass. Looking northward from the top of Ralston Hill. The Odd Fellows Lodge building is under construction at the right. The small houses spaced along the right-hand side of the street, are valve houses. They contain a fire hydrant and fire hose. About 1904. *Courtesy Kate Shaffer Hardy.*

Fig. 142 – The second school building in Cass was located on Spruce Street. This picture was taken in 1909. The Principal, Burley Williams, is standing in front of the second window from the right. *Courtesy Mary Shaw.*

Fig. 143 – Cass jail and city hall. The council room is upstairs. The jail has four cells and is heated by a coal stove. It was built about 1921. Photograph, 1984.

Fig. 144- Cass Grade School. The north wing, right, was built in 1915, the south wing was added in 1916. Each wing had four rooms. The school was heated by coal stoves in each room until the early 1920s when central steam heat was installed. 1942. *Courtesy Nellie Maude Smith.*

Fig. 145 – The Cass Presbyterian Church was built on Front Street in 1905. The original membership was fifteen persons. The bell was donated by the West Virginia Spruce Lumber Company. Membership grew to 136 active members in 1940. The Cass Presbyterian Church was dissolved on June 30, 1970. The building was given to the people of the town of Cass for a Community Building. *Courtesy Mertie V. Clarkson.*

Fig. 146—The Reverend Fred W. Gray, left, was Presbyterian minister at Cass from 1918 to 1929. He was followed by Rev. Timothy Pharr, right, who served from 1929 to 1941. *Both photographs courtesy Beatrice Blackhurst Sheets.*

Fig. 147 – Members of the Cass Camp of the Modern Woodsmen of America. 1910. Front row, l. to r.: Ed Jackson, Connell Gillespie, Walter Persinger, Harry Scott, Malan Kern. Back row, l. to r.: W. T. Newcome, Dr. George L. Eakle (optomestrist), ? Neal, Dr. Austin (druggist), Dr. Jarrett (dentist). *Courtesy Connell Gillespie.*

Fig. 148 – Some Sunday fun, Cass. Around 1905. *Courtesy Mary Clark Roach.*

Fig. 149 – A Sunday ride, Cass. Around 1906. Lucy Gillespie Matthews is on the back of the speeder. *Courtesy Mary Clark Roach.*

Fig. 150—Skating on the Greenbrier River. *Courtesy Beatrice Blackhurst Sheets.*

Fig. 151 – Cass Grade School pageant on the bank in front of the Presbyterian church. The part of town where blacks lived is in the background across the river. *From Viva Simmons. Courtesy Jesse Pennington.*

Fig. 152 – Outing on Elk River in motorcar. Front: Mrs. Patricia Shaffer. Back: Mr. and Mrs. Gordon Hamale.
Courtesy Kate Shaffer Hardy.

Fig. 153 – Construction forms for the cement bridge across the Greenbrier River at Cass 1917-18. *Courtesy Mrs. Fred Conrad. From the Pocahontas County Historical Society.*

Fig. 154 – Brill's Store, East Cass. 1920. The Siegel building is to the left. A pair of steps rose between the buildings.
Courtesy Mary Shaw.

Fig. 155 – View of Cass in 1918. Note the forms of the bridge. The railing is not yet built. The Company Store, was heavily damaged by fire shortly after this. *Courtesy Forest Wooddell. From the Pocahontas County Historical Society.*

Fig. 156—View of Cass in 1920. The store of the Pocahontas Supply Company was rebuilt after the fire in 1918. S. B. Nethken's Meat Market was moved closer to the company office and the store was enlarged. *Courtesy Warren E. Blackhurst.*

Fig. 157 – View of the town of Cass, about 1920. The Company Hotel is across the river on the right. Left of this is the Masonic Hall and the Presbyterian church. Behind the Masonic Hall is the original jail, the city hall and a company garage. The part of town where blacks lived is in the left foreground. The dark-roofed building behind the last row of houses on the right is the second school to be built in Cass.
Courtesy O. B. Curry. From the Pocahontas County Historical Society.

Fig. 158 – Top: Panorama of Cass, October 4, 1923. Bottom: Panorama of Cass, May 15, 1917. Note: in the time period between the two views the following changes were made: the iron bridge was replaced with the cement bridge, S. B. Nethkin's Meat Market was moved closer to the company office and the Company Store was enlarged, a large hay storage building and chicken house were built north of the store, the Luke house was built on the hill above the store. In East Cass, two buildings were added on the right at the end of the bridge. *Both photographs by Gay Studios.*

Fig. 159 – Emory P. Shaffer, General Superintendent of the West Virginia Pulp and Paper Company at Cass, his wife, Patty, and five of their children. L. to r.: Jane, Gertrude, Kate, Patsy, and Susan. On the steps of their home at Cass. 1923. *Photograph by Samuel O. Sweeny. Courtesy H. E. Matics.*

Fig. 160—James A. "Jim" Belcher was bus driver, constable, and truant officer. He lived in a house in East Cass in the Blackhurst Addition north of the swinging bridge. *Courtesy Earl W. Belcher.*

Fig. 161 – Scene in "Shorty" Brill's Restaurant in East Cass. Bananas were sold "off the stem" (see upper left), potatoes were ten cents, soup fifteen cents, coffee ten cents, and one egg ten cents. Note the spittoon under the barstools at the left.
Courtesy the Pocahontas County Historical Society.

Fig. 162 – Fred "Buck" Hamrick in "Buck's Place" in the Brill building in East Cass. Cookies, candies, and nuts were kept in the wide-mouth jars. *Courtesy Ernestine Hamrick Clarkson.*

Fig. 163 – The Methodist Episcopal Church North in East Cass. 1941. Built in 1924 along the Green Bank Road, it served as a Methodist church until World War II when the membership declined to almost zero. It was sold to the Baptist church in 1951. It was abandoned and derelict by the 1980s. *Courtesy Russell M. Clarkson.*

Fig. 164 – The Methodist Episcopal Church South was built on Spruce Street. It was dedicated on June 12, 1927, and is still serving the people of Cass. Photographed here in 1984. *Photograph by the author.*

Fig. 165—Rev. Harry Blackhurst, seated. Standing, l. to r., "Becky" Belcher, Earl Belcher, Woodrow Belcher. *Courtesy Earl Belcher.*

Fig. 166 – Dr. Frank C. Nickell, veterinary surgeon, at a log landing on Cheat Mountain. He rode the speeder from camp to camp to treat sick or injured horses. It could be lifted off the tracks if a train was met. *Courtesy F. C. Nickell and the Pocahontas County Historical Society.*

Fig. 167 – Mertie V. Clarkson, the author's mother, symbolizes the many homemakers in Cass who spent their lives working for their families. *Photograph by the author.*

Fig. 168 — Many Cass families supplemented their food supply by growing large gardens and raising massive hogs. Hogs were usually butchered on Thanksgiving Day. Here Ben Jackson, l., and Laban Wolfe, r., stand beside a freshly butchered hog. *Courtesy Lola Clarkson Jackson.*

Fig. 169 – Cass Presbyterian Church men's Sunday school class. 1941. Front row, l. to r., O. M. Shriver, C. R. Shrader, Ivan O. Clarkson, Dr. F. C. Nickell. Back row, l. to r., Robert S. Hickman, W. G. Moss, – – – Strickland, Fred McLaughlin, and E. J. Shaffer. *Courtesy Ivan O. Clarkson.*

Fig. 170 – The footlog across the slough in East Cass. Walter Clarkson's buildings are in the background. L. to r., Clyde Gilliam, Dorothy Harouff, Catherine Blackhurst, Beatrice Blackhurst, Ruth Blackhurst, Don Harouff, and Harry "Buzz" Blackhurst. 1929. *Courtesy Beatrice Blackhurst Sheets.*

Fig. 171 — Cass was a great place to visit. Here George Roy, the author's son, plays brakeman on a flatcar. 1960. The brake is tightened by winding a chain, attached to the brake, around the stem, as shown. The brake stem can be laid down, out of the way, to allow a log loader to be moved from car to car. *Photograph by the author.*

Fig. 172 – Women's Sunday school class, Methodist Episcopal Church. In front from left: – – –, Mrs. Thompson, Mrs. (Copen) Morris, Rella Tacy, Lola (Clarkson) Jackson, Nola Dahmer, – – –.

Fig. 173 – Many happy summer hours were spent by Cass youngsters in Blackhurst's Swimming Hole located where Deer Creek empties into the Greenbrier River. The two girls in the center are Gertrude "Trudy" Blackhurst, l., and Patricia "Patty" McPherson, r.

Fig. 174 – Derailment of C&O Locomotive No. 1505, alongside of the pulp shed of the West Virginia Pulp and Paper Company. About 1942. *Courtesy Nellie Maude Smith.*

Fig. 175—Oney Plyler in front of his store and garage in East Cass. Oney is standing to the right of the gas pump. *Courtesy Anna Plyler Ervine.*

Fig. 176 – Preston "Springy" Galford in East Cass. "Belle Cross' Place" former "Central Motel" is in the background. *Courtesy Anna Plyler Ervine.*

Fig. 177 – Mable Mauzy, l., and Susan Porter, r., in front of Kirkpatrick's Restaurant, East Cass. The Moose Lodge is upstairs. Buck Hamrick's place is on the left. About 1940. *Courtesy Ivan O. Clarkson.*

Fig. 178 – Granny's Restaurant, former Pentecostal Church, East Cass. 1984.
Photograph by the author.

Fig. 179 – Main Street Cass. Jack Kane's Grocery Store is on the right. 1984. *Photograph by the author.*

Fig. 180—One of the many attractions for visitors at Cass was the swinging bridge joining East Cass (Blackhurst Addition) with Cass. Located north of the Walter Clarkson home in East Cass. L. to r., Kimeran Ann Clarkson, Karen Sue Clarkson, and George Roy Clarkson, the author's children. 1968.
Photograph by the author.

Fig. 181—The most destructive flood to ravage East Cass peaked early in the morning of November 5, 1985. This view shows the Cass Inn, right center, and several homes in the Blackhurst Addition. *Courtesy Eugene E. Burner.*

Fig. 182 – The remaining buildings in the business section of East Cass were heavily damaged by the flood of November 5, 1985. The Cooper Building, left, the Siegel Building, center, and Brill's Store, right, were all razed by the West Virginia National Guard after the flood.
Courtesy Eugene E. Burner.

Fig. 183 – Former Mower Lumber Company Shay No. 4 with the original logo of what would become the Cass Scenic Railroad. May 28, 1961. *Courtesy Charles E. Winters.*

Fig. 184—Cass Scenic Railroad Shay No. 1 on display on the siding at the station, Cass. It was painted Chinese red. June 16, 1963. *Courtesy George A. Fizer.*

Fig. 185 – L. to r., Walter "Pop" Good, "Jack" Kane, Jesse McCalpin and Ivan O. Clarkson on one of the early runs of the Cass Scenic Railroad. July 4, 1963. *Courtesy Ivan O. Clarkson.*

Fig. 186—Cass Scenic Railroad Shay No. 4 with a load of passengers.
From the Phil Bagdon Collection.

Fig. 187 — Cass Scenic Railroad Shay No. 4 and an unidentified Shay double-head a crowded train up the Cass Hill.
Courtesy Earl Palmer.

Fig. 188 – Lined up in front of Cass Scenic Railroad Shay No. 4. L. to r., Leonard Long, Charles Queen, Kenneth Caplinger, Walter "Pop" Good, Robert Cassell, Percy F. "Bus" Long, kneeling, Ivan O. Clarkson, Clyde Galford, Kyle J. "Catty" Neighbors. *Courtesy Richard S. Carter.*

Fig. 189 – Cass Scenic Railroad Shay No. 5 and another Shay bring a load of tourists up the Cass Hill. *Courtesy D. Wallace Johnson.*

Fig. 190 – Artie Barkley, in the door, and "Doc" Carlson, at the throttle, of Cass Scenic Railroad Shay No. 5 below the crossing at the depot, Cass.
Courtesy Richard S. Carter.

Fig. 191 – Shay No. 5 of the Cass Scenic Railroad with a work train while upgrading the tracks to Bald Knob. September, 1967. *Courtesy West Virginia State Parks.*

Fig. 192 – In an attempt to acquire a diversity of geared locomotives at Cass, the state purchased Heisler No. 6 in 1966. Here "Red" McMillion, left, and Wilbur "Bud" Cassell man the train at the depot at Cass. *Courtesy Richard S. Carter.*

Fig. 193 — Trailing a magnificent plume of smoke, Heisler No. 6 is shown here on the job on the Cass Hill. *Courtesy Richard S. Carter.*

Fig. 194 – Climax No. 6 of the Middle Fork Railroad was obtained by the Cass Scenic Railroad in 1971. This acquisition completed a collection of all types of geared steam locomotives used in logging in West Virginia. June, 1957. *Courtesy of Harold K. Vollrath.*

Fig. 195—Cass Scenic Railroad Shay No. 7, with a load of passengers at Bald Knob. August 14, 1970. *Courtesy G. LeRoy Crislip.*

Fig. 196–Shays No. 7 and 4 pause at Whittaker Station. 1970. *From the Phil Bagdon Collection.*

Fig. 197–Part of the train crew on the Whittaker run, Cass Scenic Railroad. At Whittaker, 1972. L. to r., Walter "Pop" Good, conductor; Kyle J. "Catty" Neighbors, brakeman; Ben Jackson, brakeman; "Red" McMillion, engineer; and Charlie Sheets, brakeman. *Courtesy W. O. Clontz.*

Fig. 198 – In 1970, a "Pacific Coast" style, oil burning Shay was added to the roster at Cass. This was assigned Cass Scenic Railroad No. 2. This Shay was built in 1928 and weighed 90.5 tons. Artie Barkley is at the throttle. May, 1977. *Courtesy Terry E. Arbogast.*

This is THE CORRECT #2 6-28-18

Fig. 199–Cass Scenic Railroad Shay No. 3, was built in 1923. It was leased in 1970, by the Cass Scenic Railroad from the Oregon Historical Society. *Courtesy Terry E. Arbogast.*

Fig. 200 – Four Shay's in a row head up the Cass Hill. Shown here at the County Road crossing above Cass. 1985.
Courtesy Elmer E. Burris, Jr.

Fig. 201 – Three Shays and a Heisler lined up for night photography at the water tank at Cass. May 19, 1979. L. to r., Shay No. 5, Shay No. 4, Heisler No. 6 and Shay No. 2 or 3. *Courtesy Terry E. Arbogast.*

Fig. 202—Russell M. Clarkson, foreman of the dry kiln for 14 years, transfers a load of lumber to the kilns. Each load was 60 layers high, 5 feet wide, 16 feet long and contained 4,500 board feet. The average drying time for 4-quarter (1 inch) hardwood was about 10 days, 4-quarter spruce required about 7 days.

Fig. 203—Cass, with its rich history and its great potential for future interpretation of history, will be appreciated and enjoyed by future generations. Representing these is the author's granddaughter, Kathleen June McElroy. 1989.
Photograph by Karen Sue McElroy.

APPENDIX A

A BRIEF BIOGRAPHY OF JOHN G. LUKE
1857-1921

William Luke, son of a papermill worker was born near Crook of Devon, Scotland. About 1826 he emigrated to the New World. Here, as a landed immigrant, he became a workman in a New England paper mill. Thence, on to the state of Delaware, where he went to work in the Jessup-Moore Paper Company mill at Rockland. A family man, whose wife Rose (Landsay) bore him six sons and a daughter, he lived to the good age of eighty-five years.

William Luke's firstborn son, John G., was born in Springfield, Massachusetts, on April 29, 1857. At age sixteen he joined his father, by now superintendent, at the Rockland mill of Jessup-Moore. Here John stayed for seven years. During the next eight years, he moved around quite a bit, seeing service with and becoming superintendent of several paper mills. However, like many successful, ambitious men, he wanted his own organization.

Guided by zealous objectiveness John G. Luke felt that at the age of thirty-one he should remain an employee no longer if he was to realize his ambition. He must strike out on his own, having absorbed sufficient teaching from the pulp and paper industry. A forceful, likeable man with what some must have regarded as the Midas touch, he was undoubtedly an astute businessman with a convincing argument. With the aid of his father and brothers (William, David, James, Adam and Thomas), he built and put into operation a sulphite mill at the Luke Pulp Mill, Piedmont, West Virginia, in 1889. The name of the company was the West Virginia Pulp and Paper Company. John G. Luke functioned as president of the company from 1905 to 1921.

Company growth was a steady development of purchase of interests and acquisitions, coupled with relentless drive to put together an "empire" — one of the largest papermaking enterprises in the United States.

During his busy career, John G. Luke took time out for marriage and to raise a family. His first wife, Ella Hope Green from Greenville, Delaware, bore three sons and a daughter. Ella died in 1899, ten years after the Piedmont venture began. Later John G. Luke married again, this time to Miss Grace Bulkley of Arlington, New Jersey. They had a daughter, Grace Virginia.

That John G. Luke was not as long-lived as his father was unfortunate. He died following an operation for appendicitis in St. Luke's Hospital in New York City on October 15, 1921.

He possessed the driving ambition of the successful businessman and had the acumen to achieve fulfillment. He led a full and rewarding, if sometimes exacting, life and left behind him a legacy that the Lukes would continue.

APPENDIX B

A BRIEF BIOGRAPHY OF JOSEPH K. CASS

Joseph K. Cass attended the public schools in Coshocton, Ohio, and then became a student at Kenyon College, Gambier, Ohio, where he was graduated in 1868, as a civil engineer. He subsequently spent several years in railroad construction work in Michigan. Mr. Cass then became interested in the manufacturing of paper. In 1875 he entered into this business under the firm name of Morrison & Cass Paper Company. In 1899, this concern was merged with others to form a company, the West Virginia Pulp and Paper Company, which now continues paper manufacturing under the corporation name of the WESTVACO. Mr. Cass was vice-president of its board of directors. For thirty-five years he was engaged in paper manufacturing and was an official in every company with which he had been identified. He was president of the Morrison & Cass Company and also the Williamsburg Paper Manufacturing Company.

Shortly after the death of Mr. Morrison in January, 1901, Mr. Cass was elected president of the First National Bank of Tyrone, Pennsylvania, and continued as the head of this financial institution. He was looked upon as a man of exceptional business ability and his name and services were sought by many large concerns.

Mr. Cass was married in 1879 to Miss Sara M. Anderson, a daughter of Dr. John and Ann (Stevenson) Anderson. Mr. and Mrs. Cass had four children: Charles, Margaret Kerr, Joseph K., Jr. and Ann Stevenson.

He died on November 1, 1938.

APPENDIX C

A BRIEF BIOGRAPHY OF EMORY P. SHAFFER
1870-1943

Emory Peale Shaffer was born at Sinnemahoning, Pennsylvania, April 14, 1870, the son of the late Derrick Updegraff and Susan McCloskey Shaffer.

During his young manhood, he was associated with his father in lumbering operations in Cameron, Potter and McKean Counties, Pennsylvania. He attended the Central State Normal School and was a graduate of the Palms School of Business Administration in Philadelphia. From Philadelphia he went to Bayard, West Virginia, as bookkeeper for the Buffalo Lumber Company. In 1900, he went to Pocahontas County, West Virginia, as superintendent for the West Virginia Spruce Lumber Company, a subsidiary of the West Virginia Pulp and Paper Company, where he assisted in the building of the towns of Cass and Spruce, developed the operations there and successfully carried them on until his retirement in 1934.

In 1911, he married Miss Pattie V. Hannah, daughter of S. B. Hannah, Arbovale, West Virginia.

He had six children: Mrs. W. Addison Wilson, Mrs. John W. Huntington, Mrs. Frank A. Hardy, Mrs. Edward H. Stringer, Mrs. George E. Piersol of Bryn Mawr, Pennsylvania, and a son Emory. He became ill in 1940 and lived the last two years of his life in Bryn Mawr. He died on February 26, 1943.

Emory P. Shaffer

APPENDIX D

A BRIEF BIOGRAPHY OF DR. J. D. ARBUCKLE
1874-1933

Julian D. Arbuckle was a son of the late John Davis and Elizabeth VanLear Arbuckle and was born near Lewisburg, West Virginia, on August 19, 1874. He graduated from the Medical College of Virginia at Richmond and in 1900 went to Cass with his brother, Dr. J. A. Arbuckle, and Dr. Ward Randolph. They conducted the hospital of the West Virginia Pulp & Paper Company for a number of years. About 1914, he returned to Greenbrier County and built the home where he resided and which is near the homeplace on which he was born.

He was united in marriage on October 8, 1902, to Miss Anna McLaughlin. They had a family of six daughters and one son. They are Mary, Elizabeth, Margaret, Emily, Laurie, Mrs. Frank McCue and Julian D. Arbuckle, Jr.

Dr. Arbuckle was an elder in the Clifton Presbyterian Church and a member of Greenbrier Lodge, No. 42, A.F. & A.M. of Lewisburg. For ten years he served on the board of education of Lewisburg district. He died on May 3, 1933.

Dr. J. D. Arbuckle

APPENDIX E

A BRIEF BIOGRAPHY OF DR. U. H. HANNAH
1881-1943

Uriah Hevener Hannah was born April 13, 1881, at Arbovale, West Virginia, the son of Samuel Baldwin and Lizzie Hevener Hannah. He attended the Academy of Hillsboro, Hampden Sydney College and graduated from the Medical College of Virginia at Richmond in 1906. He located at Spruce as physician for the West Virginia Pulp & Paper Company. In 1914, he moved to Cass where he practiced until his death in October, 1943.

In addition to taking care of his large and widespread practice, he took time for public service as well. He served as president of the county school board and as a member for several terms. Active in politics, he was a member of the county Democratic Committee and served as Mayor of Cass for a term. He was a partner in the Pocahontas Construction Company which built a number of improved roads in the county. He dealt extensively in the cattle and sheep business and took great pride in his herd of purebred Hereford cattle on his farm at Stony Bottom.

In 1907, he was married to Laura Susanna Bock (1879-1957), the daughter of Mahlon Peter and Margaret Kimmel Bock. They had five daughters: Laura Bock, Margaret, Alice, Elizabeth and Mary Anne.

He died in October, 1943. (Margaret Gluck, in *History of Pocahontas County, W.Va. 1981.*)

Dr. U. H. Hannah

APPENDIX F

A BRIEF BIOGRAPHY OF REV. HARRY BLACKHURST
1870-1956

In 1884, at the age of fourteen, Harry Blackhurst immigrated from Tunstall, England, with his family, the Reverend Jabez and Sarah Blackhurst. They were Wesleyan Methodists, with the family interest going back to the late 1700s days of John Wesley's preachings. The ancestor, Daniel Spilsbury and his grandfather, Richard Blackhurst, were ministers in the new religion. The Blackhursts also manufactured pottery and porcelain in Tunstall at the Sanderford Works, with the "Knapper and Blackhurst" mark, until 1884 when they immigrated to America because of business difficulties.

As a young man, Mr. Blackhurst married a young lady of Minneapolis who bore him a son named Arthur. She died the next day. The maternal grandparents cared for and raised this son.

Miss Lula May Burner, of Pocahontas County, was the daughter of Mr. and Mrs. Allen Craig Burner of Green Bank. Her mother had been Virginia Cathren Clark of Augusta County, Virginia. Miss Burner, a teacher, had been invited by her brother George of Minneapolis to come stay with him and continue her studies in the profession of teaching. In June, 1890, she went to her brother's and attended school. There she met Mr. Blackhurst and in the year 1892 they married.

The Blackhursts moved to Pocahontas County in 1901 with five young children: Alice, Allen, Henry, George and William. When the young couple arrived in West Virginia, they found lumber camps springing up like mushrooms to fell the beautiful forests. Conditions were such that they felt they were needed, and also their needs could be met. Mr. Blackhurst preached in the mill at Cass on Sundays, and Mrs. Blackhurst taught school in her home. From that beginning, Mr. Blackhurst continued preaching for twenty-eight years.

At first the family moved from parsonage to parsonage. Then the Griffie Sheets property at the lower east end of Cass was offered for sale for the amount of eight hundred dollars. The land was sought and a fine house erected to house the family, then of eleven children, six more having been born in West Virginia: Theodore, Warren, Elizabeth, Harold, Homer and Francis.

Life in the Blackhurst home was usually joyful. A family equipped with strong convictions of moral rightness, compassion for those less fortunate, exceedingly good health, a wonderful sense of fun and laughter and a feeling that today is good, and tomorrow will be better.

The Reverend Mr. Blackhurst died on November 24, 1956. (May Blackhurst Freeland in *History of Pocahontas County 1981*).

Rev. Harry Blackhurst

APPENDIX G

A BRIEF BIOGRAPHY OF FRANK E. MOWER
1899-1956

Frank Edwin Mower was born at Horton, Randolph County, West Virginia, on October 31, 1899, the son of Frank Edwin and Martha Lockridge Mower. They then moved to Hendricks where the elder Mr. Mower was general manager of the Dry Fork Railroad for many years. As a young man, Frank worked in lumber camps and on railroads in West Virginia.

He was educated at the University of Virginia.

He formed the Mower Lumber Company at Charleston and opened a small sawmill on Witchen Creek, thirteen miles from Charleston, in 1925.

Lumbering and timbering operations were successively set up by him at Bartow, Grassy Meadows, Williamsburg, Marmet, Calcord, Pettus, Omar, Cass, Nallen, Durbin and Dailey, all in West Virginia.

He was also active in the building up South American connections which have resulted in expansion of the export market for West Virginia hardwoods.

During World War II, he served on the OPA Advisory Committee for the Appalachian Hardwood Lumber industry and on a like committee for the eastern softwood lumber of the Appalachian Hardwood Manufacturers, Inc.

In 1953, the operations at Cass, Dailey, Nallen and Durbin, West Virginia, with dry kilns, planing mills, flooring and dimension stock facilities, produced thirty to thirty-five million feet of lumber and wood products annually. These operations employed around seven hundred employees.

In addition to lumber and wood products manufacturing, Mower was interested in the raising of prize Hereford cattle at his Poca Dot Farm, near Charles Town, West Virginia.

In 1927, he married Dorothy K. Higgins of Charleston, West Virginia. They had two sons, Frank Edwin II and Richard Higgins.

His hobbies were hunting, fishing and flying in his Grumman Widgeon airplane.

He died on December 11, 1956.

Frank E. Mower

APPENDIX H

A BRIEF BIOGRAPHY OF
JOHN FREDERICK WEBER, JR.
1902-1980

John Frederick Weber, Jr. was born in Ronceverte, West Virginia, on February 17, 1902. He moved to Rainelle, West Virginia, when he was ten years old. He attended school in Ronceverte, Rainelle, and Williamsburg, West Virginia. He went to the Massey Business College in Richmond, Virginia. He married Lucy Gibbs in 1929 and they had two children. Fred Weber held various positions with the Meadow River Lumber Company in Rainelle, West Virginia, until 1942. In 1942, he became general manager of The Mower Lumber Company and moved to Cass, West Virginia. He was in charge of the mills at Cass, Durbin, Nallen, and Dailey. He enjoyed his work especially on Cheat Mountain. He later became vice-president and general manager of the Mower Lumber Company. In 1960, he returned to Rainelle and became assistant-general manager of the Meadow River Lumber Company. He retired in 1970 when Meadow River Lumber Company was sold. He died April 2, 1980. (Lucy G. Weber, personal communication, January 18, 1988.)

John Frederick Weber, Jr.

APPENDIX I

A BRIEF BIOGRAPHY OF
WARREN E. BLACKHURST
1904-1970

Warren Elmer "Tweard" Blackhurst was born October 10, 1904, the seventh son of Rev. Harry and Lula Burner Blackhurst. He attended elementary school at Cass and worked seven years at the Cass mill and the Extract Plant at Deer Creek. He then entered Green Bank High School, graduated in two and one-half years, and went to Glenville State Normal School, at Glenville, West Virginia. After graduating from Glenville he returned to Green Bank High School as an English and Latin teacher. He also directed plays and taught public speaking at Green Bank. In 1949, he started an annual senior class memorial tree planting which resulted in planting thousands of trees on Allegheny Mountain. He was a very popular teacher and was Pocahontas County's first teacher of the year.

His experiences around Cass combined with his literary abilities allowed him to write several books concerning the history of the Cass area. These are *Riders of the Flood, Sawdust in Your Eyes, Mixed Harvest, Of Men and a Mighty Mountain,* and *Afterglow,* published posthumously by his wife.

On June 25, 1934, he married a former student Stella Yates. They lived in the large Blackhurst house in East Cass.

After teaching at Green Bank for thirty-two years he retired and when the Cass Scenic Railroad started operating in 1963, he was narrator for several years. He and his wife were part of a corporation that leased and ran the Company Store as a gift shop, soda fountain, and restaurant. They also opened the Wildlife Museum in part of the store. This was stocked with birds and animals he had mounted as a hobby.

Tweard was active in the Methodist church, serving as Sunday school teacher and occasional minister. He was serving as county commissioner at his death on October 5, 1970. (Stella Blackhurst in *History of Pocahontas County, 1981.*)

Warren E. "Tweard" Blackhurst

APPENDIX J

TOWN GOVERNMENT OFFICIALS—CASS, WEST VIRGINIA, 1902-1986

August 2, 1902—Election on incorporation: For incorporation—38
Against incorporation—2
August 15, 1902—Order of Incorporation, Circuit Court of Pocahontas County. W. T. Newcome appointed mayor until elections could be held.

TOWN OFFICIALS, CASS, WEST VIRGINIA
1902-1985

YEAR	MAYOR	RECORDER	CHIEF OF POLICE	TOWN COUNCIL
1902	W. T. Newcome		Gum	
1903	Amos S. Gillespie	John K. Jackson	Elmer Burner	J. S. Matthews
			C. L. C. Burner	J. D. Arbuckle
			Allen Burner	B. F. Conrad
				L. J. R. Dysard
				C. L. C. Burner
1904	Wm. M. Siple	W. F. Anderson	"	C. L. C. Burner
				R. L. Rose
				J. M. Hannah
				J. C. Graves
				J. D. Arbuckle
1905	James Kirkpatrick	"	L. S. "Link" Cochran	R. L. Rose
				J. C. Graves
				Joe Hannah
				H. W. Randolph
				James Kirkpatrick
1906	"	"	C. L. C. Burner	
1907	Amos S. Gillespie	G. S. Graham		David Finger
				J. C. Graves
				J. D. Arbuckle
				J. M. Hannah
				Harper Smith

YEAR	MAYOR	RECORDER	CHIEF OF POLICE	TOWN COUNCIL
1908	"	"		George Hannah Jacob Cooper J. D. Arbuckle Robert Hivick Ed Jackson
1909	No Report			
1910	No Report			
1911	No Report			
1912	A. S. Gillespie		Luther M. Foster	
1913	No Report			
1914	A. S. Gillespie			
1915	No Report			
1916	A. S. Gillespie			
1917	Burke McCarty	A. S. Gillespie	T. J. Baker	
1918	A. S. Gillespie	George S. Graham	J. A. Belcher	
1919	"	"	L. M. Foster W. B. Bragg	
1920	"	"	J. L. Warwick	
1921	U. H. Hannah	"	L. S. "Link" Cochran	
1922	"	"	"	
1923	"	"	Jesse Warwick L. S. Cochran	
1924	J. Hobbs Rose	"	"	J. C. Graves W. F. Anderson Robert Hivick J. B. Sutton
1925	No Report			
1926	G. M. Brice	"	"	
1927	No Report			
1928	No Report			
1929	G. M. Brice	E. L. Duncan	J. A. Belcher	

1930	"	"	J. C. Wooddell	
1931	"	"	"	
1932	No Report			
1933	Alfred P. Viering	J. M. Ward	"	
1934	"	"	"	
1935	J. C. Gum	W. H. Fulks	"	
1936	"	"	"	E. J. Shafer S. E. Keyser L. B. Jones L. E. Bowling Dale White
1937	"	"	"	E. J. Shafer S. E. Keyser L. B. Jones Burke McCarty Dale White
1938	L. B. Jones	"	"	E. J. Shafer S. E. Keyser Burke McCarty Dale White
1939	L. B. Jones	E. R. Loudermilk	"	E. J. Shafer Burke McCarty J. A. Kirkpatrick S. E. Keyser J. W. Keyser
1940	"	"	"	"
1941	A. Norman Smith, Jr.	W. H. Fulks	"	Jacob Mauzy U. H. Hannah J. B. Galford J. B. Kirkpatrick J. C. Graves

YEAR	MAYOR	RECORDER	CHIEF OF POLICE	TOWN COUNCIL
1942	W. F. Anderson	"	"	E. L. Duncan
				U. H. Hannah
				J. B. Galford
				C. R. Shrader
				J. C. Graves
1943	J. A. Kirkpatrick	"	"	Jacob Mauzy
				U. H. Hannah
				J. B. Galford
				C. R. Shrader
				J. C. Graves
1944	W. F. Anderson	"	"	E. L. Duncan
				O. H. Shriver
				J. B. Galford
				C. R. Shrader
				J. C. Graves
1945	"	Fred F. McLaughlin	"	"
1946	"	J. C. Fulks	"	E. L. Duncan
				O. H. Shriver
				C. R. Shrader
				W. D. Rader
				Charles Strickland
1947	J. C. Wooddell	"	Roy F. Workman	"
1948	C. R. Shrader	"	"	E. L. Duncan
				O. H. Shriver
				W. D. Rader
				Charles Strickland
				Flosten Sampson
1949	J. C. Wooddell	"	"	E. L. Duncan
				O. H. Shriver
				W. D. Rader
				Charles Strickland

1950	C. R. Shrader	"	"	E. L. Duncan O. H. Shriver W. D. Rader Charles Strickland Arthur White
1951	J. C. Wooddell	C. J. Ware	"	Clark Phillips J. C. Fulks Flosten Sampson Russell Clarkson L. H. Camisa
1952	"	"	Emmet Tingler	"
1953	C. R. Shrader	"	"	Clark Phillips J. C. Fulks Flosten Sampson Russell Clarkson H. H. Thompson
1954	"	"	"	"
1955	Wallace Rader	"	E. J. Wooddell	K. A. James G. L. Dahmer Clifford Barkley Lyle Meeks Phil Nelson
1956	"	"	"	"
1957	P. F. Long	C. L. Barkley	Charles J. Turner	Ben Jackson G. L. Dahmer C. R. Shrader (vacancy)
1958	"	"	"	Ben Jackson G. L. Dahmer Russell Clarkson (vacancy)
1959	"	"	"	G. L. Dahmer E. M. Arbogast

YEAR	MAYOR	RECORDER	CHIEF OF POLICE	TOWN COUNCIL
				G. C. Arbogast C. R. Haislop C. R. Shrader
1960	"	"	Russell S. Cassell	"
1961	"	"	"	"
1962	"	"	"	"
1963	"	"	"	"
1964	Russell S. Cassell	P. P. Galford	"	G. L. Dahmer E. M. Arbogast Ollie Meeks Caleb R. Haislop Marvin Moss
1965	P. F. Long	Carl Davis	Roy Workman	G. L. Dahmer Clifford Barkley Glen Grandon Gene Crist Marvin Moss
1966	"	"	"	"
1967	Carl Davis	Gene Crist	"	Lyle Meeks Clifford Barkley Glen Grandon Ben Jackson
1968	"	"	"	"
1969	"	"	"	"
1970	"	"	"	"
1971	"	"	"	Glen Grandon Sharon Cassell Barbara Crist Virginia Grandon Eugene Jones

1972	"	"	"	Glen Grandon Barbara Crist Virginia Grandon Eugene Jones
1973	Russell Cassell	Jeanette White	"	Glen Grandon Virginia Grandon Eugene Jones Lyle McPherson Sharon Cassell
1974	"	"	"	Glen Grandon Virginia Grandon Lyle McPherson Sharon Cassell Kathy Bartels
1975	Carl Davis	Virginia Grandon	"	Glen Grandon Gene Crist Lyle McPherson Ernestine Clarkson Dorotha Bartels
1976	"	"	(vacancy)	Glen Grandon Lyle McPherson Ernestine Clarkson (vacancy)
1977	"	"	"	Glen Grandon Lyle McPherson Ernestine Clarkson Edythe Davis Charlotte Elza
1978	"	"	"	"
1979	"	"	"	"
1980	"	"	"	"
1981	"	"	"	"

YEAR	MAYOR	RECORDER	CHIEF OF POLICE	TOWN COUNCIL
1982	"	"	"	Glen Grandon Lyle McPherson Ernestine Clarkson Edythe Davis
1983	"	Cathy Hickson	"	Glen Grandon Lyle McPherson Edythe Davis Heida Hickson
1984	"	"	"	Glen Grandon Lyle McPherson Edythe Davis Heida Hickson Virginia Grandon
1985	"	"	"	"
1986	On July 1 the town charter was surrendered to the Secretary of State and town government ceased.			

In addition, the following town officers served:

Treasurer:	A. S. Gillespie 1921 C. P. Gillespie 1922, 1923 J. B. Sutton 1924, 1925 W. F. Anderson 1926-1932 J. M. Ward 1933, 1934 L. B. Jones 1935-1937 E. R. Loudermilk 1938 J. W. Keyser 1939, 1940 Jacob Mauzy 1941, 1943 E. L. Duncan 1942; 1944-1949 J. C. Fulks 1950-1954 K. A. James 1955, 1956 G. L. Dahmer 1957-1970 Eugene Jones 1971-1973 Fred Bartels 1974 Ernestine Clarkson 1975-1982 (vacancy) 1983 Heida Hickson 1984
Health Officer:	Dr. U. H. Hannah 1917-1943
Street Commissioner:	J. C. Graves 1921-1924; 1945 C. R. Shrader 1946, 1947, 1949 C. R. Strickland 1948; 1950, 1951 L. H. Camisa 1952-1954 Clifford Barkley 1955-1966 G. L. Dahmer 1967-1970
Chief of Fire Department:	W. F. Anderson 1917-1921 J. H. Rose 1922-1923 J. C. Graves 1926 S. E. Keyser 1939, 1940
Supt. of Water Plant:	L. S. Lockhard 1923 J. A. Kirkpatrick 1926
Postmasters were:	Jasper S. Matthews 1902-1915 Z. M. Zyers 1916-1919 Robert Hickman 1919-1923 S. F. Clark 1923-1933 Ray Fox 1933-1934 James Moyer 1934-1944 Frank C. Nickle 1945-1963 Evelyn D. Lightner 1964-1984 Maude Moore 1984-
Assistants were:	Ruth Vint Marie Dill Tina O'Brien Ruth Hamrick

From the *West Virginia Blue Book* (Formerly *West Virginia Legislative Hand Book and Manual and Official Register*. Charleston, WV: Tribune Printing and Jarrett Printing. 1902-85.

APPENDIX K

MASTERS OF THE RIVERSIDE LODGE
NO. 124, A.F. & A.M., 1903-1989

Chartered Nov. 12, 1903

Past Masters

Year	Master		Year	Master
1903	W. D. Lodge George L. Eakle		1946	Harry J. Widney
1904	George L. Eakle		1947	Ray Robertson
1905	Jasper S. Matthews		1948	W. Clarence Phillips
1906	Robert S. Hickman		1949	Elmer Duncan
1907	Cecil N. Kryder		1950	Henry L. Stokes
1908	George O. English		1951	Henry L. Stokes
1909	W. C. Kohler		1952	Allen J. Blackhurst
1910	Charles Kirkpatrick		1953	Allen J. Blackhurst
1911	Uriah Hevener		1954	Clarence J. Ware
1912	Charles Kirkpatrick		1955	Clarence J. Ware
1913	Walter S. Bullivant		1956	Ralph G. Lowe
1914	Walter S. Bullivant		1957	J. Crawford Gum
1915	Charles Kirkpatrick		1958	Harper G. Beverage
1916	W. A. Hammen		1959	Ralph G. Lowe
1917	Sterrett D. Huff		1960	Clarence J. Ware
1918	Harold L. McNickle		1961	Ralph G. Lowe
1919	H. Harlon Brown		1962	Clarence J. Ware
1920	Sterrett D. Huff		1963	Thurmond R. Cosner
1921	Samuel L. Clark		1964	Frank L. Arnott
1922	George A. Brice		1965	Oren Luther Plyler
1923	George A. Brice		1966	Troy S. Moore
1924	William M. Siple		1967	Gray Beverage
1925	Harry Blackhurst		1968	Boyd Beverage
1926	John S. Hannah		1969	Clarence J. Ware
1927	Ray W. Fox		1970	Oren Luther Plyler
1928	J. Crawford Gum		1971	Herman D. Coleman
1929	J. Crawford Gum		1972	Oren Luther Plyler
1930	George E. Lewis		1973	Oren Luther Plyler
1931	Allen J. Blackhurst		1974	Oren Luther Plyler
1932	Sidney E. Keyser		1975	Oren Luther Plyler
1933	Guilford L. Eddy		1976	Oren Luther Plyler
1934	Albert E. Harouff		1977	Winston S. Cottrell
1935	Albert E. Harouff		1978	Winston S. Cottrell
1936	Allen J. Blackhurst		1979	Lawrence C. Guthrie
1937	H. H. Hudson		1980	Winston S. Cottrell
1938	J. W. Keyser		1981	Oren Luther Plyler
1939	L. B. Jones		1982	Orville L. Williams
1940	Glenn Gragg		1983	Jimmie A. Ryder, Jr.
1941	H. Gray Beverage		1984	Earl J. Lantz
1942	Floyd Collins		1985	Jamie A. Sheets
1943	Elmer L. Duncan		1986	Lawrence C. Guthrie
1944	Richard Eye		1987	James E. Barber
1945	Howard Hevener		1988	Hunter W. Nicholas
			1989	Merle Kerr

Russell M. Clarkson, Secretary from 1952.

Information from Russell M. Clarkson, September 10, 1985; December 29, 1987;
November 25, 1988, and May 1, 1990.

APPENDIX L

WORTHY MATRONS AND WORTHY PATRONS
CASS CHAPTER #124, INSTITUTED JUNE 27, 1929
ORDER OF THE EASTERN STAR 1929-1991, CHARTERED OCTOBER 2, 1929

YEAR	WORTHY MATRON	WORTHY PATRON
1929-30	Ruth Fox	Crawford Gum
1930-31	Bessie Irvine	S. L. Clark
1931-32	Ardelia Rose	George Lewis
1932-33	Myrtle Duncan	Allen Blackhurst
1933-34	Sadie Gum	George Lewis
1934-35	Anna Eddy	Merle Irvine
1935-36	Bonnie Brooks	George Lewis
1936-37	Gertrude Ralson	Allen Blackhurst
1937-38	Emma Graham	(until 1938)
1938-39	Cora Stewart	
1939-40	Daisy Graves	George Lewis
1940-41	Pearl Harouff	(until 1943)
1941-42	Virginia Widney	
1942-43	Genevieve Doyle	
1943-44	Minnie Kramer	Allen Blackhurst
1944-45	Ruth Kramer	(until 1946)
1945-46	Lenna Robertson	
1946-47	Elizabeth McCutcheon	Lee H. Stokes
1947-48	Margaret Cole	Allen Blackhurst
1948-49	Blanche Eye	(until 1951)
1949-50	Ella Sheets	
1950-51	Audra McPherson	
1951-52	Aliece Stokes	Lee H. Stokes
1952-53	Bertha Phillips	Allen Blackhurst
1953-54	Margaret Wilson	Russell M. Clarkson
1954-55	Marie Dill	(until present)
1955-56	Beatrice Sheets	
1956-57	Pauline Galford	
1957-58	Ernestine Clarkson	
1958-59	Ethel Fulks	
1959-60	Pearl R. Clarkson	
1960-61	Lucy Crowley	
1961-62	Ruth Riley	
1962-63	Virginia Irvine	
1963-64	Grace Nelson	
1964-65	Viola Lantz	
1965-66	Maxine Foe	
1966-67	Margaret Beverage	
1967-68	Anna Vera Bennett	
1968-69	Anna Grace Ware	
1969-70	Maudie Wenger	
1970-71	Twila Rosencrance	
1971-72	Berdeen O'Brien	
1972-73	Joanne Kane	
1973-74	Bertha Plyler	
1974-75	Anna M. Elliott	

YEAR	WORTHY MATRON	WORTHY PATRON
1975-76	Katherine Garber	
1976-77	Kathleen Colaw	
1977-78	Zula Taylor	
1978-79	Marilyn Guthrie	
1979-80	Maxine Foe	
1980-81	Mary Hannah	
1981-82	Anna G. Ware	
1982-83	Zula Taylor	
1983-84	Beatrice Sheets	
1984-85	Barbara Murphy	
1985-86	Barbara Murphy	
1986-87	Maxine Foe	
1987-88	Katherine Garber	
1988-89	Beatrice Blackhurst Sheets	
1989-90	Anna Grace Ware	
1990-91	Zula Taylor	
	Pearl R. Clarkson, Secretary 1962-	

Information from Pearl R. Clarkson, September 10, 1985; December 29, 1987;
November 25, 1988, and May 1, 1990.

APPENDIX M

CASS NICKNAMES

Like many small towns, many of the people and things at Cass were given nicknames. Whether given because of envy, spite, revenge or love, these names often stuck and the individuals were known henceforth by their new appelations.

Some of the more common nicknames follow:

"Hank" Adams	"Merf" Dill
"Capt. Bill" Anderson	"Pickle" Dill
"Arby" Arbogast	"Alex" Duncan
"Bud" Arbogast	"Shorty" Duncan
"Arty" Barkley	"Chipmonk" Ervine
"Jim" Belcher	"Nubbs" Ervine
"Rosebud" Beverage	"Pie Belly" Ervine
"Granny" Bird	"Rocky" Fisher
"Bacon" Blackhurst	"Denny" or "Dinty" Flynn
"Beaty" Blackhurst	"Jake" Fuhrman
"Bud" Blackhurst	"Wint" Foe
"Buttercup" Blackhurst	"Aggie" Galford
"Buz" Blackhurst	"Gay Loft" Galford
"Catty" Blackhurst	"Mint" Galford
"Farmer" Blackhurst	"Springy" Galford
"Moats" Blackhurst	"Buster" Geiger
"Strat" Blackhurst	"Irish" Gilliam
"Ted" Blackhurst	"Pop" Good
"Tex" Blackhurst	"Newt" Gum
"Trudy" Blackhurst	"Peg-leg" Gum
"Tweard" Blackhurst	"Bull" Guthrie
"Pretty" Bracken	"Toe" Guthrie
"Shorty" Brice	"Fuzzy" Halterman
"Tink" Brice	"Tramp" Halterman
"Shorty" Brill	"Buck" Hamrick
"Bud" Burner	"Jellyroll" Hamrick
"Ikey" Burner	"Tina" Hamrick
"King Brady" Burner	"Dutch" Haptonstall
"Granny" Byrd	"Jay-Grab" Helmic
"Blacky" Calhoun	"Thorn" Hennegan
"Cockeyed" Carpenter	"Shag" Hill
"Bud" Cassell	"Bubba" Hiner
"Lying Bill" Cassell	"Sam Bo" Hiner
"Pinhead" Cassell	"Skinny" Hiner
"Puzo" Cassell	"Jack" Holiday
"Buck" Chestnut	"Peanut" Hoover
"Cider Bill" Chestnut	"Highball" Ines
"Pooge" Chestnut	"Stub" Jackson
"Link" Cochran	"Jellyroll" James
"Midnight" Cole	"Geno" Jones
"Beeby" Conrad	"Deacon" Kane
"Shakespear" Copen	"Jack" Kane
"Big Foot" Corbitt	"Red" Kane
"Slobber Dick" Cross	"Chet" Kenny
"Web" Cross	"Jap" Laurie
"Butcher Knife" Daugherty	"Bus" Long
"Paring Knife" Daugherty	"Snakebite" Long
"Egghead" Dickenson	"Shoecock" Mayes
"Chief" Dill	

"Squeaky" McFerrin
"Road Monkey Dan" McGuire
"Dobbin" McLaughlin
"Baa-Rich" McLaughlin
"Friday" McLaughlin
"Step-n-fetch-it" McLaughlin
"Red" McMillion
"Bunny" McPherson
"Patty" McPherson
"Peck" McPherson
"Polly" McPherson
"Lefty" Meeks
"Chigger" Moats
"Fats" Moss
"Catty" Neighbors
"Dolly" Nelson
"Jay Bird" Nestor
"Pug" Olliver
"Chicken Farm" Pennington
"Steamboat" Pennington
"Skinny" Petts
"Fats" Porter
"Buck" Pusey
"Bud" Pusey
"Hell's Fire" Ralston
"Nimmy" Ralston
"Nimrod" Ralston
"Tibby" Ralston
"Peg-Leg" Rider
"Peanut" Ryder
"Perky" Ryder
"Hob" Rose
"Fats" Rosewell
"Glow" Sampson
"Herb" Shafer
"Red" Shaffer
"Bub" Sheets
"Catty" Sheets
"Web" Sheets

"Dugan" Shrader
"Skeeter" Shrader
"Jim" Shifflet
"Sal" Skinner
"Beaty" Slaven
"Patsy" Slaven
"Rat" Slaven
"Hog Island" Smith
"Puny" Smith
"Tuckahoe" Smith
"Bones" Stanley
"Red" Stanley
"Toad" Stewart
"Woodpecker" Swisher
"Beanpole" Tallman
"Bulldog" Tallman
"Basgy" Taylor
"Pappy" Taylor
"Windy" Thompson
"Blue Jay" Tumblin
"Stonewall" Turner
"Butch" Viering
"Red" Ward
"Mammy" Ware
"Big Chicken" White
"Soc" White
"Temperpot" White
"Piney" Williams
"Butch" Wilmouth
"Uncle Joe" Wooddell
"Bud" Woolwine
"Dirty Bill" Wright
"Jughead" Wright
"Bevo" Wolf
"Big Six"
"Hotbox"
"Pot Belly" Alice
"Red Wing"
"Wild Filly"

NOTES

CHAPTER I

GENESIS OF A WILDERNESS

1. Dudley H. Cardwell, *Geologic History of West Virginia, Educational Series* (Morgantown, WV: West Virginia Geological and Economic Survey, 1975), pp. 1-64.

2. Hu Maxwell, "Some West Virginia Forest Conditions" in *Report of the W.Va. State Board of Agr. for the Quarter Ending June 30, 1908* (Charleston, WV: Tribune Printing, 1908), p. 33.

3. Augustus M. Van Dyke in Jack Zinn, *R. E. Lee's Cheat Mountain Campaign* (Parsons, WV: McClain Printing Company, 1974), p. 26.

4. An actual measurement of lumber sawn from an acre was 65,000 board feet. This did not count material wasted. *Marlinton* (WV) *Pocahontas Times,* June 22, 1899.

5. Sylvester Myers, *Myers' History of West Virginia,* 2 vols. (Wheeling, WV: Wheeling News Lithograph, 1915) Vol. 2, p. 400.

6. Reuben G. Thwaites in Alexander Scott Withers, *Chronicles of Border Warfare,* ed. Reuben G. Thwaites (Cincinnati: Stewart & Kidder, 1917), p. 49.

7. Myers, *History of West Virginia,* Vol. 2, p. 400.

8. J. R. Cole, *History of Greenbrier County* (Lewisburg, WV: pub. by the author, 1918), p. 11.

9. Philip M. Conley and W. T. Doherty, *West Virginia History* (Charleston, WV: Education Foundation, 1974), p. 90.

10. Myers, *History of West Virginia,* Vol. 1, p. 56.

11. Mertie V. Clarkson, Cass, WV. Personal interview, May 28, 1965.

12. William T. Price, *Historical Sketches of Pocahontas County* (Marlinton, WV: Price Brothers, 1901), p.109.

13. The spring was covered by a springhouse and a home was built nearby by the late Joseph McLaughlin. This was located on the Back Mountain Road between Cass and Stony Bottom about two miles from Cass.

CHAPTER II

RIVER DRIVES ON THE GREENBRIER

1. Roy B. Clarkson, "The Greenbrier River" in *Rolling Rivers: An Encyclopedia of America's Rivers,* ed. Richard A. Bartlett (New York: McGraw Hill, 1984), pp. 114-16.

2. William P. McNeel, "Lumber Industry in Pocahontas County" in *History of Pocahontas County, West Virginia, 1981* (Marlinton, WV: Pocahontas County Historical Society, 1981), pp. 176-83.

3. Sam Griffin, *West Virginia Central and Pittsburg Railway* (Cumberland, MD: Independent Job Room, 1899). Reprinted (Parsons, WV: McClain, 1981), p. 8.

4. Conley and Doherty, *West Virginia History,* p. 306.

5. Lillian W. Belcher, "Pocahontas County," Federal Writers Project, West Virginia Collection, West Virginia University Library, Morgantown, WV.

6. Conley and Doherty, *West Virginia History,* p. 306.

7. A. B. Brooks, *Forestry and Wood Industries* (Morgantown, WV: W.Va. Geol. Surv., Vol. 5, 1911), p. 245.

8. McNeel, "Lumber Industry in Pocahontas County," p. 177.

9. Lewisburg (WV) *Greenbrier Independent*, May 24, 1883.

10. McNeel, "Lumber Industry in Pocahontas County," p. 177.

11. W. F. Maury and W. M. Fontaine, *Resources of West Virginia* (Wheeling, WV: Register, 1876), p. 132.

12. McNeel, "Lumber Industry in Pocahontas County," p. 177.

13. McNeel, "Lumber Industry in Pocahontas County," p. 177.

14. Marlinton (WV) *Pocahontas Times*, March 23, 1899; O'Connel used a brand known as the "box-7." He said it represented the 7 Lukes involved in the paper and pulp business. (*Pocahontas Times*, May 18, 1899.)

15. McNeel, "Lumber Industry in Pocahontas County," p. 177.

16. *Pocahontas Times*, May 18, 1899.

17. U.S. Geol. Surv. Quadrangle Maps, 1977.

18. *Pocahontas Times*, May 25, 1899.

19. *Pocahontas Times*, March 27, 1902; Preparations for the log drive were being made during the spring and summer of 1901 when Elmer Burner was blasting out rocks in the Greenbrier River to allow the drive to come down (*Pocahontas Times*, March 7, 1901).

20. McNeel, "Lumber Industry in Pocahontas County," p. 177; for interesting, well-written accounts of river drives on the Greenbrier, see Warren E. "Tweard" Blackhurst, *Riders of the Flood* (New York: Vantage Press, 1954).

21. Brooks, *Forestry and Wood Industries*, p. 149.

22. Letterhead, St. Lawrence Boom & Manufacturing Company, June 3, 1901. Records of the West Virginia Pulp and Paper Company (W.Va. P.&P. Co.), West Virginia and Regional History Collection, West Virginia University Library, Morgantown, WV. All future references to letters, letterheads or telegrams are from this source unless otherwise noted.

CHAPTER III

EARLY LOGGING AT CHEAT BRIDGE

1. Shavers Fork of Cheat River was known as Cheat River by natives of the area and by persons working there. All future references, in this book, to Shavers Fork will call the stream Cheat River.

2. Conley and Doherty, *West Virginia History*, p. 197.

3. Conley and Doherty, *West Virginia History*, p. 253.

4. Jack Zinn, *R. E. Lee's Cheat Mountain Campaign* (Parsons, WV: McClain, 1974), pp. 16, 146-53.

5. D. D. Brown, Collection, Vol. 5. West Virginia & Regional History Collection, West Virginia University Library, Morgantown, WV.

6. Brown Collection, Vol. 5.

7. *Randolph County Deed Book 17: Elkins, WV*, p. 316; *Pocahontas County Deed Book 18: Marlinton, WV*, p. 191.

8. *Randolph County Deed Book R:* p. 422.

9. Brooks, *Forestry and Wood Industries*, p. 264.

10. *Pocahontas Times*, Jan. 3, 1901.

11. Charlie Cromer, Cheat Bridge, WV. Interview by Phillip Bagdon, Jan. 3, 1976.

12. Michael Koch, *The Shay Locomotive Titan of the Timber* (Denver: World Press, 1971), p. 385.

13. Cromer, interview by Bagdon, Jan. 3, 1976.

14. Cromer, interview by Bagdon, Jan. 3, 1976.

15. Charleston (WV), *Charleston Gazette-Times*, Jan. 3, 1901.

16. *Pocahontas County Deed Book 30:* 94: The land, buildings, equipment and supplies were formally transferred by John G. Luke to the W.Va. P.&P. Co. of West Virginia on July 1, 1901, *Pocahontas County Deed Book 31:* p. 401.

17. D. L. Luke, letter to S. A. Slaymaker, July 7, 1900.

18. Cromer, interview by Bagdon, Jan. 3, 1976.

CHAPTER IV

RAILROADS INTO THE MOUNTAINS

1. Roy B. Clarkson, *Tumult on the Mountains: Lumbering in West Virginia— 1770-1920* (Parsons, WV: McClain, 1964), p. 82-86.

2. R. Clarkson, *Tumult on the Mountains*, p. 82-86.

3. McNeel, "Railroads in Pocahontas County," in *History of Pocahontas County, West Virginia, 1981* (Marlinton, WV: Poca. Co. His. Soc., 1981), p. 169-75.

4. J. M. Callahan, *History of West Virginia*, 3 Vols. (Chicago: Amer. His. Soc., 1923), Vol. 1, p. 440.

5. *Poor's Manual of Railroads—South Atlantic Group* (New York; Poor's Railroad Manual, 1902), p. 214.

6. McNeel, "Railroads in Pocahontas County," p. 169.

7. McNeel, "Railroads in Pocahontas County," p. 169.

8. Emory P. Shaffer, letter to Samuel A. Slaymaker, Dec. 21, 1900.

9. McNeel, "Railroads in Pocahontas County," pp. 169-75.

10. William Price McNeel, *The Durbin Route* (Charleston, WV: Pictorial Histories Pub. Co., 1985), pp. 31, 32.

11. *Pocahontas Times*, Feb. 21, 1901.

12. *Pocahontas Times*, Mar. 7, 1901.

13. McNeel, "Railroads in Pocahontas County," pp. 169-75.

14. McNeel, *Durbin Route*, p. 75; parlor car service (parlor/baggage combined) was added on June 7, 1910, and in Aug. 1912, a full parlor car was added to accommodate the demand. This remained until 1918 when World War I caused a drastic curtailment of branchline service. Tom Dixon, "Parlor Car to Durbin," *C&O Historical Newsletter*, Jan. 1973, pp. 10-14.

A typical schedule, June 2, 1912, as follows:

Southbound	141	143
Winterburn	6:00 am	1:20 pm
Durbin	6:20	2:45
Cass	7:00	3:25
Marlinton	8:02	4:30
Renick	9:25	5:50
Ronceverte	10:40 am	7:00 pm

Northbound	141	143
Winterburn	8:10 pm	12:55 pm
Durbin	7:45	12:30
Cass	7:05	11:50
Marlinton	6:00	10:45
Renick	4:39	9:25
Ronceverte	3:30 pm	8:15 am

Other scheduled stops were Bartow, Boyer, Hosterman, Sitlington, Clover Lick, Clawson, Buckeye, Watoga, Seebert, Denmar, Beard, Droop Mt., Spring

Creek, Anthony, Keister, North Caldwell and Whitcomb. There were also numerous flag stops. (McNeel, *Durbin Route.*)

15. *Pocahontas Times,* Jan. 1, 1903; C&O freight tonnage originating at Cass, for the fiscal year ending June 30, 1913, was 177,266 tons. During the succeeding fiscal years ending June 30, 1914, 1915 and 1916, the following tonnages originated at Cass: 202,437, 221,857 and 199,430 tons. McNeel, *Durbin Route,* p. 44.

16. Raymond Hicks, "The West Virginia Central & Pittsburgh Railroad," *Railway and Locomotive Historical Society Bulletin* 113:6-31.

17. David B. Reger, *Randolph County* (Morgantown, W.Va.: W.Va. Geol. Surv., West Virginia University, 1931), p. 7.

18. *Poor's Manual of Railroads—South Atlantic Group* p. 243.

19. Reger, *Randolph County,* p. 7.

CHAPTER V

FORMATION OF THE WEST VIRGINIA PULP AND PAPER COMPANY

1. The writer is grateful to H. E. Matics' unpublished manuscript, *The Westvaco Story, 1888-1975,* and to *Westvaco CFM News,* Covington, Va., Winter 1980-Winter 1981, for facts cited in this chapter unless otherwise stated.

2. William Luke later became manager of Jessup and Moore's Rockland Mill, a position he held until 1895 when he retired at the age of sixty-six. He was also active in organizing the Shenandoah Pulp Company and the Harper's Ferry Pulp Company, both at Harper's Ferry, W.Va., and became director of the Union Bank of Wilmington, Del.

3. It was later estimated that Tucker Co. had over 50,000 acres of spruce; Randolph Co., 140,500 acres; Pocahontas Co., 220,000 acres; Greenbrier Co., 33,500 acres and Mineral Co., 25,000 acres (A. B. Brooks, *Forestry and Wood Industries,* p. 374).

4. *Pocahontas County Deed Book 30,* p. 94; land purchases continued and by 1920, 140,009 acres (170,000 acres according to *Westvaco CFM News,* Spring, 1980, p. 10) had been acquired at the headwaters of the Greenbrier, Elk and Cheat Rivers (James D. Lacey & Company, N.Y.; unpublished report "General Report and Summary of Detailed Estimates, West Virginia Pulp and Paper Company Lands, Pocahontas, Randolph and Webster Counties, W.Va." 1920, pp. 10-12).

5. In 1922, the town of West Piedmont, Md., was renamed Luke, the name it bears today (*Westvaco CFM News,* Summer, 1980, p. 9).

6. *Pocahontas Times,* Jan. 4, 1900.

7. McNeel, *The Durbin Route,* p. 14.

8. *Pocahontas Times,* May 18, 1899.

9. Letterhead of the West Virginia Pulp and Paper Company (W.Va. P.&P. Co.), Aug. 9, 1900.

10. W.Va. P.&P. Co. of W.Va. continued in business until June 30, 1910, when all its property in West Virginia was conveyed to the Delaware Company (*Pocahontas County Deed Book 45,* p. 35).

11. *Westvaco CFM News,* Spring, 1980, p. 9.

CHAPTER VI

EARLY PLANS FOR CASS

1. *Pocahontas County Deed Book 29,* p. 93.

2. Letterhead, Thos. M. Williamson to Slaymaker, Dec. 20, 1899; S. E. Slay-

maker & Co. moved to 540 Drexel Building, Philadelphia and, after Oct., 1900, their address was 307 Broadway, N.Y.

3. Brown Collection, Vol. 4.

4. Records of the W.Va. P.&P. Co., Mar. 4, 1902.

5. Elkins (W.Va.) *Inter-Mountain,* May 27, 1900.

6. Letterhead, Aug. 8, 1900.

7. George F. Willis' letter to Slaymaker, Oct. 2, 1900.

8. *Westvaco CFM News,* "History of Westvaco, Part 2," 1980, p. 10.

9. *Pocahontas County Deed Book 30,* p. 330.

10. David L. Luke, letter to Slaymaker, Mar. 21, 1900.

11. D. Luke, letter to Slaymaker, May 24, 1900.

12. Shaffer, letter to Slaymaker, July 3, 1900.

13. D. Luke, letter to Slaymaker, July 10, 1900.

14. John G. Luke, letter to Slaymaker, Nov. 27, 1900.

15. Thomas Luke, letter to Slaymaker, Dec. 13, 1900; Dec. 17, 1900; W. Luke letter to Slaymaker, Jan. 16, 1901.

16. J. Luke, letter to Slaymaker, Dec. 13, 1900; W. Luke letter to Slaymaker, Jan. 16, 1901.

17. D. Luke, letter to Slaymaker, Dec. 13, 1900.

18. Adam K. Luke, letter to Slaymaker, Oct. 16, 1900; J. Luke letter to Slaymaker, Dec. 22, 1900.

19. *Pocahontas Times,* Oct. 4, 1900; Jan. 3, 1901; Feb. 27, 1901; Mar. 7, 1901.

CHAPTER VII

THE LOGGING RAILROAD

1. *Pocahontas Times,* Nov. 23, 1899.

2. D. Luke, letter to Slaymaker, Jan. 8, 1900.

3. J. Luke, letter to Slaymaker, Feb. 17, 1900.

4. U.S. Geological Survey Quadrangle Map, Cass Quadrangle, 1977. The bench marker at the Company Store reads 2,452 feet.

5. George Deike, "Greenbrier, Cheat & Elk No. 12," *Log Train* 1.1-2(1982): 6. Deike, letter to the author, Mar. 15, 1988.

6. U.S. Geological Survey Quadrangle Map, Cass Quadrangle, 1977.

7. Shaffer, letter to Slaymaker, June 27, 1900; A. S. and J. H. Robertson, under the company name A. S. Robertson & Bro., operated two circular mills, one on Mill Run, a tributary of Leatherbark and the other between the present Dill Farm and the Back Mountain Road. Lumber for Camp #1 and thousands of crossties for the lumber railroad were sawn by these mills (Neighbors, pers. comm., 1970).

8. J. Luke, letter to Slaymaker, June 30, 1900.

9. Shaffer, letter to Slaymaker, June 27, 1900.

10. Shaffer, letter to Slaymaker, July 3, 1900.

11. Shaffer, telegram to Slaymaker, July 6, 1900.

12. *Pocahontas Times,* July 12, 1900.

13. Kyle Neighbors, Cass, WV, 1971, Phil Bagdon Collection.

14. Shaffer, letter to Slaymaker, July 17, 1900.

15. Shaffer, letter to Slaymaker, July 20, 1900.

16. Shaffer, letter to Slaymaker, Aug. 2, 1900.

17. Shaffer, telegram to Slaymaker, Aug. 10, 1900.

18. Shaffer, letter to Slaymaker, Aug. 10, 1900.

19. Shaffer, letter to Slaymaker, Aug. 24, 1900.

20. Shaffer, letter to Slaymaker, Aug. 24, 1900.

21. Shaffer, letter to Slaymaker, July 17, 1900.

22. Shaffer, letter to Slaymaker, July 21, 1900; Huttonsville, Randolph County, was over fifty miles away and everything had to be hauled to Leatherbark in wagons over Cheat Mountain on the Parkersburg-Staunton Turnpike (now U.S. Route 250).

23. Shaffer, letter to Slaymaker, July 25, 1900.

24. Shaffer, letter to Slaymaker, July 25, 1900.

25. Shaffer, letter to Slaymaker, Aug. 29, 1900.

26. Shaffer, letter to Slaymaker, Aug. 30, 1900; Sept. 6, 1900.

27. W.Va. Spruce Lbr. Co. (W.Va. S.L. Co.), Cass, W.Va., letter to W.Va. S.L. Co., Philadelphia, Pa., Sept. 5, 1900; Sept. 18, 1900.

28. Shaffer, letter to Slaymaker, Sept. 6, 1900.

29. Records of the W.Va. P.&P. Co., Sept. 6, 1900.

30. J. Luke, letter to Slaymaker, Aug. 30, 1900.

31. D. Luke, letter to Slaymaker, Sept. 5, 1900; T. Luke, letter to Slaymaker, Oct. 1, 1900.

32. Shaffer, letter to Slaymaker, Oct. 1, 1900.

33. Shaffer, letter to Slaymaker, Sept. 18, 1900.

34. This refers to land owned by Dr. C. L. Austin, dentist.

35. E. P. Shaffer uses the spelling Linnan for this man's name (Shaffer to Slaymaker, Sept. 25, 1900; Blackhurst uses the spelling Lenan. Warren E. Blackhurst, *Of Men and a Mighty Mountain* (Parsons, W.Va.: McClain, 1965), pp. 12-14.

36. Shaffer, letter to Slaymaker, Sept. 25, 1900.

37. Shaffer, letter to Slaymaker, Sept. 25, 1900.

38. Shaffer, letter to Slaymaker, Sept. 22, 1900.

39. Shaffer, letter to Slaymaker, Oct. 30, 1900.

40. Shaffer, letter to Slaymaker, Nov. 3, 1900.

41. Shaffer, letter to Slaymaker, Oct. 26, 1900.

42. Records of the W.Va. P.&P. Co., nd.; the Lukes and others occasionally made hunting trips while visiting the job at Cass. Some of these guns were undoubtedly used on these trips (D. L. Luke, letter to Slaymaker, Nov. 1, 1900). It is improbable that the number of guns ordered were intended solely for hunting.

43. Wm. W. Supplee, Supplee Hardware Co., 503 Market St., Philadelphia, letter to Slaymaker, Oct. 13, 1900.

44. Shaffer, letter to Slaymaker, Oct. 22, 1900; Oct. 29, 1900.

45. Shaffer, letter to Slaymaker, Oct. 4, 1900.

46. Shaffer, letter to Slaymaker, Oct. 26, 1900; Oct. 30, 1900.

47. Shaffer, letter to Slaymaker, Nov. 22, 1900.

48. Shaffer, letter to Slaymaker, Oct. 30, 1900; Nov. 3, 1900.

49. J. Luke, letter to Slaymaker, Oct. 30, 1900.

50. This was on the site of the present Cheat Mountain Lodge.

51. D. Luke, letter to Slaymaker, Nov. 1, 1900.

52. J. Luke, letter to Slaymaker, Dec. 5, 1900.

53. J. Luke, letter to Slaymaker, Dec. 13, 1900.

54. D. Luke, letter to Slaymaker, Nov. 8, 1901.

55. Shaffer, letter to Slaymaker, Nov. 27, 1900.

56. Shaffer, letter to Slaymaker, Nov. 28, 1900.

57. D. Luke, letter to Slaymaker, Dec. 3, 1900.

58. Shaffer, letter to Slaymaker, Dec. 10, 1900.

59. Shaffer, letter to Slaymaker, Dec. 12, 1900.

60. Shaffer, letter to Slaymaker, Dec. 13, 1900; Dec. 15, 1900; Dec. 19, 1900.

61. D. Luke, letter to Slaymaker, Dec. 11, 1900; Dec. 13, 1900.

62. Shaffer, letter to Slaymaker, Dec. 15, 1900.

63. T. Luke, letter to Slaymaker, Nov. 5, 1901.

64. Shaffer, letter to Slaymaker, Nov. 8, 1901; Nov. 11, 1901; the pesthouse was located on company land on the east side of the river near where the house later occupied by the Jim Belcher family was built. It was used as a quarantine building.

65. C. F. Moore, letter to Slaymaker, Dec. 20, 1900.

66. Moore, letter to Slaymaker, Dec. 20, 1900; the Pocahontas Supply Company, a subsidiary, was formed in June, 1900. Its formation and operation are covered in Chapter 13.

67. Shaffer, letter to Slaymaker, Sept. 22, 1900.

68. Shaffer, letter to Slaymaker, Oct. 26, 1900; Nov. 22, 1900.

69. Shaffer, letter to Slaymaker, Nov. 27, 1900.

70. Shaffer, letter to Slaymaker, Dec. 15, 1900.

71. Shaffer, letter to Slaymaker, Dec. 17, 1900; Dec. 22, 1900.

72. Shaffer, letter to Slaymaker, Dec. 21, 1900.

73. Shaffer, telegram to Slaymaker, Dec. 21, 1900.

74. Shaffer, letter to Slaymaker, Dec. 26, 1900; bolts were purchased from the Lake Erie Iron Company. Angle bars and spikes were purchased from the Tredegar Iron Works, Richmond, Va. (Shaffer, letter to West Virginia Spruce Lumber Company, Jan. 3, 1901).

75. M. Williams, Stearn's Mfg. Co., Erie, Pa., letter to Slaymaker, Jan. 11, 1900.

76. A. Luke, letter to W.Va. Spruce Lbr. Co., Dec. 20, 1900.

77. Michael Koch, *Shay Locomotive-Titian of the Timber* (Denver: World Press, 1971), p. 402.

78. Kyle Neighbors, *The Lima Shays on the Greenbrier, Cheat & Elk Railroad Company* (Parsons, W.Va.: McClain, 1969), p. 1; "Old Barney" was traded to North Fork Lumber Company, Nottingham, W.Va., in 1915 for a 70-3 Shay tons CN 1519 that was built in 1905, and designated for second No. 1 (Neighbors, *Lima Shays*). "Old Barney" was scrapped Mar. 31, 1931 (Koch, *Shay Locomotive*, p. 402).

79. Rastus (pseud.), *Pocahontas Times*, Feb. 14, 1901.

80. *Pocahontas Times*, Feb. 14, 1901.

81. *Pocahontas Times*, Jan. 3, 1901.

82. Shaffer, letter to Slaymaker, Jan. 6, 1901; Jan. 8, 1901.

83. D. Luke to Slaymaker, Jan. 8, 1901.

84. Tredegar Iron Works, letter to W.Va. Spruce Lbr. Co., Jan. 11, 1901.

85. Shaffer, letter to Slaymaker, Jan. 10, 1901.

86. Shaffer, letter to Slaymaker, Jan. 15, 1901.

87. Shaffer, letter to Slaymaker, Jan. 18, 1901.

88. Shaffer, letter to Slaymaker, Jan. 28, 1901.

89. W.Va. S.L. Co. to Slaymaker, Jan. 30, 1901.

90. George A. Miller, letter to W.Va. S.L. Co., Dec. 3, 1900.

91. Moore, letter to Slaymaker, Dec. 20, 1900; W. A. Luke, letter to Slaymaker, Dec. 28, 1900; T. Luke, letter to Slaymaker, Jan. 19, 1901; J. G. Luke, letter to Slaymaker, Dec. 1, 1900.

92. W.Va. S.L. Co., Cass, W.Va., letter to W.Va. S.L. Co., New York, Jan. 28, 1901.

93. Savidge, letter to Slaymaker, Jan. 22, 1900.

94. Savidge, letter to Slaymaker, Jan. 22, 1900.

95. D. Luke, letter to Slaymaker, Dec. 17, 1900.

96. Shaffer, letter to Slaymaker, Jan. 11, 1901.

97. *Pocahontas Times*, Feb. 28, 1901.

98. Shaffer, letter to Slaymaker, Jan. 28, 1901.

99. Gerry Futej and Max Robin, "The Ubiquitous 40′ Wood Flat Car," *The Log Train* 2.1(1983): 12-17.

100. W.Va. S.L. Co., Cass, W.Va., letter to W.Va. S.L. Co., N.Y., Oct. 17, 1901.

101. W.Va. S.L. Co., Cass, letter to W.Va. S.L. Co., N.Y., Jan. 28, 1900 (telegram).

102. *Pocahontas Times*, Feb. 2, 1901.

103. "Woodsman" (pseud.), *Pocahontas Times*, Apr. 11, 1901.

104. "Rastus" (pseud.), *Pocahontas Times*, Feb. 14, 1901.

105. D. Luke, letter to Slaymaker, Jan. 19, 1901.

106. *Pocahontas Times*, Mar. 13, 1901.

107. *Pocahontas Times*, Mar. 28, 1901.

108. Records of the W.Va. P.&P. Co., Sept., 1901.

109. T. Luke, letter to Slaymaker, Dec. 9, 1901.

110. T. Luke, letter to Slaymaker, Oct. 13, 1901.

111. J. G. Luke, letter to Slaymaker, Jan. 31, 1901.

112. Shaffer, letter to Slaymaker, Jan. 8, 1902.

113. Shaffer, letter to Slaymaker, Jan. 24, 1902.

114. Neighbors, 1970, Bagdon Collection.

115. *Westvaco CFM News*, "History of Westvaco, Part 2," Spring, 1980, p. 9.

116. *Pocahontas Times*, Nov. 4, 1903.

117. Shaffer, letter to Slaymaker, Oct. 1, 1901.

118. D. Luke, letter to Slaymaker, Oct. 2, 1901; Shaffer, letter to Slaymaker, Oct. 22, 1901; *Pocahontas Times*, Oct. 10, 1901.

119. Shaffer, letter to Slaymaker, Oct. 18, 1901.

120. Shaffer, letter to Slaymaker, Mar. 12, 1902.

121. Shaffer, letter to Slaymaker, Oct. 22, 1901; Tabor was replaced by E. C. Hunter as woods superintendent. Hunter resigned in February, 1903, and E. A. Watson took over (*Pocahontas Times*, Feb. 12, 1903).

122. Sanville & Lingo, Philadelphia, Pa., letter to W.Va. S.L. Co., Oct. 11, 1901; Sanville & Lingo, letter to W.Va. S.L. Co., Oct. 23, 1901.

123. Shaffer, letter to Slaymaker, Dec. 2, 1901.

124. Shaffer, letter to Slaymaker, Feb. 13, 1902.

125. G. H. Deike, III, *Logging South Cheat, the History of the Snowshoe Resort Lands* (Youngstown, Ohio: the author, 1978), p. 8.

126. *Pocahontas Times*, July 4, 1901.

127. *Pocahontas Times*, Sept. 24, 1903.

128. *Pocahontas Times*, July 4, 1901.

129. Joseph K. Cass, letter to Slaymaker, Dec. 17, 1901.

130. Shaffer, letter to Slaymaker, Jan. 30, 1902; this is the accident alluded to in the *Pocahontas Times* report on page 98.

131. *Pocahontas Times*, Feb. 6, 1902.

132. Shaffer, letter to Slaymaker, Feb. 1, 1902.

133. Neighbors, 1972, Bagdon Collection.

134. Shaffer, letter to Slaymaker, Jan. 30, 1902; Feb. 10, 1902; Feb. 13, 1902.

135. Shaffer, letter to Slaymaker, Feb. 28, 1902; Apr. 2, 1902.

136. Deike, *Logging South Cheat*, p. 18.

137. Shaffer, letter to Slaymaker, Mar. 7, 1902.

138. Shaffer, letter to Slaymaker, Mar. 3, 1902; *Pocahontas Times*, Mar. 27, 1902.

139. *Pocahontas Times*, Mar. 27, 1902.

140. E. A. Shipe, letter to Slaymaker, Mar. 11, 1902.

141. Shaffer, letter to Slaymaker, Mar. 4, 1902.

142. Koch, *Shay Locomotive*, p. 407.

143. Shaffer, letter to Slaymaker, Mar. 4, 1902.

144. Records of the W.Va. P.&P. Co., nd.

145. Shaffer, letter to Slaymaker, Apr. 30, 1902.

146. Records of the W.Va. P.&P. Co., June 18, 1902; W.Va. S.L. Co., Cass, letter to W.Va. S.L. Co., N.Y., June 18, 1902.

147. Williamson, letter to W.Va. S.L. Co., N.Y., May 1, 1902.

148. Deike, letter to the author, Mar. 15, 1988.

149. Koch, *Shay Locomotive*, p. 408.

150. Neighbors, *Lima Shays*, p. 3; No. 3 was used almost continuously until it was retired in the early 1930s. It was scrapped in 1946 (Koch, *Shay Locomotive*, p. 408).

151. The Steel Rail Supply Co., N.Y., letter to W.Va. S.L. Co., N.Y., Mar. 17, 1902.

152. *Pocahontas Times*, Mar. 27, 1902.

153. *Pocahontas Times*, Nov. 12, 1903.

154. *Pocahontas Times*, May 21, 1903.

155. Koch, *Shay Locomotive*, p. 410. Deike, letter to the author, Mar. 15, 1988.

156. Neighbors, *Lima Shays*, p. 2; second No. 2 was scrapped at Cass in 1946, Koch, *Shay Locomotive*, p. 410.

157. *Pocahontas Times*, Oct. 13, 1904.

158. Koch, *Shay Locomotive*, p. 412.

159. Neighbors, *Lima Shays*, p. 4.

160. Deike, *Logging South Cheat*, p. 18.

161. *Pocahontas Times*, Apr. 27, 1911.

162. The name and post office from the original location of Spruce, now called "Old Spruce," was moved to the new location which was about one mile away.

163. Deike, *Logging South Cheat*, p. 23.

164. *Pocahontas Times*, Mar. 16, 1905.

165. Deike, *Logging South Cheat*, p. 23.

166. Neighbors, 1971, Bagdon Collection.

167. *Pocahontas Times*, Dec. 7, 1905.

168. *Pocahontas Times*, Jan. 18, 1906.

169. Deike, *Logging South Cheat*, p. 23.

170. Koch, *Shay Locomotive*, p. 415.

171. Neighbors, *Lima Shays*, p. 6.

172. George Deike, letter to the author, Mar. 15, 1988. Deike believes No. 6 was not purchased until 1910. Climax No. 6 was later renumbered to No. 9. According to Neighbors, it was used with the steam shovel on the Big Cut. Engineer was Oscar Hennington. (Neighbors, *Lima Shays*).

173. Koch, *Shay Locomotive*, p. 424; Deike, *Logging South Cheat*, p. 9.

174. Neighbors, *Lima Shays*, p. 6.

175. Deike, *Logging South Cheat*, pp. 24-26.

176. *Pocahontas Times*, Nov. 4, 1909.

177. Brooks, *Forestry and Wood Industries*, pp. 104, 267; *Pocahontas Times*, Apr. 27, 1911.

178. *Pocahontas Times*, June 4, 1908.

179. Galford, Preston "Springy," interview by Bagdon, June 11, 1976. Hostling was a good job during the boom years for most of the engines were in use most of the time. After the depression there were often three or more engines to take care of and the hostler's job became a busy one.

180. Switches on the GC&E were not locked; however, the C&O switches at Cass were locked and the conductor of the log train had to unlock them before going onto the C&O track for shifting in logs to the mill or other train movements.

181. Galford, interview by Bagdon, June 18, 1976.

182. Toward the end of the West Virginia Pulp and Paper operations, someone named this the "Million Dollar Spring." They had figured out that, with three-day and two-night runs, with each having an engineer, fireman, conductor, and three brakemen, it cost three dollars per day for a 15-minute break. This supposedly added up to a million dollar loss to the company (Neighbors, 1972, Bagdon Collection).

183. Charlie Cromer, May, 1971, Bagdon Collection.

184. Galford, interview by Bagdon, June 18, 1976; some sources say the limit was eleven cars (Mark Jones, "Reminiscing with Cletis Johnson—an Employee at Spruce in the '20s," *The Log Train* 2.2, 1983). Compared with what the 70- and 80-ton Shays do now, eleven cars is most likely for 100-3 Shays No. 8 and 11. No. 12 could handle thirteen cars. Deike, letter to the author, Mar. 15, 1988.

185. Galford, interivew by Bagdon, June 18, 1976.

186. Galford, interview by Bagdon, June 11, 1976.

187. Galford, interview by Bagdon, June 18, 1976; Walter Good came from Jenningston to Cass in 1927 and was engineer until the job closed in 1960. He then became engineer for the Cass Scenic Railway for several years.

188. William Simmons, interview by Bagdon, Aug. 31, 1975.

189. Paul Bradley, interview by Bagdon, 1974.

190. Galford, interview by Bagdon, May 25, 1976.

191. Russell Hamrick, interview by Bagdon, July 17, 1975; according to Galford, conductors were paid ninety dollars a month and engineers received one hundred dollars (or sometimes more) a month. (Galford, interview by Bagdon, June 1, 1976.)

192. Deike, letter to the author, Mar. 15, 1988. The crown sheet had to be kept covered with water at all times to prevent flash steaming and an explosion. Ivan Clarkson, per. inter., May 31, 1984.

193. Labbe & Goe, *Railroads*, p. 135.

194. Labbe & Goe, *Railroads*, p. 135.

195. Ivan Clarkson, per. inter., July 2, 1983.

196. Switch locks were made by Wilson Bohanna Co., Marion, Ohio; from specimen.

197. The low of −34° was recorded at Snowshoe on Cheat Mountain on Jan. 19, 1985. (*Pocahontas Times*, Jan. 24, 1985.) On Christmas Day, 1983, it was −27° at Snowshoe with a wind chill factor of −70° (*Pocahontas Times*, Jan. 5, 1984). Harvey Cromer, a very reliable observer and reporter, said it was −44° on Cheat one winter (no date given). (Harvey Cromer as told to Maurice Brooks. M. Brooks, per. conv., Jan. 29, 1987).

198. Robert O. Weedfall, *West Virginia Weather*, Charleston, W.Va.; West Virginia Dept. of Agr., nd.

199. Weedfall, *West Virginia Weather*.

200. Odey Cassell, interview by Bagdon, Jan. 6, 1976.

201. George Deike, 1975. (Information is from the National Weather Service, Elkins, W.Va.)

202. Paul H. Price and David B. Reger, *Pocahontas County, W.Va.*, County Reports, Geological Survey (Morgantown, W.Va., 1929), pp. 119, 132.

203. *Pocahontas Times*, May 17, 1908.

204. Reger, *Randolph County*.

205. *Pocahontas Times,* Dec. 1, 1910.

206. During the period 1910-1928, annual production of the Hopkins Mine ranged from 9,060 tons in 1910 to 53,419 tons in 1923, the year of the highest production (Reger, *Randolph County,* pp. 444-51).

207. W.Va. Dept. of Mines Annual Report, 1914, pp. 113, 126, 150, 208, 315, 552.

208. Reger, *Randolph County,* pp. 621, 622.

209. George Fizer, "Coal and Cass," *The Log Train* 2.1 (1983), pp. 22-25.

210. *Pocahontas Times,* Feb. 10, 1910.

211. H. E. Matics, "The Westvaco Story: A History of the Company and its People." Unpublished mms. (1976), pp. 1-114.

212. *Pocahontas Times,* Nov. 4, 1909; *Pocahontas County Deed Book 45,* p. 336.

213. *Pocahontas Times,* Nov. 4, 1909.

214. *Pocahontas County Deed Book 46,* p. 288.

215. *Pocahontas County Deed Book 46,* p. 288.

216. Charlie Cromer, interview by Bagdon, Jan. 6, 1976.

217. *Pocahontas Times,* Dec. 1, 1910.

218. *Pocahontas Times,* June 2, 1910.

219. This was located on Cheat River about two miles from Cheat Bridge. It was of log cabin style and had two adjacent fish ponds. Well-known visitors in later years were Harvey Firestone, Thomas A. Edison, and Henry Ford.

220. *Pocahontas Times,* June 16, 1910.

221. Koch, *Shay Locomotive,* p. 440.

222. Neighbors, *Lima Shays,* p. 7.

223. Koch, *Shay Locomotive,* p. 440.

224. Shay No. 8 holds the speed record from Spruce to Cass, made February 22, 1922, the night the Cass mill burned. The distance of 8.1 miles was covered in 27 minutes (Neighbors, *Lima Shays,* p. 9, 1969).

225. Koch, *Shay Locomotives,* p. 445.

226. Neighbors, *Lima Shays,* p. 10.

227. According to Koch, No. 11 was converted in the Cass shops to a 4-truck engine. This reference was undoubtedly concerning No. 12. No. 11 was scrapped in the Cass Shop in August, 1946 (Koch, *Shay Locomotive,* p. 445); Koch lists most of the Cass Shays that are gone as scrapped in 1946. However, according to Deike, Nos. 2 and 3 were cut up about 1930-31 and Nos. 8 and 11 were scrapped in 1939. Deike, letter to the author, Mar. 15, 1988; all locomotives were equipped with oil or acetylene head lamps until they were replaced with electric lamps during the period 1918-20. Replacements were made during regular maintenance visits of the engines to the Cass Shop (Galford, interview by Bagdon, June 18, 1976).

228. Neighbors, *Lima Shays,* p. 11.

229. This engine bore the No. 1 through the remainder of the logging operations and became the Cass Scenic Railroad No. 1. After eighteen years service there, it was leased to the Baltimore and Ohio Museum in 1981, as part of an agreement to get the 162-ton Western Maryland Shay No. 6 leased from the Museum to Cass Scenic Railroad (John P. Killoran, *The Cass Collection,* 2 Vols., Scott Depot, W.Va.: Trackage Rights, Inc. 1982), p. 52; Two Locomotives for Baltimore. *The Log Train,* 6.1 (1988).

230. *Pocahontas Times,* Oct. 15, 1914.

231. *Pocahontas Times,* Jan. 14, 1909.

232. *Pocahontas Times,* Jan. 21, 1909.

233. *Pocahontas Times,* Aug. 4, 1911.

234. *Pocahontas Times*, May 9, 1912.

235. *Pocahontas Times*, Apr. 3, 1913.

236. *Pocahontas Times*, Oct. 30, 1913.   .

237. *Pocahontas Times*, July 15, 1914.

238. Marlinton (W.Va.) *Marlinton Journal*, Jan. 19, 1916.

239. *Marlinton Journal*, May 31, 1917.

240. *Pocahontas Times*, Aug. 29, 1918.

241. *Pocahontas Times*, Aug. 15, 1914.

242. Deike, *Logging South Cheat*, p. 29.

243. Cromer, interview by Bagdon, Jan. 6, 1976.

244. Futej and Robin, "Ubiquitous 40' Wood Flat Car," *The Log Train* 2.1 (1983)12.

245. Futej and Robin, "Ubiquitous 40' Wood Flat Car," *The Log Train* 2.1 (1983)12.

246. Reger, *Randolph County*, p. 622.

247. Reger, *Randolph County*, pp. 620, 621.

248. Reger, *Randolph County*, p. 618.

249. Reger, *Randolph County*, pp. 449-51.

250. Reger, *Randolph County*, pp. 618, 619.

251. Reger, *Randolph County*, pp. 612, 613.

252. Reger, *Randolph County*, p. 661.

253. George Fizer, "Coal and Cass Continued," *The Log Train* 3.3(1985) pp. 4, 5.

254. Galford, interview by Bagdon, June 11, 1976.

255. Cromer, interview by Bagdon, Jan. 3, 1976.

256. Galford, interview by Bagdon, May 25, 1976.

257. Matics, "The Westvaco Story," p. 107.

258. Edward M. Killough, *History of the Western Maryland Railroad Company* (Baltimore, Md.: Voluntary Relief Press of the Western Maryland Railroad Co. 1940), p. 54.

259. *Pocahontas County Deed Book 65*, pp. 226-229.

260. Koch, *Shay Locomotive*, p. 463; Raymond F. Schuck Curator, Allen County Museum, Lima, Ohio, letter to the author, May 28, 1986.

261. Neighbors, *Lima Shays*, p. 12.

262. Deike, "Greenbrier, Cheat & Elk No. 12." *The Log Train* 1:6-12.

263. Koch, *Shay Locomotive*, p. 417. According to Deike, Shays No. 13 and 14 were both purchased in 1923. See End Note No. 276.

264. Neighbors, *Lima Shays*, p. 13.

265. Galford, interview by Bagdon, June 11, 1976.

266. Galford, interview by Bagdon, June 11, 1976.

267. R. Hamrick, interview by Bagdon, Aug. 18, 1975; Deike, letter to the author, Mar. 15, 1988.

268. *Pocahontas Times*, Feb. 8, 1923.

269. The statement has been made that 22 men were "killed on the job in the woods in 1922" (Deike, *Logging South Cheat*, p. 30). This writer found evidence of only one man killed in 1922.

270. *Pocahontas Times*, Feb. 1, 1923.

271. *Pocahontas Times*, Oct. 18, 1923.

272. *Pocahontas Times*, Dec. 20, 1923.

273. *Pocahontas Times*, June 12, 1924.

274. *Pocahontas Times*, Dec. 23, 1926.

275. Galford, interview by Bagdon, May 25, 1976.

276. Koch, *Shay Locomotive*, p. 433. "Extant records, in Mower's possession, show that No. 13 and No. 14 were both bought in 1923, for $2800 each including a car of parts." Deike, letter to the author, Mar. 15, 1988.

277. Neighbors, *Lima Shays*, p. 14.

278. Not the same as Whittaker on Cass Hill.

279. W.Va. P.&P. Co. Records, Mar. 3, 1908.

280. Slaymaker, letter to E. J. S. Hoch, Mar. 4, 1908.

281. Slaymaker, letter to D. C. Cannon, Aug. 9, 1907.

282. Slaymaker, Report on Innes Property, Nov. 23, 1907. Records of W.Va. P.&P. Co.

283. Slaymaker, letter to Cannon, Aug. 9, 1907.

284. W. A. Cobb, letter to Slaymaker, Nov. 28, 1907.

285. Slaymaker, letter to J. A. Innes, Dec. 6, 1907.

286. L. T. McFadden, letter to Slaymaker, Dec. 14, 1907.

287. Slaymaker, letter to J. A. Whiting, Dec. 10, 1907.

288. Slaymaker, letter to Innes, Jan. 8, 1908.

289. Whiting, letter to Slaymaker, Jan. 10, 1908.

290. Slaymaker, letter to E. E. Clark, Feb. 13, 1908.

291. Slaymaker, letter to Whiting, Feb. 14, 1908.

292. Whiting, letter to Slaymaker, Apr. 25, 1908.

293. Slaymaker, letter to McFadden, May 4, 1908; May 7, 1908.

294. Slaymaker, letter to Whiting, May 23, 1908.

295. Slaymaker, letter to Clark, June 10, 1908.

296. McFadden, cashier, The First National Bank, Canton, Pa., letter to Slaymaker, Mar. 7, 1908.

297. *Pocahontas County Deed Book 38*, p. 183.

298. Matic's manuscript.

299. *Pocahontas Times*, Sept. 22, 1910.

300. *Pocahontas County Deed Book 46*, p. 288.

301. *Pocahontas County Deed Book 52*, p. 180.

302. *Pocahontas Times*, Sept. 22, 1910.

303. *Pocahontas Times*, Apr. 13, 1911.

304. *Pocahontas Times*, Feb. 20, 1913.

305. David B. Reger, *County Reports: Webster County and Portion of Mingo District, Randolph County, South of Valley Falls of Elk River* (Morgantown: W.Va. Geol. Surv., 1920), pp. 2, 3.

306. *Pocahontas Times*, Dec. 1, 1910.

307. *Pocahontas Times*, Dec. 1, 1910; A. O. Baxter, letter to O. W. Connet, Dec. 29, 1928.

308. Marlinton (W.Va.) *Pocahontas Independent*, Aug. 7, 1913.

309. Deike, *Logging South Cheat*, p. 29.

310. "The material in this cut is principally a red shale, and has disintegrated since it first was taken out, and it has been necessary to remove large amounts which have come down from the slopes," Baxter, letter to Connet, Dec. 29, 1928.

311. Baxter, letter to Connet, Dec. 29, 1928.

312. Deike, *Logging South Cheat*, p. 28.

313. *Pocahontas Independent*, July 1, 1914.

314. *Pocahontas Independent*, Aug. 5, 1914.

315. Baxter, letter to Connet, Dec. 29, 1928.

316. *Pocahontas Times*, Oct. 17, 1912.

317. *Pocahontas Times*, Apr. 27, 1911.

318. Baxter, letter to Connet, Dec. 29, 1928.

319. *Pocahontas Independent*, May 6, 1914.

320. Killough, *History of the Western Maryland Railroad Company, Revised Edition*, p. 54.

321. *Pocahontas Times*, Nov. 4, 1914; Jan. 1, 1914.

322. Cromer, interview by Bagdon, May, 1971.

323. W.Va. Geological Survey Map, Webster County, 1919.

324. *Pocahontas Times*, Sept. 11, 1913.

325. S. S. "Si" Sharp & Eunice Gibson, interview by Bagdon, May 21, 1975.

326. Bagdon Collection, n.d.

327. *Pocahontas Times*, Sept. 21, 1916: *Marlinton Journal*, Sept. 20, 1916.

328. Deike, *Logging South Cheat*, pp. 28, 29.

329. R. Hamrick, interview by Bagdon, Aug. 18, 1975.

330. *Pocahontas Times*, Feb. 15, 1923.

331. *Railway Age Magazine*, 1923.

332. The distinction between main line and spurs was not always easy to make. If the track between Cass to Spruce and from Spruce to Bergoo on the Elk Division and from Spruce to Cheat Junction on the Cheat River Division are counted as main line, this amounts to about eighty-one miles. The mileage of spurs in operation at any one time is impossible to calculate.

333. Deike, "Greenbrier, Cheat & Elk No. 12," p. 7.

334. R. Hamrick, interview by Bagdon, May 22, 1975.

335. Deike, "Greenbrier, Cheat & Elk No. 12," p. 7.

336. Deike, "Greenbrier, Cheat & Elk No. 12," p. 7.

337. R. Hamrick, interview by Bagdon, May 22, 1975.

338. R. Hamrick, interview by Bagdon, May 22, 1975.

339. G. Hamrick, *Webster Echo.*

340. R. Hamrick, interview by Bagdon, Aug. 18, 1975.

341. Records of the W.Va. P.&P. Co., Nov. 1918; Jan. 1919. An interesting account of a runaway (Shay No. 11) on the Cass Hill is given by Ellet C. Smith in "The Day the Log Train Ran Away." The *Sunday Gazette-Mail,* June 18, 1978.

342. Records of the W.Va. P.&P. Co., June, 1919.

343. Neighbors, April, 1972, Bagdon Collection.

344. *Pocahontas Times*, Dec. 6, 1920.

345. *Pocahontas Times*, June 22, 1922.

346. *Pocahontas Times*, Feb. 18, 1926.

347. *Pocahontas Times*, Feb. 17, 1927.

348. Reger, *Webster County*, p. 459.

349. George Fizer, "Coal and Cass," *The Log Train* 2.1(1983):25; Deike, letter to the author, Mar. 15, 1988.

350. Laban Wolfe, interview by Bagdon, May 26, 1976.

351. Galford, interview by Bagdon, June 11, 1976. Deike claims that the incomplete records do not show that more than three engines were actually put on a train out of Slatyfork and two were the usual. Deike, letter to the author, Mar. 15, 1988.

352. Neighbors, Apr., 1972, Bagdon Collection; McNeel, *Durbin Route,* pp. 40, 125.

353. Harry Wanless, interview by the author, July, 1988.

354. Galford, interview by Bagdon, June 11, 1976.

355. Records of the W.Va. P.&P. Co., Mar., 1919.

356. Deike, *Logging South Cheat,* p. 34.

357. Deike, *Logging South Cheat,* p. 34.

358. *Pocahontas Times*, Apr. 27, 1922.

359. *Pocahontas Times*, Feb. 14, 1921.

360. *Pocahontas Times*, Feb. 28, 1924.

361. *Pocahontas Times*, Mar. 26, 1925.

362. *Pocahontas Times*, May 13, 1926.

363. Galford, interview by Bagdon, June 11, 1976.

364. No. 10 was resold several times finally ending up in Darrington, Washington (Koch, *Shay Locomotive,* p. 445).

365. Shop Records of the W.Va. P.&P. Co.

366. In September, 1942, Shay No. 14 was badly damaged in a runaway with seven loaded coal hoppers at Vindex, Md. It was then rebuilt, with a short stack and other modern features, at Hagerstown, Md. It was retired in 1950 and scrapped at Ridgeley in 1954 (Neighbors, 1970, Bagdon Collection; Fizer, Bagdon Collection, 1969; Koch, *Shay Locomotive,* 1971, p. 433).

367. According to Koch, *Shay Locomotive,* p. 441, No. 8 and No. 11 were scrapped at Cass on Aug. 19, 1946.

368. Neighbors, 1971, Bagdon Collection.

369. Shop Records of the W.Va. P.&P. Co.

370. Ivan Clarkson, per. inter., Aug. 16, 1975; according to Kyle Neighbors, when the No. 12 was rebuilt to a 4-truck engine, the shop crews weighed each additional part and the total added mass was forty-two tons, making a total weight of 392,000 pounds or 196 tons. The conversion from a 3-truck to a 4-truck engine changed the length of No. 12 from about sixty-five feet to about eighty feet long over the coupler faces.

371. Koch, *Shay Locomotive,* p. 417.

372. Shop Records of the W.Va. P.&P. Co. indicate the date No. 12 was wrecked was 1950, however, Deike believes it was in 1942 or 1943 or possibly 1945.

373. Koch, *Shay Locomotive,* p. 455.

374. Bradley, interview by Bagdon, June 7, 1976; Galford, interview by Bagdon, June 11, 1976.

375. Reger, *Randolph County,* pp. 7, 8.

376. *Randolph County Deed Book 129,* p. 375.

377. H. A. Fansler, Elkins, W.Va., interview by Bagdon, May 19, 1975.

378. Fizer, builders nameplate and letter from W. Raymond Hicks. Letter, Sept. 29, 1986.

379. Fizer, "Rod Type Locomotives of the Greenbrier, Cheat & Elk Railroad." *The Log Train* 2.2(1983):16.

380. *Pocahontas County Deed Book 65,* pp. 226-28.

381. Records of the W.Va. P.&P. Co., Oct. 2, 1929.

382. Ted Fearnow, "History of the Elk River Trout," *Wild Wonderful West Virginia,* Aug., 1972, pp. 21-24.

383. Records of the W.Va. P.&P. Co., May, 1929.

384. Reger, *Randolph County,* p. 8.

385. William Simmons, interview by Bagdon, Aug. 19, 1975.

386. *Pocahontas Times,* May 3, 1928.

387. Deike, *Logging South Cheat,* p. 36. This may be the same skidder referred to on p. 118.

388. *Pocahontas Times,* May 11, 1933.

389. *Pocahontas Times,* Feb. 17, 1938.

390. Deike, *Logging South Cheat,* p. 38.

391. Ben Jackson, interview by Bagdon, July 5, 1975.

392. Bedford "Buck" Chestnut, interview by Bagdon, June 15, 1976.

393. *Pocahontas Times,* Apr. 24, 1941.

394. I. Clarkson, per. inter., July 2, 1983.

395. Woodrow Sharp, interview by Bagdon, May 28, 1976; one other 5,000-foot haul was made earlier at Falling Spring (Ed Howell, interview by Bagdon, Jan. 3, 1976).

396. Neighbors, *Lima Shays,* p. 16; this engine was later used on the Whit-

taker Run by the Cass Scenic Railroad. The engineer was Clyde Galford (Neighbors, *Lima Shays*, p. 16). It is still in use at Cass.

397. Koch, *Shay Locomotive*, p. 456; Raymond F. Schuck, curator, Allen County Museum, Lima, Ohio, letter to the author, May 28, 1986.

398. W.Va. P.&P. Co., Wood's Foreman's Notebook, Nov. 17, 1941-Apr. 3, 1942.

399. *Pocahontas Times*, Jan. 7, 1943.

400. Deike, *Logging South Cheat*, p. 40; the last of the old camps was Camp 82 (Cheat River series) high on the mountain north of the Big Cut (Deike, p. 40).

401. Deike, *Logging South Cheat*, p. 40.

402. Stanley Wooddell, interview by Bagdon, May 21, 1975.

403. Deike, *Logging South Cheat*, p. 42.

404. Deike, *Logging South Cheat*, p. 42.

405. Forrest Griffin, interview by Bagdon, May 26, 1976.

406. Griffin, interview by Bagdon, Aug. 18, 1975.

407. Simmons, interview by Bagdon, Aug. 18, 1975.

408. *Pocahontas Times*, July 4, 1946.

409. Deike, *Logging South Cheat*, p. 45.

410. Woodrow Sharp, interview by Bagdon, May, 1976.

411. Warren "Doodle" Brown, interview by Bagdon, May 27, 1976.

412. Chestnut, interview by Bagdon, June 10, 1976.

413. Carl Summerfield, interview by Bagdon, Aug., 1967.

414. Shop Records of the W.Va. P.&P. Co., Aug. 16, 1975; the W.Va. P.&P. Co. had a conveyor that could be used to bring coal up to the boiler room for use when the mill was down and no wood scrap available. This was torn out by Mower; hence, the need to use No. 5 for steam in 1958.

415. Paul Dolkos, interview by Bagdon, Aug. 10, 1975. Deike believes that seven cars seems like the right load up the hill. Deike, letter to the author, Mar. 15, 1988.

416. Artie Barkley, interview by Bagdon, Aug. 20, 1975.

417. Neighbors, 1971, Bagdon Collection.

418. Brown, interview by Bagdon, May 27, 1976.

419. Rocky Fisher, May 26, 1968, Bagdon Collection.

420. Chestnut, interview by Bagdon, May 26, 1976; Sharp, interview by Bagdon, May 28, 1976.

421. Max S. Robin, "Railroad Logging on Cheat Mountain in 1980!" *The Log Train* 2.2(1983):18-20.

422. John P. Killoran, *The Cass Collection, Volume 2: The Logging Years (1901-1960).* (Scott Depot, W.Va.: Trackage Rights, 1983). 54 pp.

423. *Pocahontas Times*, Jan. 7, 1988; Apr. 7, 1988.

424. Summary partly made by George Deike from Kadelak George, *Lima, The History,* 1987. Hirsimaki; partly from Koch, *Shay Locomotive.*

CHAPTER VIII

WOODS OPERATIONS

1. During the early 1900s, forestry schools required their senior students to visit and report on some phase of the logging industry. In January, 1910, Herman Work, a senior in forestry at Pennsylvania State University, visited the Cass job. He lived several days at Camp 15 on Cheat Mountain. Unless otherwise stated, the details in this account of life in the woods are taken from his report, a copy of which was given to the author by H. E. Matics.

2. Camp 1 was the camp built at Cass for track workers; *Pocahontas Times,* Feb. 7, 1901.

3. *Pocahontas Times,* Aug. 28, 1902; Sept. 11, 1902; Dec. 4, 1902; Feb. 12, 1903. Local "reporters" often used names such as "Uncle Waldo," "A Woodsman," and "Comical Jim."

4. *Pocahontas Times,* July 4, 1901.

5. Letter from W.Va. Spruce Lumber Company (WVSLC), Cass to WVSLC, N.Y., Dec. 17, 1901; Camps 2 and 3 were the first of many such camps. They were numbered consecutively for a time but, as a camp cut out and was moved to a new location, it sometimes kept the same number. Also, later, as new areas were opened to logging, as in the Elk River watershed, numbers were started at 1 again. The highest numbered camp was eventually to be 99 (Deike, *Logging South Cheat,* 1978). However, as explained above, this is not a true indication of the total number of camps built.

6. *Pocahontas Times,* Sept. 24, 1903.

7. "A Woodsman," *Pocahontas Times,* Feb. 6, 1901.

8. "Comical Jim," *Pocahontas Times,* June 19, 1902.

9. WVSLC, Cass to WVSLC, N.Y., Dec. 17, 1901; Dec. 18, 1901.

10. Deike, *Logging South Cheat,* p. 15.

11. *Pocahontas Times,* Mar. 27, 1902.

12. Deike, *Logging South Cheat,* p. 15.

13. Stanley Wooddell, interview by Bagdon, May 21, 1975.

14. Stanley Wooddell, *Pocahontas Times,* Mar. 20, 1975.

15. *Pocahontas Times,* Mar. 9, 1905.

16. *Pocahontas Times,* Aug. 28, 1902.

17. It cost twelve to fifteen hundred dollars to construct a new camp.

18. Connell Gillespie, per. inter., Oct. 13, 1960.

19. A number of horses were lost on Cheat by azoturia, a kidney disease caused by keeping the horses on full feed when they were not working daily. When they were put out for hard work, the affected animals went down in their hindquarters. This was often fatal but some animals recovered after a year's careful treatment.

20. Gillespie, per. inter., Oct. 13, 1960.

21. Gillespie, per. inter., Oct. 13, 1960.

22. Reed W. Griffith, per. inter., Mar. 2, 1961; E. C. Wyatt, per. inter., Jan. 17, 1958.

23. Wages in this chapter are as they existed in 1910 according to Work.

24. Gillespie, per. inter., Nov. 10, 1960.

25. A roller towel was an endless piece of cloth about ten feet long and fifteen inches wide, hung over a wooden roller. It was used by each man in turn rolling the towel along to find a dry spot.

26. In many camps, bunks were made of 1"x6"x7' lumber nailed around the side and ends to 2"x4" corner posts. They had straw ticks, no sheets or pillowcases but plenty of wool blankets. The bunks were in tiers of two with enough room to allow the lower occupant to crawl in and out easily (Gillespie, per. inter., Nov. 10, 1960). Many bunks were double and the lobby hog directed a new man to his bed and showed him which side to sleep on.

27. The name "wood-hick" or "hicks" was almost universally applied to the men working in the woods.

28. *Pocahontas Times,* Jan. 12, 1905.

29. E. C. Wyatt, letter, Jan. 17, 1958.

30. H. H. Farquahar, "Cost of mountain logging in West Virginia," *Forestry Quarterly* 7: (1909) 255-269.

31. The term "canthook," as used on Cheat, usually referred to a peavy.

32. Farquahar, "Cost of mountain logging in West Virginia," pp. 255-269.

33. C. P. Gillespie, letter, Nov. 10, 1960.

34. Farquahar, "Cost of mountain logging in West Virginia," pp. 255-269.

35. Farquahar, "Cost of mountain logging in West Virginia," pp. 255-269.

36. Farquahar, "Cost of mountain logging in West Virginia," pp. 255-269.

37. Gillespie, letter, Nov. 10, 1860.

38. Brown Collection, W.Va., and Regional History Coll., WVU Library. Stuart Nethkin traveled throughout the East and Midwest in search of good horses. E. P. Shaffer, a lover of good horses, attended fairs when possible for the same reason. Horses were shipped in stockcars and unloaded at Cass.

39. Brown Collection, W.Va., and Regional History Collection, WVU Library, Morgantown, W.Va.

40. Odey Cassell, interview by Bagdon, Jan. 6, 1976.

41. *Pocahontas Times,* Jan. 18, 1906.

42. Forrest Griffin, interview by Bagdon, May 26, 1976.

43. Cassell, interview by Bagdon, Jan. 6, 1976.

44. Marlinton, W.Va., *Pocahontas Independent,* June 10, 1914.

45. One grab manufacturer was D. H. Lanagan, Gaines, Pa. From specimen.

46. Gillespie, letter, Nov. 10, 1960; Ralph C. Bryant, *Logging* ((N.Y.: John Wiley & Sons, 1914)), p. 435.

47. Farquahar, "Cost of mountain logging in West Virginia," pp. 255-269.

48. Gillespie, letter, Nov. 10, 1960.

49. Laban Wolfe, interview by Bagdon, May 26, 1976.

50. Deike, *Logging South Cheat,* p. 50. Company records show Camps 10, 11, 14, 16, 46, 47, 48, 49, 51, 53 and 55 operating in 1919.

51. W. W. Sutton and Henry Galford worked on the first skidway on Cheat loading logs the "canthook" way.

52. I. Clarkson, per. inter., May 34, 1984.

53. Deike, *Logging South Cheat,* p. 20.

54. Shaffer, letter to Slaymaker, Dec. 15, 1901.

55. W.Va. S.L. Co., letter to Slaymaker, Feb. 13, 1902.

56. Shaffer, letter to Slaymaker, June 15, 1902.

57. From specimen; Deike, *Logging South Cheat,* p. 20.

58. Deike, *Logging South Cheat,* p. 29.

59. Deike, *Logging South Cheat,* p. 29.

60. William Simmons, interview by Bagdon, Aug. 18, 1975; company records, Nov. 1, 1913; Oct. 31, 1914; June 30, 1919.

61. Deike, *Logging South Cheat,* p. 30.

62. Shop records of the W.Va. P.&P. Co.

63. Stanley Wooddell, *Pocahontas Times,* Feb. 10, 1975.

64. Pat Ellisy and Ed Howell, interview by Bagdon, Jan. 3, 1976.

65. Ellisy and Howell, 1975.

66. W.Va. P.&P. Co. Shop Time Book for September, 1923, show the following names under "#2 skidder": Robert Howell, George Howell, Lottie Howell, O. S. Hitt. and J. R. Hitt. They were rebuilding this skidder.

67. Howell, interview by Bagdon, Jan. 3, 1976.

68. Woodrow Sharp, interview by Bagdon, May 28, 1975.

69. Ellisy and Howell, interview by Bagdon, Jan. 3, 1976.

70. Howell, interview by Bagdon, Jan. 3, 1976.

71. Records of W.Va. P.&P. Co., Mower Lumber Company office, Durbin, W.Va.

72. Ellisy and Howell, interview by Bagdon, Jan. 3, 1976.

73. Shop records, W.Va. P.&P. Co.

74. Invoice, W.Va. P.&P. Co., Mower Lumber Company office, Durbin, W.Va.

75. Ellisy and Howell, interview by Bagdon, Jan. 3, 1976.

76. Howell, interview by Bagdon, Jan. 3, 1976.

77. Howell, interview by Bagdon, Jan. 3, 1976.

78. I. Clarkson, per. inter., Aug. 16, 1975.

79. Howell, interview by Bagdon, Jan. 3, 1976.

80. Howell, interview by Bagdon, Jan. 3, 1976.

81. *Pocahontas Times,* Mar. 6, 1924.

82. Howell, interview by Bagdon, Jan. 3, 1976.

83. Skidder whistles were made by Lunkenheimer. From specimen.

84. Woods foreman's notebook Nov. 17, 1942-Apr. 3, 1943. From Neighbors Collection.

85. Charlie Cromer, interview by Bagdon, Jan. 3, 1976.

86. *Marlinton Journal,* May 1, 1941.

87. Howell, interview by Bagdon, Jan. 3, 1976.

88. Ellisy, interview by Bagdon, Aug. 22, 1974. This may be the same skidder referred to on page 90.

89. R. Hamrick, Aug. 9, 1975.

90. R. Clarkson, *Tumult on the Mountains,* 1964, Figure 227.

91. James D. Lacey & Company, New York, N.Y., unpub. report, "General Report and Summary of Detailed Estimates, W.Va. P.&P. Co. Lands, Pocahontas, Randolph & Webster Counties, W.Va." Sept. 30, 1920.

92. *Pocahontas Times,* June 19, 1952.

93. Bedford "Buck" Chestnut, interview by Bagdon, June 10, 1976.

94. W.Va. P.&P. Co. Shop Time Book, Aug. 1944-Sept. 9, 1945.

95. Johnny Varner, interview by Bagdon, n.d.

96. D. P. Given, "The Coldest and the Highest."

97. Woodrow Sharp, interview by Bagdon, May 28, 1976.

98. Sharp, interview by Bagdon, May 28, 1976.

99. Masonic Record, A.F. & A.M. Lodge 124, Cass, W.Va. From Russell M. Clarkson.

100. Sharp, interview by Bagdon, May 28, 1976.

CHAPTER IX

TOWN OF SPRUCE

1. W.Va. P.&P. Co., Cass, W.Va., letter to W.Va. P.&P. Co., N.Y.

2. Shaffer, letter to Slaymaker, Apr. 29, 1902.

3. This was later known as Old Spruce.

4. Price and Reger, *County Reports: Pocahontas County, W.Va.,* p. 531.

5. U.S. Postal Service, W.Va. P.&P. Co. records.

6. *Pocahontas Times,* Sept. 22, 1904.

7. Thomas Luke, letter to Slaymaker, Jan. 11, 1902.

8. *Pocahontas Times,* Sept. 22, 1904.

9. *Pocahontas Times,* Dec. 29, 1904.

10. Harry E. "Shorty" Duncan, *Do I Want to Go Home?* (Charleston, W.Va., printed by the author, 1977), p. 11.

11. Duncan, *Do I Want to Go Home?,* p. 11.

12. *Pocahontas Times,* Feb. 9, 1905.

13. Matics Mms., pp. 49, 50.

14. Matics Mms., pp. 49, 50.

15. *Pocahontas Times*, Dec. 29, 1904.

16. Matics Mms., p. 50.

17. *Pocahontas Times*, Dec. 29, 1905.

18. History of Westvaco, Part 2, p. 11.

19. *Polk's Directory*, 1904-05.

20. *Polk's Directory*, 1906-07.

21. *Pocahontas Times*, Aug. 30, 1906.

22. Margaret Hannah, "Dr. U.H. Hannah Family" in *History of Pocahontas County, 1981.* (Marlinton, W.Va., Pocahontas County Historical Society, Inc., 1981), p. 314.

23. *Pocahontas Times*, June 4, 1908.

24. *Pocahontas Times*, June 11, 1908.

25. *Pocahontas Times*, Sept. 23, 1915.

26. Duncan, *Do I Want to Go Home?*, p. 9.

27. Duncan, *Do I Want to Go Home?*, p. 11.

28. *Polk's Directory*, 1918-19.

29. Duncan, *Do I Want to Go Home?*, p. 12.

30. Records of the W.Va. P.&P. Co., 1929.

31. T. M. Phare, interview by Bagdon, May 19, 1975.

32. *History of Pocahontas County*, p. 108.

33. *Pocahontas Times*, June 30, 1988.

CHAPTER X

THE LUMBER OPERATIONS

1. It was the practice that assistance in planning the buildings of a mill was provided by the company from which the mill would be purchased; D. L. Luke, letter to Slaymaker, May 24, 1900.

2. J. Luke, letter to Slaymaker, July 6, 1900.

3. J. Luke, letter to Slaymaker, July 20, 1900.

4. Shaffer, letter to Slaymaker, Aug. 2, 1900.

5. Shaffer, letter to Slaymaker, Aug. 5, 1900.

6. Shaffer, letter to Slaymaker, Aug. 8, 1900.

7. Shaffer, letter to Slaymaker, Aug. 24, 1900; Sept. 4, 1900.

8. Shaffer, letter to Slaymaker, Sept. 20, 1900.

9. Shaffer, letter to Slaymaker, Nov. 14, 1900.

10. Shaffer, letter to Slaymaker, Oct. 15, 1900; this dam was later praised in the *Pocahontas Times* of May 1, 1902, which reads, "There are two dams across the Greenbrier River. One is built by a company that says the public be damned as far as fish are concerned. They allow the water to fall in a perpendicular stream eleven feet; too far for anything short of a flying fish to overcome. The company is too powerful to be even indicted for unlawful obstruction of the stream and too contrary to allow some of us fishermen to fix their dam so that a fish can climb it. We refer to the St. Lawrence Boom and Manufacturing Company of Ronceverte.

"At Cass there is a saw mill that is the pride of the county. The Company has a dam across the river and the water issues from the dam on a sluiceway which even the most enfeebled sucker could climb. In arranging the dam this way they have shown a consideration for the public which we appreciate" (*Pocahontas Times*, May 1, 1902). This dam was later modified and did prevent fish from moving upstream (Sam Harouff, as told to Ivan Clarkson).

11. Records of the W.Va. P.&P. Co., Aug. 9, 1900.

12. Seyferts, letter to Slaymaker, Nov. 21, 1900.

13. Seyferts, letter to Slaymaker, Dec. 2, 1900.

14. *Pocahontas Times,* Apr. 4, 1901.

15. *Pocahontas Times,* June 20, 1901.

16. Shaffer, letter to Slaymaker, Dec. 1, 1901.

17. Shaffer, letter to Slaymaker, Oct. 18, 1901.

18. Shaffer, letter to Slaymaker, Oct. 22, 1901.

19. Shaffer, letter to Slaymaker, Dec. 7, 1901.

20. Shaffer, letter to Slaymaker, Nov. 8, 1901.

21. D. L. Luke, letter to Slaymaker, June 29, 1900.

22. Shaffer, letter to Slaymaker, Dec. 8, 1901. The original mill at Cass had six smokestacks when completed (photographs).

23. Records of the W.Va. P.&P. Co., Oct. 1, 1901.

24. Shaffer, letter to Slaymaker, Dec. 25, 1901.

25. Shaffer, letter to Slaymaker, Jan. 8, 1901.

26. Shaffer, letter to Slaymaker, Jan. 10, 1901.

27. Shaffer, letter to Slaymaker, Jan. 14, 1901.

28. Shaffer, letter to Slaymaker, Oct. 25, 1901.

29. Savidge, letter to Slaymaker, Nov. 11, 1901.

30. Shaffer, letter to Slaymaker, Jan. 10, 1901.

31. Shaffer, letter to Slaymaker, Dec. 23, 1901.

32. Shaffer, letter to Slaymaker, Jan. 24, 1902.

33. Shaffer, letter to Slaymaker, Jan. 25, 1902.

34. Shaffer, telegram to Slaymaker, Jan. 25, 1902.

35. Shaffer, letter to Slaymaker, Jan. 25, 1902.

36. Shaffer, letter to Slaymaker, Jan. 28, 1902.

37. Shaffer, letter to Slaymaker, Jan. 30, 1902.

38. Shaffer, letter to New York office, Jan. 30, 1902.

39. Shaffer, letter to Slaymaker, Feb. 1, 1902.

40. Shaffer, letter to Slaymaker, Feb. 8, 1902; the problem of ice on the logs was solved by running steam pipes into the pond and warming the water.

41. Shaffer, letters to Slaymaker, Feb. 1, 1902; Feb. 8, 1902; Feb. 11, 1902.

42. Shaffer, letters to Slaymaker, Feb. 13, 1902; Feb. 14, 1902; Feb. 15, 1902.

43. Shaffer, letter to Slaymaker, Feb. 15, 1902.

44. Shaffer, letter to Slaymaker, Mar. 4, 1902.

45. Shaffer, letter to Slaymaker, Mar. 7, 1902.

46. Shaffer, letter to Slaymaker, Mar. 6, 1902.

47. Shaffer, letter to Slaymaker, Mar. 11, 1902.

48. Shaffer, letter to Slaymaker, Mar. 12, 1902.

49. Shaffer, letter to Slaymaker, Mar. 26, 1902; lath became a major item of sale. Hemlock and cull spruce were used. One car held as many as 76,700 laths (Records W.Va. P.&P. Co., June 26, 1902).

50. Shaffer, letter to Slaymaker, Mar. 17, 1902.

51. Shaffer, letters to Slaymaker, Mar. 25, 1902; Mar. 26, 1902; Apr. 1, 1902; Apr. 9, 1902; Apr. 28, 1902.

52. Shaffer, letter to Slaymaker, Apr. 28, 1902.

53. W.Va. P.&P. Co., Cass, letter to Slaymaker; apparently Leatherbark, at least in floodtime, entered the Greenbrier at a point several hundred yards south of the present mouth. This left a series of low places between the present depot and the shop area (Ivan Clarkson, per. inter., Sept., 1984); the author's mother, Mertie V. Clarkson who was born at Leatherbark in 1884, remembered watching turtles in a pond north of the present depot (Ivan Clarkson, per. inter., Nov. 28, 1985).

54. W.Va. P.&P. Co., Cass, letter to Slaymaker, May 2, 1902.

55. Shaffer, letter to Slaymaker, Jan. 10, 1902.

56. Shaffer, letter to Slaymaker, Feb. 21, 1902.

57. Shaffer, letter to Slaymaker, Apr. 12, 1902.

58. Shaffer, letter to Slaymaker, Apr. 4, 1902.

59. *Pocahontas Times,* Jan. 29, 1903; the second mill was not added until Feb., 1905 (*Pocahontas Times,* Feb. 5, 1905).

60. *Pocahontas Times,* Jan. 29, 1903.

61. *Pocahontas Times,* Aug. 20, 1903; Mrs. Dewey Hiner, daughter-in-law of Elliott Hiner, claimed this accident occurred on a mill at Dunlevie (Mrs. Dewey Hiner, as told to Ernestine Clarkson, Nov., 1985).

62. *Pocahontas Times,* Sept. 15, 1904.

63. *Pocahontas Times,* Dec. 21, 1907.

64. *Pocahontas Times,* Apr. 27, 1911.

65. John Bledsoe, "Kitty Hawk and Cass," *The Log Train* 2:8.

66. *Pocahontas Times,* May 7, 1908.

67. *Pocahontas Times,* May 7, 1908.

68. *American Lumberman.* Cheat River Valley Spruce. Oct. 1, 1910. pp. 48-50.

69. *American Lumberman.* Cheat River Valley Spruce. Oct. 1, 1910. pp. 48-50.

70. *Pocahontas Times,* Mar. 3, 1915.

71. Allen Blackhurst, per. inter., Aug. 23, 1975.

72. This was the first time that land and timber were recognized to be important enough to have a man at the corporate level in charge of procurement. Charles W. Luke's influence was to be felt in the company for many years to come.

73. Herman Work remained with the company until he retired in 1953.

74. Lacey, report to W.Va. P.&P. Co.

75. Matics mms., p. 103.

76. Sam Waugh, Bagdon Notebook, May 19, 1975.

77. United States Geol. Surv., Cass Quadrangel Maps, 1977.

78. Neighbors, Bagdon Notebooks, 1970.

79. *Pocahontas Times,* "Million Dollar Fire," Mar. 2, 1922.

80. Fearnow, 1972.

81. Neighbors, Bagdon Notebooks, May 17, 1975; Unless otherwise noted, dimensions for the new mill and other buildings were supplied by Harry F. Clark of Connellsville, Pa., who made extensive measurements of the mill in the 1970s.

82. William Simmons, per. inter., June 6, 1985.

83. Simmons, per. inter., June 6, 1985.

84. Simmons, per. inter., June 6, 1985.

85. Connell P. Gillespie, letter to the author, Nov. 10, 1960.

86. Records of the W.Va. P.&P. Co., Oct. 19, 1925.

87. Gillespie, letter to the author, Nov. 10, 1960.

88. The jack slip was an inclined trough leading from the pond to the mill. The bull chain, a heavy, endless chain with cleats or weld every four feet, ran at the bottom of the trough and pulled the logs up to the mill.

89. Ben Jackson was log scaler for many years. During the Mower years, logs were cut double-length in the woods. The scaler had to cut them to standard length by means of a 6-foot chain saw.

90. The resaw was a 7-foot Clark band mill. It was purchased, used, by Connell Gillespie in North Carolina for $100. Installed in 1927-28, it replaced the gang saw (Simmons, June 6, 1985).

91. Brown Collection, Vol. 6 (Morgantown, W.Va., West Virginia Collection, Library); the gang saw was sold to a Parkersburg mill where it later was destroyed in a fire (Simmons, per. inter., June 6, 1985).

92. *Pocahontas Times,* Apr. 26, 1923.

93. Records of the W.Va. P.&P. Co., Oct. 31, 1925.

94. Simmons, interview by Bagdon, Jan. 6, 1976.

95. Shaffer, letter to Slaymaker, July 30, 1925; Simmons, interview by Bagdon, Aug. 19, 1975.

96. *Pocahontas Times,* Nov. 14, 1918.

97. *Pocahontas Times,* June 19, 1924.

98. *Pocahontas Times,* Dec. 25, 1924.

99. *Pocahontas Times,* Feb. 18, 1926.

100. *Pocahontas Times,* May 30, 1929.

101. B. Jackson, per. inter., Mar. 9, 1984; Tombstone, Oliver Cemetery.

102. Ivan Clarkson, per. inter., July 5, 1975.

103. *Pocahontas Times,* Dec. 17, 1936.

104. W.Va. P.&P. Co., Jan. 1, 1940-Dec. 31, 1940.

105. *Pocahontas County Deed Book, No. 79,* pp. 36-84.

106. Fred Weber, interview by Bagdon, Aug. 12, 1974; the Mowers were also interested in farming. They owned Pok-a-Dot Farms in Charleston, W.Va., and Deerfield, Va. A prize winning bull, Starduke, was purchased by them for fifty-three thousand dollars.

107. Louis H. Camisa, letter to the author, Jan. 14, 1989.

108. *Pocahontas Times,* Apr. 20, 1911.

109. *Pocahontas Times,* Mar. 5, 1925: Receipt given to the author by William Sampson.

110. *Pocahontas Times,* Nov. 15, 1934.

111. Puffenbarger, interview by Bagdon, May 26, 1976.

112. *Pocahontas Times,* Oct. 22, 1936.

113. *Marlinton Journal,* Sept. 25, 1952.

114. Puffenbarger, interview by Bagdon, May 26, 1926.

115. The Monongahela National Forest was established by a presidential proclamation by Woodrow Wilson on Apr. 28, 1920, and was expanded by later proclamations.

116. McKim, C. R. *50 Year History of the Monongahela National Forest.* n.p. 1970. Ch. 6.

117. Paul Bradley, interview by Bagdon, June 7, 1976.

118. Simmons, interview by Bagdon, Jan. 6, 1976.

119. *Pocahontas Times,* Apr. 21, 1955.

120. Weber, interview by Bagdon, Aug. 12, 1974.

121. Copy of Notice, June 25, 1960.

122. I. Clarkson, per. inter., Aug. 25, 1974.

123. *Pocahontas Times,* Aug. 4, 1960.

124. The Ritter Lumber Company was merged with the Georgia Pacific Lumber Company a short time after the lumber purchase. Edward "Puzo" Cassell, per. inter., June 1, 1986.

125. Woodrow Sharp, interview by Bagdon, May 28, 1976.

126. Cassell, per. inter., June 1, 1986.

127. I. Clarkson, per. inter., July 25, 1974.

128. *Pocahontas Times,* Aug. 11, 1966.

129. *Pocahontas Times,* Aug. 24, 1978.

130. *Pocahontas Times,* Feb. 18, 1982; June 3, 1982.

CHAPTER XI

MACHINE SHOPS

1. Simmons, interview by Bagdon, Aug. 18, 1975.
2. Allen J. Blackhurst, per. inter., Aug. 23, 1974; E. J. "Herb" Shafer remained as foreman of the shop at Cass until he retired at age seventy. He was born in Pennsylvania. His popular slogan was "born in Pennsylvania, raised in Maryland, and worn out in West Virginia," "Herb" Shafer was a just and considerate foreman. One of the most disagreeable jobs done in the shop was riveting the spar pole for a skidder. During this operation, a man had to crawl inside the pole to back up the rivets—a deafening, smothering feat. This task was often foisted onto a new worker. On one occasion, no one would agree to go into a skidder tower and Herb said, "Well, if there isn't anyone to do it, I'll do it myself" (Allen Blackhurst interview, Aug. 23, 1974). Mr. Shafer retired in 1949 (Mary Shafer Shaw, letter, Oct. 8, 1986).
3. Simmons, interview by Bagdon, Jan. 6, 1976.
4. I. Clarkson, per. inter., June 6, 1985.
5. A. Blackhurst, per. inter., Aug. 23, 1974.
6. Neighbors, Bagdon notebooks, 1971.
7. W.Va. P.&P. Co., Shop Time Book, Apr., 1914.
8. Shop Time Book, Feb., 1920, and July, 1920.
9. Shop Time Book, July, 1931.
10. Shop Time Book, Dec. 16, 1934.
11. Shop Time Book, 1940.
12. Shop Time Book, Jan. 1 to June 30, 1942.
13. Shop Time Book, June 15, 1942, to July 1, 1943.
14. Shop Time Book, Sept. 1, 1945, to Oct. 1, 1946.
15. Russell Clarkson, per. inter., July 5, 1984.
16. I. Clarkson, diary, July 18, 1957.
17. A. Blackhurst, per. inter., Aug. 23, 1974.
18. *Pocahontas Times,* July 21, 1972.

CHAPTER XII

THE EXTRACT PLANT

1. Edwin Palaszynski, "The Deer Creek Extract Plant," *Log Train* 3, No. 3: 6.
2. Matics, unpub. manuscript.
3. Palaszynski, "Deer Creek Extract Plant."
4. *Pocahontas Independent,* Apr. 29, 1914.
5. Matics, unpub. manuscript, p. 94.
6. Records of the W.Va. P.&P. Co., 1924.
7. Matics, unpub. manuscript.
8. Ether Tyson, per. inter., Nov. 18, 1985.
9. I. Clarkson, per. inter., Mar. 11, 1984.
10. Neighbors, Bagdon interview, 1970.
11. *Pocahontas Times,* Mar. 7, 1929.
12. B. Jackson, per. inter., Nov. 18, 1984.
13. Records of the W.Va. P.&P. Co. and May 4-27, 1920.

CHAPTER XIII

THE POCAHONTAS SUPPLY COMPANY

1. Shaffer, telegraph to Slaymaker, July 6, 1900.
2. Shaffer, letter to Slaymaker, Sept. 22, 1900.
3. Shaffer, letter to Slaymaker, Nov. 28, 1900.
4. C. F. Moore, letter to Slaymaker, Dec. 20, 1900.
5. "Rastus," *Pocahontas Times*, Jan. 24, 1901.
6. Slaymaker to West Virginia Spruce Lumber Company.
7. R. B. Clarkson and Kenneth L. Carvell, "West Virginia's Logging Railroad—Its Past and Present." Northeastern Logger, Dec. (1961): p. 63.
8. I. Clarkson, per. inter., Aug. 16, 1975.
9. Photograph, 1917.
10. I. Clarkson, per. inter., Aug. 16, 1975.
11. Nodie Bascomb and Harold Lee, May 27, 1982.
12. *Pocahontas Times*, Mar. 21, 1918.
13. W. Simons, interview by Bagdon, Aug. 18, 1975.
14. Charles Sheets, interview by Bagdon, Aug. 18, 1975.
15. B. Jackson, per. inter., Oct. 15, 1984.
16. W.Va. P.&P. Co. records
17. The following list of Company Store employees was compiled from information from Dorothy Tacy, Ivan Clarkson, Ernestine Clarkson and Ben Jackson.
Managers: Robert S. Hickman (45 years); Mabe, H. H. Thompson, Robert Wright
Assistant Manager: Burke McCarty
Druggists: Dr. Wildhide, Dr. Ayers and Harry Hill.
Clerks and other workers in the Company Store were:

Cal Stoffer	"Pye-bellig" Ervine
Jimmy Moyers	Ikie Burner
Roy Stewart	George Oliver
John Kane	Pearl Harouff
John Slavins	Crawford Gum
Anna Seitz	Stanley Roupe
Dorothy Tacy	Robert Fleming
Edythe Davis	Jesse Martin
Charles Sheets	Edwin Doyle
Floyd Wright	Mike Mauzy
Jake Mauzy	Kay Martin
Maggie Wymer	Fay Turner
Lois Meeks	Margaret Jackson
Margaret Eary	Gay Miller
Beulah Dahmer	Pauline Dahmer
Juanita Dahmer	Grace Leatherwood
Dorothy Lee Meeks	Ernestine Clarkson
Margaret Eary	Burl McLaughlin
Catherine Sheets	Gertrude Moss
Maggie Vint	

18. *Pocahontas Times*, Sept. 1, 1960.

CHAPTER XIV

S. B. NETHKIN AND COMPANY

1. *Pocahontas Times,* Jan. 21, 1901.
2. Shaffer, letter to Slaymaker, Apr. 12, 1902.
3. Shaffer, letter to Slaymaker, Apr. 12, 1902.
4. W.Va. S.L. Co., Cass to W.Va. S.L. Co., N.Y., May 13, 1902.
5. W.Va. S.L. Co., Cass, letter to W.Va. S.L. Co., N.Y., May 30, 1902.
6. Letterhead 1902; Neighbors, Bagdon notebooks, July, 1971; this building was later occupied by the post office.
7. Records of the W.Va. P.&P. Co.
8. I. Clarkson, per. inter., May 31, 1984.
9. This barn, the largest barn in Pocahontas County, was burned on Sept. 13, 1930. It was full of hay and other feed and contained much valuable machinery. All was a total loss (*Pocahontas Times,* Oct. 16, 1930). It was rebuilt as rapidly as possible.
10. S. S. "Si" Sharp and Eunice Gibson, interview by Bagdon, May 21, 1975.
11. Records of the W.Va. P.&P. Co., July 19, 1920.
12. Galford, interview by Bagdon, May 11, 1976.

CHAPTER XV

THE TOWN OF CASS

1. *Pocahontas County Deed Book No. 20:* 72.
2. *Pocahontas County Deed Book No. 25:* 363.
3. *Pocahontas County Deed Book No. 15:* 170. Robert Curry, an elder in the German Baptist Church, was drowned while attempting to ford Leatherbark Run on horseback during a flood.
4. *Pocahontas County Deed Book No. 20:* 71.
5. *Pocahontas Times,* May 1, 1902.
6. The Burner house is still standing, just north of the old church in East Cass.
7. M. Clarkson, per. inter., May 2, 1965; foundations of the Galford house are visible east of the former C&O Railroad slightly south of the bridge across Cold Run.
8. This road can still be followed along its original route from the old Rt. 250 above Durbin southward to Stony Bottom, Clover Lick and Edray on Rt. 219 north of Marlinton.
9. The location of this school was on Jim McLaughlin's farm. It was on a branch of Cold Run in the next hollow north of the Cass Cave hollow. It is marked today by a grove of Balm of Gilead trees (x *Populus gileadensis* Rouleau) remaining from a tree planted before 1900 (Mertie Clarkson, per. inter., May 2, 1965). This school operated until about 1908 when it burned. Two teachers at the school were Frank Hamrick and Mamie Hannah (Monta McLaughlin letter, Oct. 10, 1984).
10. M. Clarkson, per. inter., May 2, 1965.
11. Brooks, *Forestry and Wood Industries,* p. 243.
12. Neighbors, Phil Bagdon notebooks, May 21, 1975.
13. *Pocahontas County Deed Book No. 22:* 378; this land was bounded and described as follows:

BEGINNING at a White Oak on Chestnut Ridge, corner to Fifty-six (56) acres, conveyed to Allen Galford, on the old Knox Line and with the same,

N. 67 E. 106 poles to a Chestnut and Dogwood and fallen Maple,

N. 88° E. 84 poles to a stake with 2 Walnuts, Sugar and Chestnut pointers, on a line of the seven acre tract, and with the same,

N. 35° W. 14 poles to a beech stump,

N. 24° E. 2 poles to a Birch and Spruce on the bank of Leatherbark Creek, thence down the Creek,

S. 70° E. 20 poles, S. 22° E. 6 1/2 poles to a poplar and Spruce,

S. 16 1/2° E. 32 1/2 poles to three elms,

S. 50 1/2° E. 8 1/2 poles to a Sycamore,

S. 60° E. 20 poles to the edge of Greenbrier River, thence down the river, S. 17° W. 22 poles,

S. 42° W. 42 poles to a stake on the old Knox line, thence with the same

S. 13° W. 20 poles, crossing the river to a Black Oak and fallen Lynn, an original corner of said Knox survey and corner to A.C. Burner, thence with his line.

N. 24° W. 12 poles, crossing the river to a Gum on the river bank, S. 45° W. 34 poles to a White Oak,

S. 38° W. 25 poles, crossing the river to two small Birches,

S. 43° E. 15 poles to a small Red Oak,

S. 55° W. 8 poles to a small White Pine,

S. 63° W. 27 poles to a stake and Chestnut pointer,

S. 55 1/2° W. 22 poles, to 2 Birch Saplings,

S. 68° W. 5 poles to a stake on the said Knox Line, and with the same,

N. 40° W. 28 poles, crossing the river to a sycamore, old corner, thence up the bank of the river,

N. 44° E. 8 poles passing a Chestnut and Dogwood Saplings at 4 poles to 3 Chestnut Sprouts corner to said fifty-six acre tract, and with the same,

N. 37 1/2° W. 167 poles to a small White Oak on the brow of Chestnut Ridge, N. 22° W. 12 poles to the beginning.

14. *Pocahontas County Deed Book No. 25:* 396.
15. *Pocahontas County Deed Book No. 29:* 93.
16. *Pocahontas County Deed Book No. 32:* 1.
17. Lester Burner in W. W. Sutton, *Pocahontas Times,* Feb. 2, 1963.
18. Shaffer, letter to Slaymaker, July 6, 1900.
19. Shaffer, letter to Slaymaker, Aug. 5, 1900.
20. B. Jackson, per. inter., Mar. 10, 1984.
21. Shaffer, letter to Slaymaker, Sept. 22, 1900; Sept. 28, 1900.
22. Records W.Va. P.&P. Co., 1901; 1902.
23. Elkins (W.Va.) *Inter-Mountain,* May 24, 1900, quoting the *Covington Sentinel; Pocahontas County Deed Book No. 30:* 330.
24. Shaffer, letter to Slaymaker, Aug. 2, 1900; Records of the W.Va. P.&P. Co., 1900.
25. Matics, unpub. mms., pp. 28-29. The local tradition concerning the name Cass states that Joseph Cass promised to build an opera house in the town if the town was named after him. (Margaret Hannah Gluck, per. inter., Jan. 26, 1989.)
26. Shaffer, letter to Slaymaker, Aug. 30, 1900.
27. Shaffer, letters to Slaymaker, Sept. 20, 1900; Sept. 25, 1900; Charlie Cromer, interview by Bagdon, Jan. 6, 1976.
28. Records of the W.Va. P.&P. Co., Sept., 1901.
29. The route couldn't be agreed upon and the road down Deer Creek was not constructed until 1904 (*Pocahontas Times,* Jan. 21, 1904).
30. Shaffer, letter to Slaymaker, Oct. 4, 1900.
31. *Pocahontas Times,* Oct. 18, 1900.

32. D. Luke, letter to Slaymaker, Jan. 19, 1901; The first postmaster was J. L. Matthews [R. L. Poke Directory (Detroit: R. L. Polk, 1902-03. pp. 148-149.)].

33. *Pocahontas Times*, Mar. 7, 1900.

34. See copy of town plat, Fig. 123.

35. The toilets were two-seaters with a small hole for children and a larger one for adults. They were supplied with large wooden boxes to receive wastes. Access to the boxes was by way of a hinged door located at the bottom of the toilet on the backside facing the alley. These boxes were emptied once a month by a man who dumped the contents into a wagon, called facetiously a "Honey" wagon, and hauled it away. His charge was one dollar per house. The work was done after midnight by the light of a coal oil lantern. For many years this necessary, but onerous, task was performed by Frank "Hog Island" Smith who lived north of the mill on an island in the Greenbrier. This was not considered a very high class occupation by town inhabitants but it was fully as important to the town's well-being as was any other job in town. Toilet tissue was an unknown item; however, mail-order catalogues or newsprint made satisfactory substitutes.
The woodshed had a small door that swung open at the proper height for unloading wood or coal in from a wagon, later a truck.

36. Roy C. Siple, tape recording, July 10, 1984.

37. Records of the W.Va. P.&P. Co., June 12, 1901.

38. Records of the W.Va. P.&P. Co., Oct. 5, 1901; Oct. 10, 1901.

39. W.Va. S.L. Co., Cass, letter to W.Va. S.L. Co., N.Y., Nov. 6, 1901.

40. Shaffer, letter to W.Va. P.&P. Co., Oct. 16, 1901.

41. Shaffer, letter to Slaymaker, June 2, 1902.

42. *Pocahontas Times*, June 11, 1903; *Marlinton Journal*, Apr. 27, 1933.

43. John 13:34, 35. (*A new commandment I give unto you, that ye love one another as I have loved you, that ye also love one another. 35. By this shall all men know that ye are my disciples. If ye have love one to another.*) *Holy Bible, Revised Standard Version* (N.Y.) Thomas Nelson and Sons. 1946. p. 122.

44. Lex, *Pocahontas Times*, Jan. 31, 1901.

45. Rastus, *Pocahontas Times*, Feb. 21, 1901; Rev. McLaughlin continued to preach at Cass on the second and fourth Sundays and at Old Spruce on the fourth Sunday of each month until 1903 (*Pocahontas Times*, June 11, 1903).

46. *Pocahontas Times*, May 29, 1902.

47. The suspension bridge was condemned by the Town Council in Sept., 1902, because it didn't have wire along its sides (*Pocahontas Times*, Oct. 2, 1902).

48. *Pocahontas Times*, Mar. 7, 1901: *Pocahontas Times*, Mar. 13, 1901.

49. McNeel, *Durbin Route*, p. 87.

50. Shaffer, letter to Slaymaker, Jan. 30, 1902.

51. Shaffer, letter to Slaymaker, Feb. 21, 1902.

52. Shaffer, letter to Slaymaker, Feb. 25, 1902.

53. Shaffer, letter to Slaymaker, Feb. 26, 1902.

54. Shaffer, letter to Slaymaker, Mar. 24, 1902.

55. Shaffer, letter to Slaymaker, Mar. 28, 1902.

56. *Pocahontas Times*, Aug. 14, 1901.

57. R. D. Wood and Son to W.Va. S.L. Co., Nov. 27, 1901.

58. R. D. Wood and Son to W.Va. S.L. Co., Nov. 12, 1901; Nov. 26, 1901; by Jan., 1904, water had been piped all over town and the houses had been painted.

59. W.Va. S.L. Co., Cass, letter to W.Va. S.L. Co., New York, Dec. 24, 1901.

60. Shaffer, letter to Slaymaker, Feb. 7, 1902.

61. *Pocahontas Times*, Feb. 13, 1902.

62. Shaffer, letters to Slaymaker, Feb. 27, 1902; Mar. 23, 1902; W.Va. S.L. Co., Cass, letter to W.Va. S.L. Co., N.Y., June 5, 1902.

63. *Pocahontas Times,* Sept. 4, 1902.

64. W.Va. S.L. Co., Cass, letter to W.Va. S.L. Co., N.Y., Dec. 19, 1901.

65. *Pocahontas Times,* June 4, 1903.

66. Henry Ward Randolph in *History of Pocahontas County,* p. 166.

67. Randolph in *History of Pocahontas County,* p. 166.

68. After the Greenbrier General Hospital at Ronceverte, Greenbrier County, was completed prior to October, 1907 (*Pocahontas Times,* Oct. 17, 1907), the Cass Hospital was changed over to a residence. E. P. Shaffer and his family lived there until the early 1920s. The Joe Hannah family lived in it for many years. In 1948, it was changed into a boardinghouse run by Mrs. Ollie Ervine and Mrs. Shears.

69. Randolph in *History of Pocahontas County,* p. 166.

70. Dr. Randolph remained at Cass until the end of 1905 when he left to take courses in surgery in London and Vienna (*Pocahontas Times,* Jan. 4, 1906). He later established a practice in Richmond, Va., where he died in 1978 at the age of ninety-nine (*History of Pocahontas County,* p. 166).

71. *Pocahontas Times,* Aug. 21, 1902; Sept. 4, 1902; May 7, 1903; Jan. 17, 1907.

72. *History of Pocahontas County,* p. 95.

73. *Pocahontas Times,* Aug. 7, 1902.

74. From copy of original court order.

75. Polk's Directory, 1902.

76. Polk's Directory, 1904-05, p. 151.

77. During its early years, the young, boisterous town grew from a population of less than 100 in 1900 to 496 in 1910 and 1,195 in 1920 (*Pocahontas Times,* Sept. 23, 1920). By 1920, these figures were augmented by several hundred persons living on each side of the river south of the incorporated part of town and by multitudes of loggers, track workers and trainmen on weekends coming in from the woods camps.

78. *Pocahontas Times,* Feb. 19, 1903.

79. *Pocahontas Times,* Aug. 21, 1902.

80. Warren Blackhurst, *Of Men and a Mighty Mountain.* (Parsons, W.Va.: McClain, 1965), p. 71.

81. *Pocahontas Times,* Oct. 2, 1902. Other sources name W. T. Newcome as mayor in 1902.

82. *Pocahontas Times,* Oct. 9, 1902.

83. *Pocahontas Times,* Feb. 19, 1903; Samuel Cooper later opened another store in East Cass that was operated by his son, Jacob, until 1923.

84. *Pocahontas Times,* Jan. 15, 1903; Mr. and Mrs. Sutton later returned to Cass and became two of the most respected residents. Mr. Sutton was undertaker, justice of the peace, member of the town council and constable.

85. *Pocahontas Times,* Feb. 19, 1903.

86. Charles Lee Clark (Bud) Burner.

87. One shooting was that of Craig Ashford in the arm, the other was the killing of Jeff Houchins in self-defense while in the discharge of his duties as constable (*Pocahontas Times,* Apr. 23, 1903). Neither of these events occurred at Cass; *Pocahontas Times,* Apr. 30, 1903.

88. *Pocahontas Times,* July 2, 1903; July 23, 1903.

89. *Pocahontas Times,* July 7, 1904.

90. *Pocahontas County Deed Book No. 48,* p. 418.

91. Russell M. Clarkson, In *History of Pocahontas County,* p. 45; the lodge and the Order of Eastern Star #124 continue to use this building for meetings and socials.

92. The Reverend Mr. Watkins had been preaching at Cass since the first Sunday of July, 1903 (*Pocahontas Times,* July 2, 1903).

93. *Pocahontas Times,* Mar. 16, 1905. The first sermon was preached by Rev. G. W. Nickell. His text was John 17:20,21: (*Neither pray I for these alone, but for them also which shall believe on me through their word: That they may all be one; as thou Father, art in me, and I in thee, that there may be one in us; that the world may know that thou hast sent me.*) (*Pocahontas Times,* Mar. 16, 1905).

94. Ministers to serve in longest capacity at this church were Fred W. Gray, D.D., 1918-29 and James T. Pharr, 1929-41. One of the mainstays of the church was Allen J. Blackhurst who was elected elder in 1925 and served in many capacities for over forty years (Beatrice Sheets, *History of Pocahontas County,* p. 126). Ray Fox and other dedicated Sunday school teachers left a lasting impression on their many students (Harry E. Duncan, *Do I Want to Go Home?*), p.19. The church building was remodeled in 1923. It was partially destroyed by fire in March, 1927, and was repaired and remodeled that same year. Membership grew to 136 active members in 1940. It had outpost work at Spruce and Raywood during the active years of those towns.

Some of the active religious workers to go out from the Cass Presbyterian Church were: Rev. T. L. Harnsbarger, missionary to Africa; Mrs. Alice (Hannah) Brown, a missionary-teacher in Africa; and Rev. Lewis Lyle.

Membership declined after 1940 to less than 20 and the Cass Presbyterian Church was dissolved on June 30, 1970. The building was turned over to the Presbytery of Greenbrier which gave it to the people of the town of Cass for a community building.

Roll of Ministers: Rev. Asa Watkins, D.D., 1904-07; Rev. W. W. Bain, 1907-10; Rev. J. S. Kennison, 1910-12; Rev. Louis A. Kelly, 1912-15; Rev. Fred W. Gray, D.D., 1918-29; Rev. James T. Pharr, 1929-41; Rev. H. M. Jefferson, 1941-44; Rev. B. B. Breitenhirt, 1945-48; Rev. H. G. Keys, 1949-52; Rev. George Bowman (Supply), 1953; Rev. J. D. Arbuckle, 1953-56; Rev. W. Denver Lively, 1963-66; Rev. Thomas E. Henderson, 1966-70. During the thirty-five years prior to 1970, the minister at Liberty Church at Green Bank served as minister at Cass. Beatrice (Blackhurst) Sheets, *History of Pocahontas County,* p. 126; Thomas E. Henderson in *History of Pocahontas County,* p. 132).

95. *Pocahontas Times,* Mar. 2, 1904.

96. Margaret Hannah Gluck, Jan. 26, 1989.

97. This was later a poolroom, a 5 and 10 Cent Store and a store run by Tex Blackhurst, Kane's Grocery Store and Simmon's Grocery.

98. *Pocahontas Times,* Feb. 20, 1902; later Ben Conrad, Ver Bolden and, still later, Walter H. Vint, drove dray. He was succeeded by Roy Vint, the last person to drive a horse-drawn dray in Cass.

99. I. Clarkson, per. inter., May 30, 1984.

100. Camps on Elk River were supplied meat by a slaughterhouse located near Slatyfork at a location since called Slaughter Pen Hollow.

101. W. Blackhurst, *Of Men and a Mighty Mountain,* p. 14.

102. Measurements of the foundation laid bare by the flood of Nov. 4, 5, 1985.

103. *Pocahontas Times,* Jan. 22, 1903.

104. B. Jackson, per. inter., May 22, 1983; The icehouse was torn down about 1932 by Walter G. Clarkson (Ivan Clarkson, per. inter., May 30, 1984). In the 1930s, an ice machine was built by the company behind S. B. Nethkin and Company. Here, blocks of ice were frozen and brought down a slide between Nethkin's Meat Market and the Company Store for loading on a truck and delivery. Home iceboxes had a top compartment in which ice chunks were placed. Floyd Wright delivered ice for many years. Charlie Sheets was the next delivery man. He also delivered feed, etc. from the Company Store and delivered

coal. Coal was unloaded from railroad cars into bins located west of the depot. This was then loaded into a truck by Mr. Sheets, weighed on scales in the same vicinity and delivered, on order, to customers. Coal houses had a small swinging window at a convenient height through which the coal was shoveled.

105. *Pocahontas Times*, May 5, 1904; June 30, 1904.

106. These included eight Italians killed by dynamite at Dunlevie; Lee Burner, who was killed at Durbin when the train "spooked" his horse causing a runaway; a man who committed suicide by throwing himself under a moving train on the C&O above Durbin; and an employee of the Coketon Lumber Company at Fishing Hawk who was killed while trying to apply brakes to a load of lumber and fell in front of the car (*Pocahontas Times*, Aug. 17, 1905).

107. *Pocahontas Times*, Aug. 17, 1905; violence between foreigners and Americans was common and soon after the above incident, a slaughter of foreigners by over one hundred armed men was narrowly averted at Tioga, Nicholas Co., W.Va. (*Pocahontas Times*, July 5, 1906). Other, fatal, incidents between foreigners and Americans also occurred (*Pocahontas Times*, July 5, 1906; May 5, 1906).

108. Marlinton (W.Va.) *Marlinton Messenger*, Jan. 4, 1906.

109. *Pocahontas Times*, Jan. 18, 1906.

110. McNeel, *Durbin Route*, p. 93; *Pocahontas Times*, Feb. 15, 1906.

111. *Pocahontas Times*, July 12, 1906.

112. Bottled by G. H. Mumm and Company (*Pocahontas Times*, Aug. 30, 1906; Sept. 6, 1906); C. L. C. Burner denied that any intoxicating drinks were found in a building owned by him and stated that he had only one warrant to serve which netted very little whiskey (*Pocahontas Times*, Oct. 25, 1906).

The *Pocahontas Times* used every opportunity to find fault with Burner.

113. *Pocahontas Times*, Sept. 6, 1906.

114. *Pocahontas Times*, Sept. 27, 1906.

115. *Pocahontas Times*, Jan. 3, 1907; *Marlinton Messenger*, Jan. 4, 1907.

116. The The other brick building in Cass was the home of J. B. Sutton; patented on June 9, 1903. Inscription on blocks obtained after the flood of November 4, 5, 1985.

117. *Pocahontas Times*, Feb. 20, 1908.

118. *Pocahontas Times*, Nov. 7, 1907.

119. The McLaughlin Church served from 1907-40. Ministers were: the Reverends Mr. Lawrence, Ehols, McNeil, Arbogast, Shires, Sponogaugel and Burr (partial list).

Some of the persons attending were: Joe and Sallie McLaughlin and their children, Mamie, Monta, Ward and Pearlie; Griffie and Bertie Sheets and their children, Ollie, Mary, Johnny, Arnold, Wilbur, June and Winfred; Walter and Mertie Clarkson and their children, Vallie, Ivan, Lola, Odie, Glenna and Kyle; John and Allie Tallman and their children, Ethel, Elbert, Ralph, Ruth and Russell; Warwick Simmons and family Anna, Charles, Henry, Lillie, Floyd, Viva, Beulah and Leva; Charles and Grace Tacy and their children, Bessie, Florence and Jessie; Dallas and Birdie Tacy and children, Grace, Ollie, George, Beryl and Olliver; Brown Gum, Harry Gum, Harper Gum; Johnnie Varner and Frank Varner; Willie Byrd.

The McLaughlin Church closed in 1940 and was sold in 1944 and torn down (Monta McLaughlin, letter, Oct. 10, 1984).

120. *History of Pocahontas County*, p. 95.

121. *Pocahontas Times*, Sept. 17, 1908.

122. The Cold Run School met the needs of farm families in this area from 1909 to 1940. Some of the teachers were: Floyd Winter, Frances Hardesty, Willie

Fertig, Vaughn Geiger, Leta McLaughlin Adams, Gladys McLaughlin, Mary Warwick, Ruby Bailey and Grace Arbogast.

Some of the persons attending this school were: Owen, Harry and Parker Curry; Porter, Rice and Price McLaughlin; Mamie, Monta, Ward and Pearlie McLaughlin; Ethel, Eela, Ruth, Annanera, Elbert, and Russell Tallman; Charlie, Henry, Floyd, Lillie, Viva, and Beulah Simmons; Bessie, Florence and Jesse Tacy; Grace Painter; George, Johnny and Ollie Olliver; Bertie, Beryl and Grace Tacy; Neva, Arthur and Clyde Galford; Charles Sheets; Harry and Harper Gum; Leta and Garland McLaughlin; Zeta and Roy McLaughlin (Monta McLaughlin, letter to the author, Oct. 10, 1984).

123. Some of the teachers in this school were Lottie Burner, Ora Hendricks, Duncan, McComb, Hazel McMillion and Edgar Shinaberry. Among the students were Fred Shinaberry, Charlie Gum, Casy Geiger, Lela Gum, Cordy Gum and Lewis Cassell.

124. *History of Pocahontas County*, p. 95.

125. Gluck, Jan. 26, 1989; *Pocahontas Times*, May 18, 1911; Mr. and Mrs. Shaffer had six children: Jane, Gertrude, Kate, Patsy, Susan and Emory.

126. *Pocahontas Times*, Aug. 7, 1911.

127. Simmons, per. inter., June 6, 1985; this is the present Back Mountain Road leading northward from Cass to Durbin.

128. *Pocahontas Times*, Mar. 28, 1912. Dr. Nickell charged $1.50 plus medicine for a trip to visit a horse at the barn at Cass. A visit to the woods to see a horse was $10.00 plus medicine. (Company records, Dec. 1, 1918.)

129. *Pocahontas Times*, Mar. 24, 1912; June 7, 1912; Dec. 8, 1912. (Marlinton, W.Va.) *Republican News*, June 25, 1913.

130. *Pocahontas Times*, Dec. 20, 1912.

131. McNeel, *Durbin Route*, corrections addendum for first printing, Nov. 1986.

132. *Pocahontas Times*, Feb. 13, 1913.

133. *Pocahontas Times*, Feb. 13, 1913; *Republican News*, Feb. 14, 1913.

134. *Republican News*, June 25, 1913; the practice of everyone drinking from a common cup or dipper hung beside a bucket of water was continued in the logging camps, on the mill and in private homes for the duration of the operations at Cass.

135. *Pocahontas Times*, July 24, 1913.

136. *Pocahontas Times*, July 24, 1913. The *Republican News* reported this man's name as "Jerome" (*Republican News*, July 25, 1913).

137. *Pocahontas Times*, June 25, 1913; July 26, 1913.

138. *Pocahontas Times*, Oct. 30, 1913.

139. *Pocahontas Times*, Apr. 30, 1914; Feb. 11, 1915.

140. Emma Susan (Wade) "Granny" Bird was a midwife who helped many Cass babies enter the world. She also helped with sick people whenever needed (Dorothy Tacy, letter, Apr. 18, 1980).

141. Calomel is mercurous chloride, H_2Cl; other doctors to practice in Cass were Dr. Newsom, Dr. Miller, Dr. York, Dr. Price, Dr. McCutcheon, Dr. Roark, Dr. Bennett, Dr. Crabtree and Dr. Pittman. The doctor's office in later years was located in the old Company Office building (Ben Jackson, per. inter., Oct. 15, 1984; Dorothy Tacy, letter, Apr. 18, 1986).

142. Druggists were Dr. Ayers, Dr. Wilhide and Dr. Harry Hill (Jackson, per. inter., Oct. 15, 1984; Dorothy Tacy, letter, Apr. 18, 1986); the drugstore also contained a soda fountain which was a favorite gathering place for young people. Dr. Hill was famous for his good cokes. Gluck, Jan. 26, 1989.

143. B. Jackson, per. inter., Oct. 15, 1984; Gluck, Jan. 26, 1989. After the middle 1930s, there was no longer a dentist at Cass. Most people went to Dr. Charles S. Kramer at Marlinton.

144. *Pocahontas Times*, Sept. 18, 1913.

145. (Marlinton, W.Va.) *Pocahontas Independent*, Nov. 18, 1914.

146. *Pocahontas Independent*, Feb. 4, 1915.

147. *Pocahontas Times*, Feb. 4, 1915; This location is where Odessa Kane now lives.

148. *Pocahontas Times*, Feb. 25, 1915.

149. *Pocahontas Independent*, Feb. 24, 1915.

150. *Pocahontas Times*, Feb. 25, 1915.

151. *Pocahontas Times*, Apr. 22, 1915.
William Kitchen pleaded guilty and was sentenced to five years in the penitentiary for bigamy (*Marlinton Journal*, Apr. 14, 1915).

152. *Pocahontas Times*, June 30, 1915.

153. *Pocahontas Times*, Apr. 15, 1915; Apr. 22, 1915; Aug. 5, 1915; the Max Curry story at Cass was completed when his real estate in Cass was sold for debts in August, 1915 (*Marlinton Journal*, Aug. 4, 1915). Curry was one of over 60 criminals pardoned on Mar. 7, 1917, by outgoing Governor of West Virginia, Henry D. Hatfield (*Marlinton Journal*, Mar. 17, 1917). Curry had served less than two years of his sentence.

154. Edwin Palaszynski, "The Deer Creek Extract Plant." *Log Train*, 1985. 3.3.6.

155. *Pocahontas Times*, May 16, 1901; Polk's Directory 1904-05, p. 151.

156. *Pocahontas Times*, Aug. 11, 1904.

157. Polk's Directory 1918-19, p. 153.

158. Bruce Nelson, *Pocahontas Times*, Dec. 4, 1980; about 1940, the Mountain Inn closed and it was converted into apartments.

159. Common drinking dippers were made illegal in public places by the West Virginia Legislature in 1913 (*Republican News*, Apr. 25, 1913).

160. Nelson, *Pocahontas Times*, Dec. 4, 1980.

161. James Breakeiron managed the River View in the early 1920s and Sid Church managed it until about 1930. Scott Rose then lived in it but did not run it as a hotel (Nelson, *Pocahontas Times*, Dec. 4, 1980).

162. Nelson, *Pocahontas Times*, Dec. 4, 1980; Around 1930 the name of the Central Hotel was changed to the Alpha Hotel. In later years it was run by Mr. Cross's daughter, Belle, and was known as "Belle's Place." She operated it until the 1940s. It burned in the late sixties (Dorothy Tacy, letter, Oct. 14, 1986).

163. Nelson, *Pocahontas Times*, Dec. 4, 1980; after Burner, James Breakeiron operated the Loggers' Home for a time followed by Mike Mauzy in the mid-twenties. Stanley Roberson then came from Durbin to operate it. It closed in 1936 and stood empty until it was torn down about 1939 by the owner, Dr. Allen Burner of Durbin (Nelson, *Pocahontas Times*, Dec. 4, 1980; Eugene Burner, letter, Sept. 30, 1986).

164. Nelson, *Pocahontas Times*, Dec. 4, 1980.

165. *Pocahontas Times*, Jan. 3, 1907.

166. W. Blackhurst, *Of Men and a Mighty Mountain*, p. 76.

167. Rev. Harry Blackhurst moved to Cass in September, 1907. He was assigned the Arbovale Methodist Church from 1903-07, Dunlevie and Winterburn from 1907-08 and back to the Arbovale Methodist in 1910 (*Pocahontas Times*, Dec., 1907; *History of Pocahontas County*, p. 124; *Pocahontas Times*, June 7, 1915).

168. *Pocahontas Times*, June 17, 1915.

169. *Pocahontas Times*, Nov. 4, 1915.

170. *History of Pocahontas County*, p. 95.

171. W. Blackhurst, *Of Men and a Mighty Mountain*, p. 42.

172. *Pocahontas Times*, Nov. 4, 1915.

173. *Pocahontas Times*, Mar. 4, 1915.

174. *Pocahontas Times,* June 22, 1916.

175. *Pocahontas Times,* Nov. 4, 1915.

176. *Polk's Directory,* 1916-17.

177. *Pocahontas Times,* Nov. 4, 1915.

178. Roy C. Siple, letter to the author, Apr. 26, 1979.

179. A "dead man" was a large log buried deeply and covered with rocks. The cable from the bridge was dulled around the log.

180. Measurement, Aug. 18, 1985.

181. John Slavin and later Charlie Sheets had large gardens on this land for many years.

182. *Pocahontas Times,* Feb. 24, 1916; Mar. 19, 1916.

183. *Pocahontas Times,* July 13, 1916; Gluck, Jan. 26, 1989.

184. Gluck, Jan. 26, 1989.

185. *Pocahontas Times,* Dec. 21, 1916.

186. Gluck, Jan. 26, 1989.

187. *Marlinton Journal,* Feb. 21, 1917.

188. *Marlinton Journal,* Feb. 14, 1917.

189. Page Hamrick ran this business until 1926 when "Buck" Hamrick took it over (Ernestine Clarkson, Aug. 18, 1986).

190. *Pocahontas Times,* Mar. 1, 1917.

191. *Pocahontas Times,* Mar. 15, 1917.

192. *Pocahontas Times,* Apr. 19, 1917; the steel bridge was built in 1908 and replaced a wire swinging bridge. It was removed to near Campbelltown where the Brownsburg Road crosses Stanley Creek (*Pocahontas Times,* Apr. 19, 1917).

193. *Pocahontas Times,* July 18, 1918; the builder's nameplate on the cement bridge reads, "The Concrete Steel Bridge Co., Designers and Builders, Clarksburg, W.Va., 1917."

194. *Pocahontas Times,* May 10, 1917.

195. R. Hamrick, interview by Bagdon, May 22, 1975.

196. Charles N. Gum's body was returned on October 21, 1921, and was reburied by the Moose Lodge of Cass and Marlinton (*Pocahontas Times,* Nov. 13, 1921). *Pocahontas Times,* Nov. 17, 1988; *History of Pocahontas County,* pp. 48, 49.

197. *History of Pocahontas County,* pp. 48, 49; *Pocahontas Times,* July 26, 1917.

198. *Pocahontas Times,* July 27, 1916.

199. *Pocahontas Times,* Sept. 27, 1917; Nov. 1, 1917. A short history of Green Bank High School is found in the *Pocahontas Times,* July 14, 1988.

200. *Pocahontas Times,* Jan. 24, 1918.

201. *Pocahontas Times,* Jan. 31, 1918.

202. *Pocahontas Times,* Mar. 14, 1918; Mar. 21, 1918.

203. *Pocahontas Times,* Apr. 11, 1918.

204. *Pocahontas Times,* Mar. 21, 1918.

205. *Pocahontas Times,* Mar. 28, 1918.

206. *Pocahontas Times,* May 30, 1918.

207. *Pocahontas Times,* May 16, 1918.

208. In 1939, the Reverend Mr. Gray's collection of twenty thousand specimens of lichens, bryophytes and other plants was acquired by the Herbarium at West Virginia University at Morgantown [Weldon Boone, *History of Botany in West Virginia* (Parsons, W.Va.: McClain, 1965), p. 57].

209. Allen J. Blackhurst, per. inter.; this troublesome weed is known most places as Race Weed. Its Latin name is *Galinsoga ciliata* (Raf.) Blake.

210. Gluck, Jan. 26, 1989.

211. *Pocahontas Times,* July 18, 1918.

212. McNeel, *Durbin Route*, p. 93; *Pocahontas Times,* July 25, 1918.

213. *Pocahontas Times,* Oct. 31, 1918.

214. *Pocahontas Times,* Nov. 21, 1918.

215. *Pocahontas Times,* Dec. 26, 1918; Saphronia James was convicted of second-degree murder in April, 1919 (*Pocahontas Times,* Apr. 17, 1919). However, it was later shown that Eliza Crawford was killed by Charlie "Jellyroll" James, who was sent to prison for the murder (*Pocahontas Times,* Dec. 28, 1922).

216. Industrial Workers of the World. Paraphrased by opponents as "I Won't Work."

217. *Pocahontas Times,* Mar. 27, 1919.

218. *Pocahontas Times,* Apr. 10, 1919.

219. *Pocahontas Times,* Aug. 10, 1919.

220. Records of the W.Va. P.&P. Company, Aug., 1920.

221. Records of the W.Va. P.&P. Company, Jan. 1, 1920.

222. Records of the W.Va. P.&P. Company, Oct. 23, 1919.

223. Unless otherwise stated, names of persons living in various sections of town and other facts in this section, unless otherwise noted, are from: Dorothy Tacy, letter, Apr. 28, 1986, April 10, 1990; Ivan Clarkson, per. inter., Aug. 18, 1985; Ben Jackson, per. inter., May 31, 1984; Gluck, per. inter., Jan. 20, 1989.

224. This was called "Chestnut Ridge" in the original town plat.

225. "Buck" Hamrick took this over from his brother Page in 1926. On Jan. 9, 1941, the upstairs living quarters burned. This building was torn down. On the site a church was built by the Apostolic faith. George Alikakos bought the church and used it for storage for a time. Finally, it became "Granny's," a restaurant run by Avis Seldomridge. The flood of Nov. 4-5, 1985, washed this off its foundation and it broke up and was washed away.

226. The Kirkpatricks ran the "Greasy Spoon" until the 1940s. Georgia Ryder and her daughter, Mary Lee, next ran it. They were followed by a succession of people including Maggie Vint, Calvin Meeks and his wife, Roy Workman and his wife. The building was purchased by Jack Kane who had it torn down in the 1950s.

227. Dale White's grocery was converted into a dance hall. It was later torn down.

228. MacDonald's clothing store was taken over by Hoxie Meeks. He lived in the rear of the building and had a men's clothing store in front. It was later turned into a liquor store, run by Hoxie Meeks and then by Randy Taylor. A robbery occurred in the store in the late sixties and, not long afterward, the building partially burned and was torn down.

229. Brill's store was built around 1914. It was a popular restaurant and later a dry goods and clothing store. Roy Stewart clerked there for a time. The store was then closed for a time until a man from Romney opened it. Next it became secondhand store run by Walker. In 1943, Buck Hamrick bought the Brill building and ran a pool hall and restaurant. The family lived downstairs and in the back rooms upstairs. In May, 1961, Buck sold the building to Charles Gum who ran it as "Charlie's Place." He sold it to Geno Jones in June, 1969, who sold to Bernard and Jack Lane. Lane sold it to Jessie Brown Beard and Stella Blackhurst. It was a community used-clothing store and storage building. After the 1985 flood, the building caught afire when the adjacent Siegel building was being burned and was damaged so badly it was razed.

230. The Siegel Building was built around 1906. It was made of cement blocks from the Miracle Hollow Block Company. Siegel and later Siegel-Finger Company ran a clothing store in the upstairs of this building. Downstairs was the Old Home Restaurant run by Tex Blackhurst and others. After being burned out,

across the street Buck Hamrick lived and had a restaurant downstairs before moving to the Brill Building. Traveling preachers used the downstairs for services for a time before 1942. Alfred Collins had a theatre upstairs for a time in the early 1940s (Dorothy Tacy, letter, Oct. 4, 1986). The Greenbrier Repertory Theatre also occupied the building. It next became The Whistle Stop, a store featuring model trains. It was damaged so badly in the 1985 flood that it was condemned and razed.

231. The Cooper Building was originally a clothing store downstairs with living quarters upstairs. Later, Preston "Springy" Galford lived upstairs and had a garage and a beer parlor downstairs. Still later, it was a whiskey store. Then George Alikakos opened up a store for homemade ironware. The lower floor was unoccupied when the flood of 1985 damaged the building so severely that it was razed and burned.

232. The Logger's Home Hotel was empty for many years and became known as the "White Elephant." It was torn down by its owner, Alan E. Burner, around 1939.

233. This house burned.

234. The Central Hotel was later known as Belle's Place. It was closed in the 1950s and later burned.

235. John Reda's store was torn down in the 1940s.

236. For several years this was used as a State Store run by Tony Ware and Thermond Cosner. It was robbed in the late sixties and was later torn down.

237. The Sid Church home still remains in the curve of the Green Bank Road.

238. *Pocahontas Times*, Jan. 29, 1920.

239. Georgia Dougherty Robinson, per. inter., Aug. 17, 1985. The term "Nigger" used in the preceding paragraph in no way expresses a bias of the author. It is used to give historical accuracy only.

240. Measurements by the author, Aug. 17, 1985.

241. Robinson, per. inter., Aug. 17, 1985.

242. Ether Tyson and Maggie Myers Tyson, per. inter., Nov. 28, 1985.

243. E. Tyson and M. Tyson, per. inter., Nov. 28, 1985.

244. E. Tyson and M. Tyson, per. inter., Nov. 28, 1985.

245. Original plats, Pocahontas County Courthouse, Marlinton, W.Va.

246. *Pocahontas Times*, May 20, 1915.

247. Eugene Burner, letter, Sept. 30, 1986.

248. This is now the Cass Inn. The Cass Inn was established around 1970 by Robert and Nancy Clements. Next, Delbert Cosner and his wife ran it, then Penny Crist and her husband.

249. Gluck, Jan. 26, 1989.

250. Wallace and Wallace started a funeral business at Lewisburg. Bodies were taken there for embalming and returned for the "wake" and funeral. A funeral home was opened by Wallace and Wallace at Arbovale and the custom of having a wake at the home and a funeral in the church was gradually discontinued. The funeral director for many years was Paul Findlay.

251. *Pocahontas Times*, Nov. 3, 1921; July 30, 1922.

252. *Pocahontas Times*, May 1, 1919; Sept. 4, 1919; July 21, 1921; Apr. 5, 1923; June 21, 1923; May 3, 1923.

253. Gluck, Jan. 26, 1989.

254. *Pocahontas Times*, Aug. 25, 1921.

255. *Pocahontas Times*, May 12, 1921.

256. *Pocahontas Times*, July 19, 1920.

257. *Pocahontas Times*, Dec. 16, 1920.

258. *Pocahontas Times*, Jan. 6, 1921.

259. *Pocahontas Times,* Apr. 13, 1922.

260. *Pocahontas Times,* Nov. 16, 1922.

261. *Pocahontas Times,* Dec. 28, 1922.

262. B. Jackson, per. inter., May 22, 1983.

263. *Pocahontas Times,* Dec. 28, 1922; Apr. 12, 1923; May 9, 1923; Oct. 11, 1923; June 19, 1924.

264. McNeel, *Durbin Route,* p. 49.

265. *Pocahontas Times,* Oct. 11, 1923.

266. Later known as Sheet's Cave; now known as Cass Cave.

267. *Pocahontas Times,* Aug. 2, 1923.

268. *Pocahontas Times,* Aug. 30, 1923.

269. Gluck, Jan. 26, 1989.

270. *Pocahontas Times,* Nov. 15, 1923.

271. *West Virginia Blue Book,* 1924.

272. Church Cornerstone, May 29, 1984; *Pocahontas County Deed Book No. 13,* p. 254.

273. *Pocahontas Times,* Apr. 10, 1924; the Reverend Mr. Blackhurst remained as minister of the church until around 1944 when the congregation became so small the church was closed. The building was sold in 1951 and became the First Baptist Church of Cass (*Pocahontas County Deed Book No. 28,* p. 32).

274. L. Jackson, per. inter., May 31, 1984.

275. *Pocahontas Times,* Jan. 3, 1921.

276. *Polk's Directory,* 1923-24.

277. *Pocahontas Times,* Apr. 10, 1924. L. Jackson, per. inter., Oct. 15, 1982.

278. *Pocahontas Times,* June 19, 1924.

279. *Pocahontas Times,* Sept. 18, 1924.

280. *Pocahontas Times,* Jan. 22, 1925.

281. Valley Clarkson Wilkes, per. inter., June 10, 1981; B. Jackson, per. inter., May 22, 1983.

282. *Pocahontas Times,* Dec. 3, 1925.

283. *Pocahontas Times,* Feb. 12, 1925.

284. *Pocahontas Times,* Feb. 26, 1925.

285. *Pocahontas Deed Book No. 14,* p. 109; *Pocahontas Times,* May 26, 1927; the Cass M. E. Church South was a part of the Green Bank Methodist Circuit. Ministers who served there are: Rev. L. S. Shires, 1926-27; Rev. George E. Pope, 1927-31; Rev. R. D. Marshall, 1931-35; Rev. R. B. Moore, 1935-39; Rev. Quade R. Arbogast, 1939-52; Rev. Jack Justice, 1952-53; Rev. J. B. Hanlon, 1953-summer; Rev. Okey Cooper, 1954-55; Rev. Ed Thomas, 1955-57; Rev. Charles E. Potts, 1957-60; Rev. Paul Pepoon, 1960-61; the Rev. Mr. Markley, 1964-71; Rev. Ezra Bennett, 1971-74; Rev. Kenneth Montgomery, 1974-76; Rev. T. Gregory Lewis, 1976-79; Rev. Eddie Kyle, 1979 (*History of Pocahontas County,* p. 131).

286. *Pocahontas Times,* Nov. 3, 1921.

287. *History of Pocahontas County,* p. 95; Gluck, per. inter., Jan. 26, 1989.

288. The Junior High Department remained until 1932 when the ninth grade students were trucked to Green Bank High School (*Pocahontas County History,* p. 95).

289. *Pocahontas Times,* May 20, 1926.

290. *Pocahontas Times,* Oct. 11, 1928.

291. Gluck, per. inter., Jan. 26, 1989.

292. *Pocahontas Times,* Feb. 12, 1925.

293. *Pocahontas Times,* Feb. 18, 1926.

294. *Pocahontas Times,* May 13, 1926.

295. After Mr. Hamrick quit plowing, Levi Galford, also with a team of oxen, took over. He was followed by "Tick" Wooddell who used a tractor.

296. B. Jackson, per. inter., May 31, 1984.

297. Gluck, per. inter., Jan. 26, 1989; I. Clarkson, per. inter., May 31, 1984.

298. *Pocahontas Times,* May 20, 1926; May 27, 1926; June 10, 1926; Aug. 26, 1926; July 26, 1928.

299. *Pocahontas Times,* Oct. 11, 1928.

300. *Pocahontas Times,* July 26, 1928.

301. *Pocahontas Times,* Dec. 6, 1928.

302. Gluck, per. inter., Jan. 26, 1989.

303. *Pocahontas Times,* May 2, 1929; John Philip Sousa's first radio performance was sponsored by the Chevrolet Motor Company to celebrate the selling of over a half million new 6-cylinder cars in four months time. (*Pocahontas Times,* May 2, 1929).

304. When radios became more common in later years, many persons listened to the early morning broadcasts from WSM Nashville, WLW Cincinnati and KDKA Pittsburgh and thrilled to the Sons of the Pioneers singing, "Cool Water," "Drifting Tumbleweeds," "Kentucky," and other favorites. "Death Valley Days," narrated by Ronald Reagan and "Gang Busters" provided excitement and drama. On Saturday nights the "Grand Ole Opry" with Minnie Pearl, Roy Acuff, Grandpa Jones, The Carter Family and many others entertained the entire family.

305. Gluck, per. inter., Jan. 26, 1989.

306. *Pocahontas Times,* Sept. 14, 1939.

307. *Pocahontas Times,* Feb. 21, 1929.

308. *Pocahontas Times,* Aug. 15, 1929.

309. McNeel, *Durbin Route,* p. 95.

310. *Pocahontas Times,* Oct. 17, 1929.

311. *Pocahontas Times,* Oct. 17, 1929.

312. Pearl R. Clarkson, letter to the author, Sept. 10, 1985.

313. Thomas Dixon, "Parlor Car to Durbin," C&O Historicasl Newsletter, Jan. 1973.

314. *Pocahontas Times,* July 10, 1930.

315. Gluck, per. inter., Jan. 26, 1989; Harry E. Duncan, *Do I Want to Go Home?,* p. 14.

316. *Pocahontas Times,* Apr. 17, 1930.

317. *Pocahontas Times,* Aug. 7, 1930.

318. *Pocahontas Times,* Aug. 28, 1930.

319. Ruth Taliercio Wagner, letter to the author, Dec. 22, 1984.

320. *Pocahontas Times,* Dec. 31, 1931.

321. Later telephone operators were Eva Smith, Miss Conebs, Peggy Thomas, Caroline Tacy, Grace (Geigher) Galford, Mary Geigher, Madeline Barlow, Dolly Nelson, Betty Tacy, Lorene Thomas, Ruth Carpenter, Ramona Summerfield, and Virginia Terry (Dorothy Tacy, letter, Apr. 18, 1986; Ivan Clarkson, per. inter., Mar. 10, 1984).

322. *Pocahontas Times,* June 2, 1932.

323. I. Clarkson, per. inter., Mar. 10, 1984.

324. B. Jackson, per. inter., Oct. 15, 1984.

325. *Pocahontas Times,* May 12, 1932.

326. *Pocahontas Times,* June 2, 1932.

327. *Marlinton Journal,* Mar. 9, 1933.

328. *Marlinton Journal,* May 11, 1933.

329. Duncan, *Do I Want to Go Home?,* p. 17.

330. B. Jackson, per. inter., May 29, 1984.

331. Gluck, per. inter., Jan. 26, 1989.

332. *Pocahontas Times,* Feb. 11, 1932; May 5, 1934; May 17, 1934.

333. *Pocahontas Times,* July 11, 1932.

334. *Pocahontas Times,* July 11, 1936.

335. Duncan, *Do I Want to Go Home?,* p. 22.

336. *Pocahontas Times,* June 29, 1933.

337. *History of Pocahontas County,* p. 165.

338. Duncan, *Do I Want to Go Home?,* p. 17.

339. *Pocahontas Times,* Apr. 26, 1934; June 7, 1934.

340. *Pocahontas Times,* Apr. 20, 1911.

341. *Pocahontas Times,* Nov. 15, 1934.

342. Receipts of William Simmons from William M. Sampson.

343. Receipts of Simmons from Sampson.

344. *Pocahontas Times,* July 1, 1935; July 8, 1935; original copy of Picnic Notice.

345. I. Clarkson, per. inter., Sept. 29, 1985. This cemetery is now overgrown with brush. There are many tombstones still standing, but the graves of the disinterred remains could not be located in 1988.

346. *Pocahontas Times,* Jan. 17, 1935.

347. Ernestine Clarkson, per. inter., May 30, 1984.

348. *Pocahontas Times,* Jan. 9, 1936; Feb. 13, 1936.

349. *Pocahontas Times,* Feb. 20, 1936.

350. *Marlinton Journal,* Sept. 8, 1932.

351. Gluck, per. inter., Jan 26, 1989.

352. Simmons, per. inter., June 6, 1985.

353. *Marlinton Journal,* Aug. 5, 1937; Gluck, per. inter., Jan. 26, 1989.

354. *Pocahontas Times,* Sept. 17, 1936; Dec. 17, 1936.

355. Jennings Bradford, per. inter., Apr. 15, 1985.

356. *Pocahontas Times,* Feb. 4, 1937.

357. B. Jackson, per. inter., Oct. 15, 1984; I. Clarkson, per. inter., May 6, 1985.

358. *Pocahontas Times,* Mar. 25, 1937.

359. *Pocahontas Times,* Mar. 25, 1937; Oct. 14, 1937.

360. *Pocahontas Times,* Aug. 5, 1937.

361. *Pocahontas Times,* Feb. 21, 1938.

362. *Marlinton Journal,* July 8, 1973.

363. *Pocahontas Times,* July 14, 1938.

364. Gluck, per. inter., Jan. 26, 1989.

365. *Marlinton Journal,* Nov. 10, 1938.

366. *Pocahontas Times,* Mar. 23, 1939.

367. *Marlinton Journal,* July 8, 1937.

368. *Pocahontas Times,* Dec. 21, 1939.

369. *Marlinton Journal,* Oct. 15, 1939.

370. *Pocahontas Times,* July 27, 1939.

371. *Pocahontas Times,* Oct. 26, 1939; *Marlinton Journal,* Oct. 26, 1939.

372. Upon Mr. Kane's death in 1945, his sons Ernest "Red" and John M. Jr. "Jack" took over his business. Jack continued to run the store until he died in 1980. His wife, Odessa, sold the business to Benny Simmons in 1984.

Natives of Cass remember well the meat and sausage prepared by butcher "Ted" Blackhurst. Maggie Vint Meeks, "Polly" McPherson, Johnny Varner and "Beaty" Slavin were longtime clerks. Sam Jackson delivered groceries in the early days. Ollie Meeks worked filling shelves (Ben Jackson, per. inter., Oct. 15, 1984).

373. E. Clarkson, per. inter., June 5, 1985.

374. *Pocahontas Times,* Aug. 29, 1940; persons injured in the wreck were: Ruth Hamrick, age thirteen, fractured right leg and bruises; Mrs. John Reda,

severe chest injuries; Ernestine Hamrick, tooth knocked out; Lucille Ervine, Evelyn Long and Ruby Miller, cuts and bruises (*Marlinton Journal*, Aug. 22, 1940).

375. *Marlinton Journal*, Oct. 31, 1940; Nov. 7, 1940.

376. *Marlinton Journal*, May 1, 1941.

377. M. Clarkson, per. inter., May 2, 1942.

378. I. Clarkson, per. inter., July 2, 1983; Bud Wolfe, per. inter., Feb. 22, 1985.

379. *Pocahontas Times*, Aug. 17, 1944.

380. *Pocahontas Times*, Oct. 26, 1944; Apr. 26, 1945; June 27, 1945; Nov. 17, 1988.

381. *Pocahontas Times*, June 21, 1945.

382. *Pocahontas Times*, Apr. 15, 1943; a brief biography of E. P. Shaffer is found in Appendix C.

383. *Pocahontas Times*, Aug. 26, 1943.

384. *Pocahontas Times*, Dec. 2, 1943.

385. B. Jackson, per. inter., Oct. 15, 1984; Joe Wooddell left as town policeman in 1947 (*W.Va. Blue Book*, 1947). A listing of other town policemen is found in Appendix I.

386. W.Va. P.&P. Co. Shop Time Book, Aug., 1944-Sept. 1, 1945.

387. *Pocahontas Times*, Aug. 21, 1947.

388. Anna Plyler Ervine, letter to the author, Nov. 10, 1985. In 1947, Oney sold the store to Stewart Swink and Eldon Galford. About a year later he bought it back and ran it as a store and garage until 1966. His daughter Anna and her husband, Dewey Ervine, ran the store about eleven months then sold to Caleb Haislop. In 1966 or 1967, Charles Gum bought the building and put in a tavern. In 1980, he sold to Van Roberts who, in turn, sold to a Tumblin in 1985.

389. *Pocahontas Times*, Jan. 16, 1947.

390. Gluck, per. inter., Jan. 26, 1989.

391. *Pocahontas Times*, Sept. 8, 1949; E. Clarkson, per. inter., Aug. 18, 1985.

392. *History of Pocahontas County*, p. 95; *Pocahontas Times*, Nov. 11, 1988.

393. Ether Tyson, per. inter., Nov. 22, 1985.

394. An even greater loss, perhaps, in the foundry fire was the diary of Allen J. "Farmer" Blackhurst. Farmer had kept a diary of events concerning the lumber job from the time he started working there in 1912.

395. *Pocahontas Times*, Jan. 15, 1953.

396. *Pocahontas Times*, May 31, 1956.

397. *Pocahontas Times*, May 31, 1953.

398. *Pocahontas Times*, Aug. 30, 1951; July 12, 1951; July 26, 1951; Aug. 21, 1951; Aug. 23, 1951.

399. W. Blackhurst, *Riders of the Flood*, 199 pp.

400. McNeel, *Durbin Route*, p. 82.

401. *Pocahontas Times*, Jan. 19, 1956; the Salk polio virus was announced on April 12, 1955, at a medical meeting at the University of Michigan but it was not available in quantity until 1956. Douglas Hand, "1955: The Making of Polio Vaccine," *American Heritage of Invention and Technology*, 1985. 1: 54-57.

402. *Pocahontas Times*, Nov. 29, 1956.

403. *Pocahontas Times*, Dec. 13, 1956.

404. *Pocahontas Times*, Mar. 6, 1958.

405. McNeel, *Durbin Route*, p. 57.

406. McNeel, *Durbin Route*, p. 57: During the next three decades, steam locomotives occasionally ran on the Greenbrier line in connection with the Cass Scenic Railroad. On December 9, 1964, Meadow River Lumber Company Shay No. 7 was acquired by the Cass Scenic Railroad and ran under its own power to

Cass. On Dec. 14, 1966, a second Meadow River engine, Heisler No. 6, made the same trip.

The Cass to Durbin section of the line was used many times by Cass Scenic Railroad engines en route to or from the Forest Festival in Elkins, the Strawberry Festival in Buckhannon or hauling tourists along the Greenbrier River. Regularly scheduled trips to Durbin were begun on July 7, 1984, operating on Saturdays, Sundays and Tuesdays.

This portion of the track was extensively damaged by the flood of Nov. 4-5, 1985, forcing cancellation of this run in 1986. Plans were made to repair the track and reinstitute this popular trip. These plans have not been carried out.

A steam-powered locomotive returned to the Greenbrier line in the summer and fall of 1971 when the former Reading Railroad No. 2102 pulled nine Ronceverte-to-Durbin excursion trains. This was the largest 2-cylinder locomotive to operate on the Greenbrier.

The last steam engine to run on the Greenbrier line below Cass was Cass Scenic Railroad Heisler No. 6 which pulled a special train to Pioneer Days in Marlinton from July 6-8, 1978 (McNeel, *Durbin Route*).

407. McNeel, *Durbin Route*, p. 82.

408. Notice, June 25, 1960.

409. *Pocahontas Times*, Aug. 4, 1960.

410. R. Clarkson, *Tumult on the Mountains*, pp. 34, 35 and map.

411. *History of Pocahontas County*, p. 151.

412. W. Blackhurst, *Sawdust in Your Eyes*.

413. R. Clarkson, *Tumult on the Mountains*, 410 pp.

414. W. Blackhurst, *Of Men and a Mighty Mountain*.

415. *Pocahontas Times*, Feb. 25, 1965.

416. *Pocahontas Times*, May 12, 1966; Sept. 1, 1966.

417. I. Clarkson, per. inter., Apr. 24, 1985.

418. *Pocahontas Times*, Mar. 6, 1969.

419. *Pocahontas Times*, July 23, 1970.

420. W. Blackhurst, *Mixed Harvest*.

421. W. Blackhurst, *Afterglow*.

422. *Pocahontas Times*, Feb. 25, 1971.

423. *Pocahontas Times*, May 13, 1971; May 27, 1971; July 19, 1973; June 27, 1974.

424. *Pocahontas Times*, Sept. 14, 1972.

425. *Pocahontas Times*, Sept. 13, 1973; Jan. 17, 1974.

426. (Richwood, W.Va.) *Nicholas County News Leader*, Feb. 5, 1975.

427. Marlene Chittum, letter to the author, July 7, 1984.

428. *Pocahontas Times*, Sept. 15, 1983.

429. *Pocahontas Times*, Mar. 21, 1974.

430. *Pocahontas Times*, Dec. 11, 1975.

431. McNeel, *Durbin Route*, p. 124.

432. *Pocahontas Times*, Jan. 8, 1976.

433. *Pocahontas Times*, Feb. 19, 1976.

434. *Pocahontas Times*, July 1, 1976.

435. *Pocahontas Times*, July 1, 1976.

436. *Pocahontas Times*, Jan. 20, 1977.

437. Duncan, *Do I Want to Go Home?*

438. I. Clarkson, per. inter., Apr. 24, 1985.

439. An excellent 2-page photograph of this waterfall is found in the National Geographic 125: p. 825, June, 1964; *Pocahontas Times*, Sept. 1, 1977.

440. *Pocahontas Times*, Aug. 10, 1978.

441. *Pocahontas Times*, Nov. 2, 1978.

442. *Pocahontas Times*, Jan. 4, 1979.

443. *Pocahontas Times*, Jan. 4, 1979; Ivan Clarkson, per. inter., July 2, 1983.

444. *Pocahontas Times*, June 21, 1979.

445. *Pocahontas Times*, Sept. 13, 1979; Sept. 20, 1979; Oct. 18, 1979.

446. *Pocahontas Times*, Jan. 18, 1979; Apr. 5, 1979.

447. *Pocahontas Times*, Apr. 26, 1979; EPA is the Environmental Protection Agency; ARC is the Appalachian Regional Commission; FHA is the Farmer's Home Administration; Jan. 1, 1982.

448. *Pocahontas Times*, Jan. 1, 1981.

449. *Pocahontas Times*, Feb. 12, 1981.

450. Karen Clarkson, unpub. mms., 1981.

451. *Pocahontas Times*, July 28, 1981.

452. *Pocahontas Times*, May 7, 1987.

453. *Pocahontas Times*, Oct. 1, 1981.

454. *Pocahontas Times*, Jan. 3, 1983.

455. *Pocahontas Times*, Dec. 22, 1983.

456. *The Log Train* 1:1-2. 1982.

457. *Pocahontas County Deed Book No. 170*, p. 403, Willis Hertig, per. inter., May 5, 1983.

458. *Pocahontas Times*, Jan. 6, 1983.

459. I. Clarkson, per. inter., Aug. 18, 1985.

460. *Pocahontas Times*, Apr. 26, 1984.

461. I. Clarkson, per. inter., Oct. 1, 1984.

462. *Pocahontas Times*, Dec. 6, 1984.

463. *Pocahontas Times*, Mar. 14, 1985.

464. E. Clarkson, per. inter., Aug. 18, 1985.

465. Marvin O. Hill, "National Weather Service Report," *Pocahontas Times*, Jan. 2, 1986.

466. Truman Miller, "There's No New Thing Under the Sun" in *Pocahontas County Floods*, compiled by Craig Smith (Marlinton: Pocahontas County Historical Society, 1986), pp. 31-33.

467. Snider, Mary. Letter to the author, Feb. 23, 1988.

468. *Pocahontas Times*, May 14, 1987.

469. *Pocahontas Times*, Aug. 20, 1987; Nov. 12, 1987. Officers of the CVF & RC were President Mike O'Brien; Rescue Chief, Willa Queen.

470. *Pocahontas Times*, Nov. 12, 1987.

471. *Pocahontas Times*, Jan. 7, 1988.

472. *Pocahontas Times*, Oct. 8, 1987.

473. *Pocahontas Times*, Dec. 8, 1988.

474. *Pocahontas Times*, June 23, 1988.

475. *Pocahontas Times*, July 14, 1988; Nov. 24, 1988.

CHAPTER XVI

CASS SCENIC RAILROAD

1. John P. Killoran, *The Cass Collection, Vol. 1* (Scott Depot, W.Va.: Trackage Rights, 1982), p.4.

2. I. Clarkson, per. inter., Aug. 19, 1975.
3. I. Clarkson, per. inter., Aug. 19, 1975.
4. Woodrow Sharp, interview by Bagdon, May 28, 1976.
5. I. Clarkson, per. inter., Aug. 16, 1975.
6. James Comstock, (Richwood, W.Va.) *West Virginia Hillbilly,* Oct. 15, 1960.
7. Comstock, *W.Va. Hillbilly,* Oct. 15, 1960.
8. Comstock, *W.Va. Hillbilly,* Oct. 15, 1960.
9. Comstock, *W.Va. Hillbilly,* Oct. 15, 1960.
10. Russell Baum, *W.Va. Hillbilly,* Oct. 22, 1960.
11. Comstock, *W.Va. Hillbilly,* Oct. 15, 1960.
12. *Pocahontas Times,* Oct. 27, 1960.
13. *Pocahontas Times,* Nov. 24, 1960; *W.Va. Hillbilly,* Dec. 3, 1960.
14. *Pocahontas Times,* May 4, 1961.
15. *Pocahontas County Deed Book No. 108,* pp. 310-320.
16. *Pocahontas Times,* May 14, 1961.
17. *Pocahontas Times,* June 29, 1961.
18. The West Virginia Conservation Commission was replaced by the Department of National Resources on July 1, 1961.
19. *Pocahontas County Deed Book No. 108,* p. 310.
20. In the publicity surrounding the acquisition of the Cass Scenic Railroad, some persons were given credit and other deserving persons were omitted. In an attempt to set the record straight, Jim Comstock wrote the following to show how various persons formed links in a chain of events leading up to the purchase.

"I won't be long on this. I just want to give you some links and may the Lord help me for the missing ones. Most important man was the Pennsylvania, Ralph Baum. Remember? He was a steam buff and he came down for the last ride in the Mower cut-out. He spent the night at Bill Sperry's motel and told Bill that it was a shame to lose that railroad when other places were buying them up as tourist attractions. That makes Bill most important man because he didn't simply yawn and agree, he got on the phone and called me. 'You are covering the legislature for your paper,' he said. 'Tell them to buy the Cass Railroad.' Next day I went to see the governor and that made me most important man. But a Republican in West Virginia doesn't do a thing like that on his own. That makes J. C. Cruikshank most important man because I asked him to go along and be my ticket. I don't know of another soul who would have gone on a wacky mission like this. The governor became the most important man because he said to see Warden Lane, then head of the Conservation Department which for some crazy reason had control of such things. Warden then became most important man, until J. C. stepped in again and became most important by introducing the resolution to buy the thing. He got it again when somebody reported to me that he had strong words with the governor, who feared criticism for such a purchase. 'I didn't know I voted for a coward,' J. C. supposedly told him. Then Howard Pauley became most important man for a bit of finangaling on the passing of the resolution, and Hans McCourt became most important for something he did with budget juggling. Then Jack Kane was most important man for urging and fighting night and day. Those are the links, or a pitiful small few of them" (Comstock, *W.Va. Hillbilly*).

21. *Pocahontas Times,* Jan. 24, 1963.
22. As it turned out, weekend crowds flocking to Cass in 1963 to ride the scenic railroad left the State with no alternative but to operate No. 1 in late summer as a helper engine. Doubleheading with No. 4, it provided the extra power required to push a heavily loaded tourist train up the steepest part of the tracks without causing potential danger of a runaway train.

23. Previously the home of S. D. Huff.

24. *Pocahontas Times,* June 20, 1963.

25. *Pocahontas Times,* July 4, 1963.

26. *Pocahontas Times,* July 25, 1963.

27. *Pocahontas Times,* July 25, 1963.

28. *Pocahontas Times,* Aug. 15, 1963.

29. *Pocahontas Times,* Mar. 5, 1964.

30. *Pocahontas Times,* Mar. 12, 1964.

31. *Pocahontas Times,* May 14, 1964.

32. *Pocahontas Times,* May 14, 1964.

33. *Pocahontas County Deed Book No. 112,* p. 231.

34. *Pocahontas Times,* June 4, 1964.

35. *Pocahontas Times,* July 9, 1964.

36. I. Clarkson, per. inter., Mar. 11, 1984.

37. *W.Va. Hillbilly,* Nov. 28, 1964; July 24, 1964.

38. *Pocahontas Times,* Oct. 15, 1964.

39. *Pocahontas Times,* Dec. 17, 1964. Raymond F. Schuck, letter to the author, May 28, 1986.

40. R. Clarkson, *Tumult on the Mountains;* W. Blackhurst, *Riders of the Flood;* W. Blackhurst, *Sawdust in Your Eyes.*

41. *Pocahontas Times,* July 12, 1965; Aug. 26, 1965.

42. *Pocahontas Times,* July 29, 1965.

43. A study outlining these ideas headed by Rev. Clifford M. Lewis, SJ of Wheeling College assisted by Roy B. Clarkson and others was presented to the State DNR. No action was taken on these plans.

44. *Pocahontas Times,* July 12, 1965.

45. *Pocahontas Times,* Apr. 28, 1966.

46. *Pocahontas Times,* July 7, 1966.

47. *Pocahontas Times,* July 7, 1966.

48. *Pocahontas Times,* Dec. 8, 1966.

49. *Pocahontas Times,* Dec. 8, 1966.

50. *Pocahontas Times,* Nov. 23, 1967.

51. *Pocahontas Times,* May 16, 1968.

52. *Pocahontas Times,* Nov. 6, 1968.

53. *History of Pocahontas County,* p. 8.

54. The *Inter-Mountain:* Dec. 3, 1970. As of this writing, 1988, it had not been refurbished and was stored on the sidetrack near the Cass Shop.

55. The *Inter-Mountain,* Dec. 3, 1970; Killoran, *The Cass Collection,* Vol 2: 55; Fizer, George A., adding to the roster at Cass. *The Log Train* 6.3 (1989).

56. Koch, *Shay Locomotive,* p. 457; Killoran, *The Cass Collection,* Vol. 2: p. 55; Fizer, *The Log Train* 6.3 (1989).

57. *Pocahontas Times,* Sept. 3, 1972.

58. *Pocahontas Times,* May 13, 1971.

59. *Pocahontas Times,* May 27, 1972.

60. Koch, *The Shay Locomotive.*

61. *Pocahontas Times,* June 8, 1972.

62. *Pocahontas Times,* June 8, 1972.

63. *Pocahontas Times,* July 27, 1972.

64. *Pocahontas Times,* July 27, 1972.

65. *Pocahontas Times,* July 19, 1973.

66. *Pocahontas Times,* Nov. 8, 1973.

67. *Pocahontas Times,* Nov. 6, 1986.

68. *Pocahontas Times,* May 8, 1975.

69. All of these structures have since been destroyed by fire. To date nothing has been done concerning these ideas for a logging museum at Cass. Although in 1983, the state did purchase the grade school building for the purpose of establishing such a museum (Willis Hertig, Deputy Director, DNR, May 9, 1983; per. inter., *Pocahontas County Deed Book No. 10,* p. 403).

70. (Charleston, W.Va.) *Charleston Gazette,* May 24, 1976; *Pocahontas Times,* July 1, 1976.

71. *Pocahontas County Deed Book No. 140,* 19-38.

72. *Pocahontas Times,* May 12, 1977.

73. *Pocahontas Times,* Aug. 25, 1977.

74. *Pocahontas Times,* Nov. 3, 1977.

75. *Pocahontas Times,* Aug. 10, 1978.

76. *Pocahontas Times,* May 17, 1979.

77. *Pocahontas Times,* May 17, 1979.

78. *Pocahontas Times,* Sept. 4, 1980; *The Log Train* 5.3 (1987): 2-20. For a detailed account of the construction, acquisition, moving and restoration of Western Maryland Shay No. 6 see the following: Bartels, Fred, The Birth of the Big Six; *The Log Train* 5.3 (1987); Bartels, Western Maryland Shay No. 6 – from Baltimore to Cass; *The Log Train* 5.4 (1988); Bartels, Restoration of the Big Six; *The Log Train* 6.1 (1988); Two Locomotives for Baltimore; *The Log Train* 6.1 (1988).

79. N.p., *Cass Chronicle 3* (No. 1): Summer, 1981; n.p., *Chessie News,* June, 1980. Schuck, letter to the author, May 28, 1986.

80. McNeel, *Durbin Route,* p. 70.

81. *Pocahontas Times,* Jan. 1, 1981.

82. *Pocahontas Times,* June 3, 1982.

83. Mark Jones, *Pocahontas Times,* Mar. 31, 1983.

84. *Pocahontas Times,* June 30, 1983.

85. *Pocahontas Times,* July 14, 1983.

86. Snider, Mary, letter to the author, Feb. 23, 1988.

87. *Pocahontas Times,* Sept. 15, 1983.

88. *Pocahontas Times,* Sept. 29, 1983.

89. *Pocahontas Times,* Nov. 3, 1983.

90. *Pocahontas Times,* Mar. 1, 1984.

91. *Pocahontas Times,* May 24, 1984.

92. *Pocahontas Times,* May 24, 1984.

93. *Pocahontas Times,* May 24, 1984.

94. Snider, letter to the author, Feb. 23, 1988.

95. *Pocahontas Times,* Dec. 6, 1984.

96. *Pocahontas Times,* July 24, 1986. As of 1988, the tracks from Cass to Durbin have not been repaired and there seems little hope of their ever being repaired.

97. Snider, letter to the author, Feb. 23, 1988.

98. *Pocahontas Times,* Nov., 1985.

99. *Pocahontas Times,* May 24, 1986; Jeff Harpold, "Cass Scenic Railroad of West Virginia." *Wonderful West Virginia* 50(6): Aug., 1986. pp. 2-7.

100. Snider, letter to the author, Feb. 23, 1988.

101. *Pocahontas Times,* Feb. 5, 1987.

102. *Pocahontas Times,* Apr. 2, 1987; *Running Extra.* Mountain State Railroad and Logging Historical Association, Mar., 1987.

103. Snider, letter to the author, Feb. 23, 1988.

104. *Pocahontas Times,* Oct. 22, 1987; *Running Extra.* Mountain State Railroad and Logging Historical Association Newsletter. Oct.-Nov., 1987.

105. *Running Extra.* Oct.-Nov., 1987; *Pocahontas Times,* Jan. 14, 1988.

106. *Pocahontas Times,* Apr. 7, 1988.

107. *Pocahontas Times,* May 5, 1988; Aug. 18, 1988.

108. *Pocahontas Times,* Sept. 8, 1988; Sept. 29, 1988.

109. *Pocahontas Times,* Apr. 7, 1988; June 16, 1988; *Sunday Gazette-Mail,* June 12, 1988, "The First Cass Railroad Festival, June 17-19, 1988" supplement prepared by the Advertising and Promotions Division of the West Virginia Department of Commerce.

110. *Pocahontas Times,* Nov. 24, 1988.

WORKS CITED

BOOKS

Blackhurst, Warren E. *Riders of the Flood*. New York: Vantage Press, 1954. 199 pp.

— — —. *Sawdust in Your Eyes*. Parsons, W.Va.: McClain, 1963. 216 pp.

— — —. *Of Men and a Mighty Mountain*. Parsons, W.Va.: McClain, 1965. 216 pp.

— — —. *Your Train Ride Through History*. Parsons, W.Va.: McClain, 1968. 17 pp.

— — —. *Mixed Harvest*. Parsons, W.Va.: McClain, 1970. 202 pp.

— — —. *Afterglow*. Parsons, W.Va.: McClain, 1972. 231 pp.

Boone, Weldon. *History of Botany in West Virginia*. Parsons, W.Va.: McClain, 1965. 196 pp.

Bryant, Ralph Clement. *Logging*. New York: John Wiley & Sons, 1914. 590 pp.

Callahan, James Morton. *History of West Virginia, Old and New*, 2 Vols. Chicago: American Historical Society, 1923. 723 pp. and 648 pp.

Clarkson, Roy B. *Tumult on the Mountains—Lumbering in West Virginia 1770-1920*. Parsons, W.Va.: McClain, 1964. 410 pp.

— — —. "The Greenbrier River" in *Rolling Rivers: An Encyclopedia of America's Rivers*. ed. Richard A. Bartlett. New York: McGraw-Hll, 1984. pp. 114-18.

— — —. "Flora of the Monongahela National Forest." Dissertation, West Virginia University, 1960. 616 pp.

Cole, J. R. *History of Greenbrier County*. Lewisburg, W.Va.: published by the author, 1918. 347 pp.

Conley, Phil and William T. Doherty. *West Virginia History*. Charleston, W.Va.: Education Foundation, 1974. 494 pp.

Deike, George H., III. *Logging South Cheat. The History of the Snowshoe Resort Lands*. Published by the author, 1978. 55 pp.

Duncan, Harry E. *Do I Want to Go Home?* Charleston, W.Va.: published by the author. 34 pp.

Griffin, Sam. *West Virginia Central and Pittsburg Railroad*. Parsons, W.Va.: McClain, 1981. 100 pp.

Holy Bible, Revised Standard Version. New York: Thomas Nelson & Sons, 1946. 997 + 293 pp.

Killoran, John P. *The Cass Collection, Vol. 1*. Scott Depot, W.Va.: Trackage Rights, 1982. 52 pp.

— — —. *The Cass Collection, Vol. 2*. Scott Depot, W.Va.: Trackage Rights, 1983. 54 pp.

Killough, Edward M. *History of the Western Maryland Railway Company*, Rev. ed. Baltimore: Voluntary Relief Press of the Western Maryland Railway Company, 1940. 128 pp.

Koch, Michael. *Shay Locomotive—Titian of the Timber*. Denver: World Press, 1971. 488 pp.

Labbe, John T. and Vernon Goe. *Railroads in the Woods*. Berkeley: Howell-North Books, 1961. 269 pp.

Maury, W. F. and W. M. Fontaine. *Resources of West Virginia*. Wheeling, W.Va.: Register Company, 1876. 430 pp.

McClintic, C. F. ed. *Historical Booklet, Greenbrier County, 160 Anniversary, 1778-1938*. Charleston, W.Va.: Jarrett Printing Company, 1938. 52 pp.

McKim, C. R. *50 Year History of the Monongahela National Forest*, n.p., 1970. 66 pp.

McNeel, William P. "Lumber Industry in Pocahontas County" in *History of Pocahontas County, West Virginia, 1981*. Marlinton, W.Va.: Pocahontas County Historical Society, 1981. pp. 176-83.

– – –. "Railroads in Pocahontas County" in *History of Pocahontas County, West Virginia, 1981*. Marlinton, W.Va.: Pocahontas County Historical Society, 1981. pp. 169-75.

– – –. *The Durbin Route – The Greenbrier Division of the Chesapeake & Ohio Railway*. Charleston, W.Va.: Pictorial Histories Publishing Company, 1985. 142 pp.

Miller, Truman. "There's Nothing New Under the Sun" in *Pocahontas County Floods Through 1986* compiled by Craig Smith, 1985, Marlinton, W.Va.: Pocahontas County Historical Society, 1986. pp. 31-33.

Myers. Sylvester. *Myer's History of West Virginia*, 2 Vol. Wheeling, W.Va.: Wheeling News Lithograph Company. Vol. 1, 560 pp.; Vol. 2, 490 pp.

Neighbors, Kyle. *The Lima Shays on the Greenbrier, Cheat and Elk Railroad Company*. Parsons, W.Va.: McClain, 1969. 13 pp.

Poor's Railroad Manual Company. *Poor's Manual of Railroads*. New York: Poor's Railroad Manual Company, 1902. 1640 pp.

Polk, R. L. and Company. *West Virginia State Gazetteer and Business Directory*. Detroit: R. L. Polk and Company, 1888-89 to 1923-24.

Price, William T. *Historical Sketches of Pocahontas County*. Marlinton, W.Va.: Price Brothers, 1901. 622 pp.

Sell, Jesse C. *History of Blair County, Pennsylvania*. Chicago: n.p. 1911.

Thwaites, Ruben Gold in *Chronicles of Border Warfare* by Alexander Scott Withers, ed. Ruben G. Thwaites. New edition. Cincinnati: Robert Clarke, 1895. 447 pp.

Zinn, Jack. *R. E. Lee's Cheat Mountain Campaign*. Parsons, W.Va.: McClain, 1971. 230 pp.

ARTICLES

Bartles, Fred. ''The Birth of the Big Six.'' *The Log Train*. 1987. 5.3:3-8.

– – –. "Western Maryland Shay No. 6 – from Baltimore to Cass." *The Log Train*. 1988. 5.4:3-13.

– – –. "Restoration of the Big Six." *The Log Train*. 1988. 6.1:3-5.

– – –. "Two Locomotives for Baltimore." *The Log Train*. 1988. 6.1:7-18.

Bledsoe, John. "Kitty Hawk and Cass." *Log Train*. 1983. 2.1:8.

Clarkson, Roy B. and Kenneth L. Carvell. "West Virginia's Logging Railroad – Its Past and Present." *Northeastern Logger*, Dec. 1961. pp. 20, 21, 62, 63.

Deike, George H., III. "Greenbrier, Cheat, and Elk No. 12." *Log Train*. 1982. 1.1:6-12.

Dixon, Tom. "Parlor Car to Durbin." *C&O Historical Newsletter*. Jan. 1973. pp. 10-14.

Farquahar, H. H. "Cost of Mountain Logging in West Virginia." *Forestry Quarterly*. 1909. 7:255-269.

Fearnow, Ted. "History of Elk River Rainbow." *Wonderful, West Virginia*. Aug. 1972. 36.6:21-24.

Fizer, George. "Coal and Cass." *Log Train*. 1983. 2.1:22-25.

Futej, Gerry and Max Robin. "The Ubiquitous 40' Wood Flat Car." *Log Train*. 1983. 2.1:12-17.

Hamrick, Gordon. "Land That Time Forgot." *Wild, Wonderful West Virginia*. 1971. 35.4:11, 12.

Hand, Douglas. "The Making of the Polio Vaccine," *American Heritage of Invention and Technology.* 1985. 1:54-57.

Harpold, Jeff. "Cass Scenic Railroad of West Virginia." *Wonderful West Virginia.* 1986. 50.6:2-7.

Hicks, Raymond. "The West Virginia Central and Pittsburg Railroad." *Railway & Locomotive Historical Society Bulletin.* 1965. 113:6-31.

Jones, Mark. "Reminiscing With Cletis Johnson—an Employee at Spruce in the '20s." *Log Train.* 1983. 2.2:6.

n.a. "Cheat River Valley Spruce." *American Lumberman.* Oct. 1, 1910. pp. 48-50.

n.a. "History of Westvaco." *Westvaco CFM News:* Part I, Winter 1980. pp. 2-4; Part II, Spring 1980. pp. 9-12; Part II, Summer 1980. pp. 8-12; Part IV, Fall 1980. pp. 5-9; Part V, Winter 1981. pp. 5-7.

Palaszynski, Edwin. "The Deer Creek Extract Plant." *Log Train.* 1985. 3.3:6.

Robin, Max S. "Railroad Logging on Cheat Mountain in 1980!" *Log Train.* 1983. 2.2:18-20.

Sparks, Richard. "Technical Musings on . . . a Giant Shay." *Log Train.* 1983. 2.2: 14-15.

NEWSPAPERS

Allegheny Journal [Marlinton, W.Va.]. Apr. 26, 1973-May 23, 1974.

n.a. *Cass Chronicle and Railroad Gazette,* Vol. 3, No. 1, n.p. 1981.

Charleston Gazette [Charleston, W.Va.]. Dec. 12, 1956.

Charleston Gazette Times [Charleston, W.Va.]. Jan. 3, 1901.

Greenbrier Independent [Lewisburg, W.Va.]. Mar. 11, 1971-May 24, 1983.

The Inter-Mountain [Elkins, W.Va.]. Dec. 1-20, 1970.

Marlinton Journal [Marlinton, W.Va.]. Mar. 24, 1914-Apr. 23, 1973.

Marlinton Messenger [Marlinton, W.Va.]. Jan. 4, 1906-Dec. 8, 1911.

Pocahontas Independent [Marlinton, W.Va.]. Jan. 1912-Dec. 1915.

Pocahontas Times, [Marlinton, W.Va.]. May 10, 1883-Jan., 1990.

Republican News [Marlinton, W.Va.]. Dec. 8, 1911-Jan. 30, 1914.

Webster Echo [Webster Springs, W.Va.]. Jan. 1980-July 1, 1986.

West Virginia Hillbilly [Richwood, W.Va.]. Oct. 15, 1960-Nov. 28, 1964.

GOVERNMENT PUBLICATIONS AND RECORDS

Brooks, A. B. *Forestry and Wood Industries.* Morgantown, W.Va.: W.Va. Geological Survey, Vol. 5, 1911. 481 pp.

Cardwell, Dudley H. *Geologic History of West Virginia.* Morgantown, W.Va.: W.Va. Geologic and Economic Survey, Vol. 64, 1975. 64 pp.

Hopkins, A.D. "The spruce in West Virginia" in *Report of the W.Va. State Board of Agriculture for the Quarter Ending June 30, 1908.* Charleston, W.Va.: Tribune Printing, 1908. 131 pp.

Pocahontas County Deed Books. Courthouse, Marlinton, W.Va.

Price, Paul H. and David B. Reger. *County Reports: Pocahontas County.* Morgantown, W.Va.: W.Va. Geological Survey, 1929. p. 531.

Randolph County Deed Books. Courthouse, Elkins, W.Va.

Reger, David. B. *County Reports: Webster County and Portion of Mingo District, Randolph County, South of Valley Fork of Elk River.* Morgantown, W.Va.: W.Va. Geological Survey, 1920. 682 pp.

– – –. *County Reports: Randolph County.* Morgantown, W.Va.: W.Va. Geological Survey, 1931. 989 pp.

Weedfall, Robert O. *West Virginia Weather.* W.Va. Dept. of Agriculture, Charleston, W.Va. n.p., n.d.

West Virginia Blue Book (Formerly *West Virginia Legislative Hand Book and Manual and Official Register*). Charleston, W.Va.: Tribune Printing and Jarrett Printing. 1916-1985.

West Virginia State Department of Mines. Annual Report, 1914 . Charleston, W.Va. n.p.

UNPUBLISHED MANUSCRIPTS AND RECORDS

Belcher, Lillian W. Pocahontas County. Federal Writer's Project, Boxes 75, 78. West Virginia and Regional History Collection, West Virginia University Library, Morgantown, W.Va.

Brown, D. D. D. D. Brown Collection of Lumber Activities in West Virginia. West Virginia and Regional History Collection, West Virginia University Library, Morgantown, W.Va.

Clarkson, Karen. 1981. Survey of population and business activity in Cass, West Virginia. 8 pp.

Harper, Enid. Pocahontas County Federal Writer's Project, Box 77. West Virginia and Regional History Collection, West Virginia University Library, Morgantown, W.Va.

Matics, H. E. 1976. The Westvaco Story: A History of the Company and Its People. 114 pp.

Smith, Samuel G. Pocahontas County. Federal Writer's Project, Box 77. West Virginia and Regional History Collection, West Virginia University Library, Morgantown, W.Va.

Sterling, E. A. 1920. General Report and Summary of Detailed Estimates, West Virginia Pulp & Paper Company Lands, Pocahontas, Randolph and Webster Counties, W.Va. James D. Lacey & Company, New York.

West Virginia Pulp and Paper Company Records, forty-four boxes and microfilm reels. West Virginia and Regional History Collection, West Virginia University Library, Morgantown, W.Va.

West Virginia Pulp and Paper Company Machine Shop Records. In private hands, Cass, W.Va.

PERSONAL INTERVIEWS AND LETTERS

Interviews by Phil Bagdon:

Artie Barkley	Ben Jackson
Paul Bradley	Kyle "Catty" Neighbors
Warren "Doodle" Brown	T. M. Phare
Odey Cassell	Frank Puffenbarger
Bedford "Buck" Chestnut	S. S. "Si" Sharp
Charlie Cromer	Woodrow Sharp
Paul Dolkos	Charles Sheets
Pat Ellisy	William Simmons

Rocky Fisher
Preston "Springy" Galford
Eunice Gibson
Forest Griffin
Reed W. Griffin
Russell Hamrick
Ed Howell

Carl Summerfield
Johnny Warner
Sam Waugh
Fred Weber
Laban Wolfe
Stanley Wooddell

Interviews by the author:
Allen J. Blackhurst
Jennings Bradford
Eugene Burner
Edward "Puzo" Cassell
Ernestine Clarkson
Ivan Clarkson
Mertie Clarkson
Russell M. Clarkson
Reed W. Griffith
Connell P. Gillespie
Willis Hertig
Ben Jackson

Lola Clarkson Jackson
Harold Lee
Georgia Daugherty Robinson
Roy C. Siple
William Simmons
Ether Tyson
Maggie Myers Tyson
Harry Wanless
Jim White
Valley Clarkson Wilkes
Bud Wolfe
E. C. Wyatt

Letters to the author:
Eugene Burner
Louis H. Camisa
Marlene Chittum
Harry Clark
Anna Plyler Ervine
George A. Fizer
Colin Gillespie
Connell P. Gillespie
Reed W. Griffith

Charles Gum
Gordon Hamrick
Monta McLaughlin Mace
H. E. Matics
Raymond F. Schuck
Roy C. Siple
Dorothy Tacy
E. C. Wyatt

INDEX